Frontiers of Alcoholism

FRONTIERS OF ALCOHOLISM

Edited by

Morris E. Chafetz, M.D.
Director of Clinical Psychiatric Services, Massachusetts General Hospital; Associate Clinical Professor of Psychiatry, Harvard Medical School

Howard T. Blane, PH.D.
Associate Psychologist, Massachusetts General Hospital; Assistant Professor of Psychology, Harvard Medical School

Marjorie J. Hill, PH.D.
Formerly of the Massachusetts General Hospital, now Associate Coordinator, Office of Alcoholism, Department of Health and Welfare for the State of Alaska

Science House · 1970 · New York

Copyright, © 1970, Science House, Inc.

All rights reserved. No part of this book may be reproduced in any form without permission in writing from the publisher, except by a reviewer who wishes to quote brief passages in connection with a review.

Library of Congress Catalog Card Number: 79-91171
Standard Book Number: 87668-026-0

FORMAT BY HARVEY DUKE

Manufactured by Haddon Craftsmen, Inc.
Scranton, Pennsylvania

Introduction

The research and clinical programs described in the pages to follow arose out of the belief that alcoholics can be helped by psychoanalytically oriented psychotherapy. A corollary belief is that the fatalism of practitioners toward treating alcoholics may in part be explained by widely prevalent attitudes toward the use of alcohol and those who suffer from alcoholism. These attitudes, ranging from self-righteous, destructive punitiveness to derisive laughter at another's debility, reinforce certain characteristics commonly seen in the alcoholic himself: a need to be rejected and a fear of becoming involved with others. The results of interaction between social attitudes and individual propensities have been with us for many years; only recently has a more rational attitude toward the problem begun to develop. The alcoholic is seen by many as a willful partner of evil, or at least a willing victim; attitudes of hopelessness and despondency are pervasive even among the increasing number of people who see alcoholism as an illness unrelated to moral lapses.

In the first half of this volume we have addressed ourselves to the evolution of our theoretical positions and empirical work. In our earliest work (Chapter 1, Section 1A) we were concerned with the effectiveness of psychoanalytically oriented psychotherapy in the treatment of alcoholic problems. Under what conditions was it effective? What modifications of technique were necessary? What additions to technique seemed advisable? How was our psychodynamic conception of the alcoholic related to changes in therapeutic parameters? We were also interested in developing ways of describing alcoholics that, while doing little violence to a psychoanalytic understanding in depth, would be in keeping with observable behaviors and employ a non-technical language that is part of common experience (Chapter 1, Section 1B).

The first study (Chapter 2, Section 2A) is a demographic and diagnostic examination of the flow of patients with alcoholic problems through the emergency service of a large metropolitan general hospital. An unpublished finding of this survey was that patients nominally referred for continuing outpatient treatment of their alcoholism failed to act upon this recommendation. On the basis of this we began to investigate ways of facilitating the alcoholic's search for treatment and of enhancing his interest in being helped. The first two of these experiments-in-action (Chapter 2, Sections 2B and 2C) confirmed and reconfirmed the thesis that alcoholics will enter into and remain in treatment if they are approached initially with respect and with due regard to the psychological and social aspects of their illness. We have continued to make similar investigations as a means of evaluating the introduction of innovative techniques into our clinical services (Chapter 2, Sections 2D, 2E, and 2F).

Having demonstrated that alcoholics would enter into and stay in treatment, we wished to examine some of the factors that militated for or against such an effect when treatment efforts were held constant. Here we discovered an interplay of several factors at behavioral, social, and situational levels of analysis. These included overt dependency and counterdependency, socioeconomic status, whether the patient was brought to the emergency service by the police and, having arrived at the emergency service, whether he was hospitalized (Chapter 3, Sections 3A, 3B, 3C, and 3D). The relationship between brief hospitalization and entering treatment is important for immediate application, while the relationship between lower-middle social class position and therapeutic engagement has implications for social action programs.

While we intentionally examined internal and external facets of the alcoholic's life situation that bear on his response to therapeutic overtures, it was a fortuitous circumstance that we were able to identify and understand some of the attitudes in the professional community that act to vitiate the alcoholic's own efforts. The entire investigation of attitudes (as described in Chapter 4, Sections 4A, 4B, 4C, and 4D) rested on one of those happy but rare instances in science when one takes advantage of a puzzling anomaly; in this instance, we noted that case flow was about one half what we had expected, and wondered why the referring physicians were missing so many cases. Curiosity led us to discover that the physicians did not refer all alcoholics because the basis of their referral was a stereotype that excluded about half of the alcoholics who came to the emergency service. This stereotype favored the relatively physically healthy but severely socially deteriorated alcoholic, even though the alcoholics who were not referred showed signs of social deterioration when compared with a group of nonalcoholics. Finally, we were able to demonstrate that even the doctor's tone of voice (with the content of what he says electronically filtered out) is related to whether the alcoholic enters treatment: an angry tone is associated with not entering and an anxious tone with entering treatment.

In our studies we used a definition of establishing a therapeutic alliance that, however operationally satisfactory, was an index, not a suitable substantive statement. Our sense of dissatisfaction led us to become more and more interested in other measures of therapy outcome, and resulted in a review of the literature of studies that evaluate psychological methods of treating alcoholics (Chapter 5, Section 5A). The next section gives detailed reports on techniques that may be applied by those requiring high rates of follow-up in clinical investigations that use repeated measures.

The first half of the book, then, deals with a series of studies that arose from a central program of research. The second describes several directions, including clinical action and research and evaluation projects that are the direct and indirect consequences of the earlier work.

We had demonstrated the practicality and effectiveness of a particular clinical approach in reaching alcoholics who would otherwise be lost to rehabilitative efforts, and there were indications that, with minor modifications, the approach might prove effective for general psychiatric patients who seek help at a general hospital emergency service. We expanded the operations of our teams to cover the entire caseload of alcoholics, and finally the entire caseload of all psychiatric patients (Chapter 6, Sections 6A and 6D). Simultaneously, we endeavored to develop and describe new clinical techniques of treatment (Chapter 6, Sections 6B and 6C), and to investigate the effectiveness of our approach in a rural general hospital serving a large, but thinly populated region (Chapter 6, Section 6E).

One of the more important observations made during our research was that existing models of treatment of alcoholism, whether primarily psychological, social, or physical, can at best represent only holding operations. This is so because prodromal and early alcoholics are rarely seen in treatment centers; the typical client is a late-stage alcoholic who is already severely and perhaps irreparably disorganized in one and often more aspects of his life. If we are to make any demonstrably noticeable inroads on the incidence and prevalence of alcoholism, our efforts must be increasingly centered on prevention. Sections 7A and 7C of Chapter 7 are directed at two different ways of setting up secondary prevention programs; the one focuses on a youthful high-risk population, the other on casefinding through a public health nursing organization. The importance of attitudes toward alcohol use and alcoholism in affecting social drinking behavior and in particular behavior toward alcoholics was clearly apparent from the literature and some of the findings of our early research. The description of these attitudes in Section 7B of Chapter 7 and an understanding of their relation to prevention may have significant consequences in ameliorating alcohol problems.

In the final chapter, we have included three papers, two pointing to broad avenues of social action for prevention (Sections 8A and 8B), the other an analysis of the psychological functions served by alcohol based on recent observations (Section 8C), and bringing to full circle some of the issues raised in the initial chapter.

Morris E. Chafetz, M.D.
Howard T. Blane, Ph.D.
Marjorie J. Hill, Ph.D.

Acknowledgments

In any book editors and authors can acknowledge only some of the many contributions that result in a finished work. Those who have contributed directly to this book are Harry Abram, Elliot Brown, Eleanor Clark, Fred Frankel, Joseph Golner, Elizabeth Hastie, Richard Kasschau, Alfred Koumans, William McCourt, Jack Mendelson, William Meyers, Carole Miller, Susan Milmoe, James Muller, Willis Overton, Jr., Robert Rosenthal, Estelle Singer, Charles Taylor, and Irving Wolf. The assistance of Lorraine Lyman and Diane Finer in helping with the organization of the manuscript is gratefully acknowledged as is our debt to Nancy Jacobs for her expert typing of the manuscript.

We can express our thanks only in a general way to the many people in the Massachusetts General Hospital, the Division of Alcoholism of the Commonwealth of Massachusetts, the National Institute of Mental Health, the numerous community resources, and most of all, to the patients, who allowed our work to continue and allowed us to go on learning.

M.E.C.
H.T.B.
M.J.H.

We further express our appreciation to the following publishers for permission to reprint, with changes, the following copyrighted material.

The American Medical Association
FRANKEL, F. H., M. E. CHAFETZ, and H. T. BLANE, "Treatment of Psychosocial Crises in the Emergency Service of a General Hospital," *Journal of the American Medical Association*, 195:626–628, 1966.

The American Psychiatric Association
BLANE, H. T., J. J. MULLER, and M. E. CHAFETZ, "Acute Psychi-

atric Services in the General Hospital. II. Current Status of Emergency Psychiatric Services," *American Journal of Psychiatry*, October supplement, 124:37–45, 1967; Copyright, 1967, by the American Psychiatric Association.

BLANE, H. T., "Trends in the Prevention of Alcoholism," *Research Report*, 24:1–9, 1968.

The American Psychological Association

SINGER, E., H. T. BLANE, and R. KASSCHAU, "Alcoholism and Social Isolation," *Journal of Abnormal and Social Psychology*, 69:681–685, 1964; Copyright, 1964, by the American Psychological Association.

MILMOE, S., R. ROSENTHAL, H. T. BLANE, M. E. CHAFETZ, and I. WOLF, "The Doctor's Voice: Postdictor of Successful Referral of Alcoholic Patients," *Journal of Abnormal Psychology*, 72:78–84, 1967; Copyright, 1967, by the American Psychological Association.

Journal of Clinical Psychology

BLANE, H. T., and W. R. MYERS, "Social Class and the Establishment of Treatment Relations by Alcoholics," *Journal of Clinical Psychology*, 20:287–290, 1964.

Massachusetts Department of Public Health

BLANE, H. T., "The Personality of the Alcoholic," in *The Role of the Nurse in the Care of the Alcoholic Patient in A General Hospital*, Division of Alcoholism, Massachusetts Department of Public Health, 1960.

The National Association for Mental Health, Inc.

BROWN, E., and C. TAYLOR, "An Alcoholism Treatment Facility in a Rural Area," *Mental Hygiene*, 50:194–198, 1966.

The New York Academy of Sciences

CHAFETZ, M. E., "Alcohol Excess," *Annals of the New York Academy of Sciences*, 133:808–813, 1966.

• • •

Acknowledgments

Nursing Outlook
BLANE, H. T., and M. J. HILL, "Public Health Nurses Speak Up About Alcoholism," *Nursing Outlook,* 12:34–37, 1964.

Psychological Reports
CHAFETZ, M. E., and H. T. BLANE, "Alcohol Crisis Treatment Approach and Establishment of Treatment Relations with Alcoholics," *Psychological Reports,* 12:862, 1963.
KOUMANS, A. J. R., and J. J. MULLER, "Use of Letters to Increase Motivation for Treatment in Alcoholics," *Psychological Reports,* 16:1152, 1965.
KOUMANS, A. J. R., J. J. MULLER, and C. F. MILLER, "Use of Telephone Calls to Increase Motivation for Treatment in Alcoholics," *Psychological Reports,* 21:327–328, 1967.

Quarterly Journal of Studies on Alcohol
CHAFETZ, M. E., "Practical and Theoretical Considerations in the Psychotherapy of Alcoholism," *Quarterly Journal of Studies on Alcohol,* 20:281–291, 1959; Copyright, 1959.
MENDELSON, J. H., and M. E. CHAFETZ, "Alcoholism as an Emergency Ward Problem," *Quarterly Journal of Studies on Alcohol,* 20:270–275, 1959; Copyright, 1959.
BLANE, H. T., and W. R. MYERS, "Behavioral Dependence and Length of Stay Among Alcoholics," *Quarterly Journal of Studies on Alcohol,* 24:503–520, 1963; Copyright, 1963.
BLANE, H. T., W. F. OVERTON, and M. E. CHAFETZ, "Social Factors in the Diagnosis of Alcoholism. I: Characteristics of the Patient," *Quarterly Journal of Studies on Alcohol,* 24:640–663, 1963; Copyright, 1963.
WOLF, I., M. E. CHAFETZ, H. T. BLANE, and M. J. HILL, "Social Factors in the Diagnosis of Alcoholism. II: Attitudes of Physicians," *Quarterly Journal of Studies on Alcohol,* 26:72–79, 1965; Copyright, 1965.
HILL, M. J., and H. T. BLANE, "Evaluation of Psychotherapy with Alcoholics: A Critical Review," *Quarterly Journal of Studies on Alcohol,* 28:76–104, 1967; Copyright, 1967.

CHAFETZ, M. E., "Alcoholism Prevention and Reality," *Quarterly Journal of Studies on Alcohol,* 28:345–348, 1967; Copyright, 1967.

The Williams and Wilkins Company

CHAFETZ, M. E., H. T. BLANE, H. S. ABRAM, J. R. GOLNER, E. LACY, W. F. McCOURT, E. CLARK, and W. MYERS, "Establishing Treatment Relations with Alcoholics," *Journal of Nervous and Mental Disease,* 134:395–409, 1962.

CHAFETZ, M. E., H. T. BLANE, H. S. ABRAM, E. CLARK, E. L. HASTIE, and W. F. McCOURT, "Establishing Treatment Relations with Alcoholics: A Supplementary Report," *Journal of Nervous and Mental Disease,* 138:390–393, 1964.

CHAFETZ, M. E., "The Effect of a Psychiatric Emergency Service on Motivation for Psychiatric Treatment," *Journal of Nervous and Mental Disease,* 140:442–448, 1965.

Table of Contents

Introduction v
PART I. UNDERSTANDING AND FACILITATING PSYCHOTHERAPY WITH ALCOHOLICS
  1. The Alcoholic: Psychodynamics and
     Personality Structure 3
     A. Practical and Theoretical Considerations
        in the Psychotherapy of Alcoholism 6
     B. The Personality of the Alcoholic 16
  2. Engaging the Alcoholic to Enter into
     Treatment 31
     A. Alcoholism as an Emergency Ward Problem 37
     B. Establishing Treatment Relations with
        Alcoholics I 42
     C. Establishing Treatment Relations with
        Alcoholics II 60
     D. Alcohol Crisis Treatment Approach and
        Establishment of Treatment Relations 64
     E. Use of Letters to Increase the
        Motivation for Treatment 67
     F. Use of Telephone Calls to Increase the
        Motivation for Treatment 68
  3. The Context of Entering and
     Staying in Treatment 75
     A. Behavioral Dependence and Length of
        Stay in Psychotherapy 78
     B. Mode of Entry and Subsequent Hospitalization in Relation to Establishment of
        Treatment Relations 85
     C. Social Class and Establishment of
        Treatment Relations 88
     D. Social Isolation, Social Dependence, and
        the Formation of Treatment Relations 92
  4. Recognizing Alcoholics: Social and
     Professional Attitudes 103
     A. Social Factors in the Diagnosis of Alcoholism:
        Characteristics of the Patient 106
     B. Social Factors in the Diagnosis of Alcoholism:
        Attitudes of Physicians 128
     C. The Doctor's Voice: Postdictor of Successful
        Referral of Alcoholic Patients 136

       D. Alcoholism and Social Isolation 144
  5. Evaluative Studies 157
       A. Evaluation of Psychotherapy with Alcoholics: A Critical Review 160
       B. Techniques of Follow-up 186

PART II. NEW DIRECTIONS IN RESEARCH AND CLINICAL ACTION

  6. Broadening the Clinical Base: Around-the-Clock Psychiatric Services 203
       A. The Effect of a Psychiatric Emergency Service on Motivation for Psychiatric Treatment ... 207
       B. Treatment of Psychosocial Crises in the Emergency Service of a General Hospital .. 213
       C. Modalities of Intervention in a Psychiatric Emergency Service 219
       D. Current Status of Emergency Psychiatric Services in General Hospitals 229
       E. An Alcoholism Treatment Facility in a Rural Area 242
  7. Trends in Prevention 255
       A. Trends in the Prevention of Alcoholism 258
       B. Public Health Nurses Speak up About Alcoholism 267
       C. Public Health Nurses and the Care of Alcoholics: A Study of Attitude Change ... 278
  8. Making Alcohol Use and Problems Respectable . 293
       A. Alcohol Excess 296
       B. Alcoholism Prevention and Reality 305
       C. Clinical Syndromes of Liquor Drinkers 309
Conclusion 322
Appendix A. Tables 325
Appendix B. Auxiliary Materials for Public Health Nurse Study 351
Appendix C. Annotated Bibliography of Studies Evaluating Psychotherapeutic Techniques, 1952–1963 357
Bibliography 395
Index 415

PART ONE: UNDERSTANDING AND FACILITATING PSYCHO-THERAPY WITH ALCOHOLICS

# Chapter 1
The Alcoholic: Psychodynamics and Personality Structure

In the early 1950's the medical and caretaking professions showed heightened recognition of the need to assume responsibility for the care and study of alcoholism, and in 1953 the Commonwealth of Massachusetts founded its third Alcohol Clinic, at the Massachusetts General Hospital.

This clinic had two major purposes: to investigate the effectiveness of psychoanalytically oriented psychotherapy in the treatment of alcoholism, and to evolve therapeutic techniques for the treatment of alcoholism that might be employed by other disciplines involved in the treatment of the alcoholic. Although the value of psychoanalytically oriented psychotherapy had been established in the treatment of a number of psychological disturbances, the literature had repeatedly stressed the ineffectiveness of this form of treatment in the care of the alcoholic.

An early survey of patients in the Alcohol Clinic indicated what seemed to be a reasonable rate of "successes." We present these data fully recognizing the limitations of such "evaluative" surveys, the lack of clear or universal criteria for "success," and the bias of those who apply the criteria. In 1959 the clinic reported that out of 600 referred patients in five years, 25 percent had developed and maintained a continuous therapeutic relationship. These 125 patients were studied during long-term psychoanalytically oriented psychotherapy, by social anamnesis, and by psychological tests. Of these cases, more than 60 percent achieved satisfactory results; that is, drinking was brought under greater control than the patient had ever achieved prior to treatment. The patients' behavior patterns were more mature in dealing with day-to-day living, and their response to anxiety was considered to be more realistic by both patient and therapist. Although the remaining patients did not meet these criteria for satisfactory results, many of them achieved what may be considered to be some beneficial alteration of their drinking patterns.

The two papers that follow stem in large part from studying these patients. In them, we formulate a psychoanalytically oriented approach to understanding persons with alcoholic problems; we develop treatment techniques that are rather more active, directive, controlling, and therapist-involved than those of traditional psychoanalytically oriented psychotherapy; and we examine the personality of the alcoholic from the vantage points of a number of key psychological factors.

1.A. Practical and Theoretical Considerations in the Psychotherapy of Alcoholism

Alcoholism is a growing medical problem toward which the medical profession has only recently directed any sustained energies. Present-day thinking views alcoholism as a symptom of an underlying personality disorder, with psychological factors leading to the self-destructive use of this toxic agent. The maintenance of psychological dependence on alcohol is seen as hinging upon a combination of emotional, physiological, and pharmacological factors, and the end result for the individual is usually oblivion or illness. The psychiatric implications of alcoholism have led psychiatrists to assume a more active role in the search for efficient methods of dealing with this immense problem. The purposes of the present report are to present psychodynamic hypotheses derived from long-term psychotherapeutic relationships with alcoholics, and their implications for modification of psychotherapy with alcoholics.

Review of the alcoholism literature reveals many theories based on dynamic formulations. Freud alluded to strong oral childhood influences as a cause of excessive drinking and considered change of mood to be the most valuable contribution of alcohol to the individual.[1] His thesis was that under the influence of alcohol the adult regresses to a childhood level in which he derives pleasure from thinking that is unrelated to logic. In later papers Freud spoke of a reactivation of repressed homosexual traits, and considered this to be the reason why men disappointed by women frequented bars.[2]

Brill considered alcoholism as a flight from homosexual impulses, incestuous thoughts, and masturbatory guilt.[3] Jones suggested that alcoholism is a symptom of epilepsy and psychosis,[4] while Glover

Section 1.A. written by Morris E. Chafetz, M.D.
Notes to Chapter 1 will be found on page 28.

related addiction to sadistic drives and oedipal conflicts.[5] Sachs viewed alcoholism as the compromise between hysterical and obsessive-compulsive neuroses,[6] while Rado suggested that alcohol addiction is mainly a problem of depression, the alcohol producing pharmacologically a magical sense of elation craved by the patient.[7] Menninger emphasized the self-destructive drives of the alcoholic and termed alcoholism "chronic suicide."[8] Feelings of inadequacy, internalized fears of failure, and deficiencies in social relationships are the main forces operating in the alcoholic according to Klebanoff.[9] Tiebout believes that the alcoholic has an unconscious need to dominate, together with feelings of loneliness and isolation,[10] while Knight considers that the addictive alcoholic basically suffers from a character disorder distinguished by excessive demandingness and an inability to carry out sustained effort and to express feelings of hostility and rage; alcohol is utilized to satisfy and pacify the alcoholic's frustrated needs.[11]

Classification of Alcoholic Patients

In our clinic alcoholic patients are classified into two broad categories; the reactive and the addicted. While we recognize the limitations of classification systems, we have utilized these categories to aid us in the definition of the problem presented by each patient.

Reactive or neurotic alcoholics have relatively normal prealcoholic personality structures; retrospective examination of their life patterns reveals reasonable adjustment in the areas of the family, education, work, and social demands, with a reasonably progressive movement toward realistic goals. These patients use alcohol to excess when temporarily overwhelmed by some external stress situations, usually of long duration. An episode of excessive drinking has a determinable onset, runs a course consistent with tension release, and may terminate through some measure of control exercised by the individual. Some reactive alcoholics become so involved in their neurotic drinking that they regress to a state approximating that of the malignant or addicted alcoholic, making differentiation of the two groups extremely difficult. Reactive or neurotic alcoholics can be treated with psychotherapeutic techniques similar to those used with other neurotic disorders.

The alcohol addict presents a somewhat different picture. Examination of the life history of the addict shows gross disturbances in his prealcoholic personality, with difficulties in adjustment during the early years manifested in relationships within family, in school, at work, and in attempts at marital adjustment. There is no clearly defined point at which loss of control over drinking occurred, and there is usually minimal observable external stress associated with the onset of a drinking episode. Needs for drinking arise from within the individual and, to the casual observer, seem to have no rhyme or reason. Drinking bouts usually continue until sickness or stupor ensues; drinking and the events surrounding it are usually self-destructive.

While each patient must be studied individually to understand the personal dynamics behind his addiction, certain dynamic factors are common to alcohol addicts and are related to the psychotherapeutic approach proposed in this paper.

The evidence provided by our patients suggests that by psychoanalytic classification addictive alcoholism is an oral perversion.[12] An oral perversion results from traumata that occur during the earliest stage of psychosexual development, at the time when the individual's means of achieving security and release from tension was through stimulation of the oral cavity. The tendency to fixation at the oral level may be heightened by constitutional factors tending toward increased intensity of oral drives. A great deal of energy is expended in drinking, eating, smoking, pill-taking, and the like; there may be emphasis on the mouth in sexual activity, and there is a predominance of oral imagery in fantasy production. One patient who had been in therapy for five years was asked by a friend what her therapist looked like, and could only remember that he had a beautiful mouth, though she could describe no other feature. Because the addictive alcoholic gratifies his instinctual oral wishes directly and without anxiety, we view addictive alcoholism as a perversion rather than as a neurotic mechanism, which is the disguised anxiety-ridden converse of a perversion.

In our patients, the fixation at this early level of emotional development seems to be the result of deprivation in a significant emotional relationship during the early years of life. This deprivation usually involved the death, or the emotional or physical absence, of a key figure during the early period of development. Many of the addicted alcoholics were abandoned, illegitimate children. Others were children of psychotic mothers. Still others had a parent die shortly before or after their own birth, while some were the progeny of parents who were severely alcoholic during the patient's early years. A few addicted alcoholics were the children of excessively indulgent or overly protective mothers, with underlying disguised hostility existing in both cases.

Fundamentally, the common thread running through these patients' early relationships was the absence of a warm, giving, meaningful relationship with a mother-figure during this period of development. A very similar situation is frequently observed in the early relationships of schizophrenics. Certainly, the similarity between the primitive fantasies and behavioral patterns of addicted alcoholics and schizophrenics cannot be readily dismissed. Sherfey has reported that up to 68 percent of the case histories of some groups of alcoholics reveal a significant family figure who depended on alcohol in an unhealthy way.[13] It might be proposed that one of the main reasons the addictive alcoholic does not use frank schizophrenic mechanisms to escape unpleasant reality is that significant people with whom he relates and identifies handle their desire to escape via alcohol. Possibly, therefore, the symptom choice in these two primitively deprived classes is environmentally and culturally determined.

The loss or lack of a meaningful relationship with a mother-figure may help us to understand some of the unconscious drives motivating the alcoholic. Just as the infant seeks through ingestion to quiet the emptiness and soothe the pangs that threaten his security, so does the alcoholic seek this gratification by stimulation of the oral mucosa, by imbibing massive amounts of ethanol and by seeking peaceful oblivion, symbolically attempting to achieve the blissful infantile state. Many patients, after their drinking has become controlled, express their envy of their intoxicated brethren who continue to achieve alcohol-induced oblivion. The main devastating unconscious wish with which the alcoholic must deal seems to be his passive-dependent wish for reunion with an all-giving mother-figure.

The loss of a loved parental figure early in life may be responsible for the depression that is the main affect present in the addictive alcoholic. This severe underlying depression, expressed through feelings of emptiness and loneliness, and seen in such a phrase as "something important is missing," results in the utilization of one of the alcoholic's characteristic defense mechanisms—denial. There is no more striking example of denial than the intoxicated alcoholic who declares that he does not have a problem. Asked whether he drinks, the reply is "a little"—another denial. When confronted by his intoxicated state the familiar response is, "I can stop any time I want to." Denial constitutes the main method by which alcoholics deal with life. They deny their feelings of inferiority, depression, lack of self-respect, and dependence on alcohol.

Severe, ever-present, deeply penetrating depression pervades all of the alcoholic's personality and all of his reactions in the search for oblivion. For the addict, alcohol is an easy method of achieving control over feelings of helplessness and deprivation. At the same time it substitutes symbolically something he feels he can control. The object loss during the oral stage results in primitive, excessive demands that are ultimately insatiable. Consequently, interpersonal relationships eventually, but inexorably, lead to a sense of rejection in the patient, a reawakening of the original loss and rejection he experienced as an infant. The pain, depression and loss of self-esteem that alcoholics experience reproduce the rage experienced by a deprived infant, a rage so intense and all-consuming that the infant will seemingly destroy himself rather than relent. So it is with the alcoholic. The rage has a murderous ferocity and intent, and rather than destroy another, the alcoholic internalizes his anger and consumes it in drink. As one patient succinctly put it: "It is more socially acceptable to get stinking drunk than to murder someone."

The alcoholic's fixation at the oral stage suggests a possible explanation for his lack of satiation. In mature love, the instinctual wish is gratified but the object is preserved. In the oral stage, the instinctual wishes are gratified by incorporation and the love object is destroyed. The continued consumption of alcohol is a symbolic acting out of the oral conflict; each drink gratifies the instinctual wish but destroys the love object; hence a new one must be found and satiation is never achieved.

Issues in Treatment

If one accepts the preceding psychodynamic formulation for the addictive alcoholic, the difficulties of treating him become apparent. Most primitive disorders are treated within the protective and supportive confines of an institution. Not only does the addicted alcoholic suffer from a primitive psychological disorder, but there is a great tendency to act out conflict situations. Hence, the attempt to treat him psychotherapeutically on an ambulatory basis can be fraught with danger. The danger, we believe, lies in two main failings on the part of therapists. The first is the tendency of most psychiatrists to maintain a rather rigid therapeutic approach; their training has emphasized the limits of their role and their behavior. The second is in the overgeneralized classification of alcoholics as patients who suffer from hopeless character disorders and hence are untreatable.

The psychotherapist who is prepared to deal with the alcoholic must be prepared to be a pioneer in his approach to each case; for example, he must reach out to a reluctant patient. Fundamentally, he must be a warm, kind, interested individual who can at the same time set and maintain reality-oriented limits; he must not and cannot assume moralizing and punitive attitudes. Since we are dealing with a disorder of early personality development, words are of little use; it is not what we say to the alcoholic, but what we really feel and do that will determine the outcome. Alcoholism, as a preverbal disorder, must be treated by action—by "doing for" the patient. These primitive individuals want to be loved, want to be treated, and want to grow emotionally. Yet all of their emotional life experience warns and threatens them against entering into relationships in which rejection is the inevitable outcome.

Action or "doing" therapy means, for example, that if the patient requires physical treatment, then hospitalization and medical care should be readily provided. Prescriptions for vitamins or disulfiram may be meaningful when the patient is seeking evidence of the tangible support. In other words, in the early relationship the therapist must be very active; the passive, nondirective therapist who follows his usual psychoanalytically oriented therapeutic approach with alcoholics soon has no patients to treat.

In all therapeutic situations dealing with primitive problems a positive relationship is of prime importance. Without this firm bond between therapist and alcoholic no exploratory approach can hope to succeed. This bond may take a few interviews or several years to develop, but it cannot be bypassed. When it appears to be firm the patient will test it again and again, and even when the tests are passed the bond will be tested further. To ensure such a bond the patient must be offered help again and again, no matter how often he fails and resorts to alcohol.

Since the addictive alcoholic patient is fundamentally hostile, his behavior is unconsciously designed to arouse negative feelings and to invite retaliation. Hostility and retaliation must be constantly guarded against by all treatment personnel. Counterhostility is frequently expressed by being nice or excessively permissive. The absence of controls by the therapist is poorly tolerated by, and threatening to, the patient who is already leaning heavily toward loss of control. It indicates to the patient a lack of understanding of his basic problem, and intensifies the identification of loss of control with loss of contact with reality, resulting in disintegration of personality.

Anxiety in the therapist is interpreted by the patient as evidence of insecurity and uncertainty of control. The hostility present in the therapist who is rigid, harsh, and punitively controlling is self-evident. An attitude of tolerant acceptance with consistent firmness is healthy and reassuring. The therapist must maintain a position of constancy and absolute honesty, acknowledging to the patient mistakes, errors, and feelings arising within him as soon as he becomes aware of them. When the patient makes a demand, an oversimplified but safe question to ask oneself is: "Am I doing this really for the patient's good, or to make him like me?" This question will be especially pertinent when the patient, besides inviting punishment, attempts to seduce the therapist into prescribing drugs or granting other dependency gratifications.

While the therapist must be an active, continually supporting substitute for the alcohol, he cannot help being aware of the insatiable demands of alcoholic patients. Few human beings can long endure the pressures, hostility, and acting out of conflicts commonly endured in treating alcoholics. Thus these patients are most appropriately treated within a team setting that includes the psychiatrist, the social worker, and the psychologist. The all-important social worker should be available to help with the financial, family, and social pressures that commonly arise to interfere with treatment. The psychologist, with his particular way of understanding people, makes his contribution to the team's formulation of problems and predictions. Medical facilities should be readily available so that the patient can be prevented from utilizing physical symptoms and demands for medical treatment as a weapon against the therapist. A division of labor brought about through the team approach aids in the delineation of the physiological needs, the socioenvironmental demands, and the underlying emotional upheavals with which the therapist works. Thus, the task of the therapist becomes somewhat more manageable, the possibilities for arousal of his counterhostility are minimized, and the patient is more readily confronted with reality. The therapist who must dominate his patients to compensate for his own insecurity, and the one whose motivation is to be loved by all, will rarely deal successfully with the addictive alcoholic.

When a satisfactory relationship has been successfully developed, the therapist must gradually wean the alcoholic from his dependency need to a recognition and acceptance of reality factors. Once the drinking is controlled, the therapist must avoid the tendency to continue his now outgrown protective attitude. He must be prepared to encourage his patient to carry out tasks, to make decisions and, consistent with the patient's abilities, to meet and deal with reality in a mature manner. Situations that reactivate emotional reactions associated with the patient's original rejection are common pitfalls that therapists must avoid. These pitfalls include missing or canceling appointments without adequate warning to the patient, tardiness, making promises and not keeping them, and telling the patient untruths. Such events tend to be interpreted as rejection; they can lead to a catastrophic setback in the progress of therapy and to renewed acting out.

In formulating a course of psychotherapy for a patient, one must establish realistic goals. For some patients a supportive relationship and the provision of external aid in control over drinking is all that can be tolerated. Others may require partial custodial care and more continuous support. For many others, however, an intensive, exploratory uncovering psychotherapeutic approach with resolution of the transference may be tolerated. The goals must be set within the abilities and the capacities of the patient; they should be based upon a team evaluation of the patient's make-up and many clinical hours of amending and confirming preliminary formulations.

Denial must be dealt with quickly and as often as it becomes recognizable in the treatment setting, since the recognition of denial allows the patient to be more aware of his problem and his role in its causation. Denial mechanisms must equally be confronted and handled when they appear among caretaking personnel. For example, for years the Alcoholism Clinic at Massachusetts General Hospital was called "Psychiatry A." This name was an inadvertent means of strengthening the patient's denial and no objection was evoked from our patients when the clinic was truthfully renamed the "Alcohol Clinic."

An important aspect of the psychotherapy of the addictive alcoholic involves the first contact with him. This contact is not usually made by the therapist but by a secretary, a social worker, or a house officer in an emergency ward. Here the battle may be won or lost. Initial rejection is a constant hazard. Major examples of rejection are permitting the patient to be treated as a second-class citizen who waits around, or handling him gruffly and with little interest. Also, merely pushing some medication at the patient and discharging him outright hinders the establishment of a supporting therapeutic relationship. The importance of early contact was strikingly illustrated by a patient who had come to the emergency ward on many occasions while she was intoxicated but who had refused to accept follow-up care in the clinic. A turning point came on the occasion when a volunteer worker, while serving coffee to the employees in the emergency ward, included the patient in her distribution. As a result, the patient made an appointment in the clinic, which was kept, along with subsequent appointments, and she was successfully treated. She frequently told her therapist that the turning point for her had been the fact that someone had considered her as an equal, demonstrating this by including her in the coffee service. This incident also underlines again the action or "doing" aspect of the early treatment of the addictive alcoholic.

Alcoholics Anonymous has shown itself to be a helpful adjunct in our work. Since we and others have conceived of alcoholism as the result of an object loss, the loss of a mother-figure that must be symbolically replaced by alcohol, we have looked at A.A. in this frame of reference. A.A. is an uncritical, acting group, since all members are themselves alcoholics. It is an action or "doing" group and evokes a spiritual conversion with its implied maternal reunion. In other words, it tends toward being a "good," nonrejecting object. A. O. Ludwig has pointed out that the compulsiveness of A.A. workers in helping other alcoholics not to drink resembles the compulsiveness they formerly exhibited in their drinking pattern.[14] Thus the effectiveness of A.A. is understandable within our psychodynamic formulation of alcoholism.

Summary

Alcohol addiction has been described as a result of early emotional deprivation in relation to a significant parental figure, the symbolic and psychological replacement of which is achieved through alcohol. The symptom-choice of alcoholism seems to be culturally and environmentally determined. It is proposed that treatment is most effective when managed so as to establish a warm, giving relationship within the limits of reality.

1.B. The Personaltiy of the Alcoholic

In any branch of psychology, but particularly in that dealing with the abnormal personality, almost everyone considers himself to be an expert; so it is with alcoholism. In nearly all social groups the professional who works with alcoholics can expect to be confronted with curiosity and admiration for dealing with such a difficult and serious social problem, and to be the recipient of a great deal of information as to what alcoholics are *really* like.

Everyone knows about alcoholics, from the popular press, from experience with an acquaintance, friend, or relative who has a drinking problem, and in the case of caretakers, from their professional experience with patients who are alcoholic.

Everyone knows about alcoholics, yet we who work in the field, who attempt to obtain precise knowledge of the alcoholic in the interests of treatment and of prevention, feel less certain about what alcoholics are like. We do know that there are vast differences among individual alcoholics, and that these differences depend on a wide array of factors, such as social and cultural backgrounds, intelligence and education, the stage to which drinking behavior has progressed, and so on. However, we also know that there are certain personality characteristics, traits, and consistent patterns of behavior that occur commonly among alcoholics.

These traits are not present in all alcoholics, but are common enough to warrant description. Nor are they of equal intensity; that is, the patterning and organization of the traits varies from individual to individual. Further, some or all of these traits are seen in persons who are not alcoholic; indeed, if we examine ourselves we are apt to see these traits, the difference being that they are transitory, or that they are not centrally important to us, or that they don't rule us to the point that they prevent us from doing what we want to do or make us do what we don't want to do, as occurs in the case of the alcoholic.

Section 1.B. written by Howard T. Blane, Ph.D.

We do not know precisely the "whys" of becoming alcoholic. Certainly, the etiology of the disease is not any simple and single cause-and-effect relationship, although such relationships have often been suggested as explanations. Currently, we believe that alcoholism is the product of a complex combination of factors, some of which we know more about than others. Stated in the most general terms, this position says that a person with a certain psychological and probably physiological background, who lives in a particular society and culture, will, under specified circumstances, in all likelihood become alcoholic. We know quite a bit about some of the terms of this formulation. For example, we know that alcoholism among Jews and Chinese is almost nonexistent, but has a high incidence among the Irish and Scandinavians. Another example, less convincing than the first, is that alcoholics frequently have alcoholic parents; it is obvious, though, that not all alcoholic fathers have alcoholic children.

In any event, it is because we know relatively so little about why people become alcoholic and also because the several theories of etiology lack conviction that I have decided not to go any further into them, but to describe some of the personality characteristics that are commonly seen in alcoholics, and tell you why I think a knowledge of these characteristics is important.

Personality Characteristics

Perhaps the most commonly observed trait among alcoholics is what we refer to as *low frustration tolerance*. This means that when a wish, or request, or desire, or demand of the alcoholic is not gratified immediately, when its object is not achieved, the alcoholic tends to react with anger, with insistence that his wish be fulfilled, or by withdrawal from the frustrating situation. Most of us have the capacity to delay gratification as well as the ability to tolerate great degrees of frustration, but this kind of delay and tolerance is virtually foreign to the alcoholic. Let me illustrate. An alcoholic has an appointment to see his physician for a medical ailment; when he arrives, the doctor is examining another patient and is behind schedule; the alcoholic expostulates with the doctor's secretary; he had an appointment at 2:30; he hasn't got all day; he has to be some place else shortly; and so on. Alternatively, he waits for a few minutes and then quietly leaves, probably carrying his resentment with him. In addition, the alcoholic is very apt to interpret ordinary frustrations as personal rejection rather than in terms of reality. This sort of reaction occurs in the most mundane situations: when service in a restaurant is slow, when there is a delay in obtaining an ordered drink, and so on. It is not difficult to imagine how such behavior, frequently repeated by the alcoholic, affects his relationships at home or on the job.

A second trait seen in many alcoholics is their *sociability*. They are frequently engaging individuals who enjoy the company of convivial groups, and they can be charming companions. They have a lively sense of humor and are often good story tellers. However, the alcoholic's social charm usually includes a need to impress others with his worth, his adventures, his accomplishments in life, and with well worked-out reasons for his failures. Upon closer examination, this sociability, genuine and likable as it is, rarely occurs within the context of any deeply positive emotional relationship, but is superficial in the sense that anyone who comes into contact with the alcoholic will be the recipient of feelings of good fellowship and camaraderie. This sociability frequently and paradoxically coexists in alcoholics who are unable to maintain permanent, mutually satisfying relationships with wife, parents, or friends, or whose significant relationships are shot through with guilt, hostility, threats of rejection, and mutual recriminations.

A third characteristic of the alcoholic, which again presents an apparent paradox, is his *feelings of inferiority combined with attitudes of superiority*. Attitudes of superiority are readily observable in the alcoholic's general behavior. Although the expression of these feelings may take many forms, they are most often limited to the following kinds of behavior: (1) The alcoholic acts as if he assumed that it is his right to get preferential treatment in life, and that the satisfaction of his needs and desires comes before that of others. We have already discussed indications of this in his low frustration tolerance. (2) He speaks of his importance, either his own personal importance or that which he derives from his association with important and influential people. He may dwell on his past accomplishments and exploits, or tell you of some important figure who is or has been a close friend, and what this person has done or is going to do for him.

The alcoholic's feelings of inferiority are seldom directly expressed by him or directly observed by others. This, of course, is quite understandable, since no one likes to admit to himself or to others that he feels less adequate than his fellowmen. Our first line of evidence is indirect: People who habitually have to impress others (and thus themselves) with their own worth frequently suffer from doubts as to their ability, adequacy, and so on. With our second line of evidence we feel more secure: A recurrent observation in prolonged psychotherapy with alcoholics is that they eventually bring up violent feelings of hatred toward themselves, and speak convincingly of their lack of worth and inadequacy. These are not isolated or specific feelings of the sort that we have when we are annoyed at ourselves for being unable to do some specific task. On the contrary, the alcoholic perceives his failure to accomplish even the most commonplace goal as confirmation of what he has known all along—that he feels just plain no good through and through. Further, this feeling can occur despite the most blatant evidence to the contrary; the alcoholic may have all sorts of substantial achievements to his credit and be a person of considerable success, but nevertheless pervasive feelings of worthlessness and low self-esteem accompany his every thought and action.

Another occasion on which the alcoholic expresses feelings of being no good is either in the midst of an alcoholic spree or when he has just stopped drinking, is physically ill, and is filled with guilt and remorse over his drinking behavior. Recently one of our psychiatrists was seeing an alcoholic patient in the emergency ward. The patient insisted that the doctor call him "Bum," and was obviously perturbed when the doctor naturally refused and continued to address him as "Mister." When questioned, the patient elaborated convincingly and with feeling on why he ought to be called Bum and did not deserve to be called Mister.

Most of the time, of course, the alcoholic tries to avoid feelings of low self-esteem, and part of his avoidance technique is to impress not only others but himself with his own worth. In other words, we see his feelings and fantasies of superiority in part at least as a defense against perceiving his feelings of worthlessness. We also suspect, however, that some of his feelings of superiority stem from a more basic source in his personality structure.

Most alcoholics are *fearful* individuals. This may seem to contradict what I have said about their sociability and their often garrulous need to impress others. The contradiction, however, is only apparent, since the alcoholic's sociability is confined to certain situations and does not appear in others, and the fearfulness behind his attempts to impress others is frequently all too readily evident.

What is the alcoholic afraid of? Experience in therapy with alcoholics shows that their fears and anxieties can be numerous, and highly individual with respect to the person's unique life experiences and background. For our purposes, it is primary to take note that the alcoholic is afraid of anything that poses a challenge to him and to his abilities. This overall formulation covers a wide range of behaviors. Thus, the alcoholic is fearful of trying to obtain a job that is within his abilities and for which his past experience well equips him, especially if he feels the job to be a worthy one. This is one reason why alcoholics are often found working in menial jobs, as for instance, dishwashers, kitchen helpers, or janitors, even though they may be reasonably well educated and have training for jobs that are higher in the occupational scale. The alcoholic is also fearful of entering into relationships in which he feels demands may be made upon him involving responsibility and mutuality; by mutuality I mean respect for the other person, as well as trust in his respect for you. In the kinds of sociability I described before, such mutuality and responsibility are minor aspects and may often be nonexistent.

The alcoholic's fearfulness in human relationships is in large part the reason for the immense difficulty experienced in engaging him in a treatment relationship. This anxiety places the professional person in a most awkward position with regard to reaching the alcoholic. To be treated with respect is frightening to him, and he may react with either defensive anger or attempts to run from the relationship as speedily as he can. To be treated with disrespect, derision, open hostility, or a moralizing attitude is what the alcoholic expects, for it confirms his view that he is worthless and that the world is hostile, not understanding, and not to be trusted. It is this self-created conception of the world that the alcoholic uses as a major reason for his continued drinking behavior. If he is able to accept the respect of others, this is already an excellent sign of potential recovery, and is a first step to discontinuing drinking. The alcoholic seems aware of this, and while some part of him would like not to be alcoholic, another and nearly always stronger part is tremendously fearful of not being an alcoholic. For these reasons the alcoholic shies violently away from any potentially mutually respectful relationship.

Another aspect of the alcoholic's fearfulness has to do with testing himself and his capabilities. He won't shut up and he is afraid to put up. He is well able to tell others of his capacities, but this is bravado in the service of warding off feelings of inadequacy and helplessness. When it comes to the point of doing things that he feels will in a reality and action setting test his statements, the alcoholic becomes quite fearful, and under these conditions will more likely than not resort to flight. Should he get into a situation that he feels is a test, he is apt to take the view that he has failed and will respond with depression or increased drinking. The alcoholic often impresses one as an expert at garnering failure, and as one who is equally expert in rationalizing failure as due to unavoidable external circumstances, such as his being victimized by a hostile environment. When he suffers a set-back in reality or merely in his own mind's eye, he is frustrated and responds accordingly.

I want to emphasize again that the failures or defeats that the alcoholic feels he has suffered consist from our point of view of the minor irritations, the petty annoyances that beset us daily. However, they do assume major proportions in the alcoholic's mind, and he reacts to them as we might to a major blow in life. One can only guess what a burden life must be to the alcoholic, and what a Kafka-like nightmare he exists in. The writings of someone like Edgar Allan Poe, himself an alcoholic and drug addict, become understandable in these terms.

The fifth personality variable commonly seen among alcoholics involves *dependency* and its various expressions. While many alcoholics would not be described as dependent on the basis of their surface behavior, clinical and therapeutic experience teaches us that dependent needs are nearly always of central importance in the alcoholic's personality makeup.

One group of patients, who quite openly seek to be taken care of and to be given to, we infer to have strong dependent needs for which they seek direct gratification. Alcoholics in this group expect and actively try to get others and the environment to meet their needs. They show a marked lack of initiative, will do little on their own, and appear to function most adequately under the firm and close guidance of those around them. They are often drifters who develop relationships with a dominant man or woman who will protect and take care of them. From the caretaker's viewpoint, these patients are usually "good" patients.

A second extreme group of patients includes alcoholics who are quite the opposite to the above. Relationships that involve any open expression of dependent behavior are avoided. They see themselves as quite capable of taking care of themselves, usually deny any problems involving drinking, and pride themselves on their masculine physical prowess. The statement "he can drink like a man" is among their highest forms of praise. That they do seek gratification of dependent needs is apparent, however, though such expressions are indirect. The bonhomie of the tavern, the sometimes maudlin avowals of friendship, and indeed the dependency on alcohol itself are examples of this. We infer that this type of alcoholic has intense dependent needs, the direct satisfaction of which is extremely unacceptable and frightening to him. The basic fear seems to be that directly dependent behavior makes him look like a little boy, like a "sissy"; in other words, he fears that expressed dependency will drastically alter his tenuous image of himself, will destroy his identity as a man.

A third group of alcoholics lies midway between the extremes I have just described. These patients fluctuate, according to circumstances and their current life situation, between denial of dependent needs and displays of direct gratification. In terms of reaching them therapeutically, we find for several reasons that they promise more than either of the groups above. First, they are not so frightened of their dependent wishes that they have to deny them completely. Second, they are not apt to regress to a severe state of dependent behavior, either because their needs are not so intense or because of the fear they do have of complete expression of dependent behavior. Third, they are still in an active and painful state of conflict, the hoped-for alleviation of which may prompt them to seek help. Both of the other groups have in a very real sense resolved the conflict, one by denying its existence, the other by regressing to marked dependent behavior. Fourth, the very fact that these individuals vary their behavior with respect to dependent needs implies a certain flexibility, which is a positive sign. Despite the notion that these alcoholics are potentially more therapeutically rewarding, their behavior can be confusing and annoying because it is so contradictory. On one occasion, an alcoholic of this type may actively seek help and wish to be taken care of, and on the next deny that he ever requested anything, state he is quite capable of taking care of any problems he might have, and so on. These patients often present management problems with respect to hospital care.

Implications For Caretakers

Let us now look at some of the implications of these traits in terms of the alcoholic's relationships to the world, with special reference to his contacts with caretaking personnel.

With the possible exception of the alcoholic's difficulty in maintaining mutually satisfying relationships, the traits I have described are commonly seen as a natural part of the developmental process in children, and for this reason alcoholics are often described as "infantile," "immature," or "regressed" personalities. Much of their behavior is reminiscent of that seen in small children; it is as if either they had never "grown up" psychologically, or alternately that some stumbling block occurred in their adulthood that resulted in a return to earlier, more childhoodlike modes of behavior and of coping with problems.

When I spoke of the alcoholic's attitudes of superiority, I indicated that it was in part a defensive reflection of feelings of inadequacy; I also said that his superiority has a more basic source. This source is more understandable when we assume that certain aspects of the alcoholic's personality are analogous to those seen among children. Small children are egocentric; that is, from their viewpoint the world revolves around them, and has no reason for existing other than for the satisfaction of their wishes. This childhood egocentrism carries with it implications of omnipotence, and is borne out by fantasies of children containing themes of being all-powerful. We assume that much of the "acting superior" of alcoholics has an analogous origin. Alcoholics, like children, are highly egocentric and have fantasies of omnipotence. The case is similar for low-frustration tolerance: it is a common observation that children, if their wishes are not satisfied on the spot, react with rage, temper tantrums, or sullen withdrawal. Part of growing up is the learning of methods to delay gratification, to put off immediate satisfaction for the sake of later and perhaps more rewarding outcomes; this is, to build up tolerance for frustration. The alcoholic, as we have seen, is unable to tolerate frustration and, like the child, reacts with rage or withdrawal.

The child, because of his relative physical helplessness and because he is egocentric and demands satisfaction of all his needs, is highly dependent. If his needs to be taken care of are not met he is frustrated, and will more often than not respond with indications of anger and pain. However, as the child grows older he becomes more and more interested in doing things for himself, refuses the assistance of others, and shows evidence of marked strivings for independence, self-sufficiency, and autonomy. Certain stages in his development are characterized by kaleidoscopic shifts between dependence and independence. Against this background of the childhood vicissitudes of dependent needs one may view the alcoholic and his ways of coping with similar needs.

The central point I wish to make about the analogies between the child and the alcoholic is this: Such behaviors in a child are considered "normal" and by and large acceptable, but analogous behaviors in an adult are highly unacceptable and a source of anxiety in others. This is a major reason why many people react to the alcoholic with contempt, amusement, or moral indignation.

The often contradictory behavior of the alcoholic, his tendency to express hostility when his needs are frustrated, and his apparent lack of human dignity when drinking heavily, serve to provoke hostility in those around him. Much of the time he acts as though he wished for hostility and rejection from others, and as though he wished to destroy relationships with others. The entire life pattern of the alcoholic points toward a gradual self-destruction: the marital instability of alcoholics is well known; the deterioration of occupational achievement is apparent in many; physical disintegration of serious proportions may occur; and decline of intellectual and other mental faculties is frequently severe. This pattern has been called "slow suicide" by some, and yet the alcoholic persists in this self-destructive process. Because of the evident self-destructive aspects of his life, and because of the positive association between alcoholism and suicide, some investigators have postulated a self-destructive urge as a basic factor in the alcoholic's motivational makeup.

The view may also be taken that the alcoholic's self-destructive behavior is an outcome rather than a cause of his commitment to alcohol and its effects. This conception holds that the alcoholic has discovered a solution to his conflict through excessive alcoholic intake. Though this solution is painful to him, involves loss of self-respect, estrangement from others, and gradual destruction, he feels it is less painful than dealing directly with his conflicts. Part of the pathos of the alcoholic is that while slowly killing himself, physically and emotionally, he feels that he is saving himself from a threat that exists only in his fantasies, but not in outer reality.

The traits I have mentioned are not meant to be all-inclusive, but are intended as general and for the most part easily observable guideposts. Other lists of traits could have been made; for instance, I could have spoken of orality, depression, ambivalence, latent homosexuality, and so on. However, I wanted to describe common and observable characteristics.

Another point concerns the variable expression of the behaviors discussed. Important in this connection is that the traits I have mentioned may be more or less apparent according to the stage of alcoholism, and also depend on whether the alcoholic is drinking heavily at the time he is seen. When he is not drinking, for example, a spree drinker may be a dependent, mildly fearful individual who appears quiet and unassuming; on a spree, however, garrulous expressions of self-importance, anger at supposed slights, and defensive expressions of independence become primary behaviors.

You will have noticed that I have not described the personality of alcoholics within the more standard classifications of the mentally ill, such as the neuroses, or the schizophrenias, or the mood disorders. The reason for this is that a number of studies have shown that when alcoholics are given formal psychiatric diagnoses, these diagnoses tend to fall throughout the range of possible diagnoses. Students of alcoholism have often attempted to devise meaningful diagnostic categories; their success, however, has been minimal. For example, one system divides chronic drinkers into four classes, the social, the reactive, the neurotic, and the addictive, in order of severity of social disintegration and psychological disturbance. In practice, however, the majority of chronic drinkers who are seen in hospitals, clinics, or other caretaking agencies fall into the addictive group, with very few neurotic drinkers, and almost no social or reactive drinkers. Even among the addictive group of alcoholics, wide individual variations in personality makeup are known to occur.

You have seen how adept alcoholics are at provoking hostility or derision in others; I have also indicated how angry or derisive attitudes on the part of others confirm the alcoholic in his conception of the world, thus reaffirming the life pattern that the alcoholic uses as a justification for excessive drinking behavior. Obviously such attitudes are antitherapeutic. When on the other hand, the alcoholic is treated matter-of-factly, with the same respect as that shown toward other patients, he may feel uncomfortable, he may fight against it, he may withdraw from it, but it nevertheless has a positive, and potentially beneficial, meaning to him.

In dealing with alcoholics in hospitals and clinics, awareness of their diminished capacity to withstand frustration as well as their fearfulness can be an important aid. Waiting and delays are inevitable in these settings, and often result in withdrawal or anger. To explain to the alcoholic when and why he will have to wait is an easy antidote, and can serve to reduce tension and decrease the alcoholic's notion that a delay is something directed toward him personally. The patient's fearfulness can often be reduced by describing what procedures are to be done and the reasons for them. In my own work with alcoholics I find that they are initially quite fearful, and I have found that giving them straightforward explanations as to the reasons for the consultation reduces anxiety.

Because of the alcoholic's low frustration tolerance, he has a great deal of difficulty in keeping to the rules and regulations necessary in caretaking settings, since rules by their very nature involve frustration, however minimal. Violation of rules can be most disturbing to caretakers, and can also disrupt the organization of a ward or clinic. To change regulations just for alcoholics, or to be overly permissive with regard to rules, is as much an error as to react punitively with regard to infractions. Either of these means to the alcoholic that he is misunderstood, and he has as little trust in permissive as in punitive persons. He needs and seeks the controls and limits against which he struggles, and in this he again reminds one of the small child. He will repeatedly attempt to break rules to test the limits of the situation he is in. But limits must be set and adhered to, and if it is made clear to the alcoholic that the setting of limits is not punitive but ultimately in his best interests, he less often finds it necessary to exceed limits. For instance, in psychotherapy with alcoholics the patient will not be seen if he is intoxicated when he comes to an interview, nor are persistent phone calls permitted. These rules serve to reduce the patient's dependency and his attempts to involve the therapist in his feelings of low self-esteem.

The insistent demands of the alcoholic and his intense unconscious attempts to provoke rejection and hostility require that treatment be carried on in a team setting involving psychiatrists, psychologists and social workers, physicians, nurses and ward personnel, and the administrative and other nonmedical personnel with whom the patient must interact. Among the guiding principles of this staff should be knowledge and understanding of the alcoholic's fear of establishing meaningful relationships, his low frustration tolerance, his need for controls, and his dependency. Alcoholics are sick people, and when we see them in a hospital setting they are usually physically as well as psychologically ill. The tendency to focus on physical aspects of the disease is understandable. When this happens, however, only some of the results of the illness are treated; if the psychological aspects are ignored a major part of the illness is left untreated. The patient often realizes this and feels that his problem is not understood, so he is less likely to enter or continue treatment when he is discharged.

Notes

1. S. Freud, *Three Contributions to the Theory of Sex* (4th ed.; Washington, D. C.: Nervous and Mental Disease Publishing House, 1930), pp. 43-74.
2. S. Freud, *Contributions to the Psychology of Love. The Most Prevalent Form of Degradation in Erotic Life* (1912), in *Collected Papers* (London: Hogarth, 1925), Vol. 4, pp. 203-216; *Mourning and Melancholia* (1917), in *Collected Papers* (London: Hogarth, 1925), Vol. 4, pp. 152-170.
3. A. A. Brill, "Alcohol and the Individual," *New York Medical Journal*, 109:928-950, 1919.
4. E. Jones, *Papers on Psychoneurosis* (Baltimore: Ward and Co., 1938).
5. E. Glover, "The Etiology of Drug Addiction," *International Journal of Psycho-Analysis*, 13:298-328, 1932.
6. H. Sachs, "The Genesis of Perversions" (abstract), *Psychoanalytic Review*, 16:74, 1929.
7. S. Rado, "The Psychoanalysis of Pharmacothymia," *Psychoanalytic Quarterly*, 2:1-23, 1933.
8. K. A. Menninger, *Man Against Himself* (New York: Harcourt Brace, 1938).
9. S. G. Klebanoff, "Personality Factors in Symptomatic Chronic Alcoholism as Indicated by the Thematic Apperception Test," *Journal of Consulting Psychology*, 11:111-119, 1947.

10. H. M. TIEBOUT, "The Role of Psychiatry in the Field of Alcoholism. With Comment on the Concept of Alcoholism as a Symptom and as Disease," *Quarterly Journal of Studies on Alcohol,* 12:52-57, 1951.
11. R. P. KNIGHT, "The Psychodynamics of Chronic Alcoholism," *Journal of Nervous and Mental Disease,* 86:538-548, 1937.
12. A. O. LUDWIG, "Some Factors in the Genesis of Chronic Alcoholism and Their Bearing on Treatment," in *Papers Presented at the Physicians Institute on Alcoholism of the National State Conference on Alcoholism, March 9-10, 1956* (Boston, 1957).
13. M. J. SHERFEY, "Psychotherapy and Character Structure in Chronic Alcoholism," in O. Diethelm (ed.), *Etiology of Chronic Alcoholism* (Springfield, Illinois: Charles C Thomas, 1955), pp. 16-42.
14. A. O. LUDWIG, personal communication.

Chapter 2
Engaging the Alcoholic to Enter into Treatment

The Massachusetts General Hospital is typical of many university-affiliated hospitals in large cities in that its emergency service operations are divided between treating traditional medical and surgical emergencies, and serving as a community clinic. Each year an increasing number of patients whose major presenting physical complaints are directly related to the use of alcohol come to the hospital. Because of this we were asked, some years after the inception of the Alcohol Clinic, to conduct a survey of the alcoholic population in our emergency service. In this primarily demographic study, reported in Section A, we asked who these patients are, where they come from, what their needs are, and what services an emergency service can provide for them.

An unpublished finding of this study was that less than one percent of alcoholic patients seen in the emergency service ever came to the Alcohol Clinic for treatment, although theoretically all such patients were referred. At first our conclusion was that these patients did not desire any therapeutic endeavor, but inevitably we were struck by a wide gap between our theory and practice. Theoretically, we felt that the successful care of the alcoholic patient requires a continuous nonfragmented, action-oriented, nonrejecting, nonhostile relationship. But what happened in practice? On entering the emergency service, the patient was seen by the following individuals: an admitting clerk, the chief medical officer, a specialist if there were complications, a financial officer, a nurse, a social worker, and any other physicians and paramedical personnel who might be called into the case. If the patient survived this and wanted to go to the Alcohol Clinic (which was at that time located in another building), he would have to go to an admitting officer in the Out-Patient Department, be seen by a financial officer, go upstairs to the Clinic, where he would be seen by the clinic secrétary, a psychiatric social worker, possibly the psychiatric resident on call that day, and with an appointment being made for the patient to see a psychiatric resident for evaluation; if the patient kept this appointment, his name was placed on a waiting list for treatment. Assignment to a permanent therapist occurred in four to six weeks, with a doctor different from any he had seen during his previous contacts. The alcoholic must deal with perhaps a dozen different individuals and innumerable delays with accompanying chances for hostility and rejection, even though he may have originally come to the emergency service as an individual desperately needing a steady and secure relationship.

Recognition of the extreme discrepancy between emergency service procedures and clinical practice in the Alcohol Clinic, revealed an opportunity to submit our ideas about treatment to actual test in a clinical setting. Project support from the National Institute of Mental Health enabled us to carry out such a test. In the project we defined alcoholism as a chronic behavior disorder manifested by repeated drinking of alcoholic beverages to an extent that interferes with the drinker's health or his social or economic functioning. Implicit in this definition is an emphasis on the uncontrolled, self-destructive, and dependent behavior that we usually refer to as "addiction." The general purpose of the project was to effect an interruption of this behavior by utilizing the patient's dependency needs constructively. Since most alcoholics do not exercise their own initiative in seeking out treatment, we assumed that the situation in which the alcoholic has to seek aid via an emergency service signifies both a timely and appropriate point at which to attempt the establishment of a therapeutic relationship. Historically, the alcoholic in the emergency facilities of our nation's hospitals has received scant attention and interest. One obvious reason for this is the crisis-dominated atmosphere of these overtaxed facilities. A second and more subtle explanation, however, may be inferred from attitudes toward alcoholism common in our society, attitudes that may well affect the medical handling of alcoholic patients. A third possible factor in the failure to "reach" the alcoholic through emergency services is that these services fail to take account of the fact that the symptom of alcoholism must be viewed within the patient's social setting, as well as within the medical setting.

Since our goal was to initiate and maintain contact at a time when the alcoholic is highly dependent upon the hospital, that is, when he comes to an emergency service for medical treatment, we proposed an approach involving assistance both in the emergency service setting and in the patient's social setting. We proposed the use of "alcoholism treatment catalysts," represented by a psychiatrist physically present at all times in the emergency service, and a psychiatric social worker to negotiate with the patient and his family outside the hospital, in the patient's social environment. The specific roles of these "catalysts" is described in Section B.

The project was designed as an experiment to compare groups of patients receiving these special services with groups of patients treated in the manner usual in the emergency service. Our hypothesis, stated in the form of a prediction, was that:

> The experimental group that has received the special effects of the combined interest and activities of the social worker and emergency [service] psychiatric resident will differ significantly from the control group, which has not received this special attention, with respect to the incidence of initial visits to the alcoholism clinic and with respect to the total number of visits to the alcoholism clinic by patients in each group, and further that the difference will be in a single direction, namely that the experimental group will have more first visits and more total visits.

Substantiation of the hypothesis would mean that the findings could have widespread application throughout the country, where metropolitan general hospitals in large cities might well utilize emergency service contacts of alcoholic patients as a significant adjunct to their alcoholism clinic facilities and treatment operations.

The project was initiated in 1959. Its major findings were reported in the paper reprinted in Section 2B. A report of a replication of the original investigation with a group of alcoholics less socially isolated than those in the first study is presented in Section 2C. Other studies with patients who enter or go through the medical social system in different ways are reported briefly in Sections 2D, 2E, and 2F.

Not all patients who are seeking help with alcohol problems come to a clinic or emergency service; frequently the first tentative contact is made by telephone. The call may be from a patient, but often such calls are made by family members or relatives. Usually the decision to contact a treatment facility is made in the heat of a domestic crisis, with a sense of desperation that informs us that the parties involved feel helpless to cope with the predicament they are in. The call also signals an admission that outside help is required. Such a situation appears to be a propitious point at which to intervene immediately and actively not only to relieve the crisis but hopefully to form a therapeutic alliance whereby the forces underlying the eruption of crises may be dealt with. The usual procedure for handling these calls at our clinic was little different than that used in most outpatient settings. The secretary obtained the information necessary to arrange an appointment for evaluation, then mailed an appointment slip to the patient; this procedure required several contacts with the patient, and took at least two to four weeks. By the time the patient was able to start treatment the crisis that had motivated the phone call had passed, and the patient had often lost interest in entering treatment. Having demonstrated the importance of the initial contact with patients entering an emergency service, we undertook another study (Section 2D) utilizing telephone calls as the point of intervention.

Other patients may come to an outpatient clinic or walk-in service for help with a problem that requires inpatient care before the underlying issues can be dealt with. When the clinic or service does not provide such care routinely, it becomes necessary to involve other institutions. This makes for a complication in care in that referral and rereferral procedures must be instituted. If the patient is not to be lost at these crucial points, caution must be exercised. Many patients who come to the Massachusetts General Hospital with alcoholic problems request or require a voluntary admission to Bridgewater State Hospital, a correctional institution with a rehabilitative orientation where alcoholics may be admitted by self-request or by court commitment. After detoxification and discharge from Bridgewater we request the patient to return to us for continuing treatment on an outpatient basis. As an extension of our interest in enhancing motivation to enter and to continue in treatment, we undertook two studies (Sections 2E and 2F) with patients referred to

Bridgewater, the point of intervention in both occurring immediately prior to discharge, the technique of intervention being a letter to the patient in one study and a telephone call to the patient in the other. Of additional interest is the inclusion in both studies of a clinical measure of sobriety as a dependent variable.

2.A. Alcoholism as an Emergency Ward Problem

The steady increase in the number of patients utilizing emergency facilities in general hospitals has been reported and explained in part as a result of increased public acceptance of the general hospital as a health center of the community.[1] The treatment of patients with alcoholism alone or in combination with other disorders has always been a difficult problem for physicians who work on general hospital emergency facilities. Some hospitals have been so overwhelmed by the incidence of admissions to emergency services that they have established special alcoholic units; a small number of hospitals, particularly in large cities, have attempted to provide specific diagnostic and therapeutic programs for alcoholic patients. A few pioneering hospitals have attempted to establish broad therapeutic programs for alcoholic patients, with encouraging initial results.[2] Adequate facilities for alcoholics have, however, been described as "almost nonexistent in most general hospitals."[3]

The recognition that alcoholism constitutes a serious medical and public health problem has resulted in increased demands that hospitals open their doors to these patients. The necessity for wide-range facilities is obvious. In the emergency service the alcoholic should be able to receive treatment for his acute problems and their secondary complications, and ideally, to establish his first contact with an alcoholism clinic for long-term rehabilitation. Most emergency rooms, however, have been concerned only with sobering up the patient, treating his medical complications, and then rapidly

Section 2.A. written, in collaboration, by Jack H. Mendelson and Morris E. Chafetz.
Notes to Chapter 2 will be found on page 70.

discharging him. Because of the high rate of relapse among alcoholics, efforts to effect changes in the treatment orientation adopted by most emergency service staffs are difficult. The present study undertook to observe alcoholic patients directly in an emergency service setting and gather information in three fundamental areas: (1) Who are the alcoholic patients? (2) Where do they come from? (3) What are their needs? In reporting data from any small population group, it is necessary to recognize that differences will occur from locale to locale. The role of this pilot study is of a hypothesis-seeking nature and recognizes the limitations of any broad generalizations.

Procedure

It has always been difficult to obtain information about alcoholics admitted to general hospital emergency facilities. This is in part related to the general reluctance of staff personnel to record the diagnosis of alcoholism, perhaps because of anticipated medicolegal complications that might arise from official recordings of such a diagnosis. It was therefore necessary to establish a reliable and yet unofficial method of obtaining admission data. Arrangements were made in the Emergency Ward of the Massachusetts General Hospital for the entry of names, addresses, and identifying hospital (unit) numbers of all alcoholic patients; this material was available only to the study group.

The alcoholic population was divided into two groups.

Group 1. Patients in this group were admitted to the emergency ward with a history of alcoholism and were either acutely intoxicated or suffering from symptoms of alcohol withdrawal. These patients came to the emergency service chiefly for problems connected with alcohol, and not for other surgical or medical problems.

Group 2. Patients in this group were admitted to the emergency service with a history of alcoholism and showed evidences of intoxication at the time of admission. The prime motivating factor for admission to the emergency service for these patients, however, was a variety of surgical or medical problems, not alcoholism alone. More than one-half of this group entered with traumatic injuries consisting mainly of fractures, contusions, and lacerations; many of these injuries were the result of automobile accidents. A quarter of these patients entered with a febrile illness of pulmonary origin. Other conditions, in the order of frequency of appearance, were gastrointestinal illnesses, dermatological problems, and cardiac and hepatic disease.

The study began on July 1, 1957, and was completed on September 15, 1957. The 100th case of Group 2 was admitted on August 17, 1957. At the time the 100th case of Group 1 was admitted on September 15, 1957, an additional 31 cases of patients in Group 2 had also been recorded. Thus the total number of cases involving alcoholism seen during the 2½ months was 231, indicating a yearly rate of more than 1,000 admissions. On admission, the names, addresses, and unit numbers of all patients were recorded. Other data presented here were obtained from a study of the patients' hospital records.

Results

The 100 consecutive cases of Group 1 patients consisted of 80 males ranging in age from 19 to 64 years, with an average age of 42; 11 females ranging in age from 20 to 53 years, with an average age of 37; and 9 readmissions, 8 males and 1 female. The duration of excessive drinking of these patients ranged from 1 to 31 years (average 8 years) for males and from 2 to 16 years (average 12 years) for females.

The 100 consecutive cases of Group 2 patients consisted of 68 males ranging in age from 18 to 70 years with an average age of 39; 24 females ranging in age from 24 to 55 years with an average age of 35; and 8 readmissions, 6 males and 2 females. The duration of excessive drinking in Group 2 patients ranged from 3 months to 28 years for males (average 4 years) and from 1 to 8 years for females (average 5 years).

In both groups the number of female patients was smaller than the number of males but the proportion of males was higher in Group 1. The age range and average age of females was lower but their average duration of excessive drinking was greater.

The majority of the subjects (71 percent) lived within the metropolitan Boston area, or, more specifically, within a 15-mile radius of the hospital; 16.5 percent lived outside this area, some coming from as far as Washington, D. C.; 4 percent reported that they were homeless and had no address (one patient gave the Boston Common, a public park, as his address).

Discussion

The wide age range of the sample and the variety of the illnesses observed in Group 2 indicate that alcoholic patients seeking aid in a general hospital emergency service are characterized by a number of problems associated with the somatopsychic pathology of alcoholism. It is therefore obvious that facilities for treating these patients cannot be geared to a specific population, age, or socioeconomic group. The problems may range from those encountered in late adolescence to those of old age. The high ratio of male to female patients encountered in both groups suggests that alcoholism is more prevalent among men, but greater average duration of excessive drinking of the females in both categories seems to indicate that women may be more reluctant to seek therapy early; the longevity of their illness may therefore impede therapeutic measures.

The large number of patients in both groups who came from the immediate vicinity of the hospital does not necessarily reflect a particularly high incidence of alcoholism in that area, since most of the patients who come to the hospital, clinics, and emergency service for a variety of other surgical and medical problems are from this area. The fact that patients in the hospital area will utilize emergency room facilities for problems involving alcoholism indicates that resources for the treatment of alcoholism will be used when they are readily available. The geographical data also indicate that general hospital emergency services must be prepared to treat patients from distant areas and make suitable arrangements for their return.

Four percent of the cases observed were homeless individuals, and a major aspect of their care consisted in making suitable social service arrangements for the provision of housing and food after discharge. The large number of cases (8.5 percent) readmitted during the short period studied emphasizes the high rate of relapse in alcoholic patients.

Emergency service treatment of the intoxicated alcoholic patient is uniquely difficult because of the hostile feelings these patients tend to evoke. At the time of admission, the alcoholic tends to be dirty, disheveled, disturbing, and demanding, and caretaking personnel react toward these patients with attitudes reserved for delinquents. Frequently the alcoholic patient is admitted to the emergency service during the early hours of the morning, which may result in a disinterested, hostile attitude on the part of the admitting physician. Since we are culturally oriented to treat people who are sick and suffering, the implied pleasure the alcoholic supposedly received from his drinking tends to result in moralizing and punitive attitudes. Psychotherapeutic experiences with alcoholics in our Alcohol Clinic have shown that the initial contact with the addicted patient will have a significant influence on the establishment of a healthy therapeutic relationship. Since most alcoholic bouts terminate in stupor or sickness requiring medical care, it is apparent that the emergency service of a general hospital is a logical locale for establishing the first important contact with alcoholic patients.

Fundamentally, the successful rehabilitation of the alcoholic patient begins with treatment of the acute manifestations of alcoholism and the secondary complications due to prolonged excessive use of alcohol. The average alcoholic patient, when he presents himself for treatment, arrives in a state of despair and is usually physically debilitated. Only resolute and immediate action in the direction of strong support can penetrate his defensive shell. For this reason, the interest of the admitting officer in the emergency service may be the vital key to contact with him, eventually and ideally leading to prolonged treatment. Furthermore, since the admitting physician is usually faced with the problems of adequate disposition of the cases of alcoholism he treats, it is important that the medical services dealing with the problem of alcoholism have a close working relationship with available social service facilities within and outside the hospital. When physicians who are involved in treating alcoholics in the emergency service understand the problem and are aware of the facilities available for suitable disposition they can often react toward these patients in a helpful way.

2.B. Establishing Treatment Relations with Alcoholics I.

Lindemann has dealt theoretically with the concept of crisis as it relates to significant, and often typical, events in the individual's life history.[4] Using his thesis as a starting point, we assume that: (1) an individual's initial contact with a medical institution reflects a physical, psychological, and/or social crisis; and (2) motivation for treatment is higher at times of crisis than at times of noncrisis. A corollary of the second assumption is that motivation for treatment is not only greater for the immediate crisis, but also for the broader pathology from which the crisis may have arisen. It follows that the alcoholic's initial contact with a medical facility represents a crisis in which motivation for treatment for both the presenting complaint and for alcoholism is higher than usual.

Viewed within this conceptual framework, the mere fact of admission to an emergency service furnishes an unusual opportunity to effect a rehabilitative relation with the alcoholic. In order to maximize this positive motivation to the point at which treatment relations will be initiated and maintained, certain conditions of care must be met, based on a conception of alcoholism as a behavioral disorder involving the individual and his social environment. In handling the initial contact, consistent respect for the alcoholic's tenuous feelings of self-esteem and constructive utilization of his dependency needs are essential; this means treating him with respect and consideration, reducing the frequency of frustrating situations, and gratifying his requests. Constructive utilization of dependency needs does not imply indiscriminate giving, but gratification that

Section 2.B. written, in collaboration, by Morris E. Chafetz, Howard T. Blane, Harry S. Abram, Joseph H. Golner, Elizabeth Lacy, William F. McCourt, Eleanor Clark, and William Meyers.

Notes to Chapter 2 will be found on page 70.

serves to establish and further the patient's trust and confidence in the caretaker. In the initial meeting, the alcoholic must be offered a relationship with caretakers that promises to continue and that is available as frequently as the patient needs it. This approach alleviates the alcoholic's notorious difficulty in interpersonal relations as well as his reaction to the frustration of not getting help immediately when he wants it. The help given must be as active as possible, because the alcoholic responds more to action than to words. Finally, since alcoholism involves the individual's social environment, the patient must be approached in his social setting outside the hospital. The necessity for full utilization of initial contacts with alcoholics if one is to establish treatment relations has been described in terms very similar to ours by Jean Sapir.[5] She emphasizes gratification of dependency needs, care by the same person, decreasing frustration, and increasing self-esteem.

Procedure

The method we proposed consists of a two-step approach. The initial step, at the intrapersonal level, is taken by a resident psychiatrist in the emergency ward. Simultaneous extramural and interpersonal levels are handled by a psychiatric social worker, who negotiates with the patient and his family in the patient's environment. The efforts of the members of these treatment teams center around meeting the conditions listed above: utilization of the alcoholic's dependency needs, consideration for his lowered self-esteem, reduction of frustration, continuity of care, and communication through action. More specifically, the psychiatrist and social worker show the patient that he is always welcome, and that he will be met with interest and respect whatever his problems. Each patient is made aware that the psychiatrist is "his doctor" and the social worker is "his social worker." During his stay in the emergency service and as an outpatient in our alcohol clinic, as well as in the community, every patient is closely followed by the team members. Direct contact with the patient is increased, and every attempt is made to avoid an impersonal approach, rejection, or hostility in contacts with other hospital personnel. Many problems presented by the patients are dealt with at a concrete level, and include such things as obtaining lodging for homeless patients, help in making financial arrangements, or getting the patient a shave or a meal. Through such concrete and personal ways of gratifying dependency needs we aim to show each patient our interest in him as an individual and in his current and future well-being.

We chose the emergency service as the place to test the effectiveness of the method because many alcoholics make initial contact with the hospital through the emergency service, but do not follow through on treatment by seeking outpatient care. These patients represent a group that is neglected at both research and clinical levels.

Our first job was to familiarize the psychiatrists, social workers, and other project personnel with the thinking that led us to undertake the project, and to discuss our clinical and theoretical viewpoints with them. Since it was clear that this could not be done *in vacuo,* over a period of eight weeks we selected some fifteen emergency service alcoholic patients as pilot cases. Our experience with these patients enabled us to modify our thinking and our clinical approach; the approach was at that time and has since remained highly flexible and geared to each patient's unique life situation.

Because we wanted to ensure utmost coordination among the treatment teams, personnel of the emergency service, and other hospital services, we undertook to explain and discuss methods and goals of the project with individuals and groups at various levels of administrative and professional hierarchies of the hospital departments involved. The need to develop working relations with a number of public and private agencies in the community was soon apparent; this spadework was carried out primarily by the social workers. Explanations were service-oriented at all times, and the research orientation of our efforts was muted in order to lessen the possibility that this information would get into the "grapevine" of the alcoholic subculture, since this would introduce a major uncontrolled variable into an already complex situation. We have no way of knowing how successful we were in this endeavor, but anecdotal material suggests that some alcoholics sought aid at the emergency ward because they heard one was "treated right" there. In addition to indicating that our approach appealed to alcoholics, this anecdotal feedback reinforces the notion that research carried out in a social organism changes the organism itself.

During the pilot study, team members familiarized themselves with the various methods of recording data, and suggested modifications. Although the research team included members of three different, but related, disciplines (psychiatry, social work, psychology), working relations proved to be remarkably good. This is attributed to our awareness of difficulties encountered by others,[6] to a spirit of free exchange without criticism, to high interest and enthusiasm, and to delegation of carefully delineated areas of authority and responsibility by the project director.

The study group consisted of 200 male alcoholics. Of these, 100 were assigned to an experimental group, each member of which was treated by one of the treatment teams; the other 100 patients, each of whom received no special treatment other than usual emergency service care, were assigned to a control group. Control patients were to have no direct or indirect contact with members of the research teams. As it turned out, six control patients were inadvertently seen by project personnel after entry into the project and during the one-year experimental period; they were excluded from statistical analyses. Contact with these patients was unavoidable due to the sometimes hectic activity occurring on the emergency service. A seventh control patient had been seen as a pilot study case; he, too, was not included in the statistical analysis.

Subject Selection

The first twenty patients diagnosed as alcoholic by the chief medical officer of the emergency service at the beginning of the month were alternately assigned to the experimental or control group. This procedure was repeated for ten months until a total of 200 subjects was reached. Four excluding criteria were used: (1) only men were selected; (2) patients treated in the hospital's alcohol clinic less than sixty days prior to emergency service admission were not selected; (3) patients whose residence was more than twenty miles from the hospital were not selected; and (4) patients previously selected as experimental, control, or pilot-study group subjects were not reselected in the event of subsequent readmission to the emergency service. The chief medical officer was chosen to select subjects in order to preserve as much as possible the usual pattern of emergency service care of alcoholics. This physician, who is always an advanced medical or surgical resident, sees each patient who comes to the emergency service; after the examination he refers the patient to the appropriate service. The position of chief medical officer is rotated among the residents on a monthly or bimonthly basis; fifteen residents served this function over the period of the project.

Our operational definition of an alcoholic was any individual who was diagnosed as such by the chief medical officer in the emergency service. The physician was free to use whatever criteria for diagnosis he thought appropriate, although he was given the following guide to aid in identifying alcoholics:

I. *Primary Indices*
   A. Previous diagnosis of alcoholism
   B. Alcohol on the breath
   C. Clinical evidence of intoxication
   D. Symptoms of alcohol withdrawal
   E. Presence of physical symptoms associated with "chronic alcoholism"
   F. Current employment status

II. *Historical Indices*
   A. Heavy drinking, continued or sporadic, for the past two years (heavy drinking refers to drinking patterns in excess of the sociocultural group of which the patient is a member)
   B. Impaired interpersonal relationships associated with drinking
      (1) Marital difficulties
      (2) Loss of former nonfamily associations
      (3) Change in previous religious group participation
   C. Alteration of employment status in association with increased drinking behavior

D. Alteration of social conformity behavior
   (1) Arrest history
   (2) Driving history

Independent criteria (probation records, hospitalization for alcoholism, and family reports) indicate that few false positives, that is, patients assigned to the project as alcoholic but not in fact alcoholic, were selected by using this selection procedure. However, review of records of all patients admitted to the emergency service during periods of subject selection reveal that more than 200 additional patients diagnosable as alcoholic by the above criteria were not referred to the project as subjects. Comparison of these "missed" cases with the study group is the subject of a separate report to determine patient characteristics related to differential diagnosis; attitudes of chief medical officers toward alcoholism are also reported.

The experimental period was one year, at the end of which both experimental and control subjects were followed by interview and other methods. Analysis of data includes comparisons between experimental and control groups in order to test the major predictions of the study.

Methods:

Treatment teams. Two half-time psychiatrists, one full-time and a second half-time psychiatric social worker rotated with one another to make up four treatment teams. During the period of subject selection at the beginning of each month, one or the other psychiatrist was on twenty-four hour call to the emergency service. The social workers, on the other hand, were on duty during the day, but not on weekends or evenings. Patients admitted to the service during these times were seen the following day or Monday by the social workers on an outpatient basis. When a patient was hospitalized, as was often the case, the social worker saw him on the ward at the earliest opportunity. Each team member was responsible for keeping a clinical record of his contact with each patient, for obtaining information necessary to complete a specially devised social history, and for keeping records of contacts with the patient, emotionally relevant others, and agencies involved in the team's effort with each patient. In the pilot study, it became evident that the patient's social needs were extremely varied and a challenge to the ingenuity of the social workers. The time necessary to meet these challenges was great; for every hour of direct patient-social worker contact in the emergency ward, four to eight hours of nondirect services were necessary to provide adequate handling of a patient's social problems. To arrive at a systematic picture of the extent and breadth of those complex and time-consuming activities, each social worker maintained a log of contacts with individuals and agencies, inside and outside the hospital.

Assessing patient contact. To obtain measures to test the two major predictions of the study, a record was made of each type of face-to-face contact in the clinic initiated by the patient. These included: (1) scheduled interviews with a psychiatrist or social worker; (2) attendance at group therapy meetings; (3) psychological testing; and (4) unscheduled visits to the hospital by the patient with express requests to see his doctor or social worker. Since patients have means of maintaining a relationship with the clinic other than direct contact, such things as telephone calls and letters from patients were also recorded, although these are treated separately in statistical analyses. Since it is assumed that consistent keeping of appointments is an index of strength of a therapeutic alliance, records were kept of canceled appointments and appointments that a patient failed to keep without notifying the clinic.

Follow-up. Follow-up of the 200 project cases at the end of the one-year experimental period consisted of interviews with the patient, relatives, and others, (1) to complete the social history inventory and (2) to determine patient attitudes toward the hospital and treatment. The follow-up interview was carried out by individual members of the teams; experimental cases were interviewed whenever possible by a worker with whom the patient had had no previous contact. When the patient himself was the respondent, the following attitudinal areas were investigated:

1. Attitudes toward treatment received at the hospital.
2. Attitudes toward emergency service treatment received.
3. Conceptions of ideal treatment.

4. Attitudes toward treatment received via the treatment teams (experimental cases only).

5. Patient's reasons for return or nonreturn to alcohol clinic.

6. Patient's response to description of treatment team approach (control cases only).

The actual process of following these patients after a one-year interval proved to be extremely difficult, and the methods employed are reported elsewhere (see Chapter 5, Section B).

Results

The first prediction stated that more experimental than control group patients would make initial visits to the alcohol clinic. Table 1 (Appendix A) shows that 65.0 percent of the experimental group in contrast to 5.4 percent of the control group made initial clinic visits; this finding is significant beyond the .001 level of confidence.

Our second prediction was that more experimental than control group patients would make five or more self-initiated visits to the alcohol clinic. Table 1 (Appendix A) shows that 42.0 percent of the experimental group returned to the clinic five or more times in contrast to 1.1 percent of the control group.

It may be noted that the results summarized in Tables 1 and 2 differ from those reported in previous papers.[7] These discrepancies are due to the fact that the first communication reported preliminary findings based on the first eighty-subject and four-month experimental period,[8] and the second paper presented findings on the total sample but for a six-month period.[9]

Establishment of a therapeutic relationship was operationally defined as five or more self-initiated face-to-face contacts with research team members in the course of the experimental period. Patients making one to four visits are termed "abortive" treatment relation cases. Patients who made no self-initiated personal contact with the clinic are classed as having established no treatment relation. Results by this threefold classification are presented in Table 1 (Appendix A) and show that treatment and abortive treatment relations were established significantly more often among experimental than among control cases. These results confirm the two major predictions of this investigation.

Perhaps a word is in order about our choice of five visits as signifying that patients have formed a treatment relation. Although we attribute no magical properties to the number five, we do believe that most patients who keep five or more appointments can be considered to be "in treatment." This obviously does not mean that all patients who come for four visits and then stop have not been in treatment, nor that all patients who make five or more visits are indeed in treatment. We chose a criterion of five visits as a rigorous and clinically realistic measure of classifying those patients who most probably had established treatment relations with the clinic. This choice emerged from consideration of three factors. First, others have used a criterion of five visits to differentiate "continuers" from "noncontinuers" in studies undertaken in psychiatric or alcoholic clinic samples.[10] Second, clinical experience instructs us that patients who make more than five visits tend to remain in treatment.[11] Third, patients too fearful to make more than tentative attempts to enter treatment usually make this known by canceling or not showing up for appointments well before their fifth visit.

The measure on which the major findings are based is the number of scheduled appointments kept in the alcohol clinic, plus any other patient-initiated face-to-face contacts with team personnel. As indicated earlier, patients have ways other than direct personal meetings of initiating and maintaining contact with members of the therapeutic team; these include telephone calls, letters, and greeting cards. When these indirect means are added to the more usual ways of continuing a relationship, the percentage of patients making one or more contacts in the experimental group rises from 65 to 69 percent; the percentage of treatment relations (five or more contacts) established from 42 to 45 percent. Comparative figures from the control group are not available, since we did not keep a precise record of indirect means of control-group contact. However, we do know that none of the control patients made contact by mail, and it is our impression that few, if any, telephone calls were made to the clinic by control patients.

In addition to the establishment of a therapeutic link, we were also interested in the maintenance of the relation. Consequently the number of visits by the forty-two patients who came to the clinic more than five times is presented in Table 2 (Appendix A), which shows that 40.5 percent of these forty-two patients continue on in treatment for ten or more interviews. If all types of patient-initiated contact are considered, 50.0 percent make ten or more contacts with members of the team. This suggests that patients who establish treatment relations tend to use more than one way of maintaining the alliance. Analyzing this suggestion directly, it is found that 54.8 percent of the forty-two men who established treatment relations at the criterion of five or more interviews also maintained the relationship by telephoning and/or writing to their psychiatrist or social worker.

The median number of visits for the entire experimental group is two, considerably below the numbers of median visits reported by investigators of duration of psychotherapy in general psychiatric clinics.[12] The explanation of this low number of median visits may be found in the fact that we accepted all patients for treatment, rather than using the selection procedures usually employed in psychiatric clinics. This is not the case for the studies cited. Garfield and Affleck and Rosenthal and Frank studied those cases who came for at least one treatment session.[13] The median numbers of visits reported in these two investigations are twelve and six respectively. Another study dealt with three samples of "closed treatment" cases in a federal mental hygiene clinic, and the medians were nine, nine, and five treatment sessions for each of the samples.[14] Schaffer and Myers used a more inclusive criterion; all cases were accepted for therapy, but not all patients who applied to their clinic for treatment were accepted as candidates for psychotherapy.[15] Although these investigators do not report median number of visits, examination of their data indicates that the median fell between two to four weeks of treatment (they roughly equate one week of treatment with one treatment visit). Our figure of two visits for the entire experimental group, therefore, can be compared only indirectly with these studies.

When we adopt as a criterion only those experimental patients who came for at least one visit, direct comparison with two previous investigations can be made.[16] On this basis our median number of visits is six, the same as that reported by Rosenthal and Frank,[17] although less than that of Garfield and Affleck.[18] This suggests that the clinical approach we used is approximately as effective in maintaining treatment relationships with chronic alcoholics as traditional approaches are with general psychiatric populations.

In view of the clinical observation that alcoholics miss many appointments scheduled for them, we examined the data and found that the median number of appointments scheduled for the experimental group was five. It is evident that although treatment relations were established far beyond expectancy with alcoholics in the experimental group, the problem characteristic of alcoholics—missed appointments—was still present. Even among those patients who made five or more visits to the clinic, nearly three-quarters (73.8 percent) missed two or more of the interviews formally scheduled. Stated differently, the median number of interviews scheduled for those patients who returned more than five times is eleven, in contrast to a median of seven appointments kept.

The results on return patterns, significant in themselves, attain additional meaning when the composition of the sample is considered and contrasted with samples of general psychiatric clientele reported in studies related to continuing or discontinuing treatment. The 200 men who composed the present study group were, on the average, middle-aged (mean age: 48, $S.D. = 11$), predominantly of the Catholic faith (77.1 percent), either single, separated, divorced, or widowed (79 percent). Less than half (45.7 percent) reported an employer at the time of emergency service admission, and over half (55.6 percent) were brought to the hospital by the police. The subjective complaints that led these men to come to the emergency service were classified into three categories: medical (17.5 percent), surgical (6.5 percent), and alcoholic-psychiatric (28.0 percent). No subjective presenting complaint was reported for the remainder of the group (48.0 percent). This high figure is due largely to the fact that most of the men brought in by the police saw no reason for medical attention, and were either severely intoxicated or felt coerced; in some instances, however, the admitting physician did not record the patient's initial complaint. Few men in the sample (17 percent) reported subscribing to any form of medical insurance. Of the 100 experimental cases, 29 were homeless, that is, without a place to sleep at the time of admission; 40 lived alone or in some type of social institution; the remainder lived with relatives or friends. It is of interest that although 71 percent of the men stated they had entered into marital contracts at one time in their lives, only 11 percent indicated that they were currently living with their wives.

We dealt, then, with a group of middle-aged alcoholics consisting predominantly of men without families, some of them homeless, with a high incidence of unemployment and of involvement with legal authorities. These men were largely destitute and lacking social resources; many of them had no subjective presenting complaint when they entered the emergency service. The similarity between our group and those studied by others[19] indicates that our sample was drawn from a previously well-described population of alcoholics, localized within relatively small geographic subdivisions of metropolitan centers. Our group was selected on the basis of admission to a general hospital, whereas Straus and McCarthy studied men living on the Bowery,[20] and Pittman and Gordon studied men serving sentences for public intoxication.[21] It appears that each set of investigators examined the same kind of population, but at different points in a cyclical and repetitive life style. The sociocultural characteristics of this population of alcoholics differ markedly from those of alcoholics seen in private psychiatric facilities[22] and to a lesser extent from those of alcoholics seen in public alcoholism clinics.[23] Finally, the composition of our sample of alcoholics is in marked contrast to those reported in studies investigating drop-out rates in psychiatric outpatient samples. In these studies age is typically lower, and marital stability and employment higher;[24] the element of direct coercion surrounding admission is almost completely lacking, and the presenting problem is more frequently and explicitly expressed as a direct psychological or social one. These considerations give added dimension to the results reported here.

Discussion

The results pertaining to the two predictions of this study are of major importance, for they convincingly demonstrate that individuals in a hitherto unreachable clinical group can indeed form therapeutic attachments. It cannot be emphasized too strongly that, prior to the initiation of this study, virtually no alcoholics came to the alcoholic clinic as a consequence of emergency service admission. The fact that nearly two-thirds of the experimental cases made initial clinic visits and that well over one-third made five or more visits are striking indications that interest and attention based on understanding can engage tenuously motivated alcoholics into meaningful relationships. As we have seen, these patients were frequently homeless and poverty-stricken, leading lives devoid of meaningful human contacts, and were of the type most often referred to as Skid Row alcoholics. The response of these supposedly alienated men graphically documents the necessity of developing and applying new and imaginative variations of clinical skills to mental health problems, which have often mistakenly been considered unsolvable because rigid applications of traditional approaches have failed.

Examination of other aspects of the present findings confirm the view that usual clinical approaches to difficult treatment groups (including delinquents and other socially deviant groups, as well as alcoholics) must be reexamined and revised. Reference to two studies of continuance and discontinuance of therapy in outpatient alcohol treatment settings show that the number of patients remaining in treatment is low.[25] Chafetz, using a criterion of three or more visits to define continuance, found that only 25 percent of the regular caseload at our alcohol clinic remained in treatment.[26] Fowler, using five or more interviews to define continuers, reports a figure of 28 percent.[27] It must be emphasized that the usual clinic caseload includes a high proportion of alcoholics sufficiently motivated to seek treatment by their own endeavors, at facilities specifically designed to treat problems involving excessive drinking. The currently obtained figure of 42 percent (using a criterion of five or more visits) in our experimental group compares favorably with both of these previous studies, particularly in view of the observation that the experimental patients as a group appear to be less initially motivated and less socially integrated than patients who come directly to a clinic for help. It follows that by revising traditional clinic admission and administrative policies that make for delay and fragmented relations with hospital and clinic personnel, we could be highly effective in increasing the incidence of establishing treatment relations.

Our assumption that continuity of care is crucial in maintaining relations with alcoholics is supported by the fact that only one control patient returned for five or more visits. It is worth more than passing mention that this patient was a former clinic client who in years past had had an excellent relationship with one therapist, but had discontinued treatment some time prior to the initiation of the study. His avowed purpose in coming to the emergency service was to resume treatment with his former therapist. With this exception, none of the control patients followed through to establish a treatment relationship; we believe that this is a result of lack of continuity of care. Additional support for this view is evident when the return patterns of six control patients inadvertently seen by project personnel are examined. These men were seen by project personnel in isolated contacts and in the context of extraproject clinical responsibilities of the research personnel; no attempt was made to ensure continuity of care in their contacts with these patients. Four of these six men returned to the clinic for initial visits, but none for five or more visits. It is likely that one or two of the four patients who returned for initial visits would have maintained a treatment relation had continuity of care been available. It should be noted, however, that the one control patient who had been seen as a pilot study case did not return to the clinic during the one-year experimental period, nor did he come to the clinic when he was seen as a pilot study case.

Finally, five control patients returned to the clinic for visits subsequent to emergency service admission. Since our previous survey showed that almost no patients followed through on treatment in the emergency service by presenting themselves in the alcohol clinic,[28] the return of some control patients achieves speculative, though not statistical, significance. It is likely that the return beyond expectancy of these control patients is related to changes in attitude toward treatment of alcoholism on the part of emergency service personnel as a consequence of their observation of the operation of the treatment teams. One emergency service physician, for example, who was actively hostile and rejecting toward alcoholics and contemptuous of the goals of the project, showed a complete reversal of behavior some time after the project began, and asked team members how best to treat his alcoholic patients. He explained that he had not realized that alcoholics could indeed be helped, and had learned this only by observing the treatment teams in action.

Earlier we referred to studies on continuers and discontinuers in general psychiatric outpatient settings. These studies bear an important relationship to the work reported here, even though they deal with a spectrum of psychiatric disorders in contrast to a particular diagnostic category, and despite the marked divergence between psychiatric clinic intake procedures and that described here. We refer to results indicating that early drop-out from psychotherapy in outpatient psychiatric settings is associated with low social class position.[29] This finding, as well as others, has led to two ostensibly divergent viewpoints with regard to psychiatric treatment. While fully realizing the complexity of the issue, Garfield and Affleck state:

> In view of the number of patients requesting psychotherapy and the scarcity of available therapists, the large incidence of "drop-outs" from psychotherapy represents a waste of specialized therapeuetic effort. If poor therapeutic risks can be identified prior to therapy, most of the limited therapeutic resources available might be channeled to those cases who would profit the most.[30]

They go on, however, to question the applicability of ". . . current psychotherapeutic approaches for those patients who leave therapy prematurely." This view is explicitly examined by Rosenthal and Frank:

> Insight-based forms of psychotherapy may not be the best ones for psychiatric clinic outpatients and . . . the time may be at hand for wider experimenting with other kinds of psychotherapy which have shown evidence of being adaptable with success to a clinic outpatient population.[31]

They specifically mention the effect of brief contacts with a therapist, conditioned reflex therapy, reciprocal inhibition therapy, and abreaction induced by ether. To this list may be added dynamically oriented approaches that focus on therapeutic intervention at a point of personal or social crisis, and which deal with the patient in the context of his membership in a socio-cultural system.[32] Another example is Slack's novel method of getting juvenile delinquents into treatment.[33] Returning to the aforementioned association between "dropout" rate and social class position, our study dealt with individuals who fall predominantly in class positions IV and V in the Hollingshead index of social class. This may mean that the clinical method used in this investigation has applicability to that not inconsiderable proportion of general psychiatric patients who are members of class positions IV and V and who contribute substantially to the size of terminator groups.

Outpatient clinic policies that result in exclusive screening practices are based on understandable factors—for example, understaffing, teaching needs, increasing referrals, and limited space. However, repeatedly confirmed findings that large numbers of people in psychological-social stress do not find help forthcoming, or are unable, for various reasons, to accept forms of treatment offered, are sufficient indication that systematic efforts should be made to develop and test therapeutic methods that are effective.[34] Such endeavors need not be solely intraprofessional or even interprofessional, but should involve action at community levels in order to be successfully carried out. This is clearly demonstrated in the experiences of team members in the present study.

An integral part in the therapeutic armamentarium of our approach was the use of extrahospital community facilities and services. Our endeavors at the community level bring into sharp focus an amazing lack of single-agency operations designed to treat alcoholics effectively and comprehensively, despite an apparent plethora of services and agencies for alcoholics. The *Classified Directory of Agencies Serving Alcoholics and Their Relatives in Massachusetts* (1960), for example, lists dozens of agencies in the Boston area offering services to alcoholics, ranging from alcoholism clinics to work relief for alcoholics. Seven homes and half-way houses for alcoholics are listed for the Boston area. Nevertheless, we experienced considerable difficulty in obtaining facilities tailored to meet the particular kinds of needs presented by the men we studied. This situation, which occurred despite excellent cooperative working relationships with state, local, and private agencies, involves three major factors. First, each agency has an administrative organization with rules and regulations peculiar to itself, which often restricts the generality with which its services can be offered. Many homes for alcoholics, for example, do not accept patients with any medical complications, because provision for medical care is not included within their organizational structure. A second factor is the inability of some agencies to accept patients who are unable to pay their way. For example, one hospital geared solely to treatment of chronic alcoholics required a minimum length of seven days' hospitalization at reasonable rates; the fees, however, are beyond the financial capacities of many of those addicted to alcohol. Finally, most of the agencies whose services are available deal with one particular, and often very circumscribed, area of need. For example, some agencies offer a night's lodgings and meals, others furnish clothing, yet others provide fellowship, and so on. In other words, numerous part-services are available, but few agencies offer comprehensive care aimed toward rehabilitation at medical, social, and psychological levels simultaneously. It is worthy of note that few agencies accept acutely inebriated applicants, and most agencies discharge patients who get drunk. In general, numerous services apparently available on paper do not in practical fact exist, because of restrictive admission procedures. There is evident need for coordination and cooperation at policy-making levels, in order to avoid duplication of services and to ensure the possibility of effectively comprehensive rehabilitation.

It should be noted that in this investigation intense and generally successful efforts were made, within limits of institutional structure, to provide comprehensive extramural treatment for the alcoholics studied. Our social workers informally examined the range of community services available to alcoholics in the greater Boston area, and whenever possible made special arrangements with community agents in the interests of providing smoothly comprehensive care. One dormitory-type rehabilitation center, for example, refused to readmit men who were intoxicated. After consultation with the director of this agency a plan was worked out whereby his workers would call us if one of our experimental patients applied for readmission in an inebriated state. We could then make other provisions for the patient until such time as he was able to meet the rehabilitation center's requirements for admission. A number of plans of this kind were gradually and carefully arrived at with several other community agents.

We have seen, then, that alcoholics form therapeutic attachments. In the sense that it is based on widely accepted principles of dynamic psychology, the technique we used is not new. Its uniqueness lies in its emphasis on action rather than words, on gratification rather than frustration, and on placing responsibility for achieving a therapeutic alliance on the caretaker rather than on the patient. Dynamically oriented mental health workers have preferred to offer their clients some form of insight-based psychotherapy. This professional preference is the consequence of an interlocking complex of social factors, such as training, values, prestige, and public demand, discussion of which is beyond the scope of this paper. Its consequences, however, are clear: psychologically ill persons who are unable to tolerate insight psychotherapy fall into a therapeutic void. It is not difficult to understand how these people come to be considered untreatable. In fact, they are untreatable by traditional methods. The error that many mental health workers have committed is the easy generalization that because many disturbed individuals are untreatable by one approach, they are untreatable by any approach, so they are avoided and their problems neglected. These individuals number among them not only alcoholics, but schizophrenics, the feeble-minded and brain-damaged, and delinquents both young and old, to mention a few of the more obvious examples. In our view, these people do seek to be helped, and to perceive them as untreatable is a disservice as much to ourselves as to them.

Summary

The effectiveness of a clinical approach designed to establish and maintain treatment relations with alcoholics by utilizing their initial hospital contact was tested by applying the method to 100 alcoholics (experimental group). Another 100 alcoholics comprised a control group. The conceptual and clinical backgrounds of the approach are described. The core of the approach was a team composed of a psychiatrist and a psychiatric social worker, who stressed handling of the patient's initial contact with the hospital, in this case his admission to the emergency service. They provided comprehensive medical, psychological, and social care based on understanding of the psychodynamics of the individual patient. Constructive utilization of dependency needs and continuity of care were emphasized. Measures of effectiveness were: (1) incidence of initial visits and (2) incidence of patients making five or more visits to the hospital's alcoholism clinic within the experimental period of one year. Results show that 65 percent of experimental cases made initial visits in contrast to five percent of control cases; 42 percent of experimental cases made five or more visits in contrast to one percent of control cases. These results are significant ($p < .001$). The results are compared with findings of other investigators of continuance and discontinuance in psychotherapy in both outpatient alcoholism and general psychiatric clinics. Implications of the findings for treatment not only of alcoholism but for other psychological disturbances are discussed. The problem of community resources in comprehensive treatment of alcoholism is raised.

2.C. Establishing Treatment Relations with Alcoholics A Supplementary Report

The clinical method tested and the structure of the evaluative study are the same for both investigations; the difference between

---

Section 2.C. written, in collaboration, by Morris E. Chafetz, Howard T. Blane, Harry S. Abram, Eleanor Clark, Joseph H. Golner, Elizabeth Lacy Hastie, and William F. McCourt.

Notes to Chapter 2 will be found on page 70.

the two lies in the manner employed in selecting alcoholic patients. Subject selection in the original study has been described. In the present study, two modifications were employed in an attempt to obtain a sample of emergency service alcoholics less socially isolated than that in the original investigation. The first modification, varying only slightly from the technique of the first study, involved the physical presence of one of the project psychiatrists *at the admitting desk* during the intake period in the hope that this would result in a higher rate of assignment of less socially isolated alcoholics. A four-month trial with this modification indicated no increase in such a rate of assignment. For the remaining six months, a more radical modification was adopted. The project psychiatrist reviewed the medical record and saw each man he could who was admitted to the emergency service. If signs of alcoholism were present, according to criteria listed in the previous paper, the psychiatrist asked the chief medical officer to assign the patient to the study. The marked increase in the rate of assignment that followed gave us some assurance that we were obtaining a sample more representative of the total alcoholic emergency service population than we had obtained heretofore.

One other modification of subject selection may have some bearing on the composition of the final sample. In the first study, project psychiatrists were on 24-hour call until all subjects were assigned to the study at the beginning of any one of the 10 consecutive monthly selection periods. In the second study, the psychiatrists selected subjects from 9 A.M. to 5 P.M., and sample size was reduced to 100—50 experimental and 50 control; as in the previous study, however, there were 10 monthly selection periods with alternate assignment of patients as experimental and control subjects. Also, the same excluding criteria applied in both studies.

In order to determine whether modifications of subject selection procedures resulted in a sample less socially isolated than that of the original study, we compared the two samples on three measures of social isolation: employment, marital status, and whether the patient was living with a relative. Specific predictions were that the present sample (Study 2) would show a higher incidence of employment, of being currently married, and of living with a relative than in the original sample (Study 1). Results are: (1) 61 percent of Study 2 alcoholics were employed[35] compared to 45 percent of Study 1 alcoholics ($x^2 = 4.653$, $1df$, $p < .05$);[36] (2) 26 percent of Study 2 were currently married compared to 17 percent of Study 1 alcoholics ($x^2 = 3.310$, $2df$, $p = .10$); (3) 43 percent of Study 2 subjects were living with a relative compared to 28 percent of Study 1 subjects ($x^2 = 6.330$, $1df$, $p < .01$). With the exception of marital status, then, these results support the prediction that the Study 2 sample is less isolated socially than the Study 1 sample. Further examination of marital status shows that of men who have ever entered a marital contract 36 percent are still married in the Study 2 sample, in contrast to 25 percent in the Study 1 sample ($x^2 = 2.941$, $1df$, $p < .05$).

Since two selection techniques were used in drawing the sample for Study 2, it is appropriate to ask whether subjects drawn by each of the techniques differ with respect to social isolation measures. Analysis along these lines reveals no difference between the two subsamples for employment or living with relative. There is, however, a trend ($p = .10$) for alcoholics drawn by the first technique to be more maritally stable than those drawn by the second technique; when single men are excluded from analysis, the difference between the subsamples with regard to marital status is significant ($x^2 = 6.813$, $1df$, $p < .01$).

In sum, then the present sample is less socially isolated than the original study sample, and there is evidence to indicate a difference in marital status within the present sample according to the subject selection technique used.

Results

To test whether the clinical method is effective with a sample of emergency service alcoholics less alienated than the original study sample, the same measures as those in the original study were used. We predicted that more experimental than control patients would make initial self-initiated visits to the clinic and that more experimental than control patients would establish treatment relations at a criterion of five or more self-initiated visits during the one-year study period. The findings presented in Tables 5 and 6 (Appendix A) with regard to initial visits and establishment of treatment relations indicate that the clinical approach again is highly effective in its aim.

Since there was a difference on one measure of social isolation, that is, marital status, between the two samples, we recast data on initial visits and establishment of treatment relations by subsample. Analysis reveals only random variation with respect to initial visits and establishment of treatment relations between the two subgroups.

Discussion

This replication of the original study evaluates the effectiveness of our method of establishing treatment contact with alcoholics less socially isolated than those in the original study. The findings are again striking and, indeed, show an absolute increase in percentages over the first study of alcoholics who responded to the approach with initial visits and by establishing treatment relations. This might be due to increased competence with the clinical approach or might reflect the difference in composition between the samples. That the findings on return visits were duplicated strongly suggests that meeting patients initially with understanding, sympathy, and attention to expressed needs, however concrete they may be, can assure higher rates of follow-through on treatment recommendations.

An interesting finding with respect to sample composition is that we obtained a less socially isolated group of men than the Study 1 sample with the first modification of the subject selection procedure even though rate of assignment was not increased over Study 1. There is no satisfactory explanation of this finding. It may have to do with the fact that we selected patients only during daytime hours in Study 2, rather than over 24-hour periods as in Study 1. Alcoholics admitted to the emergency service during the day may be less socially isolated than those admitted during evening hours. Another possible explanation has to do with experimenter bias.[37] The project psychiatrists were aware that we were attempting to obtain a sample of alcoholics less socially isolated than subjects in Study 1. The psychiatrists may have communicated this knowledge to the chief medical officers in such a way that rate of assignment did not increase but type of alcoholic assigned changed from Study 1 to Study 2 during the first four months of subject selection.

Finally, it is worth more than passing mention to note that as a result of our research findings, the clinical approach is now an integral part of the routine clinical services offered not only to alcoholics, but to all psychiatric patients admitted to the emergency service. Psychiatric residents rotating through the emergency service are trained in this approach, which may represent one means of treating socially and culturally impoverished patients who do not always respond to traditional psychiatric outpatient treatment procedures.

2.D. Alcohol Crisis Treatment Approach and Establishment of Treatment Relations with Alcoholics

During the course of this study, the first telephone call from an alcoholic or his relative during any week was referred to a social worker; these callers constituted the experimental group. All other calls were handled as before, making up the control group.

The role of the social worker was to respond immediately to the calls of the experimental group. When it seemed advisable, he visited the patient's home that day to evaluate family problems and, if the family wished, made a referral at that time. Alternatively the patient or his relative could be seen that day in the clinic. Psychiatric, medical, and social service consultation were provided, and immediate treatment, including individual or group therapy, was made available. These services were offered both to the patient and to family members who were also involved in the crisis. The course of treatment in the clinic included the continuing involvement of the social worker, in order to cement the relationship established in the initial contact.

A case history will serve to illustrate the type of action taken by the social worker:

Section 2.D. written, in collaboration, by Morris E. Chafetz and Howard T. Blane.

We received a call from Mrs. R., who said that her husband was seriously ill with delirium tremens, and could get no treatment. She had called another general hospital, but was unable to obtain an appointment for a week. She next called a hospital for alcoholics, but could not afford the price which was quoted to her. She then contacted a social service agency, but was told that the first available appointment would be in two weeks. When Mrs. R. called our clinic, she was immediately referred to the project social worker. Since the patient was unable to come to the hospital, the social worker made a home visit that same day. He found Mr. R. in bed, and very shaky and tremulous. Mr. R. had had a drinking problem for over 20 years; recently he had quit work, and was staying home to take care of his senile mother and retarded sister, who live with the R's. Mrs. R. is employed in a department store. The R's have three children, one of whom is receiving psychiatric treatment for chronic truancy. Mrs. R. expressed great appreciation of the social worker's visit to the home, saying it had given her a "new lease on life." She especially appreciated it because she felt that this was the right time to engage her husband in treatment.

The patient entered treatment in the clinic, and at the end of the six-month study, had kept a total of 12 appointments with the social worker. He discussed his recent losses, and the discouragement and depression he escaped by drinking. Mrs. R. had kept seven treatment appointments with another social worker at the clinic, and spoke of her family problems, which included her husband's abusiveness, her role as breadwinner for the family, and her obligation to Mr. R's family.

Through a crisis-intervention approach, the project has enabled our clinic to help this and other families find solutions to their problems through the use of community social service facilities, and through the development of the insight that changes motivation and gives hope. During the six-month duration of the project, 45 telephone calls were made requesting help. Of these 21 cases were designated as experimental and 24 as control cases. We hypothesized that more of the specially treated group of alcoholics and relatives would accept treatment recommendations than of the control, or routinely handled, group. In order to test this hypothesis we employed measures similar to those of our previous studies, and included the number of patients *and* relatives who made initial visits to the clinic, as well as the number of patients and relatives making five or more visits.

Hypotheses

We assessed the general hypothesis by means of four specific predictions, as follows:

1. A greater frequency of experimental than control patients will make initial clinic visits.
2. A greater frequency of experimental than control relatives will make initial clinic visits.
3. A greater frequency of experimental than control patients will make five or more clinic visits during a six-month period.
4. A greater frequency of experimental than control relatives will make five or more clinic visits during a six-month period.

The first three predictions were confirmed by the data; results for the last prediction were in the expected direction, but were not significant. Results for initial visits showed that 61.9 percent of the experimental patients made initial clinic visits, as opposed to 20.8 percent of the control patients. As for the relatives, 38.1 percent of the relatives of patients in the experimental group made initial visits in contrast to 12.5 percent of relatives of patients in the control group. These findings are summarized in Table 3 (Appendix A). It should be noted that we used a one-tailed test of significance. In 28.6 percent of the cases in the experimental group, both the patient and a relative visited the clinic, while this never occurred in the control group.

Because expected call frequencies were less than five for data used to test the third and fourth predictions, we employed Fisher's exact test rather than chi-square as the appropriate statistic. The findings for establishing treatment relations show that 26.8 percent of the experimental patients, as opposed to none of the patients in the control group, made five or more clinic visits during the six-month period of the study. Very few relatives in either group came for five or more visits; two relatives of patients in the experimental group did so, in contrast to none of the relatives of control group patients. The findings are shown in Table 3 (Appendix A).

The results of this study confirm and offer additional support to our previous findings; they indicate that immediate intervention in a psychological or social crisis increases the likelihood that alcoholics will enter into treatment relations, and that relatives will recognize their own roles in helping the patient. Crises seldom spring forth full-blown, but frequently represent an accumulation of events that gradually reach crisis proportions; this is probably always true in crises involving alcoholism. It may be that a telephone call requesting help from a caretaking agency is an exploratory maneuver that comes earlier than the situation that forces the patient to come into the hospital looking for help. If immediate response to such overtures can be used to involve the patient in treatment, casefinding has advanced a step, and intervention may take place before the crisis reaches its acute phase.

2.E. Use of Letters to Increase Motivation for Treatment in Alcoholics

The inability of alcoholics to accept outpatient psychiatric care is related in part to traditional referral practices. When the initial clinic contact comes during an acute alcohol crisis and includes information, services, and other concrete demonstrations of interest, alcoholics do enter treatment. One difficulty in implementing this approach is that, like many treatment agencies, we have no inpatient facilities designed to care for the intoxicated or physically debilitated individual. Many must be temporarily institutionalized elsewhere before an effective contact can be made, and many predictably fail to return. We thought a partial remedy for this enforced separation

Section 2.E. written, in collaboration, by Alfred J. R. Koumans and James J. Muller.

during the alcohol crisis would be a personal letter expressing concern for the patient's well-being and repeating our invitation to return for further assistance. We predicted that more patients receiving such letters would return than those who did not.

The sample consisted of 100 chronic alcoholic men who were referred to a public custodial hospital for alcoholics for 14 days. Fifty men selected at random received a letter. The remaining 50 subjects received no letter. Chi-square comparisons indicated no differences between the two groups in regard to age, occupation, social or marital status, contact with family, and drinking history. After an interval of two months the groups were compared for (1) incidence of return to the hospital, (2) delay between discharge from the custodial hospital and return to the out-patient facility, and (3) sobriety upon return.

Results, shown in Table 4 (Appendix A), confirmed our expectations. A letter expressing interest has a significant positive effect on the motivation of chronic alcoholics to return to a treatment situation, as measured by incidence of return, speed of return, and sobriety on arrival.

2.F. Use of Telephone Calls to Increase Motivation for Treatment in Alcoholics

As we have seen, chronic alcoholics can be motivated to accept psychiatric treatment during acute alcoholic crises. At these crucial times, concrete expressions by caretakers of interest, acceptance, and willingness to gratify real needs can result in viable, on-going treatment relationships. However, many patients are too drunk or physically debilitated to relate to on initial contact and must be referred someplace else for drying out. Since no rapport has been established, these referrals usually fail to return and the therapeutic opportunity is wasted. In the previous section we showed that a single personal letter to the alcoholic after he has been referred to a remote institution significantly increases the likelihood of his re-

Section 2.F. written, in collaboration, by Alfred J. R. Koumans, James J. Muller, and Carole F. Miller.

turning in a sober, receptive condition on his own. Interest in this result led us to consider other, equally practical techniques for drawing on the unappreciated motivational resources of this group of patients. We thought that a single phone call to chronic alcoholics who were temporarily institutionalized after initial contact at our hospital would increase their motivation for subsequent outpatient treatment here. We predicted that more patients receiving such a phone call from one of our staff would return than those who did not.

The sample included 100 chronic alcoholic men who were referred consecutively to a public custodial hospital for alcoholics for 14 days. The first 50 men referred received no phone call and the second 50 men referred had a phone call put through to them. Chi-square comparisons indicated no difference between the groups in regard to age, occupation, social or marital status, contact with family, and drinking history. Neither were there differences in these respects between this sample and that in the previous study. After an interval of two months, the groups were compared for (1) incidence of return to the hospital, (2) delay between discharge from the hospital and return to the outpatient facility, and (3) sobriety at the time of return.

Main results were that 44 percent of patients who received a telephone call returned within a week of their discharge (half of these within the first two days) in contrast to 8 percent of those who did not get a call ($x^2 = 16.84$, $df = 1$, $p < .01$); only four patients who did not receive a call returned altogether, making statistical comparison of the two groups for speed of return and sobriety on return impossible. Three of the four patients who did not receive a call returned within two days and were sober on arrival. The other came after a week and was intoxicated. Ten of the returning patients who received a call were sober on arrival. Of the remaining 12 patients who received a call, eight were drunk and four were questionably intoxicated.

The results show that a telephone call expressing interest has a significant positive effect on the motivation of chronic alcoholics to return to a treatment situation, as measured by their incidence of return. The small number of patients who returned without receiving a call made it impossible to verify statistically the appearance of more delay subjects receiving a call in this study than when letters were used. Further study is indicated to determine (1) differences in the effectiveness of these two modes of communication with chronic alcoholics and (2) psychological factors underlying such differences that increase understanding of motivations of chronic alcoholics for treatment contact.

Notes

1. E. G. SHORTLIFFE, T. S. HAMILTON, and E. H. NOROCAN, "The Emergency Room and the Changing Pattern of Medical Care," *New England Journal of Medicine,* 258:2-25, 1958.
2. J. POST, "Current Research on Problems of Alcoholism. III: Report of the Section on Internal Medical Research," *Quarterly Journal of Studies on Alcohol,* 16:544-546, 1955.
3. M. BRUNNER-ORNE, "The Role of a General Hospital in the Treatment and Rehabilitation of Alcoholics," *Quarterly Journal of Studies on Alcohol,* 19:108-117, 1958.
4. E. LINDEMANN, "The Meaning of Crisis in Individual and Family Living," *Teachers College Record,* 57:310, 1956; "The Psychosocial Position on Etiology," in H. D. KRUSE (ed.), *Integrating the Approaches to Mental Disease* (New York: Harper and Brothers, 1957).
5. J. V. SAPIR, "Relationship Factors in the Treatment of the Alcoholic," *Social Casework,* 34:297-303, 1953.
6. W. CAUDILL and D. H. ROBERTS, "Pitfalls in the Organization of Interdisciplinary Research," *Human Organization,* 10:12-15, 1951; F. C. REDLICH and E. B. BRODY, "Emotional Problems of Interdisciplinary Research in Psychiatry," *Psychiatry,* 18:233-239, 1955.
7. H. T. BLANE, "Effectiveness of a Method for Establishing Treatment Relations with Alcoholics" (abstract), *American Psychologist,* 16:366, 1961; M. E. CHAFETZ, "A Procedure for Establishing Therapeutic Contact with the Alcoholic," *Quarterly Journal of Studies on Alcohol,* 22:325-328, 1961.
8. CHAFETZ, *op. cit.*

9. BLANE, op. cit.
10. R. D. FOWLER, SR., *Studies in Alcoholism* (Montgomery, Alabama: Alabama Commission on Alcoholism, 1960); J. D. FRANK, L. H. GLIEDMAN, S. D. IMBER, E. H. NASH, and A. R. STONE, "Why Patients Leave Psychotherapy," *Archives of Neurology and Psychiatry,* 77:283-299, 1957; S. KURLAND, "Length of Treatment in a Mental Hygiene Clinic," *Psychiatric Quarterly* (Suppl.), 30:83-90, 1956; D. ROSENTHAL and J. D. FRANK, "The Fate of Psychiatric Clinic Out-Patients Assigned to Psychotherapy," *Journal of Mental Disease,* 127:330-343, 1958; L. SCHAFFER and J. K. MYERS, "Psychotherapy and Social Stratification," *Psychiatry,* 17:83-93, 1954.
11. FOWLER, op. cit.
12. S. L. GARFIELD and D. C. AFFLECK, "An Appraisal of Duration of Stay in Outpatient Psychotherapy," *Journal of Nervous and Mental Disease,* 129:492-498, 1959; ROSENTHAL AND FRANK, op. cit.; SCHAFFER AND MYERS, op. cit.; P. L. SULLIVAN, C. MILLER, and W. SMELSER, "Factors in Length of Stay and Progress in Psychotherapy," *Journal of Consulting Psychology,* 22:1-9, 1958.
13. GARFIELD AND AFFLECK, op. cit.; ROSENTHAL AND FRANK, op. cit.
14. SULLIVAN et al., op. cit.
15. SCHAFFER AND MYERS, op. cit.
16. GARFIELD AND AFFLECK, op. cit.; ROSENTHAL AND FRANK, op. cit.
17. ROSENTHAL AND FRANK, op. cit.
18. GARFIELD AND AFFLECK, op. cit.
19. For example, D. J. PITTMAN and C. W. GORDON, *Revolving Door: A Study of the Chronic Police Case Inebriate* (Glencoe, Illinois: The Free Press, 1958); R. STRAUS and R. G. McCARTHY, "Non-addictive Pathological Drinking Patterns in Homeless Men," *Quarterly Journal of Studies on Alcohol,* 12:601-611, 1951.
20. STRAUS AND MCCARTHY, op. cit.
21. PITTMAN AND GORDON, op. cit.

22. For example, R. P. KNIGHT, "The Psychodynamics of Chronic Alcoholism," *Journal of Nervous and Mental Disease,* 86:538-548, 1937; K. A. MENNINGER, *Man Against Himself* (New York: Harcourt Brace, 1938).
23. For example, R. STRAUS and S. D. BACON, "Alcoholism and Social Stability. A Study of Occupational Integration in 2,023 Male Clinic Patients," *Quarterly Journal of Studies on Alcohol,* 12:601-611, 1951.
24. GARFIELD AND AFFLECK, *op. cit.*; H. S. LIEF, V. F. LIEF, C. D. WARREN, and R. G. HEATH, "Low Dropout Rate in a Psychiatric Clinic," *Archives of General Psychiatry,* 5:200-211, 1961; ROSENTHAL AND FRANK, *op. cit.*
25. M. E. CHAFETZ, "Practical and Theoretical Considerations in the Psychotherapy of Alcoholism," *Quarterly Journal of Studies on Alcohol,* 20:281-291, 1959; FOWLER, *op. cit.*
26. CHAFETZ, "Practical and Theoretical Considerations. . . ."
27. FOWLER, *op. cit.*
28. J. H. MENDELSON and M. E. CHAFETZ, "Alcoholism as an Emergency Ward Problem," *Quarterly Journal of Studies on Alcohol,* 20:270-275, 1959.
29. F. AULD and J. K. MYERS, "Contributions to a Theory for Selecting Psychotherapy Patients," *Journal of Clinical Psychology,* 10:56-60, 1954; M. A. BAILEY, L. WARSHAW, and R. M. EICHLER, "A Study of Factors Related to Length of Stay in Psychotherapy," *Journal of Clinical Psychology,* 15:442-444, 1959; FRANK *et al., op. cit.*; R. E. GIBBY, B. A. STOTSKY, E. W. HILER, and D. R. MILLER, "Validation of Rorschach Criteria for Predicting Duration of Therapy," *Journal of Consulting Psychology,* 18:185-191, 1954; S. D. IMBER, E. H. NASH, and A. R. STONE, "Social Class and Duration of Psychotherapy," *Journal of Clinical Psychology,* 11:281-284, 1955; Lief *et al., op. cit.*; M. LORR, M. M. KATZ, and E. A. RUBINSTEIN, "The Prediction of Length of Stay in Psychotherapy," *Journal of Consulting Psychology,* 22:321-327, 1958; ROSENTHAL AND FRANK, *op. cit.*; E. A. RUBINSTEIN and M. A. LORR, "A Comparison of Terminators and Remainers in Outpatient Psycho-

therapy," *Journal of Clinical Psychology,* 12:345-349, 1956; SCHAFFER AND MYERS, *op. cit.*; SULLIVAN *et al., op. cit.*; E. A. WINDER AND M. HERSKO, "The Effect of Social Class on the Length and Type of Psychotherapy in a Veterans Administration Mental Hygiene Clinic," *Journal of Clinical Psychology,* 11:77-79, 1955.
30. GARFIELD AND AFFLECK, *op. cit.*
31. ROSENTHAL AND FRANK, *op. cit.*
32. LINDEMANN, *op. cit.*
33. C. W. SLACK, "Experimenter-Subject Psychotherapy: A New Method of Introducing Intensive Office Treatment for Unreachable Cases," *Mental Hygiene,* 44:238-256, 1960.
34. N. Q. BRILL and H. A. STORROW, "Social Class and Psychiatric Treatment," *Archives of General Psychiatry,* 3:340-344, 1960; S. I. DEAN, "Treatment of the Reluctant Client," *American Psychologist,* 13:627-630, 1958; LIEF *et al., op. cit.*; H. A. ROBINSON, F. C. REDLICH, and J. K. MYERS, "Social Structure and Psychiatric Treatment," *American Journal of Orthopsychiatry,* 24:307, 316, 1954; ROSENTHAL AND FRANK, *et al., op. cit.*
35. In this analysis, patients over 65 years of age or on pension were excluded on the assumption that they are not available to the labor force.
36. All tests of significance are one-tailed.
37. R. ROSENTHAL and K. L. FODE, "Psychology of the Scientists: V. Three Experiments in Experimenter Bias," *Psychological Reports,* 12:491-511, 1963.

Chapter 3
The Context of Entering and Staying in Treatment

The treatment-catalyst approach to patients in the project was successful with a large number of patients. Why did the technique work for some patients but not for others? Were there measurable differences between those patients who formed therapeutic alliances and those who did not? How were these differences related to our conception of treatment?

It will be recalled that the teams' efforts centered around utilization of the alcoholic's dependency needs, consideration for his lowered self-esteem, reduction of frustration, communication through action, and the offering of continuity of care. Three aspects of the clinical approach make psychodynamic sense but distinguish it from usual outpatient techniques: (1) granting, within limits imposed by reality, specific requests of the patient (e.g., requests for cigarettes, food, clothing); (2) reducing as much as possible potentially frustrating occurrences in the hospital (e.g., long waiting periods, many impersonal contacts with hospital personnel); and (3) communicating with the alcoholic by doing for him, as much as by listening to and talking with him.

Clearly, it was important to investigate variables that measured or at least reflected the critical aspects of the clinical approach. In practice, our ability to do this in an entirely satisfactory manner was hampered by the fact that questions about factors related to differential response to treatment were posed as the project progressed, not as it was originally being designed. Thus it became necessary to devise measures *ex post facto* from project, hospital, and other records. In the following sections we report studies of the association between several variables and formation of treatment relations. One variable is dependency, clearly involved in our clinical approach. Another is hospitalization at the time of admission, which we considered as concrete evidence of continuous care, doing for the patient, and showing him consideration. A third is the way the patient was admitted to the emergency service; if he were brought in by the police we considered this to represent an increase in frustration that would militate against subsequent involvement in treatment.

In addition to factors related to the type of treatment we provided, we were interested in the social and situational characteristics of the patients and how these were associated with treatment involvement. This interest was particularly stimulated as we discovered that most of our patients were drawn from lower- and lower-middle class groups, notoriously difficult to engage in treatment endeavors and notoriously undesired by the upper middle-class professionals who could provide treatment. Our concern here was whether a form of therapy that bore distinct differences from usual methods of psychological care would be effective in engaging alienated lower-class patients into treatment. This led us to investigate social class affiliation, social isolation, and social dependence in relation to the development and maintenance of a treatment alliance.

The papers reported in this section provide a look at a few of the many possible variables that interact with, and partially determine the success of any treatment method.

3.A. Behavioral Dependence and Length of Stay in Psychotherapy

Much attention has been given in the literature to the role of dependency needs in the alcoholic. Some writers feel that there is no satisfactory evidence of a common personality type among alcoholics nor of major differences in personality between alcoholics and nonalcoholics. Syme,[1] and Sutherland, Schroeder and Tordella,[2] who reviewed the literature on this subject take this position, as does the World Health Organization Expert Committee on Mental Health;[3] they admit the possibility that the failure to substantiate differences may be due to inadequacies in research methods.

Psychoanalytic writers disagree on the subject of basic personality characteristics of the alcoholic, but their formulations usually include dependency as a major component. Fenichel considers alcoholism an

---

Section 3.A. written, in collaboration, by Howard T. Blane and William R. Meyers.

Notes to Chapter 3 will be found on page 98.

impulse neurosis, rooted in an oral and narcissistic personality structure.[4] The oral fixation and homosexual tendencies caused by early childhood frustrations are acted out in a disguised form in the drinking bout. Lorand's survey found orality and homosexual strivings predominant in alcoholism, in accord with the psychoanalytic conception.[5] Rado saw the alcoholic as longing to return to the passively obtained gratifications of infancy.[6] Though K. Menninger argued that alcoholism is based on impulses of self-destruction and guilt,[7] Schilder thought that the alcoholic's need to be loved is more central than his masochistic tendencies.[8] Knight regarded alcoholism as gratifying oral and dependent needs, hostile wishes against family members, and masochistic needs.[9]

More recent work by Witkin and his colleagues considers dependency from a perceptual point of view. Perceptual dependence may be defined as a tendency to rely on established structure in the perceptual field. The rod and frame test, the body adjustment test, and the embedded figures test provide measures of perceptual dependency. Witkin and his colleagues have found that alcoholics are perceptually more dependent than nonalcoholics, as measured by these tests. At times Witkin seems to feel that perceptual dependence is an aspect of what we shall call motivational dependence—that is, dependence in interpersonal relationships, dependence as a form of orality. It is not clear to us that perceptual dependence is indeed an aspect of, or related to, motivational dependence. If it is not, then Witkin's research has not demonstrated a basic personality constellation common to alcoholics, though they have been shown to share a perceptual trait. But Witkin has a strong argument for the relatedness of the two kinds of dependence in the fact that other groups, such as ulcer patients and obese people, usually considered to be motivationally dependent, have been found to be perceptually dependent in the Witkin tests.[10]

A study by McCord and McCord has focused on motivational dependency in male alcoholics.[11] Although much of the McCords' thinking is founded in psychoanalytic conceptions and is, like these, developmental, it goes beyond the thinking of psychoanalytic writers in several ways. First, it is based on research that is replicable without problems of interobserver reliability, and that is susceptible to statistical analysis. Although one may question the relevance of the theory of categories they used for statistical analysis, the McCords' study is the first longitudinal investigation attempting to relate data obtained in childhood to adult behavior. Second, the McCords' formulation accounts for the role of aggressiveness, as well as dependency, in alcoholism, and it harmonizes insights into the individual personality with the cultural and anthropological point of view toward alcoholism. On the basis of their research, McCord and McCord conclude that alcoholism is a result of an intense conflict over dependency, rooted in erratic and unreliable satisfaction of dependency desires during childhood. The consequent fear that dependent relationships are unattainable leads to the suppression of dependent urges as the child grows up. In the background of many male alcoholics, accompanying the uncertain satisfaction of dependency needs, is the absence of suitable role models. The resulting role confusion leads to an intensified search for a stable self-image, and overacceptance of a culturally sanctioned image of masculinity as ultraindependent. A façade of intense masculinity (aggression, hyperactivity, independence, self-confidence) results as the child grows up. This is not true independence but rather counterdependence, a reaction formation against dependent needs.

According to McCord and McCord, conflict is intensified when the individual reaches adulthood, for he must relinquish some dependency needs in order to fill the adult male role. Heavy drinking is a compromise solution. Since drinking is culturally regarded as a masculine type of behavior, it can simultaneously satisfy dependent desires and maintain the alcoholic's precarious grip on a masculine self-image. But because it plays havoc with the person's work and family role, as alcoholism progresses it eventually leads to "collapse of the self-image and emergence of repressed dependent traits."

In this formulation dependency conflict, rather than mere dependency, is seen as the psychological core of the alcoholism problem. We cite it in detail because it accords so well with our clinical experience with the low social status alcoholics who come to an emergency service. Further, we see merit in this conception because it bridges the gap between dependency as a motivational or etiological construct, and behavior that logically results from conflict over dependency.

As we mentioned earlier, a very important aspect of the treatment approach we have been using is the constructive utilization of dependency needs. It is reasonable to suppose that counterdependent alcoholics may find it difficult to tolerate the giving approach used to initiate treatment relations, and may find it more difficult to tolerate the closeness of the therapeutic relationship than do overtly dependent alcoholics. This would certainly accord with the formulation of McCord and McCord, who see the pseudoindependent alcholic as one who must defend against direct and open expressions of dependency, and who can permit only indirect and covert ways of gratifying dependency needs.

Procedure

In order to investigate the effects of dependency on the establishment of treatment relations, patients were rated as either dependent or counterdependent in overt behavior. For this purpose, we defined overt dependent behavior as requests or demands for psychological or material help, passive acquiescence to requests or demands of others, pleas to be taken care of, and similar behaviors, for example, frequently asking for cigarettes. We defined overtly counterdependent behavior as resistance to proffered help, insistence on ability to do things (materially or psychologically) for or by oneself, a verbalized image of oneself as not needing anything from anyone, verbalized belief that it is useless or wrong to have faith or trust in others, and similar behaviors.

The psychiatrists and the social workers, in accordance with standard hospital procedure, made written notes concerning each contact with a patient. Neither psychiatrists nor social workers knew that their notes would later be used to rate dependence and counterdependence. Ratings of dependency were made independently by two advanced graduate students in psychology. The raters used only the transcribed notes concerning the first contact of the psychiatrist and the social worker with each patient. This was ordinarily at the time of the patient's arrival in the emergency services. Occasionally, because of an oversight of the emergency service staff, the clinical team was not summoned immediately but the patient had first been hospitalized overnight; in these cases, the first contact was made the next day on the ward. In many instances, the patient was intoxicated during the first contact.

The raters were instructed to categorize each patient as either overtly dependent or overtly counterdependent. The written definitions quoted above were furnished as a guide. No further instructions were given. The raters did not know that the study pertained to the establishment of treatment relations.

There was information sufficient to rate 99 of the 100 alcoholic patients as either predominantly dependent or counterdependent. Rating was done in two sets. The first set included 86 patients. The percentage of interrater agreement was 79.1. By discussion, the raters then resolved the 18 cases in which the ratings disagreed. The percentage of interrater agreement on the second set of 13 patients was 84.6; the raters by discussion then resolved the two cases in which the ratings disagreed. The percentage of interrater agreement on both sets combined was 79.8.

Results

We made two predictions. First, overtly dependent alcoholics will establish a therapeutic relationship (at a criterion of five interviews) more frequently than overtly counterdependent alcoholics; and second, overtly dependent alcoholics will stay in treatment for long periods (ten or more interviews) more frequently than counterdependent alcoholics. With regard to establishing treatment relations, we found that 61 percent of overtly dependent patients made five or more self-initiated visits to the clinic, in contrast to 15 percent of the patients who were rated counterdependent. As for maintaining treatment relations, we found that 27 percent of the dependent patients, in contrast to 3 percent of the counterdependent patients, remained in treatment for ten or more self-initiated visits. These findings are summarized in Table 5 (Appendix A).

These results indicate that overtly dependent alcoholics respond more positively to our method of establishing treatment relations than do overtly counterdependent alcoholics, in both forming and continuing a therapeutic alliance. Some of the difficulty counterdependent alcoholics show in establishing a relationship may be attributable to anxiety aroused by a giving approach; one could hope that new methods of establishing contact that are well suited to counterdependent alcoholics might be found. For individual patients, we have varied our approach by appealing to the alcoholic's counterdependent defense. For example, rather than asking the patient what we can do to help him, we ask him how he can help us. Can he tell us what it is like to have a drinking problem or how we might best help alcoholics? If he denies a drinking problem, we ask him if he can tell us how he has been able to avoid it, since we are as much interested in what prevents alcoholism as in what causes it. Techniques such as these have, however, been employed only casually, and at present we have no way of knowing how effective they would be if systematically applied. Slack's success in engaging presumably counterdependent juvenile delinquents in relationships associated with subsequent behavior change suggests that methods might be developed for reaching counterdependent individuals.[13]

Establishing a treatment relationship is not enough; in order to be effective, the relationship must continue. The very nature of the psychotherapeutic relationship, with its necessary closeness and temporary regression, is intolerable to counterdependent patients. Entirely new methods that allow self-direction and autonomy may have to be devised to help counterdependent alcoholics. One possibility is the use of groups run largely by the patients; another is to make opportunities available for setting up social and recreational centers or clubs run by alcoholics.

An additional aspect of this study concerns the social situation of our patients. We found, as we report elsewhere, that the most anomic and socially isolated patients (homeless, jobless, widowed, separated, or divorced, etc.) returned more frequently than more socially stable people, and that people of moderately low social class returned more frequently than people of higher social class or very low social class. These findings may be related to those of dependence-counterdependence; it is possible that social isolation and anomie cause dependent needs to be expressed overtly. The independence (or counterdependence) training of middle-class culture may be related to social class status. In any event, in considering the relation of interpersonal behaviors like overt dependence versus overt counterdependence, it is wise to keep in mind their possible social context or meaning.

One further point of interest relates to the developmental conception of McCord and McCord. According to their formulation, overt dependence occurs in a later stage of alcoholism than does counterdependence.[14] If it is assumed that the progression of the disease process of alcoholism among the men in our sample is correlated with age, then it would be expected that the men rated as dependent would be older than those rated as counterdependent. This is not borne out by our data; the mean age of the dependent group is 48.66 years, and of the counterdependent group, 49.65 years (C.R. $= 0.55$, $p = .29$). Similarly, if we assume that length of drinking history among the men in our sample is correlated with progression of the syndrome of alcoholism, then the dependent alcoholics could be expected to report a longer history of severe drinking than the counterdependent ones. Such reports are available from 55 of the dependent and 28 of the counterdependent group. The data do not confirm the expectation: the dependent alcoholics reported a mean drinking history of 19.84 years in contrast to a mean of 19.18 years by the counterdependent group (C.R. $= 0.54$, $p = .29$). It should be noted that length of drinking history was obtained from self-reports, and the dependability of the information is open to question.

Summary

We investigated dependency as a characteristic varying within the alcoholic population. We classified alcoholics as dependent or counterdependent on the basis of overt behavior and found, as we had predicted, that dependent patients respond more positively to therapeutic effort based on the constructive use of dependency needs than do counterdependent alcoholics. Our findings also indicate the need to devise treatment methods that enhance motivation in the counterdependent alcoholic.

3.B. Mode of Entry and Subsequent Hospitalization in Relation to Establishment of Treatment Relations

The manner in which an alcoholic comes to a hospital is a major determinant of his degree of involvement in and his attitudes toward subsequent interactions with the hospital and its staff. We have termed the alcoholic's manner of coming to the emergency service "mode of entry." Operationally, mode of entry refers to whether the patient was brought to the emergency service by the police or whether he came by some other means. We assume that mode of entry via the police represents an involuntary admission, involuntary in the sense that the alcoholic has no say about coming to the hospital. Sometimes the alcoholic is comatose when the police bring him in, and upon coming to, may be thankful that he was brought to the hospital. Sometimes he may have suffered an injury while severely inebriated, but resist being brought in by the police, even though he appreciates it when he sobers up. No matter what his condition at the time of admission, however, his coming to the hospital is involuntary in the sense defined.

Coming to the hospital by means other than the police is voluntary in the sense that the alcoholic takes part in the decision, albeit in many instances only minimally. He may eagerly desire help and come to the emergency service completely on his own specifically to seek out help for his alcohol problem. Or he may come in accompanied by his wife, not seeking help, but in response to a wifely ultimatum.

It is clear that mode of entry by police or by other modes is not a dichotomous category, but forms a continuum along at least two dimensions: desire for help and decision to seek aid. Desire for help and decision-making are usually less marked among men brought to the hospital by the police than among those who are not brought in

Section 3.B. written by Howard T. Blane.

by the police. What does this mean in regard to subsequent establishment of treatment relations? First, we would expect reduced frequency of formation of treatment relations when mode of entry is by police, because the desire for help is not strong. Second, we would expect resentment over the abrogation of decision-making powers among men brought to the hospital by the police, a resentment generalized by contiguity to the hospital, and expressed in a negative response to suggestions and recommendations about continuing treatment. For these two reasons we would predict a lower percentage of establishing and maintaining treatment relations among alcoholics in the police mode of entry group than in the nonpolice group.

Information about how patients come to the emergency service is routinely entered on the face-sheet filled out by emergency service clerks at the time a patient enters. We used this information to categorize patients according to mode of entry to test the hypothesis formulated above. The findings of the resulting analysis are presented in Table 5 (Appendix A), where it may be seen that patients brought in by the police establish treatment relations significantly less frequently than those who come in by other means. This is in accord with our expectations. However, maintenance of treatment relations does not differ significantly between the two modes of entry groups, even though the direction in favor of those not brought in by the police is maintained.

Another variable of importance is whether the patient was hospitalized as a consequence of his admission to the emergency service. In so far as hospitalization may be perceived by the patient as a concrete instance of concern and consideration, we would expect that it would reinforce positive attitudes toward continuing treatment after discharge. Also, hospitalization, even for brief periods, facilitates the formation of relationships between the patient and members of the treatment team. The formation of a working relationship in the hospital is the base for its continuation on an outpatient basis. We expected that patients who were hospitalized at the time of the emergency service admission would form treatment relations more often and continue them longer than alcoholics who were not hospitalized. The data in support of this expectation are presented in Table 5 (Appendix A). For the formation of treatment relations, there is a statistically nonsignificant trend in the expected direction, with 48 percent of hospitalized patients forming treatment relations compared to 31 percent of those not hospitalized. Maintenance of a treatment relationship is, however, closely associated with hospitalization. Of the 17 patients who came back to the clinic ten or more times, 16 had been hospitalized at the time they first entered the hospital's emergency service. Although the numbers are small, this is a clear indication of the usefulness of brief hospitalization in the treatment of alcoholism.

The relation between mode of entry and hospitalization is of interest. There is a significant negative association between the two variables ($x^2 = 4.34$, $p < .05$), such that men brought in by the police are less frequently hospitalized (55%) than those who come in by other means (76%). This finding is all the more impressive when one considers that the police choose to bring men to the hospital rather than to jail because there is an obvious medical problem (e.g., unconsciousness, injuries sustained in a fight or fall), so that one might expect a high incidence of hospitalization among this group. It is likely that attitudinal factors on the part of caretakers play a role in this difference in hospitalization frequencies between the two modes of entry groups.

It is also relevant to examine the association between behavioral dependency and the two factors considered in this section. Analysis reveals a marked negative relationship between dependency and mode of entry ($x^2 = 14.02$, $p < .001$), and a positive relationship between dependency and hospitalization ($x^2 = 11.34$, $p < .001$). In the first instance, counterdependent patients were brought in by the police far more often (82%) than dependent alcoholics (44%); and in the second, dependent patients were hospitalized more frequently (78%) than counterdependent patients (45%). It should be noted that the three variables are not independent, since the man brought in by the police is apt to say he does not want help and thereby be classified as counterdependent, while the one who comes in on his own asking for help will be categorized as dependent and runs better chance of hospitalization. But it does seem clear that the fate of counterdependent alcoholics includes contacts with the police and a failure to receive the best medical care, even though this failure is partly self-provoked; while dependent alcoholics less often are involved with the police and obtain medical care more readily than counterdependent alcoholics.

To sum up, alcoholics who are brought to the emergency service of a hospital by the police are less likely to form a therapeutic link with the hospital than those whose admission reflects some voluntary effort. Once having made contact with a hospital, those alcoholics who are hospitalized tend to form treatment relations more often than those not hospitalized; hospitalized patients certainly maintain treatment relations over a longer period than those not hospitalized. Associations of these variables with dependency, however, suggest that behavioral manifestations of dependency play a central role and may be prepotent over hospitalization and mode of entry in the establishment of a treatment alliance.

3.C. Social Class and Establishment of Treatment Relations

Over the past decade, a number of studies have shown an association between social class factors and stay in psychiatric outpatient treatment.[15] Although setting, method, and measures vary from study to study, there is a remarkably consistent finding that lower- and lower-middle-class patients drop out of treatment sooner (or stay in psychotherapy for shorter periods) than middle- and upper-middle-class patients. This finding has been reported for general psychiatric outpatient settings that offer some form of psychoanalytically oriented individual or group psychotherapy. Studies of dropout rates among alcoholics, on the other hand, have not focused on social class as a variable, but have demonstrated that dropout rates for alcoholics are on the whole higher than for general psychi-

Section 3.C. written, in collaboration, by Howard T. Blane and William R. Meyers.
Notes to Chapter 3 will be found on page 98.

atric patients.[16] Zax, Marsey, and Biggs examined length of stay in treatment among alcoholics in relation to several demographic variables, and although they did not focus on social class per se, they report no relation between education or occupation and length of stay in treatment.[17]

The study reported here investigates social class in relation to the establishment and maintenance of treatment relations among alcoholics. The subjects are the 100 patients assigned to the project, 42 of whom established treatment relations at a criterion of five visits within one year, and 58 of whom did not.

Procedure

The Hollingshead two-factor index of social position was used to obtain two measures of social class.[18] The first—current social class—is based on current occupation and education; the second—past social class—is based on the individuals' major occupation and education. The Hollingshead method of classification results in five social positions, with I the highest and V the lowest. Current occupation is defined as the patient's occupational status at the time of admissions to the emergency service, and major occupation as the occupation for which the patient was trained, or in which he has spent most of his working life. Past social class was used as a measure because a substantial proportion of subjects showed a downward class drift. This might mean that current social class, although a measure of actual current class position, obscures a commitment to the values, sanctions, and role expectations of a higher social class position. Measures of current social class position were available for 38, or 90.5 percent, of the patients who formed a treatment relation, and for 48, or 82.8 percent, of the men who failed to meet the criterion for establishing a treatment relation. Data to classify subjects into past social class were available for 39, or 92.9 percent, of the men who made a therapeutic alliance, and for 47, or 81.0 percent, of the patients who did not form treatment relations. Differences in numbers of unknown cases between the groups of men who established or failed to establish treatment relations are not statistically significant, either for current or past social class position.

Results

Findings with regard to current social class position and involvement in treatment may be found in Table 5 (Appendix A). Since only 3 patients were categorized as middle class (III), data were analyzed for only classes IV and V. Analysis shows that lower-middle-class patients (IV) established treatment relations significantly more frequently than lower-class patients (V). However, many patients in current social class position V were unemployed, and unemployment itself showed an association with establishment of treatment relations, (50.0% of unemployed subjects established treatment relations in contrast to 28.9% employed subjects; $x^2 = 4.29$, 1 df, $p < .05$). Therefore, we recast the current social class position data for subjects who were employed and unemployed, and found that 66.7 percent of the 9 subjects who were employed and in current social class IV had established treatment relations, in comparison to 21.1 percent of the 19 patients who were employed but in current social class V (exact two-tailed $p = .055$). There is only a chance difference between the number of current social class IV and V unemployed subjects who established treatment relations (exact two-tailed $p = .45$). The differences in establishment of treatment by social class do not hold up for maintenance of treatment relations.

The findings with regard to past social class position may be found in Table 5 (Appendix A), which shows a significant non-hierarchic association between past social class affiliation and establishment of treatment relations, such that lower-middle-class patients establish treatment relations more frequently than lower-class patients, on the one hand, and middle- and upper-middle-class patients on the other. Analyzing the data further, it becomes clear that the large difference between patients of lower-middle and lower-class origins makes the major contribution to the overall chi-square ($x^2 = 8.76$, 1df, $p. < .01$), and that the difference between lower-middle-class patients and patients of higher class backgrounds is not significant ($x^2 = 1.51$, 1df, $p. < .10$). Again, the relationship between social class and establishment of treatment relations fails to hold up for maintenance of a therapeutic alliance, although the absolute figures follow the same pattern.

Analyzing the data for occupation level independent of educational level (education bears only a random association with establishing treatment relations), we find in Table 5 (Appendix A) the same nonhierarchic association between the formation of treatment relations and occupation that obtained for past social class position. Breaking down the overall chi-square into individual comparisons we find that minor white-collar and skilled manual workers (occupational levels 4 and 5) establish treatment relations at a significantly higher rate than white-collar workers and lesser professionals (levels 2 and 3; exact test $p < .02$) on the one hand, and semiskilled and unskilled workers (levels 6 and 7; $x^2 = 8.69$, $1df$, $p < .01$) on the other. Furthermore, the overall relationship holds for the continuance of treatment relations, with minor white-collar and skilled workers staying in treatment significantly longer than semiskilled and unskilled workers ($x^2 = 5.20$, $1df$, $p. < .05$).

Since we dealt with a downwardly mobile group of men, we analyzed the data in a number of different ways to determine whether social class mobility and occupational mobility are related to establishment of treatment relations. No significant findings emerged from these analyses.

The results of this exploratory investigation show that Class IV alcoholic men respond to a specific treatment approach by establishing treatment relations more frequently than Class V alcoholics and, taking into account small frequencies, than Class III alcoholics. The findings assume importance in light of earlier reports that show that lower-middle-class psychiatric outpatients stay in treatment for shorter periods than middle- and upper-middle-class patients. On the basis of this widely reported finding, some workers suggest that "current psychotherapeutic approaches" or "insight-based forms of psychotherapy" are not suited for patients who terminate treatment prematurely, and these same workers make a plea for additional kinds of psychotherapy suited to the needs of particular outpatient groups.[19] The modifications of treatment we have used (concrete giving, reduction of frustration situations, communication through action) in treating alcoholics forms a type of psychotherapy that may be applicable to lower-middle-class psychiatric patients as well.

Of course, it is clear that the findings presented here are not definitive, especially in regard to comparisons between Classes III and IV. Further investigation with a larger sample of Class III patients as well as with samples of general psychiatric outpatients is needed.

3.D. Social Isolation, Social Dependence, and the Formation of Treatment Relations

The previous sections in this chapter have shown social class, dependent behavior, mode of entry, and hospitalization at time of admission to be related to establishment of outpatient treatment relations by project patients following initial contact in the emergency service. This paper examines social isolation and social dependence in regard to establishment and maintenance of treatment relations. We define *social isolation,* in a population of Skid-Row alcoholics, as "little close contact with others, low stability in maintaining social involvement, and few positive ties with the community at large."[20] *Social dependence,* in a population of Skid-Row alcoholics, we define as the tendency to make use of social welfare agencies and other social institutions ministering to deprived or poverty-stricken individuals.

As a context for the present study, what pattern can we see in our findings that the following factors are related to the establishment of treatment relations in our sample: residence in a deteriorated area; social class position; social isolation; social dependence; overt expression of dependent needs?

It seems likely that dependent needs keenly felt and overtly expressed permit a person to seize upon and accept proffered help and outpatient treatment. A general pattern of social dependence (putting heavy reliance on social agencies) may make it more likely

---

Section 3.D. written, in collaboration, by William R. Meyers and Howard T. Blane.
Notes to Chapter 3 will be found on page 98.

that a person would respond to an outpatient alcoholism program at a hospital. Such general patterns of social dependence and an overtly dependent or demanding attitude may tend to characterize people who are socially isolated, deprived of ordinary relationships, and intensely lonely. A great deal of research has shown that unstable, physically deteriorated areas are heavily populated by socially isolated, anomic individuals.[21]

These deteriorated or "Skid-Row" areas, with dilapidated rooming houses, cheap hotels, bars, pawn shops, and a highly transient population, are located around the edges of the central business district of a city.[22] Such areas are highest in unemployment, divorce, desertion, alcoholism, schizophrenia, vice, and other indices of social disorganization and isolation. There are many more men than women, few children, many old men, and many lone individuals.[23] These are areas to be distinguished from *stable* lower- and lower-middle-class urban residential areas, often with a population of a cohesive ethnic or religious minority group. Such areas, of which the old West End and the North End of Boston are examples, tend to have stable family structures, some degree of ethnic, religious, or linguistic homogeneity, little geographic or social class mobility, many families who were born there and have resided there all their lives, relatively few isolated individuals, and low crime rates. As a consequence, even though the physical condition of the structures may be faulty or deteriorated, there is a strong sense of community, considerable social cohesion, agreed-upon norms, and hence, relatively little anomie and social isolation.

The residents of deteriorated areas consume a share of public and private social agency expenditures vastly disproportionate to their numbers.[24] The residents are the "hard core" cases of a variety of social agencies such as family service agencies, Salvation Army Homes, adoption agencies, placement agencies for children, free clinics, hospital emergency services, and even jails, which in a sense are caretaking agencies.[25] A large proportion receive public relief payments of some kind. It may be suggested that this heavy use of caretaking agencies is in effect a substitute for the extended family and kinship relations these people lack.

Among these deteriorated areas in Boston are the Scollay Square neighborhood, the South End, the South Cove, and parts of Charlestown. Most of the patient population in the study is drawn from these areas: 59 out of 100 listed a home address in these areas, and of the remainder, almost all chose one of these areas as their usual haunt and were either homeless or shifted from rooming house to rooming house within these areas, having forsaken their family and nominal home address. Social relationships in such deteriorated areas or skid row areas are characterized by social distance from people.[26] With these conditions of social isolation and poverty among the residents of these deteriorating areas, we would expect intense feelings of loneliness and emotional deprivation and, therefore, the dependent needs that we have clinically noted in our patient population.

This physical and social background forms one base from which we can study the establishment and maintenance of outpatient treatment relations with a more or less destitute group of alcoholics. We have shown how social class factors among this population are related to the tendency to establish and maintain treatment relations; how overt expression of dependent needs is associated with the establishment of treatment relations, and how situational factors immediately preceding and following admission are related to establishment of treatment relations. The present paper examines the relation of measures of social isolation and of social dependence to the establishment and continuance of treatment relations by our patient group, and also examines the extent to which behavioral dependence is correlated with social dependence and social isolation.

Procedure

Five measures of social isolation were employed:

1. *Living with relatives.* Patients not living with the person they designated as their closest relative were considered to be more socially isolated than those living with their closest relative.

2. *Employment.* Since employment offers the possibility of social contact on the job, unemployed persons were considered to be more socially isolated than employed patients.

3. *Type of dwelling.* Homeless patients and those living in a rooming house or institution were considered to be more isolated than patients owning or renting a house or apartment.

4. *Marital status.* Single patients and patients separated, widowed, or divorced were considered to be more isolated than currently married patients.

5. *Index of social isolation.* Measures 1, 2, and 3 were each assigned a score of 1 or 0, 1 indicating social isolation and 0 indicating its absence. Scores were summed to form an index from 0 to 3.

Five measures of social dependence were used:

1. *Use of hospital.* Any admission to the Massachusetts General Hospital (a) one year or (b) five years preceding the patient's entry into the project was considered an indication of social dependence.

2. *Pension.* Patients receiving any form of regular pension (public or private) were considered to be more socially dependent than patients not receiving a pension.

3. *Social agency use.* Any listing of the patient in the Social Service Index (a list of contacts with a wide variety of social service agencies in the metropolitan area), during the five years preceding the patient's entry into the project was considered to be an indication of social dependence.

4. *Use of correctional institutions.* Patients (a) arrested or (b) imprisoned for any offense during the year preceding entry into the project were considered to be more socially dependent than patients not arrested or imprisoned during that period.

5. *Index of social dependence.* Measures 1b, 2, 3, and 4b were each assigned a score of 1 or 0, 1 indicating social dependence and 0 its absence. Scores were summed to form an index from 0 to 4.

The results for the five social isolation measures presented in Table 5 (Appendix A) show that one variable—employment—significantly distinguishes patients who established treatment relations from those who did not. Living with relatives and type of dwelling, both in the expected direction, do not reach significance ($p < .10 > .05$). Marital status is significant, but not in the expected direction. Single patients, presumably socially isolated, establish treatment relations at a significantly *lower* level than either married patients or separated, divorced, and widowed patients. There is no appreciable difference in frequency of establishing treatment relations between married patients on the one hand and separated, divorced, or widowed patients on the other. As for maintenance of treatment relations, none of the social isolation measures are related to it. Thus, while the findings are in the predicted direction, they fail to reach acceptable levels of statistical significance.

Results for the five social dependence measures presented in Table 5 (Appendix A) show two variables—pension, and the composite index of social dependence—to reach statistical significance with respect to establishment of treatment relations. The same variables, plus use of hospital (5 years prior to admission), are significant with regard to maintenance of treatment relations. All other variables are in the expected direction, but do not reach significance.

Although many of the variables fail to reach statistical significance, the presence of a consistent trend throughout all measures of social dependence and all but one measure of social isolation indicates some support for the hypothesis that the more socially dependent patient, and the more socially isolated patient, responds more often to offers of treatment than does the less socially dependent and less socially isolated patient, according to our measures.

The results presented with regard to social isolation may be viewed in the light of studies demonstrating that social isolation is a usual concomitant of alcoholism.[27] The sample investigated in this study was drawn from that segment of the alcoholic population that is most socially isolated. We know that alcoholics in general respond infrequently to offers of assistance and that they are in general socially isolated. This may well mean that those alcoholics who respond to the kind of aid we offered in this project suffer rather extreme social isolation. If so, one implication is that assignment of alcoholic patients to particular treatment forms in the clinical situation should vary in part according to the severity of social isolation the patient is experiencing.

The findings suggest the importance of examining treatment

response in particular, and response to social action programs in general at more than one level of analysis. Previous studies focused on personal, situational, and social variables; the present investigation examined social variables as they are theoretically presumed to relate to physical-environmental conditions. For each level of analysis, significant associations with the criterion variable—response to offers of therapeutic assistance—were found to obtain. However, it is not clear how the several levels of analysis interrelate, nor whether one level, or single variable within a level, is prepotent over all others in predicting formation of treatment relations. Our previous analyses suggest that behavioral dependence may be a critical variable in this regard. With this in mind, we examined the relation between social dependence and social isolation, and then the association between each of these variables and behavioral dependence.

Using the indices of social dependence and social isolation as measures, we find that the two are positively associated ($x^2 = 19.16$, 3 df, $p < .01$, with a contingency coefficient of .41).

Table 6 (Appendix A) presents associations between behavioral dependence on the one hand, and the indices of social isolation and social dependence on the other. Behavioral dependence is significantly related to social isolation, ($x^2 = 9.22$, $p < .05$), such that over two-thirds of men characterized by severe social isolation (index position 3) are behaviorally dependent, in contrast to lesser proportions in other index positions. (An anomaly is that relatively many men with a social isolation index score of zero are behaviorally dependent; the relation between social isolation and social dependence may not be linear.)

The index of social dependence is also not linearly related to behavioral dependence. However, when the data are dichotomized into low (0-1) and high (3-4) social dependence, a positive association between the two variables is apparent ($x^2 = 4.93$, 1 df, $p < .05$).

Interpretively, it would appear that behavioral dependence is not prepotent over social dependence. Social dependence is a variable in its own right, somewhat related to, but mostly independent of behavioral dependence. Most of the relationship of social dependence to the formation of treatment relations can, therefore, not be attributed to a correlation between social and behavioral dependence. In sum, social dependence, the use of social agencies and related institutions, appears to be a behavioral pattern predictive of utilization of outpatient services by alcoholics. Social isolation appears to have only a very mild relationship to establishment of treatment relations; it is hard to tell from our data whether this relationship is attributable to either the strong relationship of social isolation to social dependence, and/or to the mild relationship of social isolation to behavioral dependence.

Notes

1. L. SYME, "Personality Characteristics and the Alcoholic: A Critique of Current Studies," *Quarterly Journal of Studies on Alcohol,* 18:288-302, 1957.
2. E. H. SUTHERLAND, H. G. SCHROEDER, and C. L. TORDELLA, "Personality Traits and the Alcoholic: A Critique of Existing Studies," *Quarterly Journal of Studies on Alcohol,* 11:547-561, 1950.
3. WORLD HEALTH ORGANIZATION, Expert Committee on Mental Health, Alcoholism Subcommittee, Second Report, *World Health Organization Technical Report Series,* No. 48 (Geneva, 1952).
4. O. FENICHEL, *The Psychoanalytic Theory of Neurosis* (New York: W. W. Norton and Co., 1945).
5. S. A. LORAND, "A Survey of Psychoanalytical Literature on Problems of Alcohol: Bibliography," *Yearbook of Psychoanalysis,* 1:359-370, 1945.
6. S. RADO, "The Psychoanalysis of Pharmacothymia," *Psychoanalytic Quarterly,* 2:1-23, 1933.
7. K. A. MENNINGER, *Man Against Himself* (New York: Harcourt Brace, 1938).
8. P. SCHILDER, "Psychogenesis of Alcoholism," *Quarterly Journal of Studies on Alcohol,* 2:277-292, 1941.
9. R. P. KNIGHT, "The Dynamics and Treatment of Chronic Alcohol Addiction," *Bulletin of the Menninger Clinic,* 1:233-250, 1937.

10. H. A. WITKIN, S. A. KARP, and D. R. GOODENOUGH, "Dependence in Alcoholics," *Quarterly Journal of Studies on Alcohol,* 20:493-504, 1959.
11. W. McCORD and J. McCORD, *Origins of Alcoholism* (Stanford, California: Stanford University Press, 1960).
12. *Ibid.*
13. C. W. SLACK, "Experimenter-Subject Psychotherapy: A New Method of Introducing Intensive Office Treatment for Unreachable Cases," *Mental Hygiene,* 44:238-256, 1960.
14. McCORD and McCORD, *op. cit.*
15. F. AULD and J. K. MYERS, "Contributions to a Theory for Selecting Psychotherapy Patients," *Journal of Clinical Psychology,* 10:56-60, 1954; M. A. BAILEY, L. WARSHAW, and R. M. EICHLER, "A Study of Factors Related to Length of Stay in Psychotherapy," *Journal of Clinical Psychology,* 15:442-444, 1959; J. D. FRANK, L. H. GLIEDMAN, S. D. IMBER, E. H. NASH, and A. R. STONE, "Why Patients Leave Psychotherapy," *Archives of Neurology and Psychiatry,* 77:283-299, 1957; R. E. GIBBY, B. A. STOTSKY, E. W. HILER, and D. R. MILLER, "Validation of Rorschach Criteria for Predicting Duration of Therapy," *Journal of Consulting Psychology,* 18:185-191, 1954; S. D. IMBER, E. H. NASH, and A. R. STONE, "Social Class and Duration of Psychotherapy," *Journal of Clinical Psychology,* 11:281-284, 1955; H. S. LIEF, V. F. LIEF, C. D. WARREN, and R. G. HEATH, "Low Dropout Rate in a Psychiatric Clinic," *Archives of General Psychiatry,* 5:200-211, 1961; M. LORR, M. M. KATZ, and E. A. RUBINSTEIN, "The Prediction of Length of Stay in Psychotherapy," *Journal of Consulting Psychology,* 22:321-327, 1958; L. SCHAFFER and J. K. MEYERS, "Psychotherapy and Social Stratification," *Psychiatry,* 17:277-292, 1954; P. L. SULLIVAN, C. MILLER, and W. SMELSER, "Factors in Length of Stay and Progress in Psychotherapy," *Journal of Consulting Psychology,* 22:1-9, 1958; A. E. WINDER and M. HERSKO, "The Effect of Social Class on the Length and Type of Psychotherapy in a Veterans Administration Mental Hygiene Clinic," *Journal of Clinical Psychology,* 11:77-79, 1955.
16. M. E. CHAFETZ, "Practical and Theoretical Considerations in

the Psychotherapy of Alcoholism," *Quarterly Journal of Studies on Alcohol,* 20:281-291, 1959; R. D. FOWLER, SR., *Studies in Alcoholism* (Montgomery, Alabama: Alabama Commission on Alcoholism, 1960); M. ZAX, "The Incidence and Fate of the Reopened Case on an Alcoholism Treatment Center," *Quarterly Journal of Studies on Alcohol,* 23:634-639, 1962.

17. M. ZAX, M. MASSEY, and C. F. BIGGS, "Demographic Characteristics of Alcoholic Outpatients and the Tendency to Remain in Treatment," *Quarterly Journal of Studies on Alcohol,* 22:98-105, 1961.

18. A. B. HOLLINGSHEAD, "Two-Factor Index of Social Position" (mimeographed, undated).

19. S. L. GARFIELD and D. C. AFFLECK, "An Appraisal of Duration of Stay in Outpatient Psychotherapy," *Journal of Nervous and Mental Disease,* 129:492-498, 1959; D. ROSENTHAL and J. D. FRANK, "The Fate of Psychiatric Clinic Out-Patients Assigned to Psychotherapy," *Journal of Mental Disease,* 127:330-343, 1958.

20. E. SINGER, H. T. BLANE, and R. KASSCHAU, "Alcoholism and Social Isolation," *Journal of Abnormal and Social Psychology,* 69:681-685, 1964.

21. S. A. QUEEN and D. B. CARPENTER, *The American City* (New York: McGraw-Hill, 1953); S. RIEMER, *The Modern City* (New York: Prentice-Hall, 1952); H. W. ZORBAUGH, *Gold Coast and Slum* (Chicago, Illinois: University of Chicago Press, 1929).

22. E. W. BURGESS, "The Growth of the City," in R. E. PARK, E. W. BURGESS, and R. D. MCKENZIE (eds.), *The City* (Chicago, Illinois: University of Chicago Press, 47-62, 1925).

23. E. DURKHEIM, *Suicide* (Glencoe, Illinois: The Free Press, 1962); R. E. L. FARIS and H. W. DUNHAM, *Mental Disorders in Urban Areas* (New York: Hofner, 1939); S. A. QUEEN, "The Ecological Study of Mental Disorders," *American Sociological Review,* 5:201-209, 1940).

24. BOSTON PLANNING BOARD, *Report on the Income and Cost of Six Districts in the City of Boston* (Boston, Massachusetts,

1934); R. B. NAVIN, *Analysis of a Slum Area* (Washington, D.C.: Catholic University Press, 1934); QUEEN AND CARPENTER, *op. cit.*; ST. LOUIS PLANNING COMMISSION, *Urban Land Policy* (St. Louis, Missouri, 1936), and *A Year of City Planning* (St. Louis, Missouri, 1937).

25. QUEEN AND CARPENTER, *op. cit.*
26. FARIS and DUNHAM, *op. cit.*; R. E. PARK, "The City: Suggestions for the Investigation of Human Behavior in the Urban Environment," in R. E. PARK, E. W. BURGESS, and R. D. McKENZIE (eds.), *The City* (Chicago, Illinois: University of Chicago Press, 1925), pp. 40-56; W. I. THOMAS and F. ZNANIECKI, *The Polish Peasant in Europe and America* (New York: Alfred A. Knopf, 1918); L. WIRTH, "Urbanism as a Way of Life," *American Journal of Sociology*, 19:1-12, 1938.
27. D. B. FALKEY and S. SCHNEYER, "Characteristics of Male Alcoholics Admitted to the Medical Ward of a General Hospital," *Quarterly Journal of Studies on Alcohol*, 18:67-97, 1957; SINGER, BLANE, and KASSCHAU, *op. cit.*

Chapter 4
Recognizing Alcoholics: Social and Professional Attitudes

Solutions to the problem of alcoholism treatment and prevention can best be achieved through an understanding of the attitudes society holds toward alcoholics, treatment practices with alcoholics, understanding of the illness itself, and of the way these three elements interact.

Traditionally, alcoholism, like mental illness, has been negatively viewed by the general public and its caregivers. In recent years, however, public awareness and tolerance of emotional factors in human behavior have fostered an increasingly enlightened attitude toward alcoholism. A number of recent public opinion surveys show an apparently high acceptance of alcoholics as persons with an illness, although the depth of this acceptance is frequently questioned. One need not look far to see the extent of moralistic and punitive attitudes.

We know that only about ten percent of the estimated alcoholic population receives treatment, even in geographical areas where such help is available. Alcoholics often come to the attention of caretakers not because they are identified as having an alcohol problem, but because of a complication of alcoholism. It is evidently more respectable to be treated for cirrhosis than for alcoholism. Why? It would seem that there are forces operating at both psychological and social levels that conspire to prevent recognition of alcohol problems until they become severe. Although we commonly cite prejudice and negative attitudes as the cause of such denial, we may also profitably examine the protective functions of denial itself. Denial of a problem by the individual prevents him from anxiety and a possible disruption of ego-functioning. Denial on the part of society serves to protect the social organism from disruption and to preserve its values; one aspect of such denial by society is its practice of labeling as "alcoholic" only the individual whose behavior is so extreme and observable that he can be considered "not one of us."

What of the caretaking groups, such as physicians, nurses, and social workers? As both caretakers and members of society, do they share the popular view? It is often suggested that they do. Chafetz and Demone, for example, implicate all caretaking professions: "Not only is an ignorant, moralistic and punitive attitude rampant among lay people; it thrives among the caretaking professions as well . . . society despises [the alcoholic]; the medical profession shuns him."[1]

Our studies of alcoholics in the emergency service provided an opportunity to examine the attitudes of the physician. The following two studies indicate clearly that the physician sees the alcoholic as "not one of us." How does the patient perceive the doctor? Abram and McCourt have described patient-doctor interaction in terms of mutual expectations: "It is the interplay between the fulfillment and frustration of these expectations that determines behavioral responses in both alcoholic and physician."[2] The third paper in this chapter is a study of the response of our patients to one aspect of the doctor's behavior, his tone of voice.

Finally, we include a further analysis of the same patients, in which we focus specifically on the social isolation of the alcoholic. With this paper we add one more section to a cycle describing a self-fulfilling prophecy; the alcoholic, with his own feelings of guilt and worthlessness, seems to invite and encourage rejection by society and receives it in full measure. In what order do alcohol problems—isolation and rejection—enter the cycle? Such questions can be answered, as we shall point out in a later section, only with the intensive study of prealcoholic populations.

4.A. Social Factors in the Diagnosis of Alcoholism: Characteristic of the Patient

That psychiatric diagnosis varies in part with extrapsychiatric factors is a commonly held notion. The literature reveals little, however, to document or explore this impression. Studies of psychiatric diagnosis have been less concerned with extrapsychiatric facts than with reliability, validity, and adequacy or nonadequacy of classificatory schemes.[3] Raines and Rohmer report significant differences among the diagnoses of diagnosticians who independently evaluated the same patients.[4] They propose that these differences are a func-

Section 4.A. written, in collaboration, by Howard T. Blane, Willis F. Overton, Jr., and Morris E. Chafetz.
Notes to Chapter 4 will be found on page 149.

tion of differing frames of personal reference and they advance a "projection" hypothesis to explain the individual differences. Hollingshead and Redlich state that "a psychiatrist tends to diagnose according to his professional orientation or ideology. It is quite possible that a psychoanalyst does not report a complaint of abdominal pain in favor of sexual anxiety, whereas a directive-organically oriented therapist might emphasize the former."[5] With respect to alcoholism, Straus suggests that extraclassificatory factors exert an influence on whether or not it will be diagnosed.[6] These factors are primarily attitudinal and result from the physician's tendency to focus on physical pathology rather than social-psychological malfunctioning in reaching a diagnosis. This tendency is enhanced by a commonly held view that alcoholism is a disorder primarily of homeless, isolated, and impoverished inebriates.

The research described in Section B of Chapter 2 (Establishing Treatment Relations with Alcoholics) afforded a unique opportunity to examine empirical correlates of variations in the diagnosis of alcoholism. Since method of selection of the patients in this project involved the diagnosis of alcoholism and furnishes the data for the present missed-cases study, it will be helpful to review the details of the selection procedures. There were 10 subject-selection periods during each of which the first 20 patients diagnosed as "alcoholic" were assigned to the project. The diagnosis had to be made by one of the chief medical officers on duty in the emergency service. During these subject-selection periods a fact crucial to the present study came to light. A large proportion of patients who could be considered alcoholics were not assigned to the project by the medical officers. Questions arose as to why some alcoholics should be assigned and others not. Are there differences between missed, or nonassigned, and not missed, or assigned, patients? Do attitudes of physicians toward alcoholics and alcoholism influence their diagnostic decisions? Did attitudes of the physicians toward our project influence the ways in which they assigned patients to the study? By virtue of being able to identify the missed cases and also to examine systematically the attitudes of the physicians involved in subject selection, we are able to provide at least beginning answers to these questions. Our purpose in this paper is to examine the question about differences between missed and nonmissed alcoholics. The paper that follows deals directly with the attitudes of the physicians assigning patients to the project.

Assignment or nonassignment to the project is, we assume, the behavioral outcome of a complex interplay of factors that involve the patient, the physician, and the social system in which they meet. The manner in which the patient presents himself is a consequence of his immediate circumstances as well as his past experiences with physicians in this and other medical settings, and is crucial in determining the physician's response to him. Similarly, the physician's expectations of the patient fluctuate under varying circumstances but within the limits of his engrained attitudes. The nature of the interpersonal encounter that occurs is modified by the social setting in which it takes place. In the present report we do not concern ourselves with all the complexities of this interplay but with only two aspects: the relationships between two sets of attitudes assumed to be commonly held by physicians and certain definable characteristics of the patient, and the effect of these relationships on the decision to assign or not assign alcoholics as subjects to the study.

The first set of attitudes is the physician's preference for a medical diagnosis rather than one that indicates social and psychological malfunction. Straus has put it this way: "As a medical student, the physician learned to think of the liver, the heart, the respiratory system, the skin disease, the psychosis, or the fractured limb as the primary problem. . . . The physician prefers to classify his patients according to basic organic or body system disorders . . ."[7] Faced, then, with clear-cut medical symptomatology, the physician is likely to make a purely medical diagnosis even though, from another point of view, psychosocial pathology predominates.

The second set of attitudes is the physician's tendency to see alcoholism as a disorder that occurs primarily among socially isolated and impoverished chronic inebriates. Straus has described it this way:

> . . . Alcoholism carried such a social stigma that the condition was considered unmentionable and great efforts were made to conceal or deny its existence. Many persons found

comfort in the fallacious notion that the only real alcoholics were derelicts—the homeless, chronic inebriates of Skid Row. From this misconception it was reasoned that men or women who, despite pathological drinking, were able to retain a degree of stability in their family, job or community relationships, could not be true alcoholics because they did not fit the derelict stereotype. . . . Physicians have not been immune to these negative attitudes which have prevailed in the larger society. . . . In some respects the redefinition of alcoholism as a form of illness, a public health and medical problem, has gained more rapid and complete acceptance among the general public and alcoholics themselves than among some members of the medical profession.

The definable characteristics of patients that we studied include information that was relevant to either or both of the above attitudinal sets available to the physician at the time he examined the patient. Undoubtedly other information or behavior available to the physician, but not to us, played a more or less subtle role in the decision to assign or not assign the patient to the project. For example, the appearance of the patient is of considerable importance in forming a diagnostic impression. Since it was not possible for us to measure this or other factors of possible perceptual relevance to the physician, we limited ourselves to those factors that were available to us and that we knew were available to him.

We tested two hypotheses: (1) Nonassigned (missed) alcoholics show a lower incidence of social characteristics associated with the alcoholic-as-derelict than do assigned alcoholics. (2) Nonassigned alcoholics show a higher incidence of characteristics relevant to the physician's tendency to classify patients according to basic organic or body-system disorders than do assigned alcoholics.

Procedure

SUBJECT SELECTION

We defined a missed case as an alcoholic who entered the emergency service during the subject selection phases of the project, but who was not assigned to the project by the chief medical officer.

The specific intervals for identifying missed cases extended from 12 o'clock noon on the first day of each month (when the selection of subjects began) until such time as the last subject was assigned to the project for that month. There were 10 consecutive monthly subject-selection periods; each lasted until 20 alcoholics had been assigned to the project. The final project sample, therefore, consisted of 200 male alcoholics, 100 designated as experimental subjects, the other 100 as control subjects.

In order to determine the number of cases missed, we initiated this procedure: We examined the emergency service log book, a daily record of *all* persons admitted, and called in for review the medical records of all males 16 years of age (an arbitrarily chosen lower age limit) or older who entered the emergency service during the subject-selection phases of the project. We called in approximately 3,000 medical records for review; of these, five were not obtained and were officially listed as lost by the hospital. We first screened the records for residence, and eliminated those of patients who lived outside the project's geograpical limits—roughly 20 miles from the hospital. We then reviewed the remaining records for evidence of alcoholism. Our screening procedure differed from that of the chief medical officer's in that we based our diagnosis entirely on the medical record, whereas he assigned a patient to the project after personal contact with him as well as review of his medical record.

To determine whether an individual was an alcoholic, we used the same criteria as those available to the chief medical officer in his assignment of patients to the project. These criteria are listed on page 45. Since we undertook identification of missed cases some months after the conclusion of the original subject-selection phase, we frequently found entries in the medical records dated after the emergency service admission in question. We excluded such data from consideration and based our diagnosis on information in the medical record only up to but including this emergency service admission.

During the periods in which the assignment of the 200 subjects to the project occurred, we found that chief medical officers had failed to refer alcoholics to the project some 265 times (not persons). Of this number seven patients (17 misses) were missed more than once but in separate months, and three patients (three misses) were missed in one month but upon emergency service admission in a later month were assigned to the project. To avoid overrepresentation by one individual appearing more than once in the final missed-cases group, we considered a case missed more than once in a given month, or in separate months, as missed only once: the first time the patient was admitted to the emergency service. To maintain independence between the missed (nonassigned) and the project (assigned) groups, we arbitrarily considered cases missed but later assigned to the project as project cases. This procedure yielded a final count of 238 missed cases, and we compared this group with the assigned project group of 200 subjects.

CATEGORIZATION OF PATIENT CHARACTERISTICS

Data sources for categorizing patient characteristics were the emergency service face sheet and the physician's note only for the date for the emergency service admission in question. The face sheet is a standard form that a clerk fills out when the patient first enters the emergency service. The physician writes his note on it after he examines the patient.

The social characteristics used to test the first hypothesis are:

1. *Marital status.*
2. *Employer listed.* On admission the patient is asked by the clerk in the emergency service the name and address of his employer but is not asked whether he is currently employed.
3. *Nearest relative.* The patient is asked by the emergency service clerk the name and address of his nearest relative.
4. *Same address as nearest relative.*
5. *Public assistance.* The emergency service clerk determines from the patient whether he is receiving any form of public assistance, including social security, old age assistance, or aid to dependent children.
6. *Medical insurance.* The clerk determines whether the patient subscribes to some form of medical insurance.

7. *Mode of entry to E.S.* The clerk determines whether the patient arrived in custody of the police.

The medically relevant characteristics used to test the second hypothesis are:

1. *Previous hospital admission.* We determine whether each patient had been admitted to the hospital prior to the admission in question.

2. *Source of referral.* The clerk lists the source of referral when it involves a professional person (most often the patient's local physician) or agency.

3. *Patient's subjective complaint.* In the note that the physician writes after he has seen the patient he states the patient's subjective presenting complaint. We classify these statements into five categories: (a) Medical subjective physical complaints of patient not associated by him with drinking; these are general (e.g., "pains in my chest," "back pains") or specific (e.g., "vomiting," "rectal bleeding"). (b) Surgical complaints and requests for aid with lacerations, contusions, fractures, or wounds. (c) Alcoholic-patient seeks medication or other help to stop his drinking, to prevent delirium tremens, or to relieve symptoms attributed by him to heavy alcohol intake; or patient is referred by an individual, agency, or other clinic for an alcohol problem. (d) Psychiatric; psychological complaints unaccompanied by reference to alcohol (e.g., patient feels violent, or depressed, or afraid of what he might do). (e) No complaint; no expression of a subjective complaint is indicated in the physician's note. This occurs when a patient is brought in against his will or without seeking help and feels nothing is wrong with him, or when he is unconscious is unaware of why he should have been brought in, or when he states a complaint but the physician does not record it.

4. *Physician's diagnostic impression.* In the body or at the end of his note, the examining physician states his initial diagnostic impression. We selected the physician's primary diagnostic impression for purposes of classification; for example, for the entry "(i) question of acute and chronic alcoholism, (ii) question of diabetes,

(iii) laceration, right forehead," the statement "acute and chronic alcoholism" was used to classify diagnostic impression. The five classificatory categories are: (a) Medical; medical conditions not directly related to alcohol intake (e.g., tuberculosis, diabetes, pneumonia, epilepsy), or tentative or nonspecific impressions (e.g., "chest pain—possibility of heart disease"). (b) Surgical; contusion, fracture, wound, or laceration state indicates need for surgery, (e.g., appendicitis, severe infection). (c) Alcoholic; diagnosis of "acute" or "chronic" alcoholism or both, or any related expression (e.g., vagabond's disease), or diagnosis of delirium tremens or any related condition (e.g., alcohol withdrawal, rum fits), or medical conditions intimately related to excessive alcohol intake, (e.g., alcoholic gastritis, alcoholic neuropathy, cirrhosis), or anxiety, tremulousness, sweating not specifically related to delirium tremens or alcohol withdrawal, but mentioned in connection with a recent history of excessive drinking. (d) Psychiatric; diagnosis of neurosis or phychosis unrelated to alcohol use, or notations of anxiety, suicidal intentions, or nervousness unrelated to alcohol use. (e) No diagnostic impression; physician states that he found no indication of reason for complaint (e.g., patient complains of wrist pain, but no sprain, fracture, infection, etc., is found), or no diagnostic impression is present in the physician's note.[9]

5. *Hospitalization subsequent to present E. W. admission.*

Results

HYPOTHESIS 1

Table 7 (Appendix A) shows the difference between the groups of missed and assigned cases in those categories of patient characteristics used to examine the first hypothesis. It should first be noted that both groups are drawn predominantly from lower social strata, and probably in large degree represent marginal to submarginal economic segments of an urban population. There is a high incidence of unemployment in both groups, a relatively high incidence of men receiving public assistance, and a correspondingly low incidence of patients subscribing to medical insurance. Social isolation, as reflected in not residing with one's nearest relative, is high in both the assigned and missed groups of men. Men in both groups are on the average middle-aged (the difference between the missed group mean of 49.5 years and the assigned group mean of 48.3 years is not significant), although the range of ages is significantly broader in the missed than in the assigned group (C.R. = 4.9, $p < .001$). Thus, 29.0 percent of the missed cases are less than 30 or more than 65 years of age in contrast to 9.5 percent of assigned cases falling within these extreme age ranges (x square = 25.721, 1 df, $p < .001$). Finally, both groups are predominantly Catholic in religious affiliation (77.5 percent of the missed, and 77.1 percent of the assigned cases); few are Jewish (2.2 percent of the missed and 0.5 percent of the assigned cases), a finding in accord with reports of cultural differences in rates of alcoholism.[10]

Comparing the missed group with the assigned, it is apparent that significant differences obtain in all categories used to examine the first hypothesis. These differences may be summarized as follows:

1. *Marital status.* More missed than assigned patients report themselves to be currently married, whereas more assigned than missed patients state they are separated or divorced. When we examine only those men who have at some time been married (category 1b) the differences are even more striking. There are no differences between the groups in the single or widower categories. We conclude that the missed in comparison with the assigned group is more maritally stable.

2. *Employer listed.* Comparison of the groups as a whole reveals no difference in regard to the listing of an employer (category 2a); however, when we exclude patients not available to the labor force, that is, those 65 years of age or older or recipients of public assistance, it is evident that more missed than assigned cases list an employer. Thus the missed group is proportionately more employed than the assigned group.

3. *Nearest relative.* The difference between the assigned and non-assigned groups for nearest relative listed is significant. A larger percentage of the missed group lists a wife as nearest relative, whereas a larger proportion of the assigned group lists a sibling. Since this

result is partially dependent on marital status (patients currently married almost always list wife as next of kin), the data were recast (category 3b) to exclude from analysis patients who reported themselves as currently married. Results by this classification show that a larger proportion of missed than assigned alcoholics lists a parent or child as next of kin, and that a larger proportion of the assigned groups list a sibling. On the assumption that wives, parents, and children are psychologically closer than siblings, it may be inferred that nonassigned alcoholics showed relatively more psychological family unity. It is also of interest that a small proportion in both groups of the currently unmarried nevertheless list a wife as next of kin.

4. *Same address as nearest relative.* A significantly larger proportion of missed than assigned patients state that they have the same address as the person whom they list as next of kin. This suggests that missed cases as a group are less isolated from their families than the assigned group.

5. *Public assistance.* While both groups show an incidence of receiving public assistance greater than that of the general population, more of the missed cases receive such assistance than do members of the assigned group. We infer from this that, although both groups are in large part drawn from marginal or submarginal segments of an urban population, patients in the nonassigned group are more integrated with the social system in that they use the institutional facilities available to those requiring social welfare assistance.

6. *Medical insurance.* Medical insurance is less subcribed to in both groups than one would expect in an industrialized urban population. Nevertheless, the missed-cases group shows a significantly higher percentage of men subscribing to a medical insurance plan than does the assigned group. We view this finding as complementary to that in the category of public assistance—more individuals in the missed than in the assigned group make use of the social welfare institutions that society provides. In this sense, the missed-cases group as a whole is more integrated with the social system than the assigned group.

7. *Mode of entry to the emergency service.* Slightly more than

a third of the missed cases were brought to the emergency service under police escort, in contrast to well over half of the assigned cases. Relatively speaking, then, the missed show a significantly lesser involvement with agents of law enforcement than do the assigned cases.

The results from the variables used to examine the first hypothesis, that is, that missed cases show a lower incidence than assigned alcoholics of social characteristics associated with the alcoholic-as-derelict, consistently support this hypothesis.[11] If we view the derelict as a person isolated, both socially and psychologically, from commonly valued features of our society, alcoholics in the assigned group fit this conception to a significantly greater degree than alcoholics in the missed-cases group. Relative to assigned-group patients, missed alcoholics are more stable maritally and occupationally, more integrated with their families, and more integrated with the social systems that society provides for the welfare and protection of its members. The fact that the chief medical officers did not assign these alcoholics to the project confirms the idea that medical conceptions of alcoholism are in practice widely divergent from those stated by official organs of the medical profession.[12]

HYPOTHESIS 2

Table 20 (Appendix A) presents the differences between the groups of missed and assigned alcoholics on the variables used to examine the second hypothesis. The differences may be summarized as follows:

1. *Previous hospital admission.* The difference between the groups in this category is not significant, although the missed alcoholics tend to have a higher incidence ($p = .10$) of previous admissions than the assigned group.

2. *Source of referral.* Although the source of referral (from a professional person or agency) was listed infrequently for both groups, such listing was more frequent for the missed than for the assigned patients. We interpret this to mean that patients who are

referred in a context familiar and acceptable to the physician are likely to be considered to have a more "serious" condition than alcoholism.

3. *Subjective complaint.* The patterning of categories used to classify the patient's verbalized complaint differs markedly between missed and assigned alcoholic groups. The missed cases show a much greater proportion of medical-surgical complaints (70.1 percent) than do the assigned patients (24.0 percent); the missed alcoholics, in addition, show a much lower percentage of alcoholic complaints than the assigned patients. It is of interest that both groups show relatively high proportions of "No complaint listed," although a significantly smaller proportion of missed than assigned alcoholics fall in this category. We cannot state with any certainty what this finding may mean, since the "No complaint," as defined earlier, consists of three separate factors. There is no question that the physician's note is sometimes very scanty. This usually occurs when the physician is so busy with a rush of admissions that he does not write his notes on a number of patients until several hours after he has seen them. In this situation he can forget details of individual patients seen, and a sparsely written note results. It is our impression, however, that this occurs infrequently. The more usual situation is that the patient is not in a condition to state a complaint or does not verbalize a complaint (other than one of outrage), because he has been brought to the hospital against his will and does not perceive himself as being in need of medical aid. In any event, it is clear that men verbalizing a medical or surgical complaint had a much greater chance of being missed as alcoholics than men with an alcoholic complaint or with no complaint at all.

4. *Physician's diagnostic impression.* Classification of patients by type of physician's diagnostic impression significantly distinguishes the missed from the assigned group. The missed has a higher incidence than the assigned of individuals given a medical diagnosis, and a lower incidence of men receiving a diagnosis of alcoholism. It is of particular interest that although more than 13 percent of the missed cases received a diagnosis of alcoholism, these men were not assigned to the project. This suggests that specific attitudes of

the chief medical officers toward the project played a not unimportant role in assignment. A considerable proportion of alcoholics in both groups were classified as receiving no diagnosis, although the incidence is somewhat higher in the assigned than in the missed group. The meaning of this finding, like that of "no complaint" in the "Subjective complaint" variable, is not at all clear. In some instances the lack of a diagnosis reflects a lack of positive medical findings; in other cases, the rush and confusion of working in the emergency service; and perhaps in yet others this omission has an attitudinal-emotional basis.

5. *Hospitalization subsequent to present admission.*[13] Missed alcoholics are hospitalized at a much higher rate than assigned alcoholics. Further comparison of the groups by the median length of hospital stay shows that hospitalized missed cases were in hospital for significantly longer periods than the hospitalized assigned patients (x square $= 3.84$, 1 df, $p = .05$). This finding indicates that missed cases who were hospitalized had, in addition to alcoholism, medical conditions serious enough to require, on the average, relatively long periods of hospital stay. That these men were not assigned to the project suggests that their medical conditions negated, in the physician's mind, a diagnosis of alcoholism.

These results support the second hypothesis, that is, that missed (nonassigned) alcoholics show a higher incidence than the assigned of characteristics relevant to the physician's tendency to classify patients according to basic organic or body system disorders. The missed alcoholics, relative to assigned patients, are more often referred to the emergency service by a professional person or agency, have a higher incidence of medical-surgical subjective complaints, more frequently receive a medical diagnosis, are more frequently hospitalized subsequent to their emergency service admission, and those hospitalized spend a longer time in hospital. These results indicate that the alcoholic who presents himself at the emergency service in a manner consistent with the physician's preference for a diagnosis involving systemic disorder will not be assigned to the project as an alcoholic, and will receive specific treatment for physical pathology but not necessarily for the alcoholic context in which the physical disorder occurs.

SOCIAL AND MEDICAL INDICES

In order to determine to what degree the results just reported discriminate between missed and assigned groups when the categories are used in combination, another set of analyses was carried out. This involved the construction of three indices: social, medical, and combined social-medical.

Social integration index. Seven social variables reached statistical significance. These were mode of entry, marital status, nearest relative, same address as nearest relative, medical insurance, public assistance, and employer listed (for individuals not over 65 years of age and not receiving public assistance). Using these variables, we constructed a seven-point index of social integration by assigning to an individual a score of one for each of the following variables: (1) mode of entry: other than police; (2) marital status: married, single, or widowed; (3) nearest relative: wife, parent, or child; (4) same address as nearest relative: present; (5) medical insurance: present; (6) public assistance: present; (7) employer listed: yes. Scores for the individual were then summed, the range being 0 to 6, with lower index positions indicating less social integration.[14] Table 8 (Appendix A) presents the percentage distributions of social index positions in the missed and assigned groups. The two distributions differ significantly and show great consistency in the increasing percentage of missed cases at each successive index position from 0 through 6.[15] Although the index is not designed to tell whether a given individual is assigned or nonassigned, it may be noted that index positions 0 and 6 identify whether individuals will be assigned or nonassigned, respectively, at levels over 80 percent.

Medical index. A five-point medical index, constructed in the same way as the social integration index, was based on the four significant medically relevant variables, a score of 1 being assigned for each of the following: (1) source of referral: listed; (2) subjective complaint: medical or surgical; (3) physician's diagnosis: medical or surgical; and (4) hospitalization subsequent to emergency service admission: yes. Table 8 (Appendix A) shows the percentage distributions on the five medical index positions indicating more characteristics that fit in with the physicians' preference for a physical diagnosis. We did not include assigned experimental patients in this index because they were frequently hospitalized for purposes of their special care.[16]

Again the two percentage distributions differ significantly and show consistency in the increasing identification of missed cases at each successive index position from 0 through 4. Also, it may be noted that index positions 3 and 4 identify individuals at high levels. The chances are about 9 in 10 that an alcoholic with a medical index of 3 or 4 will be a nonassigned case.

Social-medical index. The 11 significant social or medically relevant variables were used in the construction of a combined index. As previously, we assigned a score of 1 to an individual for each variable listed in the two preceding sections. In the present index we included experimental assigned cases but did not index them for the hospitalization variable. Final index scores were obtained by summing individual raw scores and dividing by the number of variables for which the individual was scored. For example, an individual with a summed raw score of 7 for 11 variables received a final index score of 164. The possible range of index scores is .00 to 1.00. Table 8 (Appendix A) shows the percentage distributions of social-medical index scores in .10-step intervals.

The percentage distributions of the assigned and nonassigned alcoholics differ significantly and show again the consistently increasing percentage of missed cases at each successive index score. The identificatory power of the combined index is greater than that of either the social integration or medical index in that it discriminates at both higher and lower index scores. Thus, of alcoholics with combined index scores of .61 or larger, 91 percent are nonassigned; and of alcoholics with scores of .20 or less, 80 percent are assigned. Moreover, the percentage of the total sample ($N = 436$) identified at levels of at least 80 percent is greatest for the combined index. Alcoholics with combined index scores of .61 or more and .20 or less comprise 42 precent of the total sample. Corresponding values for the social and medical indices are 29 and 13 percent respectively. These findings suggest the presence of an interaction between socially and medically relevant characteristics that affects the physician's decision to assign or not assign an alcoholic. If an alcoholic has a high position on the social integration index, he is very likely not to be assigned to the project as an alcoholic. If, however, his position is low on both social and medical indices, he is very likely to be assigned as an alcoholic for special treatment. We interpreted this to mean that the physician's preference for viewing patients in terms of organic or body-system pathology takes precedence over his tendency to perceive alcoholism as a disorder that occurs primarily among derelicts. From the physician's viewpoint, an alcoholic is an alcoholic only if he is relatively well physically and if he is a derelict.

Discussion

The findings of this exploratory investigation bear out the hypotheses that alcoholism, as perceived by physicians, is a disease of derelicts and that alcoholism as a diagnosis is less preferred than diagnoses involving physical pathology. The results further indicate that physician attitudes continue to play a prominent role in the manner in which alcoholics are handled in medical settings. In addition, it is evident that the physicians indirectly involved in this study made fine distinctions within a sample drawn from a homogeneous socioeconomic population. The majority of alcoholics, assigned and nonassigned, came from lower- and lower-middle-class social strata.

Assigned alcoholics, more often than the nonassigned, were men whose social characteristics were little in keeping with a number of commonly adhered-to social forms. These men were in trouble with law-enforcing agents, isolated from the nuclear family, maritally unstable, unemployed, and they did not use societal avenues available for their own assistance. They presented themselves to the hospital without physical complaints and without demonstrable physical pathology. From the physician's point of view, then, alcoholics who are relatively well physically but disintegrated socially are indeed alcoholics. These assigned alcoholics fit previous descriptions of derelicts. Pittman and Gordon portray chronic police-case inebriates as impoverished, socially isolated, maritally unstable, and rejected by their families.[17] Similar findings were reported by Straus on homeless men[18] and by Jackson and Connor on Skid Row alcoholics.[19]

Nonassigned or missed alcoholics, as distinguished from the assigned, more often were not involved with the police, were integrated with the nuclear family, maritally stable, employed, and used socially provided resources to their own benefit. Further, they presented themselves to the hospital with medical-surgical complaints and showed demonstrable physical pathology. Thus, from the physician's viewpoint, the alcoholic who is medically ill and relatively intact socially is not an alcoholic.

In this study physicians' attitudes play a prominent role, but our findings result from a special situation in one hospital. How far may they be generalized? Straus suggests that the physicians' attitudes we have examined are pervasive: "Although general hospital wards contained many alcoholic patients, these were usually admitted because of more medically acceptable symptoms. . . . While he may have recognized that excessive drinking was an associated factor [the physician] was seldom encouraged to pursue its real implications."[20] Nor does Straus exculpate psychiatrists or hospital administrators: "Despite the pronounced emotional ramifications of alcoholism, most psychiatrists have been just as reluctant as their medical colleagues to become deeply involved in the treatment of alcoholic patients," and "the hospital administrator frequently will not admit the alcoholic unless he has some associated symptoms which are medically respectable." Jellinek notes that although hospital attitudes are changing in regard to the latter point, it was nevertheless necessary in 1956 "to call the matter of admission of alcoholics to the attention of hospital administrators."[21] Studies of medical attitudes toward alcoholism are few and have utilized relatively superficial survey methods rather than attempts to view attitudes in depth.[22] The findings of these studies are nevertheless in agreement on one major point: attitudes of physicians toward alcoholics are largely negative. The physician finds alcoholism "a nuisance in his practice";[23] alcoholics are "a nuisance" and "uncooperative";[24] and "attitudes . . . reflected a generally negative feeling toward the alcoholic."[25] These studies were made 10 to 15 years ago, yet their results are consistent with the more recent view of Straus and Jellinek and with our findings. It appears justified to conclude that our findings, obtained in a unique situation, nevertheless reflect attitudes widely held and maintained in the medical community.

The finding that the patients assigned to the project fall primarily into the category of derelict or Skid Row alcoholics has major implications for therapeutic control of alcoholism, particularly when we remember that assignment to the project held out the possibility of highly specialized, continuous and comprehensive care for those alcoholics designated as experimentals. First, the finding means that those alcoholics deemed most fit by physicians to receive specialized care for alcoholism are the very alcoholics for whom treatment attempts have in the past been most unpromising. The Skid Row alcoholic is often in the most advanced stages of alcoholism with all its physical, social, and psychological sequels; he is likely to be middle-aged or older, to have been drinking excessively for 20 years or more, to have been unemployed for a prolonged period, and to have severe physical and psychological disturbances more or less directly related to many years of excessive drinking. Korsakoff's or Wernicke's disease, polyneuropathy, cirrhosis of the liver, malnutrition, or repeated episodes of delirium tremens, or "rum fits" are likely to be present, either singly or in combination. The rehabilitation of this type of alcoholic is not impossible but is most difficult and requires extensive resources.

Second, socially intact alcoholics are not referred by physicians for specialized treatment of alcoholism, despite the fact that their prognosis is relatively good. The married alcoholic living with his spouse, still employed, and showing other signs of social stability has, once motivation for change is established, a much better chance of recovery than the alcoholic from Skid Row. Furthermore, socially intact problem drinkers do not in their treatment require as many specialized resources, such as living-in arrangements and vocational rehabilitation, as are necessary for the successful rehabilitation of derelict alcoholics. Thus alcoholic patients who might benefit most from treatment for alcoholism are least likely to be referred for it by physicians.

Third, young men acutely inebriated on admission are not assigned for specialized care for alcoholism. Most of these men come to the hospital for the treatment of injuries sustained in a fight or an automobile accident occurring under the influence of alcohol. While these men do not necessarily show signs of severe social, psychological, or physical disruption, their behavior nevertheless raises a strong suspicion of alcoholism. The preventive implications of intervention with these men are obvious. Intervention at an early age, before excessive drinking patterns are fixed and prior to social or physical deterioration, offers possibilities of distinct savings, both from human and social-economic viewpoints. Thus, it would seem that some of the hospital staff who are in a strategic position to contribute to case finding and prevention in the field of alcoholism keep the hospital from fully entering into this role.

In sum, it is evident that the way physicians see alcoholism exerts a tremendous influence on the way alcoholics are treated. The physician can serve as a case finder of alcoholics; yet until physician attitudes and knowledge about alcoholism undergo change, many alcoholics and prealcoholics will not receive treatment until the disease is so far advanced that treatment becomes highly complicated, therapeutic goals limited, and necessary resources extremely expensive.

An unanticipated and important finding of this study is the incongruence between the physician's written diagnosis and his assignment or nonassignment of patients to the project. Each of these behaviors signifies a diagnosis. The first we call a "formal" diagnosis; the second an "action" diagnosis. The lack of close association between these two types of classification can be summarized as follows. Of the 200 alcoholics assigned to the project, that is, receiving an action diagnosis of alcoholism, only 41.5 percent received a formal diagnosis of alcoholism. On the other side of the coin, of the 238 alcoholics not assigned to the project, 13 percent nevertheless received a formal diagnosis of alcoholism. We suggested earlier that this latter figure may reflect specific attitudes which the medical officers held about the project itself. With regard to the fact that many alcoholics assigned to the project did not receive a formal diagnosis, one interpretation is that alcoholism as a standard entity of medical diagnostic nomenclature is not, as Straus says, "medically respectable";[26] even alcoholics explicitly referred for treatment of their alcohol condition just as frequently as not received medical-surgical diagnoses or no formal diagnosis whatsoever. We do not intend this either as a reification of the word alcoholism or as an argument of a sterile rigidity in classificatory schemes. The above facts nevertheless reflect ambivalent medical attitudes about alcoholism as a disease entity. We suggest that physicians frequently arrive at a formal diagnosis of alcoholism by exclusion, as is the case with some other psychiatric diagnoses, and further that this diagnosis is often one of opprobrium.

We concur with the preference of Zigler and Phillips for a classificatory scheme that incorporates indices of preferred methods of treatment and prognosis.[27] As they point out, this was essentially the goal of Kraepelin. It is evident, however, that unless the present classificatory scheme for alcoholism, albeit ambiguous, is used, then the therapies and preventive measures concomitant with a diagnosis of the condition cannot come into play. This means that, practically speaking, large segments of the alcoholic population go untreated until their members reach social stages of the disease that coincide with the physician's limited expectations of what alcoholism is. How may these expectations be broadened to include all alcoholics? Official statements by organized medical groups, such as that by the American Medical Association in 1956 are, of course, important, but do not necessarily result in behavior change among physicians.[28] Teaching at medical school levels and learning by precept in clinical settings appear to us more meaningful methods of changing attitudes in regard to alcoholism. This has certainly been our experience in working with small numbers of psychiatric residents. Only when the medical community recognizes that alcoholism is an illness that manifests itself in social and psychological as well as medical symptoms, and that it is an illness that occurs at all social levels, only then will we be able to bring to bear our therapeutic armamentarium to prevent and control this ubiquitous disease.

Summary

The relationship between physicians' attitudes and action diagnosis or nondiagnosis formed the focus of this study. Two groups of male alcoholics admitted to a hospital emergency ward over a 10-month period were compared: (1) 200 alcoholics assigned by the emergency ward chief medical officers to an experimental project for treatment of alcoholism; (2) 238 alcoholics not assigned to the project but meeting criteria for diagnosis of alcoholism. We reasoned that assignment or nonassigment of alcoholics to the project varied systematically with (1) physicians' attitudes about alcoholism, that is, the physicians perceive alcoholism as a disorder occurring primarily among derelicts; and (2) their attitudes about medical diagnosis, that is, that physicians prefer a medical diagnosis to one that includes social and psychological malfunction.

Two hypotheses were tested: (1) nonassigned (missed) patients show a lower incidence than assigned patients of social characteristics associated with the alcoholic as derelict; (2) nonassigned patients show a higher incidence than assigned patients of characteristics relevant to the physician's tendency to classify patients according to basic organic or body-system disorders.

The first hypothesis was supported by the differences found between the assigned and missed groups on seven social variables. More missed (40 percent) than assigned (26 percent) patients reported themselves to be currently married, suggesting that missed patients were more maritally stable. When all those patients not available to the labor force (over 65 or recipients of public assistance) were excluded, more missed (70 percent) than assigned (59 percent) listed an employer. When all those patients currently married were excluded, a larger proportion of missed than assigned patients listed a parent or child as next of kin and a larger proportion of assigned listed a sibling. On the assumption that parents and children are psychologically closer than siblings, it may be inferred that the missed patients showed more family unity. A significantly larger proportion of missed (64 percent) than assigned (43 percent) patients stated that they had the same address as the person they listed as next of kin, suggesting that the missed patients are less isolated from their families. More of the missed (25 percent) than of the assigned (13 percent) patients received public assistance, suggesting that the missed patients were more integrated with the social system. More of the missed (39 percent) than the assigned (17 percent) patients subscribed to a medical insurance plan. Of the missed patients 35 percent were escorted to the hospital by the police, compared to 56 percent of the assigned.

The second hypothesis was supported by differences found on five medically relevant variables. There was a trend for the missed to have a higher incidence of previous hospital admissions (70 percent) than the assigned (63 percent) patients. Source of referral (professional person or agency) was more often listed for the missed (19 percent) than for the assigned (3 percent) patients, suggesting that patients who are referred in a context familiar and acceptable to the physician are likely to be considered to have a more "serious" condition than alcoholism. The missed showed a greater proportion of medical-surgical complaints (70 percent) than the assigned (24 percent) patients. More of the missed (39 percent) than of the assigned (6 percent) patients received a medical diagnosis. Of the assigned patients 41 percent and of the missed patients 13 percent received a diagnosis of alcoholism, although none of the latter were assigned to the project. Missed were hospitalized more frequently than assigned patients and were in hospital for significantly longer periods than the assigned.

On a scale of social integration, constructed from the seven social variables, the percentage distribution of the two groups differed significantly and showed great consistency in the increasing percentage of missed patients at each successive index position from 0 through 6, the lower index positions indicating less social integration. On a five-point medical index, constructed from the last four of the medically relevant variables, the percentage distribution of the two groups differed significantly and showed consistency in the increasing identification of missed cases at each successive index position from 0 through 4, the higher index positions indicating more characteristics that fit in with the physicians' preference for a physical diagnosis. On a combined social and medical index the percentage distributions differed significantly and showed again the consistently increasing percentage of missed patients at each successive index score from .00 to 1.00. Of the patients with combined index scores of .61 or larger, 91 percent were missed; and of those with index scores of .20 or less, 80 percent were assigned.

4.B. Social Factors in the Diagnosis of Alcoholism: Attitudes of Physicians

The previous report concerned itself with differences in social and medical variables between two groups of alcoholics, one composed of men formally diagnosed as alcoholic, the other of men not diagnosed as alcoholic; and showed that diagnosed alcoholics are more socially deteriorated but less physically ill than nondiagnosed alcoholics. These findings were conceptually related to two sets of attitudes assumed to be common to physicians: (1) the perception of alcoholism as a disorder occurring primarily among derelicts; and (2) the preference for a medical diagnosis over a diagnosis that includes psychosocial dysfunction. The study reported here was conducted to see if direct examination of physicians' attitudes by a semistructured interview method would reveal the presence of the two sets of attitudes we ascribed to the physician.

Fifteen physicians were involved in selecting subjects for the alcoholism treatment project, and one or another of them saw each of the 438 alcoholics who made up the diagnosed and nondiagnosed alcoholic groups. The physicians, who were on one- or two-month tours of duty as chief medical officers (essentially an admitting or screening job) to the emergency service of the Massachusetts General Hospital, were advanced medical or surgical residents. They had had at least two years' experience on the wards of the hospital prior

Section 4.B. written, in collaboration, by Irving Wolf, Morris E. Chafetz, Howard T. Blane, and Marjorie J. Hill.
Notes to Chapter 4 will be found on page 149.

to their rotation on the emergency service as admitting physicians. These residents come from all parts of the country, are highly intelligent and able, and are considered among the choicest candidates for residency training. It is of consequence to note that the percentages of all alcoholics diagnosed as alcoholics by each of the physicians are not significantly different among the groups of physicians.[29]

Procedure

One year after the time that the physicians were active in the study, each was interviewed by one of the authors of this Section (I.W.). Each interview, tape recorded, lasted approximately an hour, and followed a semistructured format, with probes at the completion of open-ended statements. Part of the interview was concerned with the physicians' experiences as residents at the Massachusetts General Hospital; the major focus, however, was on their recollections of the alcoholism treatment project, and their views of alcoholism and alcoholics, including both personal and professional experience. Specific topics included were: (1) definition of alcoholism; (2) criteria for diagnosing alcoholism; (3) causes of alcoholism; (4) personal acquaintance with alcoholics or persons with alcohol-related difficulties; (5) criteria used by the physician to assign patients to the alcoholism treatment project; and (6) possible explanations as to why some alcoholics had been diagnosed as alcoholic and assigned to the project, while others had not. Analysis of the verbatim transcripts of responses to these six subareas serves as the basis for the observations and conclusions of this report.

The interviewer was unknown to the respondents prior to the interview, and he was only peripherally identified in their minds with the hospital. It might be added that the physicians were very frank in their statements, and that any defensiveness apparent in the early part of the interview was quickly dissipated as the interview progressed.

Interview Material

Analysis of the interview protocols reveals that physicians hold complex attitudes about alcoholism and toward alcoholics, and further that these attitudes are intimately interwined with attitudes about professional goals, values, and prestige. These complex attitudes, of interest and importance in their own right, bear little apparent relationship to the focus of this report, that is, the differential diagnosis of alcoholism. Since we are unable here to summarize the wealth of material given us by the physicians on their overall attitudes toward alcoholics and alcoholism, we will content ourselves with presenting evidence from the interviews for and against the two ascribed sets of attitudes as they relate to the physicians' systematic manner of diagnosing some alcoholics but not others.

We assumed first that physicians perceive alcoholism as a disorder occurring primarily among derelicts. To place comments made by the physicians in perspective, it is well to note that we can reasonably estimate on the basis of the first study that about one-half of all alcoholics admitted to the emergency service of the hospital may be described as derelict, or Skid Row, alcoholics. The remarks quoted below indicate that the physicians who made them see alcoholism as a disorder of derelicts, but also verbally recognize that alcoholism occurs among nonderelicts. The crucial point here is that they indicate their belief that alcoholics coming to the emergency service are primarily drawn from a derelict population, a belief that is literally no more than a half-truth.

> In the emergency service, somebody comes in and it's pretty much of a snap judgment. If he looks like an alcoholic, he smells like an alcoholic; he's pretty much of a degenerate as far as his appearance is concerned—disheveled, filthy dirty, hasn't been holding down a job—you draw an immediate impression on this basis. . . . This certainly doesn't distinguish the well-dressed executive who comes in, who may be just as much of an alcoholic as the average person that gets to the emergency service, but this is the type of population [i.e., "degenerate"] we're dealing with.

> People whom I have considered alcoholic, all the time during the two months that I was there, have never been properly dressed. They have all been dirty, although there

are one or two exceptions. We see a lot of derelict and bum-type alcoholics. . . . We just get sort of used to the old sort of Bowery type of individual in the emergency service.

We noticed that weather changes would bring in a certain group. When it got real cold, we always expected two or three, as we called them "snowmen." . . . And when the weather was inclement, severe rainstorms and such, we'd always get a few brought in, soaking wet, and we'd have to dry them out. So we saw a recurrent group, a mixture of all sizes and shapes.

You can spot certain types of alcoholics at a glance. The so-called down-and-outer, who comes in acutely intoxicated, who is in ragged clothing, who has a weather-beaten face, who is obviously out-of-doors a great deal; he's unkempt, hasn't had his hair cut in a long time, frequently unshaven for several days. These people, I think it's rare when you're mistaken in calling them alcoholics, because we know the environment that they come from, they are intoxicated at the time, and we can pretty much classify them as alcoholics who are also down and out.

Once in a while alcoholics came in who were not the Scollay Square [a Skid Row area of Boston] variety. They were people in a little higher, or very high, sociological category, and often not quite so drunk, quite so belligerent or somnolent. Some of them are simply miserable and they need a place to sack out, and they get it.

Others of the physicians do not clearly state that alcoholism is a disorder of derelicts; they describe personally defined types of alcoholism, but in their definitions one may see the implication that alcoholics are socially-impoverished persons.

A chronic, indolent type problem. . . . If you get to them, maybe you revealed this dependent type person who really couldn't shift for himself . . . an infantile, dependent type person, who needed a lot of support, needed a lot and demanded a lot.

. . .

> The first type of alcoholic is brought in on a stretcher completely unconscious with the smell of alcohol on his breath, and the story that he's fallen down two flights of stairs. . . . The second alcoholic patient coming through is the jovial fellow who comes in and sits on a front bench and is up and down bothering you with minor complaints continually.

The physicians reveal that they see alcoholism as a disorder of derelicts, but they also show that they consider the alcoholic-as-derelict to be only one type of alcoholic. How do they perceive socially intact persons who have an alcohol problem and how readily do they diagnose such persons as alcoholic? The comments below indicate much more hesitancy in diagnosis with the socially intact as compared to the derelict alcoholic.

> Are you going to consider, for instance, a fellow who is vice president of the [local] bank who consumes a good fifth of the best every day after lunch to dinner time and yet eats a good dinner and carries on his business activities perfectly well an alcoholic? I don't know.
>
> I think the man who is unable to make a small income becomes more quickly defined as an alcoholic than a man who makes a larger income. . . . A man in a higher executive position isn't the constant alcoholic who drinks every day. But he maybe goes on sprees, maybe every month or two.
>
> Alcoholism is not just a medical term. It has social implications; . . . it has social stigma. [Therefore, he would be reluctant to label well-to-do persons,] whom you would have to see for a period of time before you would be able to say they are alcoholics. I've known people who've had relatives in their homes who were alcoholics for years, but they weren't aware of it for a long time. I would call that type of individual a problem drinker, but I wouldn't label him an alcoholic until I knew the specific circumstances of his situation.
>
> There are plenty of alcoholics I have seen who are not necessarily economically destitute. . . . [This doctor, how-

ever, when asked if he has known any alcoholics personally, immediately denied the fact that an alcoholic is not necessarily a derelict by saying:] This man is not a good example; . . . he was a very smart fellow and a good doctor. I think he was atypical because he doesn't fit into the things that I think of as characterizing alcoholics. One is that he was not chronic: he would be a binge drinker, but he wouldn't drink between times. Also he was economically well off, and he didn't have any social problems that I was aware of. . . . He just had this one bad trouble, when he got alcohol he couldn't stop drinking, and he would completely lose his mind over it, and eventually his life.

The comments presented above offer substantial support for the notion that physicians in a general hospital setting perceive alcoholism as a disorder occurring primarily among derelicts. It is clear, however, that they recognize the occurrence of alcoholism in other social groupings, but are more hesitant to make a definite diagnosis than in the instance of the derelict alcoholic. How may this discrepancy be resolved? We suggest that at a verbal, abstract level physicians view alcoholism as a disorder or disease that may be defined in psychological, social, and physiological terms and as a disorder that can occur in any segment of the population. This is borne out by the definitions of alcoholism given by most of the physicians. Alcoholism, for example, is "a disease in which the patient brings to the disease a particular psychiatric situation which leads him to become habituated or addicted to alcohol"; it is "a situation where a person imbibes alcoholic beverages to a point where he disables himself from the normal carrying on of his activities, his work, his home life"; it satisfies "certain physiologic and psychologic needs"; or an alcoholic is "a person who drinks by compulsion." The factors put forth in these definitions are familiar to and accepted by all those whose major professional interest is in alcoholism.

For what happens at the diagnostic level, we have no clear explanation in the interview material. It seems that there is an obvious discrepancy between the physicians' verbal behavior and their diagnostic behavior, and no clear explanation for the discrepancy is provided by the interview material. We suspect, however, that at the level of actual interaction with patients, emotionally laden perceptions and attitudes come into play that are more critical determinants of physicians' diagnostic behavior than views expressed at the abstract level. We may speculate further that social class identifications and the need to preserve the integrity of in-group solidarity may, at a sociological level, be important factors. Whether this is the case or not, we can, on the basis of the interviews and the results of the first study, revise our statement of the first attitudinal set we ascribed to physicians as follows: Physicians behave diagnostically as though alcoholism were primarily a disorder of derelicts, although in their verbal statements they see alcoholism as a disorder occurring in other social groups; they tend not to recognize alcoholics who are other than derelict, and when they do, are hesitant to make the diagnosis of alcoholism.

Our second assumption about physicians' attitudes is that they prefer a medical diagnosis to one that includes psychosocial dysfunction. The remarks quoted below tend to bear out this assumption.

> Being medical men, we regarded the acute medical-physical physiological states and emergencies as the ones that had to be treated first. Not that this is right, not that I hold to this, but this is the practice.

> All the subtle things in life, the implied things, people's sensitive problems, just go right by the resident. He's interested in hemorrhage, pain, and so forth.

> One of the main problems that the resident down there has is just to see medical, honest medical-surgical problems, without the alcoholic who comes in and wants a place to sleep.

> The pressure is on other patients. For example, somebody is there with a leg injury which is definitely obvious. We have more sympathy toward him than with this person who is only drunk.

Some of the physicians, however, adopt a different point of view, seeing their role as physicians in wider compass.

> The uses of the emergency service for other than medical purposes, it seems to me, are many. . . . If the practice of

medicine is invariably related to somatic complaints, well then, I don't see how you can expect to practice in the emergency service.

We should not show any partiality to the person who has the leg injury as compared to the person who is just plain out because of alcoholism. They are both patients. One has a different type of problem from the other.

The remarks cited above support the notion that physicians prefer a medical diagnosis to one that includes psychosocial malfunction. Again, however, the material given by the physicians clarifies for us the attitudinal set we ascribed to them. Thus it appears that the physicians focus primarily on the bodily symptoms, the physical problem; and psychosocial conditions are considered secondarily if at all. It therefore rarely occurs that the physician views the alcoholic as a person with a disease with certain physiological, psychological, and social concomitants; the typical occurrence is the diagnosis of a particular physical or systemic disorder in a person who also happens to be alcoholic.

In conclusion, the ways in which physicians perceive and report their diagnostic activity with alcoholics in the emergency service of a general hospital basically support two attitudinal sets we ascribed to them in an earlier study. The physicians' actual statements helped us to revise some of the specifics of their attitudes. The effect attitudes have on what subsequent treatment alcoholics receive is an important one and has been described in detail in our previous study. Briefly, alcoholics who are in the most severe stages of alcoholism are diagnosed and referred for treatment, whereas alcoholics who are in the less severe phases are likely not to be diagnosed or referred for treatment. As we have indicated earlier, this means that a substantial portion of the alcoholic population may not receive treatment at a time when therapy might have more beneficial consequences than in late-stage alcoholism.

Summary

Physicians' attitudes were examined in semistructured interviews to ascertain the presence of two sets of attitudes hypothesized in a previous study. The hypothesized attitudes are that (1) physicians perceive alcoholism as a disorder occurring primarily among derelicts; and (2) physicians prefer a medical diagnosis to one that includes psychosocial dysfunction. Verbatim material abstracted from the interviews supports the presence of the ascribed attitudes and offers further clarification of the attitudes. The first attitudinal set may be restated as follows: Physicians behave diagnostically as though alcoholism were primarily a disorder of derelicts, although in their verbal statements they describe alcoholism as a disorder occurring in other social groups; they tend not to recognize alcoholics who are other than derelict, but when they do, hesitate to make the diagnosis of alcoholism. The second attitudinal set may be restated as follows: Physicians focus primarily on the bodily symptom, the physical problem; psychosocial conditions are considered secondarily if at all. Thus it rarely occurs that the physician views the alcoholic as a person with an illness that has certain physiological, psychological, and social concomitants; the typical occurrence is rather the diagnosis of a particular physical or systemic disorder in a person who also happens to be alcoholic.

4.C. The Doctor's Voice: Postdictor of Successful Referral of Alcoholic Patients

"It wasn't what he said; it was the way he said it." Investigators are paying increased attention to the intuitively long-recognized ability of people to pick up and utilize what Kauffman referred to as "expressive" cues in the language of others, and to the importance of these expressive cues as clues to personality and feeling states.[30] The literature on nonverbal communication in speech has been reviewed by Kramer, Mahl and Schulze, and Starkweather.[31] For example, speech disruptions have been related to situational anxiety,[32] and reliable "global" judgments have been related to emotions in speech.[33]

An important area for research has been emotion judged from "content-filtered" speech, in which a tape is rerecorded through a

Section 4.C. written, in collaboration, by Susan Milmoe, Robert Rosenthal, Howard T. Blane, Morris E. Chafetz, and Irving Wolf.
Notes to Chapter 4 will be found on page 149.

low-pass filter to remove high-frequency sounds and thus render the words themselves unrecognizable. Starkweather found that content-filtered voices of hypertensives were judged to be higher on dominance than similarly presented voices of nonhypertensives.[34] Kramer, however, has observed that one of the problems in most studies that correlate paralinguistic ratings with independent variables is the weakness of the latter.[35] Another difficulty is that studies of emotion in speech have primarily utilized speech elicited in an experimental situation in which the speaker is asked to "act out" the emotion in one way or another. An unpublished study by Starkweather, in which 12 clinical psychologists rated excerpts from the Army-McCarthy hearings, seems to be one of the first in which emotional content was rated globally in completely spontaneously elicited speech.[36] Soskin and Kauffman demonstrated that listeners could agree to a significant extent about the emotional content of content-filtered spontaneously elicited speech samples gathered in a variety of situations—but they had no independent variables to which the ratings were related.[37]

The purpose of the present study was to relate emotion communicated in spontaneous speech to a clearly defined independent variable. Global ratings of emotion in the voices of physicians (presented under three conditions—normal tape recording, filtered tape recording, and transcript)—were used to postdict their success in referring alcoholic patients newly arrived on the emergency service of a large general hospital for further treatment at the alcohol clinic of the hospital. The influence of the initial contact with the alcoholic on the course of subsequent treatment has been stressed throughout our work. Sensitized to rejection, the alcoholic has been said to be especially aware of the subtle, unintended cues conveyed by the doctor, be they those of sympathy and acceptance or those of anger and disgust. Gottschalk and his co-workers and Pittenger, Hockett, and Danehy have in their separate work on language in psychotherapy interviews demonstrated a relationship between speech and the dynamics of an interpersonal situation.[38] The interpersonal situation of a loosely structured interview about doctors' experiences in the hospital in general and with alcoholic patients in particular is here seen as having elicited a variety of emotional responses as assessed in the speech of the doctors. These responses may be tentatively supposed to have also been elicited to some degree by the actual confrontation with the alcoholic patient, and to have affected the outcome of that confrontation.

Resident physicians at Massachusetts General Hospital during the time of the project rotated in 12-hour shifts as chief medical officers on the emergency service. In the course of the program, 15 residents were so rotated, of whom nine are represented in the material used in this study. Records were kept of the number of alcoholics, out of the total number diagnosed by each doctor during the experimental period, who sought subsequent treatment, both those assigned to the experimental group and those assigned to the control group. In the case of each group, the chief medical officer was the first link in the chain, but since his influence in the experimental group was immediately superseded by that of the psychiatrist on call, only the percentage of control group alcoholics who sought further treatment (defined as making and keeping at least one appointment at the alcoholic clinic) served as the criterion of a doctor's success at referral. The two previous studies trace a relationship between their conscious, socially held attitudes toward alcoholism and their diagnosis or nondiagnosis of alcoholic patients. The study reported here attempts to trace a relationship between doctors' feelings reflected in their speech and their success in referring alcoholic patients for continued treatment.

Interview Material

Approximately a year after the completion of the program for alcoholics, each doctor who had served as a chief medical officer during that program participated in a loosely structured, open-ended, tape-recorded interview about his experiences during the residency in general and with alcoholic patients in particular. From the full tapes available for nine of the doctors were excerpted their replies to the question, "What has been your experience with alcoholics?" or to whichever question in the individual interview most closely approximated that question. The replies varied in length from 79 to 390 words (mean number of words = 177.4 and mean length of reply = 1.5 minutes). The tape on which the interview segments were recorded was then passed through a filter modifier, passing only frequencies below the range of 410-450 cycles per second, with an attenuation of 60 decibels per octave. This procedure resulted in a content-filtered recording. With the high-frequency sounds filtered out, the doctors' voices sounded as though they were heard through a closed door—variations in pitch and volume were still discernible, but it was not possible to ascertain what was being said. Verbatim typed transcripts of each of the segments were also made. Thus there were three stimulus conditions: unfiltered tape (normal), filtered tape (tone only), and transcript (content only).

Judges

Thirty undergraduate and graduate students at Harvard-Radcliffe (29) and M.I.T. (1), 15 men and 15 women in age from 18 to 27, served as raters and were paid for their participation in the study. Ten judges (five men and five women) rated the unfiltered tape, 10 rated the filtered tape, and 10 rated the transcript.

Ratings

The method of rating was essentially the same for all three conditions. In the case of the normal and tone-only groups, the judges were told that they would be listening to excerpts from interviews with doctors who would be discussing their experiences with alcoholics, and that the study was concerned with the ability of people to infer feelings and attitudes from the voices of other people. In addition, the nature and purpose of the content filter was explained to those who rated the tape recording under this condition. They were asked to rate each of the segments on four dimensions—Anger-Irritation, Sympathy-Kindness, Anxiety-Nervousness, and Matter-of-factness-Professionalism—along a six-point scale (1 = none, 6 = quite a lot). The dimensions were not defined further. Each segment was played once and judges were given as much time as they needed after each (in no case was more than three minutes required). There was evidence of involvement in the task from all the raters. In the case of the content-only group, the judges were handed each transcript in turn and told to read it and rate it. They were required to return one before receiving another. They also were told that they were participating in a study of the ability of people to infer feelings and attitudes from the verbal productions of other people, and they were informed as well that other judges had rated the tape recordings of the interview segments. Two additional variables were included in the content-only condition: Sophistication about Alcoholism and Psychological-Mindedness. The combined rating score for each of the nine doctors on each dimension and under each condition was then correlated (Pearson r) with the percentage of control group alcoholics seeking further treatment out of the total number of control group alcoholics seen by each doctor.

Results

An overview of the results shows that the doctor's speech and tone of voice were related to his success in referring his alcoholic patients for additional treatment. Before giving the details of these findings, however, it will be useful to consider (1) the relationships among the variables employed in postdicting success in referral; (2) the correlations among channels of information; (3) the agreement among individual judges in rating vocal and verbal behavior; and (4) the agreement in judgment between the average male and average female judge.

Table 9 (Appendix A) shows the correlations among the postdictor variables for male, female, and all judges under each information channel or condition of observation. In the tone-only condition, anger was negatively related to sympathy ($p < .05$) and anxiety was negatively related to matter-of-factness ($p < .05$). In the content-only condition, anxiety was also related negatively to matter-of-factness ($p < .05$), and sophistication about alcoholism was positively related to psychological-mindedness ($p < .05$). Both the latter variables were significantly related to sympathy ($r = .80, p < .01$).

Table 10 (Appendix A) shows the correlations between mean ratings of the doctors' speech in each channel of information with the mean ratings made in the other channels. Inspection suggests that while ratings made in the different channels tended to be positively correlated, each was tapping quite different sources of variance. The median r's for the three sets of intercorrelations, com-

Recognizing Alcoholics: Studies of Social and Professional Attitudes 141

bining male, female, and total r's, were .39, .49, and .21, respectively, for normal-tone-only, normal-content-only, and tone-only-content-only. The highest median correlation was the one between normal ratings and content-only ratings, although Starkweather reported that, for the two variables he employed in a somewhat similar design (aggression and pleasure), the highest correlations were between normal and tone-only ratings (for aggression and pleasure, respectively, r's were normal-tone-only .79, .59; normal-content-only .22, .20; tone-only-content-only .17, .05).[39] This work was, however, done with speakers who were *acting out* a situation in which only one dominant emotion was to be conveyed, presumably more by voice quality than by content. Also, an examination of the results for the one variable that appoximates his "aggression" (anger-irritation) reveals a somewhat similar pattern of correlation (for total raters, normal-tone-only $r = .49$, tone-only-content-only $r = .43$). Kramer reports similar results in his work with judgments of emotion (by English-speaking raters) in normal English speech, tone-only speech, and Japanese speech; the correlation he obtained between ratings of the filtered presentation and ratings of the unfiltered presentation in English was only .16, lower than the obtained correlation (.34) between ratings of the content-filtered presentation and ratings of the Japanese presentation. He concluded that the ability to judge emotion from speech presented under "strange" or "unusual" conditions may be different from the ability to judge emotions in ordinary unfiltered speech.[40]

Table 11 (Appendix A) shows the interrater reliabilities that were estimated by computing Kendall's Coefficient of Concordance (W) for each variable within each of the three conditions. With the exception of matter-of-factness-professionalism in all conditions, and anger-irritation and sympathy-kindness in the content-only condition, interjudge relatabilities were significant at or below the .05 level.

The amount of agreement on the ratings generally is surprising when one recalls that the doctors whose voices were being rated had not been instructed to act out any emotion, that they were not in situations which might be expected to produce any specific emotions, and that the judges had been given neither training nor even explicit definitions of the attributes to be rated. It should be noted that in most comparable studies the investigators have predetermined which speech sample was to be considered "angry" and which "sympathetic," and the like. The results seem to show, most strongly in the case of the tone-only ratings, that some definite impression of a person's feeling state and underlying attitudes may be gathered from listening to his voice over a very short period of time. These findings bear out those of Soskin and Kauffman.[41] The agreement on the transcript ratings suggests that in the interview situation enough emotional cues of one sort or another were escaping into the semantic channel of the doctors' speech to permit judgment.

Table 12 (Appendix A) shows the agreement between the average male and average female judges. Correlations were remarkably variable ranging from —.07 to +.98 (median $r = .69$, $p < .05$). For at least some of the variables rated under some conditions of observation, the value of keeping tabulations separately for male and female judges is evident.[42]

Postdiction of Referral Effectiveness

As predicted, the control group of alcoholics that had not received the intensive care routine of the experimental group was the only one in which significant relationships emerged between speech ratings and doctors' success in getting patients to seek treatment.

Normal speech. As shown in Table 13 (Appendix A), the only significant relationship between speech ratings and doctors' success rates was that involving anxiety-nervousness. The ratings of anxiety by the male judges were positively correlated with effectiveness: the more anxious a doctor's voice was rated to be, the more successful the referrals he made ($r = .75$, $p \leq .02$). The ratings of anxiety by female judges were similarly positively correlated with effectiveness, though the relationship here failed to reach statistical significance ($r = .49$). For the total group of judges, male and female combined, $r = .62$, $p < .08$. Male judges' ratings of matter-of-factness–professionalism tended to be negatively associated with effectiveness ($r = -.54$), though this tendency was not significant at the .05 level. Neither ratings of anger nor ratings of sympathy in the normal condition postdicted effectiveness.

Tone only. There was a significant negative relationship between male judges' ratings of anger in the tone-only condition and effectiveness with alcoholic patients ($r = -.67$, $p < .05$, for female judges, $r = -.49$, $p > .10$, and for the total group of judges, $r = -.65$, $p = .06$). Other variables were unrelated to effectiveness.

Content only. No significant relationships emerged between the transcript ratings and success rates. There was a rather puzzling tendency for ratings of "psychological-mindedness," "sophisticated about alcoholism" (variables introduced only in the content-only condition), and sympathy-kindness to be correlated negatively with success rates and highly intercorrelated (mean intercorrelation = $+.80$). This cluster of "sophisticated-sympathetic" behavior may have given the alcoholic patient a feeling of insincerity. This interpretation seems supported by the fact that when greater sympathy was shown in the tone-only channel, alcoholic patients were more successfully influenced to seek treatment though the correlation was not significant statistically. There is a hint here that sympathetic content may be "invalidated" by an accompanying lack of sympathy in the tone of voice.

Considering the small sample of doctors for whom interview data were available, the small sample of alcoholics, and the many possible contaminating factors in the doctor-patient situation (contact with nurses, clerks, and other subsidiary ward personnel, for example), the relationships between the speech ratings and effectiveness with alcoholic patients reported above may be viewed as surprising and encouraging. The need for more systematic research is evident. The relationship between an "angry" tone of voice and lack of effectiveness with alcoholic patients who may be especially sensitized to rejection accords with clinical and anecdotal accounts of doctor-alcoholic patient encounters. The positive relationship between inferred anxiety in the "normal" (unfiltered) voice and effectiveness with alcoholic patients may relate to the notion that an effectively functioning healer whose manner of speech is perceived by others to have an anxious, nervous quality may be seen by the patient as showing greater concern. The literature on the relationship between speech disruptions and anxiety suggests one reason for the emergence of the correlation as significant for the normal ratings but not significant for the tone-only ratings. In the filtered tape recordings, words are not distinguishable, and it is not possible to tell speech disruptions from speech per se.

Interestingly for most, though by no means all, variables in the three conditions, male judges' ratings of voice qualities and attitudes were better postdictors of success than were female judges' ratings. Heinberg found that females were superior to males in guessing the situation and the emotion being acted out in ambiguous but non-content-filtered dialogues involving either a man and a woman or two women.[43] Perhaps nuances of feeling are recognized with greater ease and accuracy in the voices of members of one's own sex. A similar study involving female doctors or nurses would be of interest.

4.D. Alcoholism and Social Isolation

Early research studies of alcoholic men describe them as homeless, unemployed and destitute.[44] One striking characteristic of their situation was its extreme social isolation. That is, many alcoholic men had little close contact with others, low stability in maintaining social involvement, and few positive ties with the community at large.

Subsequent investigators questioned the universality of the reported association between alcoholism and social isolation on the grounds that the men who had been selected for study (e.g., Bowery residents) were already isolated. Studies were therefore made of groups of clinic patients who were not expected to be severely isolated.[45] Analyses of their data indicate, however, that these alcoholics were more isolated than the general population.

The present study, a further test of the hypothesis that alcoholism is accompanied by social isolation, took into account the following factors that may have biased previous results:

Section 4.D. written, in collaboration, by Estelle Singer, Howard T. Blane, and Richard Kasschau.
Notes to Chapter 4 will be found on page 149.

1. As suggested above, alcoholics available for research have often been people who are already relatively isolated. Examples are Bowery residents[46] and men serving sentences for public intoxication.[47]

2. Men identified as "alcoholic" may be more isolated than other alcoholics. Blane, Overton and Chafetz found that patients diagnosed as "alcoholic" were seriously isolated from their social community and family more often than undiagnosed alcoholic patients.[48] The latter had also shown symptoms of alcoholism at the time of examination according to separate criteria established for that purpose. Thus patients may be diagnosed as alcoholic partly because of their social isolation.

3. People who seek treatment for alcoholism may be motivated by a recent increase in social isolation, such as marital separation or loss of job, or by the fear of further isolation. At the time the data are collected, these men may therefore be more isolated than alcoholics who have not sought treatment. This factor may have biased tests involving patients treated at alcoholic or psychiatric clinics.[49]

4. The assumed or measured norms for social isolation among nonalcoholics may have been inappropriate. Since indices of social isolation, such as employment status, vary from locality to locality, subcultural group to subcultural group, or hospital to hospital, a specific estimate should be made for comparable nonalcoholics.[50] Previous studies have used either no explicit control condition or a gross one such as census data on the general population.

The subjects of the present study consisted of two groups of men previously described—the patients of one group had been diagnosed as "alcoholic" by the admitting physician, while the patients of the second group had received other diagnoses, but were classified as "alcoholic" by separate criteria developed for this purpose. It should be noted that the undiagnosed alcoholic group entered the hospital with almost exclusively medical or surgical complaints, that is, not directly because of their alcoholism, and further, that they were not identified as "alcoholic" by the examining physician. Thus, they became available for research in ways not obviously related to social isolation.

The diagnosed and undiagnosed alcoholic subjects were compared with a control group of nonalcoholic subjects. This group, like the undiagnosed alcoholic group, consisted of men who entered the emergency service of the hospital almost exclusively with medical or surgical complaints. The selection procedure is described below, but the various selection constraints were highly similar for the three groups. In this sense, the groups can be considered to belong to the same population.

It was predicted that each of the alcoholic groups, diagnosed and undiagnosed, would be more isolated than the nonalcoholic control group. Several aspects of social isolation were measured—current close social contacts, stability in maintaining social involvements, and positive ties with the community.

Procedure

The sample of patients included in the nonalcoholic group was selected from the population of men 16 years or older, living within the required areas, and admitted to the emergency service during the subject selection periods. Patients were chosen by proceeding chronologically through the admission log book of the emergency service. Whenever a diagnosed or undiagnosed alcoholic case was encountered, the next patient was selected who met the population requirements and whose record showed no evidence of alcoholism at the time of admission. This method provided an initial group of 438 patients.

The mean age of the 438 patients selected was significantly lower than those of the other two groups (43.7 years, as compared with 49.5 and 48.3 years for the diagnosed and undiagnosed alcoholic patients respectively). Since alcoholism and social isolation both may take time to develop, a spurious correlation was avoided by equating the groups on age. The means and distribution of ages were matched in the following manner. The undiagnosed group was used as a standard and the proportion of its patients falling within each five-year age interval was calculated. The 438 nonalcoholic patients were then grouped by corresponding five-year age intervals, and the calculated proportion of subjects were randomly selected from each age interval. Consequently, the relative distributions of ages for the nonalcoholic resultant ($N=176$) and undiagnosed alcoholic ($N=238$) groups were identical and were similar for the nonalcoholic and diagnosed alcoholic ($N=200$) groups.

As an incidental check of the equivalence of the groups, they were compared on prior use of this hospital. The 65.0 percent of nonalcoholic patients who had previous admissions did not differ significantly from the 62.6 percent and 70.3 percent of patients previously admitted in the diagnosed and undiagnosed alcoholic groups. The source of data was the emergency service face sheet for the day each patient had been admitted. In order to help to delineate the concept, in the present study social isolation was examined from three points of view. Each aspect was measured by relevant items of face sheet data as follows.[51]

Consideration was first given to the amount of current social contact, especially with people who are psychologically alone. (1) Currently married patients were assumed more likely to have a greater amount of such contact than single, divorced, widowed, or separated patients. (2) Patients living with their closest relative were similarly assumed to have more frequent social contact than other patients. (3) Finally it was assumed that those who listed an employer had more possibility of regular social contact than those who did not.

Social stability, defined as the ability to maintain social involvement, was also measured. (1) Separated or divorced patients were considered less stable than married or widowed patients. (2) In addition, patients who were employed when possible were assumed to be more stable. This item measured the proportion of patients who listed an employer, excluding patients over 65 years and excluding patients who had disability or similar pensions.

The third aspect of social isolation considered was the use of social resources. (1) It was assumed that people who are integrated into their community are more likely to be aware of and use its characteristic methods of dealing with their medical and financial problems than those who are not; one such resource is medical insurance, and another is the hospital itself. (2) Patients who entered on their own, or who had been referred by an agency they utilized first, were assumed to be better integrated into the community than patients brought in by the police.

Results

The results presented in Table 14 (Appendix A) show that both alcoholic groups were more isolated than the nonalcoholic control group on all three measures of current social contact. The results are similar for both measures of social contact and social stability, and for one of the two indices of utilization of social resources. These findings support the hypothesis that alcoholics are more socially isolated than comparable nonalcoholics, even when several biasing factors have been controlled.

The sole exception to the pattern just described was the insignificant difference between the undiagnosed alcoholic and control groups on use of medical insurance. Since the diagnosed alcoholics exceeded the undiagnosed group on this measure, use of medical insurance may be related only to diagnostic biases and not to alcoholism as such.

The diagnosed alcoholics were more isolated than the undiagnosed alcoholic patients on all measures except the two related to employment. These results duplicate those reported by Blane and his associates.[52] The lack of differences on employment status items suggests that the physician's biases in diagnosis were not influenced by employment status. It may also imply that loss of job is one of the first social results of alcoholism, and is therefore equal among the two alcoholic groups.

Discussion

The data confirmed the hypothesis. Alcoholics are socially isolated, even when a number of biases operative in prior research are controlled and when comparable nonalcoholics are used to determine the norms for social isolation. This finding is consistent with expectations based on previous research.[53]

The degree to which these results can be generalized depends partially upon further research. Let us consider the most limited degree first. It is felt by many that alcoholism is not a unitary phenomenon, but rather that there are several types of alcoholism defined by a variety of physiological, psychological, and social variables. Jellinek has reviewed the literature on this topic.[54] Available information about social variables suggests that the results can be generalized to lower- and lower-middle-class urban populations. If so, it may be necessary to have information sufficient to determine the subjects' types of alcoholism before conclusions should be generalized.

Wider generalization is possible, not limited by the type of alcoholism, if further research indicates that the effects of social isolation on different kinds of alcoholics are similar, regardless of how either the alcoholism or the isolation was caused, and regardless of the type of alcoholism prior to the increase in isolation.

It is plausible to expect severe isolation to have profound effects on people who already show some pathology. Thus, social isolation may itself account for some of the problems associated with alcoholism. Further, these problems may be common to other diagnostic groups with comparable degrees of isolation.

The findings bring into clearer focus a social problem examined by Blane, Overton, and Chafetz, who suggest that many alcoholics are shunted from treatment resources because of attitudes held by medical and paramedical personnel, and that alcoholics so diverted may be better treatment risks than those highly isolated alcoholics who are sent to treatment facilities.[55] The present study indicates that this undiagnosed group of alcoholics may already show some of the socially deteriorating effects of alcoholism and should therefore be afforded the opportunity of entering treatment for their condition.

Notes

1. M. E. CHAFETZ and H. W. DEMONE, JR., *Alcoholism and Society* (New York: Oxford University Press, 1962).
2. H. S. ABRAM and W. F. McCOURT, "Interaction of Physicians with Emergency Ward Alcoholic Patients," *Quarterly Journal of Studies on Alcohol,* 25:679-688, 1964.
3. For a comprehensive review of the literature on psychiatric diagnosis, see E. ZIGLER and L. PHILLIPS, "Psychiatric Diagnosis:

A Critique," *Journal of Abnormal and Social Psychology,* 63:607-618, 1961.
4. G. N. RAINES and J. H. ROHMER, "The Operational Matrix of Psychiatric Practices. I. Consistency and Variability in Interview Impressions of Different Psychiatrists," *American Journal of Psychiatry,* 3:721-723, 1955.
5. A. B. HOLLINGSHEAD and F. C. REDLICH, *Social Class and Mental Illness* (New York: John Wiley and Sons, 1958).
6. R. STRAUS, "Medical Practice and the Alcoholic," in E. G. JACO (ed.), *Patients, Physicians and Illness* (Glencoe, Illinois: The Free Press, 1958), pp. 439-446.
7. *Ibid.*
8. *Ibid.*
9. It might be supposed that all assigned cases were diagnosed in the physician's note as alcoholic and that all nonassigned cases had diagnoses other than alcoholism, but this is not the case. This interesting point is examined further in the discussion.
10. R. F. BALES, "Cultural Differences in Rates of Alcoholism," *Quarterly Journal of Studies on Alcohol,* 6:480-499, 1946; D.D. GLAD, "Attitudes and Experiences of American-Jewish and American-Irish Male Youth as Related to Differences in Adult Rates of Inebriety," *Quarterly Journal of Studies on Alcohol,* 8:406-474, 1947; C. R. SNYDER, *Alcohol and the Jews* (Glencoe, Illinois: The Free Press, 1958; New Brunswick, New Jersey: Rutgers Center of Alcohol Studies, 1959).
11. It should be noted that some of the variables that statistically differentiate assigned and nonassigned alcoholics are indices included in the list of diagnostic criteria we gave to the C.M.O.'s —for example, marital status, employment, living with nearest relative. Data from interviews held subsequently with each C.M.O. suggests that the list of criteria in itself was not frequently consulted when the C.M.O. was making a decision to assign or not assign an individual to the project. No precise statement can be made, however, about the extent to which the C.M.O.'s used the list of criteria.
12. "Hospitalization of Patients with Alcoholism (reports of Of-

ficers)," *Journal of the American Medical Association*, 162:750, 1956.
13. In this analysis we excluded the 100 experimental cases from the assigned group sample because, as part of their special treatment, experimental patients were frequently hospitalized. To include these cases would introduce an extraneous variable. In actual fact, 63 percent of the experimentals were hospitalized, usually for periods of 3 days or less. This is a significantly higher rate of hospitalization than that of the missed cases ($x^2 = 5.25$, 1 df, $p < .05$).
14. The variables "public assistance" and "employer listed" are for purposes of the index treated as one category. If public assistance is present, then employer listed is no, and vice versa. For this reason, the index as a seven-point rather than an eight-point scale.
15. In computing these percentages, we corrected for unequal sample size by using the formula $P = Pn(Pn+Pa) \cdot 100$, where Ph = proportion of nonassigned cases receiving a particular index position and Pa = proportion of assigned cases receiving a particular index position. The percentage of assigned cases identified is $100 - P$.
16. See remarks above, footnote 13.
17. D. J. PITTMAN and C. W. GORDON, *Revolving Door: A Study of the Chronic Police Case Inebriate* (Glencoe, Illinois: The Free Press, 1958).
18. R. STRAUS, "Alcohol and the Homeless Man," *Quarterly Journal of Studies on Alcohol*, 7:360-404, 1946.
19. J. K. JACKSON and R. CONNOR, "The Skid Road Alcoholic," *Quarterly Journal of Studies on Alcohol*, 14:468-486, 1953.
20. STRAUS, "Medical Practice and the Alcoholic."
21. E. M. JELLINEK, *The Disease Concept of Alcoholism* (New Haven, Connecticut: Hillhouse Press, 1960).
22. Committee on Public Health Relations, New York Academy of Medicine, "A Survey of Facilities for the Care and Treatment of Alcoholism in New York City," *Quarterly Journal of Studies on Alcohol*, 7:405-438, 1946; J. W. RILEY and C. F. MARDEN, "The Medical Professions and the Problem of Alcoholism," *Quarterly Journal of Studies on Alcohol*, 7:240-270, 1946;

R. Straus, "Community Surveys: Their Aims and Techniques; with Special Reference to Problems of Alcoholism," *Quarterly Journal of Studies on Alcohol*, 13:254-270, 1952.

23. Committee on Public Health Relations, New York Academy of Medicine, *op. cit.*
24. Riley and Marden, *op. cit.*
25. Straus, "Community Surveys."
26. Straus, "Medical Practice and the Alcoholic."
27. Zigler and Phillips, *op. cit.*
28. "Hospitalization of Patients with Alcoholism (Reports of Officers)," *Journal of the American Medical Association*, 162:750, 1956.
29. H. T. Blane, "Third-Party Selection of Subjects and Biased Samples," *Psychological Reports*, 13:133-134, 1963.
30. P. Kauffman, "An Investigation of Some Psychological Stimulus Properties of Speech Behavior," unpublished doctoral dissertation, University of Chicago, 1954.
31. E. Kramer, "Judgment of Personal Characteristics and Emotions from Nonverbal Properties of Speech," *Psychological Bulletin*, 60:408-420, 1963. G. Mahl and G. Schulze, "Psychological Research in the Extralinguistic Area," in T. A. Sebeck, A. S. Hayes, and M. C. Bateson (eds.), *Approaches to Semiotics* (London: Mouton, 1964), pp. 51-124; J. Starkweather, "Vocal Communication of Personality and Human Feelings," *Journal of Communication*, 11:63-72, 1961.
32. For example, S. A. Dibner, "Cue Counting: A Measure of Anxiety in Interviews," *Journal of Consulting Psychology*, 20: 475-478, 1956; S. H. Eldred and D. B. Price, "A Linguistic Evaluation of Feeling States in Psychotherapy," *Psychiatry*, 21: 115-121, 1958; S. Feldstein, M. S. Brenner, and J. Jaffe, "The Effect of Subject, Sex, Verbal Interaction, and Topical Focus on Speech Disruption," *Language and Speech*, 6:229-239, 1963; S. Kasl and G. Mahl, "Experimentally Induced Anxiety and Speech Disturbances" (abstract), *American Psychologist*, 13:349, 1958; G. Mahl, "Disturbances and Silences in the Patient's Speech in Psychotherapy," *Journal of Abnormal and Social Psychology*, 53:1-15, 1956.

33. For example, J. DAVITZ (ed.), *The Communication of Emotional Meaning* (New York: McGraw-Hill Book Co., 1964); J. DAVITZ and L. DAVITZ, "Correlates of Accuracy in the Communication of Feelings," *Journal of Communication*, 9:110-117, 1959; "The Communication of Feelings by Content-Free Speech," *Journal of Communication*, 9:6-13, 1959.
34. J. STARKWEATHER, "Content-Free Speech as a Source of Information About the Speaker," *Journal of Abnormal and Social Psychology*, 52:394-402, 1956.
35. E. KRAMER, "Elimination of Verbal Cues in Judgments of Emotion from Voice," *Journal of Abnormal and Social Psychology*, 68:390-396, 1964.
36. Cited by KRAMER, "Elimination of Verbal Cues. . . ."
37. W. F. SOSKIN and P. E. KAUFFMAN, "Judgment of Emotion in Word-Free Voice Samples," *Journal of Communication*, 11:73-80, 1961.
38. L. GOTTSCHALK (ed.), *Comparative Psycholinguistic Analysis of Two Psychotherapy Interviews* (New York: International Universities Press, 1961); R. PITTENGER, C. HOCKETT, and H. DANEHY, *The First Five Minutes* (Ithaca, New York: Paul Martineau, 1960).
39. STARKWEATHER, "Content-Free Speech. . . ."
40. KRAMER, "Elimination of Verbal Cues. . . ."
41. SOSKIN and KAUFFMAN, *op. cit.*
42. E. R. CARLSON and R. CARLSON, "Male and Female Subjects in Personality Research," *Journal of Abnormal and Social Psychology*, 61:482-483, 1960; J. KAGAN and H. Moss, *Birth to Maturity* (New York: John Wiley and Sons, 1962).
43. P. HEINBERG, "Factors Related to an Individual's Ability to Perceive Implications of Dialogue," *Speech Monographs*, 28:274-283, 1961.
44. S. D. BACON, "Inebriety, Social Integration and Marriage," *Quarterly Journal of Studies on Alcohol*, 5:303-339, 1944; R. STRAUS and R. G. MCCARTHY, "Non-Addictive Pathological Drinking Patterns in Homeless Men," *Quarterly Journal of Studies on Alcohol*, 12:601-611, 1951.
45. R. STRAUS and S. D. BACON, "Alcoholism and Social Stability.

A Study of Occupational Integration in 2,023 Male Clinic Patients," *Quarterly Journal of Studies on Alcohol,* 12:601-611, 1951; M. W. WELLMAN, M. A. MAXWELL, and P. O'HOLLAREN, "Private Hospital Alcoholic Patients and the Changing Conception of the 'Typical' Alcoholic," *Quarterly Journal of Studies on Alcohol,* 18:388-404, 1957.

46. STRAUS and MCCARTHY, *op. cit.*
47. PITTMAN and GORDON, *op. cit.*
48. H. T. BLANE, W. F. OVERTON, JR., and M. E. CHAFETZ, "Social Factors in the Diagnosis of Alcoholism. I. Characteristics of the Patient," *Quarterly Journal of Studies on Alcohol,* 24:640-663, 1963.
49. STRAUS and BACON, *op. cit.*; WELLMAN, MAXWELL, and O'HOLLAREN, *op. cit.*
50. S. SCHNEYER, "The Marital Status of Alcoholics. A Note on an Analysis of the Marital Status of 2,008 Patients of Nine Clinics," *Quarterly Journal of Studies on Alcohol,* 15:325-329, 1954.
51. Prior to analysis, reliability of the items was established by measuring the percentage of agreement between two independent raters. Absolute agreement ranged from 92 percent to 100 percent, with a median of 96 percent. Agreement in excess of chance ranged from .89 to 1.00, with a median of .95. W. MCCORD and J. MCCORD, *Origins of Alcoholism* (Stanford, California: Stanford University Press, 1960).
52. BLANE, OVERTON, and CHAFETZ, *op. cit.*
53. D. B. FALKEY and S. SCHNEYER, "Characteristics of Male Alcoholics Admitted to the Medical Ward of a General Hospital," *Quarterly Journal of Studies on Alcohol,* 18:67-97, 1957; STRAUS and BACON, *op. cit.*; WELLMAN, MAXWELL, and O'HOLLAREN, *op. cit.*
54. JELLINEK, *op. cit.*
55. BLANE, OVERTON, and CHAFETZ, *op. cit.* The following data (in percentages) on the nonalcoholic control group will facilitate further comparisons with the study by Blane, Overton, and Chafetz: (1) Marital status ($N=176$): single, 26.7; married, 58.5; widowed, 8.0; divorced or separated, 6.8. (2) Closest

relative (N=174): parent, 13.8; wife, 61.5; child, 12.7; sibling, 35.2; other relative, 11.3. (3) Public assistance (N=175): yes, 20.0; no, 80.0. (4) Patient's subjective complaint (N=174): medical, 60.9; surgical, 34.5; alcoholic, 0.0; psychiatric, 0.6; no complaint, 4.0. (5) Physician's diagnostic impression (N=174): medical, 51.1; surgical, 31.0; alcoholic, 0.0; psychiatric, 1.7; no impression, 16.1. (6) Subsequent hospitalization (N=176): yes, 30.7; no, 69.3.

Chapter 5
Evaluative Studies

Throughout the studies we have reported, we have been careful not to become involved in the complex and methodologically thorny issue of assessing the outcome of treatment. Implicit has been the assumption that treatment effectiveness is highly correlated with entering into and maintaining a treatment relationship, and that it is simpler, more efficient, and more economical to measure entry into and continuance of therapy than to assess the effectiveness of treatment. As we progressed in our research, we became increasingly concerned with the effect our interventions were having on the alcoholic patients who served as subjects in our studies. Using data collected for other purposes, we made some analyses of treatment effect. For example, the subjects in our first major project in the emergency service of the hospital (see Chapter 2, Section B) were drawn from a population that had high rates of arrest and imprisonment for the misdemeanor of "drunkenness." We presumed that patients who participated in our specially devised treatment approach might have fewer arrests for drunkenness after such participation. We found that this was indeed the case, but not only for our special treatment group; it was true for the "usual treatment" group, as well. Comparison of this reduction in arrests across groups revealed that there was no statistically significant difference between them. Other analyses of personal-social data collected before and after participation in the program revealed no differences. This is not particularly surprising, since the variables we were measuring had not been selected with an eye to change, but were often enduring traits or characteristics that could not change (e.g., social class of family of origin), or were highly unlikely to change in a year's time (e.g., educational level among middle-aged men). But the finding on arrests intrigued us because it was so graphically instructive with regard to the use of controls in evaluative research.

Along about this time, we were becoming more interested in secondary preventive approaches to alcohol problems. This interest, combined with our desire to have a clearer picture of the outcome of the treatment catalyst method in treating alcoholics, drew us closer and closer to designing studies to evaluate treatment effectiveness directly. Informally, we began to examine work done and reported in the past. We discovered that the literature on evaluation of psychotherapy with alcoholics was in no better state methodologically or conceptually than that on evaluation of psychotherapy generally. Gradually, our informal survey was transformed into an exhaustive search of the literature published during a twelve-year period. The distillate of this search is presented in the paper that follows. Out of the inadequacies of previous investigation have come guidelines concerning what to avoid and how to proceed in designing and carrying out evaluative research.

To supplement this paper, we have added a paper describing some of the techniques used in our own follow-up studies.

5.A. Evaluation of Psychotherapy with Alcoholics: A Critical Review

In 1942 Voegtlin and Lemere reviewed all studies published between 1909 and 1941 that evaluated any form of treatment for alcoholics. Among their conclusions they wrote: "The most striking observation is the apparent reticence with which the English-speaking psychiatrists have presented statistical data concerning the efficacy of treatment. With the exception of [two authors], the medical profession at large is unable to form any sort of opinion, from an examination of the literature alone, as to the value of conventional psychotherapy in the treatment of alcoholism in this country or England."[1]

More than 20 years later, we find that any "apparent reticence" in presentation of statistical data is gone; there is now little reluctance on the part of "English-speaking psychiatrists" to report statistics. We can still agree with Voegtlin and Lemere, however, that "we are unable to form any conclusive opinion as to the value of psychotherapeutic methods in the treatment of alcoholism." Perhaps it is unfair to expect that this should be possible. It is evident that most of the studies reviewed in the present paper are intended primarily as descriptive rather than as research reports, and that many of them

Section 5.A. written, in collaboration, by Marjorie J. Hill and Howard T. Blane.

Notes to Chapter 5 will be found on page 194.

make no claims to methodological sophistication.[2] There are, nevertheless, certain basic requirements of scientific conduct that any study of this type should attempt to meet.

1. In order to attribute change to a specific treatment, it is necessary to show that the change would not have occurred without the treatment; this requires the use of a comparison or control condition (either a nontreated group or a group treated with a form of treatment other than that under investigation).

2. In order to make treatment and control conditions truly comparable, the individual patients in each group must have had an equal chance of being assigned to the treatment or control conditions. This entails the use of a subject-selection procedure that ensures random assignment of patients to various treatment conditions.

3. In studying change in behavior it is necessary to select and define the type of behavior that is to be evaluated; this selection, however arbitrary, must be either theoretically or empirically relevant to the presumed effects of treatment.

4. It is necessary to establish reliable methods and instruments for measuring any change in behavior.

5. If a change in behavior is to be measured, it is necessary to obtain pretreatment baseline measures against which later measures, either during or after treatment, can be compared. This means that the same measures must be applied before and after treatment.

These requisites taken together have a common implication. Evaluative research is best undertaken when the evaluative program is planned prior to actual therapeutic intervention, so that the study is prospective rather than retrospective. Of the 49 studies that we reviewed, only two were prospective. The potential value of many recent studies is lost because of inability to pay satisfactory attention to one or more of the basic requirements for conducting research.

In addition to the requirements for conducting an evaluative investigation are standards for reporting a study.

1. In order to place the study in perspective, the setting in which it is undertaken should be clearly described.

2. The type of therapeutic technique or program evaluated should be specifically described so that the reader can interpret its relation to the results reported.

3. The population, procedures for selecting patients, and relevant characteristics of the samples must be reported, and when patients are dropped from or lost to study, the reasons and numbers of such omissions should be noted.

4. The nature of the measuring instruments applied, their reliability, and when and how they were applied should be described.

5. Reports of findings and any attendant statistical applications should be stated in sufficient detail to allow the reader to make his own interpretations of the data reported.

It is our intention to examine the extent to which the studies we reviewed meet each of these requirements for conducting and reporting evaluative investigations.

Requirements for Evaluative Research

CONTROL CONDITIONS

In attempting to demonstrate a causal relationship between treatment and change in behavior, two types of comparison may be used. The patient may be used as his own control—that is, pretreatment behavior is compared to posttreatment behavior; or a group of patients may be matched on significant characteristics with a group of patients (controls) who do not receive the treatment which is being evaluated. We shall look separately at these types of control and the difficulties they present in the literature reviewed.

The patient as his own control. This type of control is implicit in any study that reports its results in terms of changed behavior, whether a comparison group is used or not. The model is a straightforward sequential one—assessment before treatment, treatment, assessment after some time interval, or assessment after treatment. Forty-three of the articles we reviewed used this model, but in most of them inadequacies are apparent in one or more of the sequential steps. Briefly, the defects at each of the steps include (1) inadequate collection of pretreatment data; (2) lack of specification of treatment modalities; and (3) inadequate collection of posttreatment data. Each of these faults in execution will be discussed in detail.

Assuming good execution, what can be said of this control method as a general approach in evaluative research? On the surface the method is attractive. It is relatively easy to implement, it is economical, and it would appear that changes from pretreatment to posttreatment assessments can be attributed to intervening therapeutic manipulations. Reflection shows that this is not necessarily so. Whatever the findings, they cannot be attributed to treatment because of the inability of this method to control nontreatment variables, such as spontaneous remission, unidentifiable extratreatment factors or the sheer passage of time, that might result in changed behavior. In the absence of precise knowledge about these variables, we can only assume that they are randomly distributed in the population. Obviously, then, if we are to attribute changes in behavior to treatment rather than to nontreatment variables, an untreated control group is mandatory. One of the pitfalls of reporting findings where the patient is his own control is illustrated by an example from our own research. In a pre-post-treatment evaluation, we found a significant decrease in arrests for drunkenness among a group of 100 experimental patients. Had we not had a control group, we might have concluded that this reduction in the alcoholics' difficulties with the law was causally related to the treatment they received. However, analysis of the pre-post-drunkenness arrests of 100 control patients showed a similar reduction in arrests. Obviously the change in arrests is related to nontreatment rather than treatment variables.

Use of a control group. The second type of control that is available is a group of patients, matched on relevant characteristics with the subjects, who do not receive the treatment that is being evaluated. The type of control group found most frequently in the studies that we have reviewed is the type used to compare two or more forms of treatment. None of the studies used a nontreatment control group, which is understandable in view of the ethical problem involved in randomly assigning no treatment to persons who come to therapeutic agencies seeking help. While this ethical impediment has never been satisfactorily solved, one solution is to use the design with groups of persons who are sick but are not seeking help. Although this situation is not ordinarily encountered in a clinical center, it may be argued that to draw samples from the population of alcoholics who do not seek treatment would permit the generalization of results of evaluative research to a population greater than that which can be generalized to when the investigative focus is on that relatively small proportion of all alcoholics who do seek treatment.

Another solution in outpatient settings is random assignment of patients to treatment or to a waiting list with no formal psychotherapy but some professional attention; this method is only a partial solution since in essence it compares two types of treatment—one specific, the other nonspecific. A design that compares two treatment forms is acceptable, provided that the patients in each group are randomly assigned or matched on relevant variables. As will be shown in the section on subject selection, this constraint is infrequently followed in the studies reviewed. Other than gross demographic variables, such as age, sex, and education, the one single factor that is probably most necessary to control is that of motivation. Unless we can reasonably assume that motivation is equated between two groups, an adequate basis for comparison has not been established. It is discouraging to have to report that none of the studies reviewed controlled for motivation, although two studies made serious attempts to do so.[3] In some studies patients were free to choose among types of treatment; this clearly confounds treatment and motivation.[4] In others, the comparison group consisted of patients who made contact with a clinic but did not return, or of patients who kept fewer appointments than the minimum required for inclusion in the study. As we have seen in the previous chapter, such groups differ from groups of patients who stay in treatment for longer periods with respect to social class affiliation, social isolation, social dependency, and behavioral dependency. Most importantly they differ on motivation for treatment. It is clear that comparison groups such as these do not constitute acceptable controls in evaluative investigations, although they may be used to investigate differences between alcoholics who remain in treatment and those who do not.

Investigators who have attempted in their design to control for motivation have run afoul of the Hawthorne effect; that is, the patient's knowledge that he is a research subject as well as a patient and that he is being treated differently from other patients may have either a negative or positive effect on his motivation and therefore on therapeutic outcome. Ends and Page, in their comparison of four types of group therapy, considered their "social discussion" group to be controls.[5] We suspect that these patients, aware that they were being evaluated, cannot be considered a satisfactory "no treatment" control group. Wallerstein reports a similar effect. Although assignment to the various treatment groups in his study was random, he acknowledged that his "milieu" group cannot be considered a control group: "Many patients tended to experience placement in this group with considerable disappointment and resentment because it did not carry a specific, 'glamorized' and externally directed therapeutic device. . . . It soon became evident that specific psychologic features accompanied placement in this group and that the milieu treatment could not be conceptualized simply as a control."[6] Although Ends and Page did not report a similar finding, there is reason to suspect that it existed in their "control" groups who were probably aware that others were receiving a daily group therapy session in addition to the usual hospital treatment routine.[7]

To summarize, the majority of studies used a design with inherent inadequacies, that of the patient as his own control. A few studies employed another treatment group as a control condition, but by and large failed to meet the constraint of matching groups or alternatively of random assignment of patients to various treatments. The key variable, motivation for treatment, was not controlled in any study, although two sets of investigations made serious attempts to do so.

SUBJECT SELECTION PROCEDURES

There is no need to point out the difficulties involved in generalizing from limited and selected samples to a population. None of the studies reviewed claim to have achieved a "representative sample" of alcoholics; sampling procedures were, in large part, determined by practical considerations. The type of facility in which the programs were carried out varied widely, and was actually decisive in determining the nature of the population to be studied. What does represent a problem is that sampling procedures and sample characteristics (e.g., age, sex, education) are often not reported, and if reported, they are seldom clearly described. As an example, approximately half of the studies failed to specify the sex, or number of patients of each sex, in the sample. Since it has been reported that rates of improvement differ between men and women,[8] and that women alcoholics are "sicker" than men alcoholics, it is difficult to assess what recovery rates mean when the sex composition of a sample is not stated.

A majority of the studies used the population of a facility during a given period of time as the unit of investigation. This type of approach obviates some problems of generalization of findings and of sampling procedures, provided that the constraints of control conditions and random selection are applied. Studies that examined the population rather than samples drawn from it unfortunately failed to apply these constraints.

Other studies drew samples from a population and then investigated the effect of a treatment program (or programs) on the members of the sample. In only three instances, however, were sampling procedures developed prior to treatment, thereby permitting the possibility of random selection of patients.[9] In all other studies, after-the-fact sampling procedures precluded randomness or representative sampling. A not uncommon practice, for example, is to select patients who have remained in treatment for some specified length of time as the group for evaluative study, and then to report results as if they apply to the population of all patients who come to the facility for help or, indeed, to the population of all alcoholics. The effect of such selection procedures is acknowledged in some of the studies but is ignored in most.

Biased sampling is an innate feature of studies on the effects of treatment. First, most alcoholic populations are made up of voluntary admissions to treatment centers, and therefore of people who are differently motivated for treatment than is the general alcoholic population. When treatment is less than voluntary, there may be a bias in the opposite direction; the patients have been "selected" by society, on the basis of their behavior, as unfit to make voluntary decisions regarding treatment. As examples of extreme bias imposed by the nature of a facility, we can contrast the differences in motivation of the industrial clinic patient, who has often held his job for a good many years and whose continued employment suddenly becomes dependent on voluntary treatment,[10] and a group of male workhouse inmates, most of them committed by the courts,[11] or a group of women alcoholic prisoners.[12] We would expect these groups to vary widely in terms of treatment outcome, and must keep the type of population in mind when comparing the results reported. A glance at these four studies illustrates the difficulty in comparing results as they are reported. If we use them to compare the effects of treatment on relatively motivated and unmotivated populations, we find the differences we would expect but are unable to interpret them because we cannot separate motivational factors from differences in type of treatment and criteria of improvement.

A form of bias that is purposeful and usually acknowledged by the author is that in which certain members of a population are excluded because they are not felt to be suitable candidates for the type of treatment being studied. Ends and Page, for example, selected subjects from an alcoholic population defined by the following criteria: "male, white, within the age range of 21 to 60 . . . without severe organic pathology . . . or psychotic impairment . . . and above the 45th percentile" on the Army General Classification Test.[13] This is a highly acceptable procedure; it is explicit, defines the sample on a number of relevant dimensions, and results in a relatively homogeneous sample. It has the further advantage of establishing the first stage for replication, a step too infrequently taken in evaluative research. In comparing a study of this type with those in which the entire population of a facility is investigated, we must keep in mind that we cannot compare results in terms of type of treatment provided by the facility, but must consider the population that was treated.

Another source of bias occurs when patients are free to choose among types of treatment. Wallace compared clinical outcome between two groups, one receiving disulfiram and psychotherapy, the other receiving psychotherapy alone.[14] In selecting his samples he chose for his first group only patients who specifically requested disulfiram; the patients in his comparison group had not requested it. Consequently, we are unable to interpret his results, complicated as they are by differing motivations to enter treatment. Sometimes it is impossible to know whether patients requested specific treatment or whether it was assigned on some unspecified basis. Jensen compared patients who received a "full program" (evidently milieu, group, and individual therapy, plus a lysergide experience) with patients receiving group therapy without lysergide (some having refused it), and with a third "control" group who "received individual treatment by other psychiatrists."[15] Although his results show a strikingly greater degree of improvement in the "full program" group, he does not provide us with sufficient information regarding assignment to the three groups to make any justifiable conclusions regarding the efficacy of the three treatment programs.

Clearly, when patients are free to choose among treatments, motivation will be uncontrolled and findings uninterpretable. Several practices may be followed to ensure that patients have an equal chance of being assigned to one treatment or another. Assignment by random numbers is probably the simplest technique, although large samples will be necessary if the patient population is a heterogeneous one.[16] Systematic forms of selection that can reasonably assure randomness (e.g., every fifth admission assigned to treatment condition and every sixth to the comparison condition) may be used when sample sizes are fairly large, say over 50 patients in each sample.[17] When smaller sample sizes are required, patients or groups may be matched on relevant characteristics, with special attention paid to motivational state.

Too often we found it impossible to know on what basis patients were assigned to various types of treatment; even in one of the more methodologically careful studies it is reported that after initial screening, 96 patients were "selected on the basis of a sociometric test."[18] Since this is a well thought-out study, we are led to suspect that the assignment was also; however, we are not given enough information to decide whether the selection procedure was biasing to the results reported.

Another common difficulty is encountered when a population seems to be a sample from a larger group, but with no description of sampling procedure provided. Schmidt, for example, reports that he "used as research material a group of 20 alcohol- and drug-dependent patients, admitted on his service to a 150-bed private psychiatric hospital in a two-year period."[19] How were these 20 patients selected? Were they the total number of patients qualifying for this project during the 2-year period? They were evidently not selected on the basis of being easy to locate, since only 12 of the group responded to follow-up questionnaires. It is easy to suppose that these 20 patients constituted the entire population treated; it would be to the author's advantage, however, to specify this fact if true.

To summarize, we have seen that a certain degree of bias is inherent in evaluative research; it is nevertheless evident that a majority of the studies reviewed show, on various grounds, severe but easily remediable deficiencies in sampling procedures. In only a few instances were explicit sampling constraints employed to methodological advantage.

SELECTION AND DEFINITION OF CRITERION VARIABLES

It is often assumed that studies of therapy with alcoholics have an advantage over most evaluations of therapy in that a comparatively clear-cut criterion is built into the purpose of the treatment. Cessation of drinking or changes in drinking pattern appear to be more objective criteria than other changes that might be attributed to therapy—for example, improvement in insight, reduction of anxiety level, or changes in ego strength. In almost half of the studies we reviewed, drinking behavior was the only criterion employed; in almost all, it was the major criterion.

This near-universal reliance on abstinence as a criterion of therapeutic success has been infrequently challenged, although recently doubts have been voiced. Two major questions may be asked: Are changes or cessation of drinking behavior as easily measured as has been assumed? If measurable, is abstinence a criterion either theoretically or empirically relevant to the presumed effects of treatment?

Measurement of abstinence, no matter how it is defined, requires an assessment of drinking behavior. One group of investigators has portrayed some of the difficulties:

> The most troublesome area [in collecting and analyzing certain kinds of behavioral data] was drinking behavior, a complex activity including the following dimensions: type and amount of beverage consumed, frequency, regularity, and consequences of heavy drinking occasions, places where drinking occurs, with whom drinking is done, and variations in all of the above from one occasion to another or even within a single occasion. Drinking behavior has so many facets that no investigation of alcoholism to date has successfully incorporated them into a single index, or group of indices by which an alcoholic's drinking behavior can be adequately evaluated.[20]

Complicating this general measurement problem is the question of how dependable the source of information is; sources of data reported include the patient, his relatives, other persons who know the patient, public records, or some combination of these.

In the extrahospital situation, the patient alone can provide accurate information concerning his drinking; how dependable the information is poses a different problem. One of the characteristics often noted in alcoholics is a willingness to please, to say the right thing; another is the tendency to deny the seriousness of their drinking problem. Either of these characteristics makes evaluation based only on self-report somewhat suspect. Gibbins and Armstrong have described some of the difficulties they encountered:

"Generally patients tended to place less emphasis on the seriousness of their drinking problems, and to report fewer and shorter periods of preadmission abstinence, during the follow-up interview. Also noticeable was a tendency to exaggerate the duration of periods of abstinence following treatment. For example, patients interviewed 13 or 14 months after admission sometimes reported periods of abstinence totaling more than that."[21]

Many investigators are aware of the possibility of distortion by the patient, and have turned to relatives for infromation to substantiate or invalidate his report. As Guze's group has demonstrated, relatives, for whatever reasons, portray patients' drinking behavior in a more benign fashion than the patients themselves. Guze and his colleagues compared information elicited from patients and their relatives and found a 26 percent disagreement between responses about drinking behavior provided by alcoholic patients and their relatives; 80 percent of the disagreement involved a positive answer from the patient and a negative one from the relative. These interviews, carried out at the time of admission, showed that, "In 28 percent of all the interviews with relatives . . . the diagnosis of alcoholism would not be made and would not even be suspected from the information given."[22]

A number of studies, acknowledging the fact that the report of the patient and his relatives is not sufficient, attempt to tap other sources of information, including police and arrest records, employers, landlords, local agencies, doctors, and Alcoholics Anonymous groups. Although these sources are valuable in increasing the accuracy and scope of the information obtained, we would expect them to show even more discrepancy than was found in Guze's study. None of the studies employing a number of sources of information indicated to what extent these sources agreed.

We may conclude that abstinence, or change in drinking pattern, even when considered solely as an exercise in measurement, is not as clear-cut a criterion as one might suppose.

If one examines some of the assumptions that explicitly or, more often, implicitly underlie the choice of abstinence as a criterion, its status is further diminished. Lipscomb describes one probably prevalent rationale for its use: "Current professional thinking, volubly backed by those many agencies who believe that quantity of drinking and severity of problems are directly proportionate, admits that as of this time the best single measure of therapeutic response is abstinence. (This admission is usually made with an expression that plainly cries, 'God, I wish we could pin down some other item beside drinking.')"[23] Those investigators who feel that they are "stuck" with abstinence as a criterion may be forced into the currently untenable position of implying that a one-to-one correspondence exists between amount of alcohol consumed and severity of problems. The California group questions the use of abstinence per se as a criterion on the grounds that it "excludes partial improvement as evidence of rehabilitation" and further that it "requires a standard of conduct to which even persons in a 'normal' population are not expected to conform."[24]

The problem of choice of criteria for improvement raises the question, largely social-philosophical, regarding the values, professional orientation, and goals of various investigators. The medically oriented researcher is more likely to value symptom removal as a legitimate goal than the social scientist or the psychoanalytically oriented investigator. If, however, abstinence is not associated with better overall adjustment, symptom removal may be a case of "the operation was a success, but the patient died." While there is nothing wrong with any particular type of value orientation regarding "success," there seems to be considerable confusion about the aims of therapy, confusion that has implications not only for research tactics and strategy but also for the kinds of interpretations that can legitimately be made of reported therapeutic results. The social scientist, for example, is likely to value, and see as the end goal, some ideal concept of "mental health"; yet in his research, he tends to make symptom removal (abstinence in this case) his goal, with either an implicit or explicit assumption that this means ideal mental health. In the studies we reviewed, many of the investigators seemed to fall into this type of thinking. If symptom removal is the value and the goal, then abstinence-oriented research is appropriate. If, however, some mental-health goal is desired and valued, then the research strategy and tactics will follow a quite different pattern, and abstinence becomes just one of a complex array of factors that may be subsumed under the term "mental health." If, after careful investigation, abstinence is demonstrated to be highly correlated with these factors, then we would be justified in undertaking abstinence-oriented research. This search for correlates of abstinence seems to us to be one of the most needed research efforts in the field of alcoholism at the present time.

In our present state of knowledge, we cannot assume that abstinence reflects other psychological and social changes; the investigator who does this is in error and misrepresents his findings. Many investigators are at least implicitly aware of this problem and resolve it by including other criteria of this problem and resolve it by including other criteria of change; among those used in these studies are family relationships, occupational and economic adjustment, arrests, A.A. contacts, physical status, amount of money spent on alcohol, and performance on adjective check lists. There is no attempt to indicate whether a patient would be rated as "improved" if he had given up drinking completely but had deteriorated on other indices of adjustment. Several studies employ "scales" on which various types of behavior are rated; results are then either presented separately for each scale or lumped to indicate "improvement," although it seems logically improbable that all criteria should be given equal weight in an evaluation of improvement.

Abstinence, as we have seen, can be a meaningful criterion of improvement only when it is shown that changes in drinking behavior are correlated with other forms of adjustment. The two attempts to do this provide a major reason for questioning the use of abstinence as a criterion variable.

The first of these is a clinical study of 55 abstinent alcoholics followed at intervals of two, five, and eight years after their admission for treatment.[25] Gerard, Saenger, and Wile found, first of all, a consistent relationship between abstinence and better family relationships, physical health and social and occupational adjustment, supporting the hypothesis that "giving up drinking is associated with 'better' functioning and adjustment in the public or outer aspects of the alcoholic's life." With regard to personal and social functioning, however, the findings were less satisfactory. On the basis of clinical material in 50 cases, abstinent ex-patients were classified into 4 groups: (1) Overtly disturbed; 27 (54%) were found to be either tense, aggressive, or anxious to an uncomfortable or pathological degree, or to display overt psychotic symptoms. (2) Inconspicuously inadequate personalities; 12 (24%) were classified as having "total functioning . . . characterized by meagerness of their involvement with life and living." (3) Alcoholics

Anonymous successes; 6 (12%) "made a spectacular shift in their lives through a successful identification with A.A.," and are "as dependent on A.A. as they had once been on alcohol." (4) Independent successes; 5 (10%) had "achieved a state of self-respecting independence, of personal growth, and of self-realization."[26] Parenthetically, only 16 of the 55 patients (29%) traced the onset of their abstinence to inpatient or outpatient treatment.

The second study compared pre- and posthospitalization drinking patterns of 149 male patients, and evaluated these patterns against 20 other areas of adjustment.[27] Using a criterion of at least one 6-month category upgrading, Rossi, Stach, and Bradley found that 14 men were abstinent, 45 were drinking with mild effects, and 90 were drinking with serious effects. When differences between before-and-after treatment measures were compared for the entire group of 149 patients in 20 areas of attitude and behavior, significant improvement occurred in 7 areas, significant deterioration occurred in 4, and no change occurred in the remaining 9 areas. By inspection (that is, without any reported statistical analysis), the 14 abstinent men improved in 16 out of the 20 areas when compared with the group as a whole. Unfortunately, Rossi, Stach, and Bradley did not report before-after data separately for the abstinent, drinking-with-mild-effects, and drinking-with-serious-effects groups; this omission precludes clear-cut interpretation about the extent to which abstinence is associated with change in other areas. However, posttreatment frequencies were reported but not analyzed for each of their groups. We analyzed these posttreatment frequencies to determine the significance of differences between the abstinent and mild effects groups for each of the 20 variables. The results of this analysis show significant differences in favor of the abstinent group in only 4 of the 20 areas, using a $p < .05$ level of confidence. Though incomplete because it does not incorporate a baseline measure, our analysis nevertheless suggests that the authors' statement, "Abstinence . . . appears to be the condition associated with improved adjustment in most areas," can hardly be taken at face value.

Each of these studies indicates that cessation of drinking cannot be considered as a cure-all. Surprisingly, the Rossi, Stach, and

Bradley study shows that even in areas where we might automatically assume improvement with abstinence, namely, employment and patterns of money dealings, improvement did not, on the basis of our posttreatment analysis, occur.

One final source of information that leads one to question uncritical use of abstinence as a criterion is the clinical conjecture that cessation (or decrease) of drinking may be accompanied by the onset or increase of other symptoms equally disturbing to those with whom the alcoholic comes in contact but not tapped by the measuring instruments employed. We have no way of estimating the frequency of such occurrences, but occasional instances are reported. Lipscomb describes the type of behavior that may be encountered:

"One patient in my study group before treatment drank 365 days of the year, . . . following treatment he drank 300 days per year (if his interview testimony is correct). But . . . this individual, concurrent with stemming in part his drinking, developed ulcers, lost his wife, family and the job support he had managed to find in the interim since treatment. By the variable of drinking he was one-sixth better whereas, in fact, his total living situation had degenerated inclusive of his health."[28]

Perhaps it would be wise in evaluative studies not to employ abstinence as the measure of total therapeutic response but rather, as Lipscomb has suggested, to view it as an indicator of a positive therapist-patient relation or, alternatively, of the patient's motivation to change. It certainly appears that abstinence is only one component of a complex array of factors that must be considered if we are to speak about therapeutic outcomes without limiting ourselves to changed drinking behavior as a goal.

Two evaluative reports from industrial settings did not employ changes in drinking pattern as a criterion, but rather focused on maintenance of job absentee rates.[29] Such criteria have an attractive simplicity; unfortunately, the high rates of success reported when job maintenance is the criterion are vitiated by the fact that job maintenance is dependent on remaining in treatment. That threat of loss of job may in itself be an effective agent of some type of change is suggested by one study in which it was reported that 50 percent of men who either refused or discontinued treatment nevertheless maintained their jobs.[30] With respect to reductions in absenteeism, one is similarly unable to know the extent of the effect due to therapeutic intervention, to threat of loss of job, or to interaction between them.

In summary, the behavior most frequently evaluated is change in drinking pattern, the ideal goal being abstinence. There is considerable question as to whether changes in drinking behavior are measurable and whether decrease or cessation of drinking is a relevant measure. Other behaviors selected for measurement suffer from inadequate methodological handling.

MEASURING INSTRUMENTS AND THEIR RELIABILITY

The preponderant source of data for the studies reviewed was the interview. In many instances clinical interviews that had not been undertaken with subsequent evaluation in mind were used as basic data sources. In others interview schedules designed with specific research questions in mind were used by personnel specifically trained for the purpose. In some studies mailed questionnaires were filled out by patients. In only rare instances were specific instruments, such as attitude scales, mood scales, projective tests, or other psychological tests administered to assess change in relevant areas of behavior. Clinical outcome measures were usually global and either based on the judgment of the therapist or the pooled judgment of a clinical team. Attempts to deal with problems of reliability were on the whole lacking, although several investigators discuss some of the pitfalls involved in attaining reliability of measurement.

The problem of reliability is this: if the same measures were applied to the same behavior by two different people at the same point in time (or at two different points in time) to what extent would the results correspond?

One of the simplest types of reliability to measure is interjudge reliability, the extent to which independent observers, provided with the same information, will categorize the behavior in the same way. This information is rarely reported although sometimes it would appear to be readily available. Mindlin, for example, says that "improvement ratings constituted the pooled judgments of five clinic staff members who had contact with these patients";[31] Walcott and Straus report ratings "based on conferences between staff members of each clinic and one of the authors";[32] and Terhune says, "members of our group and a research worker have studied these records, and we believe the statements made are accurate."[33] These studies leave us to wonder whether interjudge correlations were never obtained or were of such low order that they were not reported.

Only two of the studies actually report interjudge correlation coefficients. Pfeffer and Berger report a correlation of .67 between ratings made by clinic personnel and work supervisors on criteria that were not identical but were comparable in reflecting changes in behavior that might be attributed to treatment.[34] The most satisfactory report of reliability was found in the study by Rossi, Stach and Bradley: 95 of the 149 patients in their sample were evaluated twice by different interviewers, using a 5-point rating scale. They report reliabilities ranging from .61 to .78.[35]

With the exception of these two investigations, the studies we reviewed are vague in reporting how ratings were made or the extent to which informants agreed. In some of the studies, we can infer that had attempts to obtain reliability coefficients been made, the resulting values would not have reached acceptable levels. This inference is based on the fact that extent of agreement depends, in part, on the clarity with which categories are defined, and in the studies such clarity of definition was not always present. For example, many studies use categories, such as "improved," "moderately improved," and "unimproved," without stating what criterion was used to assign a patient to a particular classification. Though this may reflect failure to report the criterion, it often appears that judgments are made on the basis of global clinical impressions, which means that acceptable levels of reliability would probably not be obtained. In other studies criteria for classification were more carefully spelled out, permitting the possibility of estimating reliability; in these instances the findings reported would have gained in significance had reliability studies been undertaken.

In summary, the studies reviewed reveal a singular lack of imagination with respect to choice of measuring instruments; the interview served as the major source of data. The concern voiced by some writers over reliability of measurement went largely unheeded in actual practice.

MEASUREMENT BEFORE AND AFTER TREATMENT

Most of the studies, as previously noted, were retrospective, and therefore the patient's pretreatment behavior was either rated as he remembered it after having been in treatment or on the basis of intake interviews not designed for subsequent research use. In many instances no attempt was made to establish any accurate picture of pretreatment behavior, so that amount and direction of change were often assessed on the basis of the therapist's or patient's judgment, and only for the posttreatment condition. This lack of sufficient or sound pretreatment data means that results of most of the studies cannot be easily interpreted, especially in view of the frequent failure of authors to acknowledge or take into account the inadequacies that exist. Although a small number of studies report the systematic collection of pretreatment data, the difficulties encountered have caused at least one group of investigators to question the validity of their own data.[36] An acceptable use of pre-post comparisons is found in three prospective studies in which psychological self-ratings were made by the patients before and after treatment, permitting a comparison of ratings.[37]

Difficulties of other kinds occur in obtaining posttherapeutic measures; namely, difficulties involved in locating and following patients and problems arising from the choice of the time interval between the collection of pre- and posttherapeutic data.

In regard to the locating-following problem, a majority of the studies report follow-up rates of less than 75 percent. In a few instances, follow-up rates are acceptably high, while in others information is insufficient to determine the percentage of follow-up. These uniformly low rates of follow-up pinpoint a source of bias in addition to those discussed earlier. It is not clear whether the bias introduced by low follow-up rates is systematic or random, although it may be argued that systematic bias occurs insofar as patients who are located and followed are probably those who have benefited from treatment.

Low follow-up rates occur primarily because of faulty techniques, the use of which are frequently justified on the grounds of lack of personnel or funds, or on the basis of a widely held conviction that alcoholics are more difficult to locate and follow than are other groups. There is no question that locating and following individuals after any extended period of time in any type of study is always difficult and that expecting 100 percent success is unrealistic. Nevertheless, adopting certain specific guidelines and procedures ensures a maximum rate of follow-up. First, follow-up rates drop rapidly with time. The shorter the time elapsed between treatment and follow-up assessment, the greater the follow-up rate. Second, the more personal the attempted follow-up contact, the greater is the follow-up rate. Face-to-face interviews, for example, result in higher follow-up rates than attempts to follow by mailed questionnaires. Third, there are numerous means of locating patients that are either matters of public record (e.g., city directory or telephone directory listings) or available to professional groups (e.g., utility company or central social-service listings). That use of procedures such as these results in high follow-up is demonstrated by the findings of two studies in which the authors of this Section participated. In the first study 88 percent of 200 alcoholic patients or their relatives were located and followed; in the second study, 98 percent were located and followed. The formal time interval between initial contact and follow-up was 1 year; follow-up was concluded at 18 months.

These two studies, as well as a few of those reviewed that had high follow-up rates, show the advantages of systematic employment of carefully thought-out techniques, but perhaps more importantly reveal that the widely held conviction that alcoholics are harder than most to locate is fallacious. What, then, of the justification that insufficient funds or personnel preclude adequate follow-up? Obviously, if the means to undertake a study are inadequate, the study itself will be inadequate. Under such circumstances it is perhaps wise to defer the study or to design it so that it fits within one's means. Among the studies reviewed, it is clear that reduction in the scope of some of them might have resulted in greater precision. As an example, Walcott and Straus report "no information" for 40 percent of their sample of 474 patients, a loss they attribute to lack of staff time.[38] Had they reduced sample size by 75 percent ($N = 118$), they would still have had a relatively large sample and would have been able to allocate staff time more efficiently to reduce their high percentage of loss.

This factor of patients lost to contact cannot fail to introduce bias into evaluative studies. Unfortunately the issue is all too frequently ignored in the studies reviewed, and results are reported as though the considerable loss of sample through faulty follow-up has no bearing on them. It is obvious, however, that it is difficult, if not impossible, to interpret findings on the effectiveness of treatment when follow-up rates are low or are not reported.

The choice of the time interval between the collection of pre- and posttherapeutic data presents a problem somewhat different from the locating-following one in that any time interval has, as we shall see, its inherent difficulties. It is apparent, however, that whatever the time interval selected, it should be the same for all patients participating in a given study, and, further, that length of treatment as well as any period that follows termination of treatment should be the same for all subjects. When meeting these requirements is not possible, as is often the case in practice, evaluative data should be analyzed and reported in a manner that systematically accounts for variations in treatment length and in time elapsed since the end of treatment.

In only three of the studies reviewed was the time interval between pre- and posttherapeutic data collection as well as length of treatment identical for all subjects.[39] The remaining studies show disparities in total length of pre-post evaluation periods, in length of treatment and in time elapsed since termination of treatment. Indeed, in some studies the time interval involved is not specified or is not clearly described. Practices include following patients at one point in time regardless of when they were admitted to a facility and grouping of patients who have terminated treatment with those still receiving treatment. In studies that follow terminated patients it is never reported what proportion stopped treatment by mutual consent of patient and therapist and what proportion dropped treatment of their own volition.

The selection of any time interval represents a compromise. The basic issue is this: a short time interval is at best a weak basis on which to predict future behavior; long-term follow-up, on the other hand, is confronted with another, largely unmeasurable factor—the unknown environmental influences contributing to the behavior that is observed. Obviously, the longer the time elapsed between termination of treatment and the follow-up study, the better the basis for a prediction that the change is a permanent one; however, it is then impossible to ascertain whether the change is due to treatment or external intervening circumstances. Complicating the problem further are the possibilities that environmental influences will either reinforce or negate beneficial changes made in therapy.

Some of the difficulties that arise are illustrated by studies specifically concerned with changes in outcome after repeated follow-up. Gerard and Saenger, in a study of the effects of various periods of follow-up, analyzed the data presented by Davies, Shepherd and Myers, Gibbins and Armstrong, and a previous unpublished study of their own, and conclude that "data presented here do not suggest that a 1-year follow-up study of patients with a drinking problem would grossly distort the picture of the relationship between the characteristics of the patient at intake, the treatment he received, and the movement of change in his functioning."[40] The continued maintenance of change, left unanswered by Gerard and Saenger, is examined in several other studies. Rossi, Stach and Bradley report that when a group of patients who showed improvement 6 to 36 months after hospitalization were reevaluated a year later, 90 percent had regressed to drinking with serious effects.[41] In another study, Rossi and Bradley used three annual follow-up surveys to determine relative stability of rated changes and found that the group initially rated "improved" remained fairly stable, while the group "motivated" to change decreased, thereby increasing the size of the "unimproved" group.[42] These findings lend support to the statement that ". . . with long-term follow-up the percentage of rehabilitated patients does fall off year by year until the fifth year."[43] Two other studies, however, report contradictory findings. Wilby and Jones report that an 18-month follow-up evaluation understated abstinence when compared with a 2-to-7-year reevaluation.[44] A similar finding is reported by Fox and Smith, who reevaluated 231 patients one year after an initial follow-up, and found that at the time of the second evaluation, 67 percent had maintained the same status as at initial evaluation, 24 percent had improved and 7 percent were worse.[45]

Obviously, these studies are of little help in establishing follow-up time intervals when conducting an evaluation study. Most of the authors used different periods of time on which to base their findings, and results are conflicting.

It seems clear, however, that investigators interested in the stability of change over time, or in permanence of beneficial change, must rely on repeated measures over at least a five-year period. In view of this, Gerard and Saenger's dictum about a one-year time interval appears reasonable. The crucial factors, as we noted above, are that length of treatment and time elapsed after treatment be controlled. Although no time interval is optimal, if investigators use roughly equivalent time intervals, it will be one step in the direction of making evaluative studies comparable, thereby enhancing our understanding of treatment effects.

To summarize, in the studies under review, collection of pretreatment data was *ex post facto* and used data sources not designed for research purposes. Collection of posttreatment data was often more systematic but resulted in bias because of poor following-locating practices and because temporal relationships between admission, length of therapy, and time elapsed since treatment were either not reported or not controlled.

Requirements for Reporting Evaluative Research

SETTING

Certainly the nature of the setting in which treatment is carried out will be one determinant of both type of treatment and type of research that can be done. The difference, for example, between treatment and carrying out a follow-up of 1,031 homeless Skid Row alcoholics[46] and a group of industrial employees attending a company-sponsored rehabilitation clinic[47] is obvious. All in all, the studies provide clear description of the settings in which they took place, and we urge only that the nature of the facility and type of population be kept in mind when evaluating differences that might appear to be due to different types of treatment.

TREATMENT

The major reason for reporting therapeutic findings is to draw some conclusion, or at least to give some indication as to the effectiveness of one kind of therapy compared to another or to none. It is abundantly clear, then, that a careful description of the treatment assessed is a necessary part of any evaluation report; this necessity is not often met. Several of the studies made no attempt to state type of treatment other than reference to "psychiatric treatment"; at the opposite extreme are those few that carefully described the treatment provided.[48] The other studies range between these two extremes, with varying degrees of clarity in describing their programs. Often, information readily available to the authors should have been included as a guide to the reader. Not only do these omissions prevent interpretation of findings, but they also lead to further omissions, such as the failure to report frequency and length of treatment.

POPULATION AND SAMPLE CHARACTERISTICS

If any judgment about the generalizability of reported results is to be made, one must have a clear notion of relevant characteristics of the population from which a sample has been drawn, and whether the sample has been selected in such a way that it can reasonably be assumed to represent the parent population. As we have observed earlier, reporting of population and sample characteristics, as well as selection procedures, has ranged from nonexistent or vague in the majority of studies to relatively precise in no more than a handful of investigations. It is obvious from reading between the lines of many studies that patients are for various reasons dropped from or lost to the study. The reasons for such omissions are rarely reported and their possible impact on findings is rarely discussed. It is a minor annoyance to be told that original sample size is 100, and then to find that results are reported for 98 patients, with no explanation of the discrepant numbers, yet the unexplained loss of two patients will not affect the general results. When, however, decreases of 20 percent or 30 percent of the original sample size occur and are neither explained nor discussed, the reader is left to wonder whether reports of outcomes have any meaning at all. Such occurrences are not infrequent in the studies reviewed. Whether evaluative reports are primarily clinical or research oriented, the author has an obligation to report at least on age and sex, how patients were selected, and any variations in choosing patients or in losing them.

MEASURING INSTRUMENTS

In an earlier section we described the importance of selecting, defining, and measuring behavior relevant to the aims of treatment. It is equally important to report clearly on the definition and measurement of the behavior selected as a criterion of evaluation. This is rarely done in the studies we reviewed. Descriptions of measuring tools are imprecise, gross, and misleading to the unsophisticated reader. When, for example, we are told that 66 percent of a group of patients remained "sober" after receiving X treatment, but are not informed as to how sobriety is defined or measured, we are unable to make any judgment about the finding reported. Does sobriety mean abstinence in the sense of total cessation of drinking? Or does it mean that the patient drinks but not to the point of intoxication? For how long a period? Was the patient (or his therapist) the source of information? Is there any evidence that the source of information is dependable? Is there any corroborating or validating information? The omission of answers to questions like these is all too frequent in the literature cited.

RESULTS

A report should provide enough information about results and their analysis to enable a reader to draw his own conclusions. Some

Methodological Aspects of Evaluative Studies

of the faults noted among the articles reviewed include the presentation of findings in percentages without a base frequency so that cell frequencies cannot be calculated; the presentation of probability values without stating the particular statistical technique applied; and the presentation of data without the application of any statistical test of differences between groups. Frequently, data are presented in such complicated ways that more time must be spent in trying to comprehend a table than in reading the entire paper. If one purpose of graphic methods of presenting data is simplification, this represents a misuse of descriptive statistics.

In summary, failure to meet requirements for reporting evaluative work is nearly as great as that for conducting evaluations. Except for the description of settings in which the various studies took place, most investigators were remiss in one or more of these requisites for scientific reporting.

CONCLUSION

Most of the studies we reviewed were descriptive in nature and made no claim to be experimental research. We were surprised, however, to find how few of the studies reported their clinical findings in clear and unambiguous ways, how few used easily applied statistical techniques, how few used readily available psychological tests as a means of measuring change, and how few built on evaluations reported in similar previous work. We rarely encountered explicitly research-oriented studies. Experimental research requires, as we have indicated, prospective ratings of patients; it requires control groups and random assignment to conditions; it requires valid and reliable measures of change. The only studies in this group that attempt to meet these criteria are those of Ends and Page and of Wallerstein.[49] Many of the reports fall into the borderlands between acceptable clinical studies and acceptable research studies. Both, of course, are necessary, and clinical studies in the past provided a fruitful source of hypotheses for the experimentally minded investigator and should continue to have a place in the literature.[50]

The bulk of the studies are gross retrospective surveys, usually with large groups of patients, as if quantity substituted for quality, with reliance on unreliable and unvalidated superficial measures and with inadequate follow-up procedures. It is for these reasons, as well as wide variations in settings and types of treatment offered, that we have made no attempt to summarize findings about "improvement." To allow the evaluation of each study on its own merits, we have prepared an annotated bibliography that includes the following information for each study: setting, purpose, subjects, controls (if any), type and length of treatment, length of follow-up, method of evaluation, and results (See Appendix C).

Finally, for the person or agency planning to embark on an evaluative study, there are a number of published sources that may be of use in avoiding the pitfalls described in this review.[51] Wherever possible, evaluative research should be designed and supervised by a person whose interests and training are primarily in research.

5.B. Techniques of Follow-Up

The alcoholism literature indicates that studies that utilize follow-up of subjects as part of their design are discouraging, in that rates of patients located are often low. Because of the relatively high rates of follow-up of the patients who served as subjects in our emergency service projects (see Sections B and C of Chapter 2), we feel that a description of the techniques we employed may be of use to other investigators.

In the first and larger study, the follow-up was service-oriented, and was carried out by the members of the treatment teams who had originally participated as clinicians in the project. Although a secretary obtained information from records, direct contact with patients or their relatives was left to the psychiatrists and social workers, each of whom was assigned five patients per month to follow and interview. Originally it was planned to have the follow-up done by a team member who had not had previous contact with the patient, in the hope of obtaining responses free of the voices of

Section 5.B. written by Elizabeth Lacy Hastie.
Notes to Chapter 5 will be found on page 194.

gratitude, hostility, or guilt. However, in the interest of interviewing as many patients as possible, this plan was not always adhered to. Every effort was made to locate each patient within a month following the one-year anniversary of his first visit to the emergency service; in general, when the efforts of one interviewer failed, patients were reassigned to another interviewer, and the search continued for the remainder of the follow-up year.

When possible, patients were interviewed at the hospital. Otherwise, the interviewer would go to the patient's home, or to the institution where he was located. Relatives were interviewed when a patient could not be located, had died, was found to suffer from brain damage affecting his memory, refused to be interviewed, or lived at too great a distance from the hospital. Only patients who lived within a fifty-mile radius of the hospital were interviewed, unless they were willing to come to the hospital for the interview. One exception was made because it was convenient for the interviewer. Patients who were located only because they came to the hospital intoxicated were kept in the hospital until sober, and this hospitalization was paid for by special funds. At the end of the first year of follow-up, it was found that only three patients (or their relatives) refused to become involved: a newly deceased patient's mother refused steadily; one patient slammed the door in the interviewer's face; a third patient with strong homicidal thoughts was so paranoid that discretion was thought to be the better part of valor.

Throughout the period of follow-up, weekly meetings were held, in which the entire follow-up staff participated. These meetings served the purpose of coordinating activities, maintaining morale, and provided an opportunity for interviewers to express their feelings about their work. Initially negative feelings were centered on the questionnaire, and the reluctance of psychiatrists and social workers to fill out schedules in front of patients, and to use a standardized questionnaire. It seemed that perhaps these interviewers were afraid of angering the patient and driving him away by demands for information, and that they would have been more comfortable using the less structured interview techniques with which they were familiar. This feeling is probably typical of social workers and psychiatrists who engage in clinical research, and has been discussed by Fellin.[52] Methods for locating patients and patient care were also topics of discussion at the meetings.

In any follow-up study, successfully locating patients depends on the adequacy of information obtained about the patients' usual behavior at the time of initial contact, and results depend on gathering adequate factual information about patients when they first appear for treatment. We tried to get name, date, and place of birth; age, name, and place of work and employer; pension type (Old Age Assistance, Veterans Administration, Veterans Services, Social Security, General Relief, Disability Assistance, etc.); place where the patient was currently living, and the names and addresses of landlord and of all close relatives and friends. We were not always able to obtain this information, and it frequently required great skill to obtain even part of it, since our patients usually were intoxicated when they entered the hospital, and were often brought in against their wills by the police, or in a comatose state. Sometimes the patients eloped from the hospital before we could obtain their names and addresses. When this minimal information was obtained, it was often unreliable. Aliases were frequent, and "address" frequently meant the place where the patient had slept the night before—Boston Common, an all-night theater, or "the weeds" (local sleeping spots for the regularly intoxicated) were often given, as were the addresses of used car lots, a mission's dormitory for homeless men, the address of a mother who had died ten years before, and a rooming house where the patient had lived months before. There were patients who did not know exactly when or where they were born, and who were reluctant to say whether they were married or not, either because they had been married several times, or because they feared suits for nonsupport. Other patients had lived and worked at so many different addresses, and lost so many days when they were drunk, that they could not remember where their last place of employment had been. (One such man was able to list forty-two jobs held in the previous year through a cousin who had done his income tax returns for him. In this case, it was probably not the number of jobs that was unusual, but that the patient could account for all of them).

The group of patients we followed was composed largely of inhabitants of Skid Row, and were thus difficult to locate. They moved frequently, held numerous low-status jobs, and often had little or no contact with relatives. On the other hand, they tended not to move out of the Boston area permanently. Mr. A's case illustrates the types of procedures used to locate patients.

Mr. A

Hospital records gave us Mr. A's latest address, which was in Boston, but he had no telephone. We used the telephone company street directory to obtain the telephone number of a neighbor whom the social worker called, only to be told that the patient had moved to another address five months ago. Using the same procedure we located a neighbor at the new address, who said that patient had moved, and that we should call the Department of Public Welfare. Public Welfare reported that assistance had been discontinued because of patient's constantly intoxicated condition, and they didn't know his whereabouts. Department of Probation records revealed that Mr. A had spelled his name in eight different ways (he was illiterate), and had six older addresses. These records provided the name and address of his wife. Mr. A's wife did not have a phone, so the worker called a neighbor, who said that she would ask the wife to call us. When Mrs. A called, an appointment was made, and she was interviewed at her home. She was a pathetic but cooperative lady, who had had a lot of medical attention at Massachusetts General Hospital. She did not know where to locate her husband, but provided the name of a man at City Hall who would know which bars her husband frequented. The worker then called the man at City Hall, and was given the name of a bar where patient could most likely be located. On arriving, the worker found that ladies were not admitted, and so asked a woman on the street about patient. She said that she would find out about him, and wrote to us about two weeks later. In this way, we found that the patient lived in many rooms on that street, that he was rarely sober, and that he was scheduled soon for an operation at City Hospital. We then asked City Hospital to notify us when patient was admitted, which they did. Patient died shortly thereafter, without an interview having been obtained.

We soon found that in addition to obtaining all the information we could about the patient, it was necessary to become familiar with the structure of the community and the agencies to which these men often turned for help. We therefore visited and got to know all the major agencies that offered services to destitute and alcoholic patients. This made our work immeasurably easier, since these agencies faced the same problems we did, and were eager to help us and to benefit from what we learned.

We found that the agencies fell into four major categories: public, social, medical, and correctional services, and that these services were administered either privately, or by city, state, or federal agencies. We also discovered that there were certain "key" agencies (for example, the Social Service Index) that listed names and addresses of people who had made use of a number of organizations, which contributed this information to the "key" agency. This service, although useful, was not infallible: names were listed as they were contributed by other agencies, such as the State Departments of Mental Health, T. B. and Sanitation, and lists were often out of date.

We had already found that each agency operated with different rules and procedures ,and we compiled a guide, to which we added at the time of follow-up. This guide, which was confidential and for the use of hospital personnel only, proved to be of great help to us and to other social workers in the hospital. With appropriate revisions, it has been continued in use since the time it was first compiled. Titled "A List of Procedures for Destitute and Alcoholic Patients in Boston," the guide provides information regarding procedures, whom to contact, how to get needed information, and other information that is often familiar to individuals, but lost when the social worker leaves an institution.

Some of the problems we have described point clearly to the need to allow enough time to be perservering, and this rule cannot be stated too strongly. Lack of sufficient time is often the cause for the low percentages of subjects found and evaluated. In general, if a small sample of patients is followed, it will be possible to make estimates of the time required to complete the follow-up and to cost account it. On the latter topic, Hill has some helpful ideas.[53] The various activities involved in follow-up should be broken down in such a way as to make it clear how long each activity takes, what activities can be carried out by trained clerical assistants, and which can be handled most effectively by professional staff. Once standard procedures have been established for gaining information, a great deal of this work can be done by clerical personnel, freeing the professional staff to use its clinical skills in eliciting information in face-to-face contacts.

Our follow-up approach was planned to be both reassuring and service-oriented. In letters asking patients to see us, we said that we wished to improve services in our emergency service, and would like their opinions of the treatment they had received. When we met the patients, we told them that we wanted to learn more about the people who use the emergency ward, and added that we thought perhaps certain people received better care than others, and that we wondered if people with certain kinds of illnesses or personalities receive different kinds of services and treatment. This approach usually led to cooperation on the part of the patient. The idea that we were interested in learning more about the people who use the emergency service made our project seem valid to other agencies, relatives and friends, when we were not able to locate the patients themselves.

The service orientation was made quite explicit in the interview; we asked the patients, for example, what they thought of the care they had received, and what they thought would have been the ideal way to be treated. It was only after this time that we mentioned that it had been recommended that the patient attend the alcohol clinic, and by this time the patient had usually mentioned it himself. It was at this point that we asked why the patient had or had not returned to the clinic.

Such an approach encompassed both our concern for our patients, and our awareness of many of their fears at being contacted. Some denied social or psychological problems, some feared legal or financial entanglements, and some were avoiding the police. Others feared confinement; "hospital," to some patients, symbolized loss of freedom and personal rights. This was especially true for the alcoholic who had been "punished" for his drinking by being "sent to a state farm" or similar institution.

Some patients expressed these fears by refusing to answer calls, or by saying that they were too busy to come for an interview. Others were overcompliant, said that they would come in any time, and did; others used this as a means of holding off the interviewer. Some accepted, and some refused home visits. Some patients were interviewed in state institutions, and although they were polite and cooperative, presented themselves blandly, and gave very meager social histories, denying serious problems. A number, however, returned to us for treatment on their release from other institutions. No matter what their initial attitude, almost all patients who were interviewed relaxed considerably during the session.

We have already specified the conditions under which relatives, rather than patients, were interviewed. In these interviews we stressed both our interest in the patient's evaluation of the treatment he received, and our wish to improve present and future patient care. Our approach in eliciting the cooperation of relatives consisted in a number of steps, listed here in the order of their effectiveness: (1) a straightforward statement of our objectives; (2) the assurance of the relative's exemption from financial or other responsibility for the patient; (3) an appeal to their sense of duty in helping the alcoholic community in general, even though they might not be interested in the patient; (4) the offer to visit them in their homes, to minimize inconvenience to them; and (5) the offer to conduct the interview by telephone. Our procedures were adjusted in accordance with what we knew about relationships between each patient and his relatives, and the attitudes we encountered ranged from firm noncooperation to wholehearted collaboration. At one extreme, we made many phone calls to arrange a home visit and then found no one home; at the other extreme, we had relatives who located and personally escorted patients to the clinic.

The varied reactions we encountered were related to the attitudes of the relatives toward the patient. Many were angry with the patient, and expressed this anger by their unwillingness to try to get some help for him. When the patient was still a member of a family unit, some relatives feared that somehow our intervention would change a status quo to which they had consciously become resigned, or which they unconsciously wished to perpetuate. For example, we interviewed the illiterate and humorous Irish mother of a confirmed "wino," her youngest son. The mother was a hard-working, deprived mother of nine, who had been orphaned at age three, and put to work at age eight on a small farm in Ireland. She described her alcoholic son's intoxicated behavior with such a combination of glee and condolence that it was not difficult to see that his behavior fulfilled some of her own needs to behave badly.

Some relatives were uncooperative because a strange interviewer, from long years of association, was identified as a hostile agent such as a bill collector, the police, or even a criminal associate. On the other hand, relatives who welcomed our follow-up interviews seemed eager to help the patient. They frequently perceived the visit as an opportunity to unburden long-denied feelings and issues to a sympathetic ear. As a result, they often felt free to ask for help with their own problems.

In addition to eliciting the cooperation of relatives in locating patients, we asked for the cooperation of many "caretakers" such as employers, ministers, doctors, managers of shelters, bartenders, and professional social agencies. Here we met with various reactions of annoyance and cooperation similar to that encountered in the relatives. The major difference between the reactions of the two groups was the more guarded and protective attitude of the caretakers. Again, with this group we were careful to identify ourselves with the hospital rather than with the Alcohol Clinic, since we feared that an affiliation with the clinic might be used by an employer or social agency to jeopardize a patient's job or his rights to public financial assistance.

In summary, we have found it possible to obtain very high rates of follow-up by the use of a few specific techniques. First, we feel that follow-up can be made more effective by making a special effort, at the time of evaluation, to obtain information designed to facilitate locating the patient at a later time. Second, we feel that weekly staff meetings are necessary, both in order to maintain morale during the often arduous task of locating patients, and to permit coordination of efforts. Obtaining the cooperation of other agencies can be of invaluable help; in order to do this, it is necessary to become thoroughly acquainted with a variety of community agencies, their policies and services. Finally, we have found a service orientation to be of inestimable help in achieving the cooperation of patients and their families.

Notes

1. W. L. VOEGTLIN and F. LEMERE, "The Treatment of Alcohol Addiction: A Review of the Literature," *Quarterly Journal of Studies on Alcohol*, 2:717-803, 1942.
2. We attempted to review all studies published in the United States and Canada from 1952 through 1963 that had as either an implicit or explicit purpose evaluation of some type of psychological intervention with alcoholics. We first screened all articles in the *Quarterly Journal of Studies on Alcohol* during the period 1952-1963, including the abstracts of the Current Literature Section; in addition we screened other articles by means of the *Index Medicus* and *Psychological Abstracts*. Any publication in which there was evidence that a group of more than 10 alcoholic patients was assessed as to degree of "improvement" during or following some form of psychological intervention (individual or group psychotherapy, casework, counseling, psychological interviewing) was included in the final review. It is unlikely that we missed any evaluative papers that appeared in the *Quarterly Journal of Studies on Alcohol* or in the abstracts of Current Literature, although we may have missed some articles that appeared in other journals but were not summarized in the Current Literature section of the *Quarterly Journal of Studies on Alcohol*. This may in part be because, other than the *Quarterly Journal of Studies on Alcohol*, no North American journal deals specifically with issues relating to alcohol. Thus, the 28 articles reviewed here that did not appear in the *Quarterly Journal of Studies on Alcohol* were culled from no less than 22 journals or other sources

that represented such varied fields as medicine, psychiatry, psychology, public health, criminology, and industry.
3. E. J. Ends and C. W. Page, "Group Psychotherapy and Concomitant Psychological Change," *Psychological Monographs*, Vol. 73, No. 480, 1959; R. S. Wallerstein and Associates, *Hospital Treatment of Alcoholism: A Comparative Experimental Study* (Menninger Clinic Monograph No. 11) (New York: Basic Books, 1957).
4. For example, S. Jensen, "A Treatment Program for Alcoholics in a Mental Hospital," *Quarterly Journal of Studies on Alcohol,* 14:468-486, 1953; J. A. Wallace, "A Comparison of Disulfiram Therapy and Routine Therapy in Alcoholism," *Quarterly Journal of Studies on Alcohol,* 13:397-400, 1952.
5. E. J. Ends and C. W. Page, "A Study of Three Types of Group Psychotherapy with Hospitalized Male Inebriates," *Quarterly Journal of Studies on Alcohol,* 18:263-277, 1957.
6. R. S. Wallerstein, "Comparative Study of Treatment Methods for Chronic Alcoholism: The Alcoholism Research Project at Winter V. A. Hospital," *American Journal of Psychiatry,* 113:223-228, 232, 1956.
7. Ends and Page, "Group Psychotherapy. . . ."
8. W. B. Terhune, "A Method of Treatment of Alcoholism and the Results," *Journal of the Kentucky Medical Association,* 54:255-260, 1956.
9. Ends and Page, "Study of Three Types of Group Psychotherapy . . ."; "Group Psychotherapy . . ."; Wallerstein, *Hospital Treatment of Alcoholism.*
10. A. Z. Pfeffer and S. Berger, "A Follow-up Study of Treated Alcoholics," *Quarterly Journal of Studies on Alcohol,* 18:624-648, 1957; A. Z. Pfeffer, D. J. Feldman, C. Feibel, J. A. Frank, M. Cohen, S. Berger, and M. F. Fleetwood, "A Treatment Program for the Alcoholic in Industry," *Journal of the American Medical Association,* 161:827-836, 1956.
11. D. F. Mindlin, "Evaluation of Theapy for Alcoholics in a Workhouse Setting," *Quarterly Journal of Studies on Alcohol,* 21:233-252, 1960.
12. D. J. Myerson, J. MacKay, A. Wallens, and N. Neiberg, "A

Report of a Rehabilitation Program for Alcoholic Women Prisoners," *Quarterly Journal of Studies on Alcohol*, Suppl. No. 1:151-157, 1961.
13. ENDS and PAGE, "Group Psychotherapy. . . ."
14. WALLACE, *op. cit.*
15. JENSEN, *op. cit.*
16. R. J. GIBBINS and J. D. ARMSTRONG, "Effects of Clinical Treatment on Behavior of Alcoholic Patients: An Exploratory Methodological Investigation," *Quarterly Journal of Studies on Alcohol*, 18:429-450, 1957; J. J. ROSSI, A. STACH, and N. J. BRADLEY, "Effects of Treatment of Male Alcoholics in a Mental Hospital: A Follow-up Study," *Quarterly Journal of Studies on Alcohol*, 24:91-108, 1963.
17. D. L. GERARD, G. SAENGER, and R. WILE, "The Abstinent Alcoholic," *Archives of General Psychiatry*, 6:83-95, 1962.
18. ENDS and PAGE, "Study of Three Types of Group Psychotherapy. . . ."
19. E. C. SCHMIDT, "Alcoholic Dependency—Disease or Dilemma," *Wisconsin Medical Journal*, 57:457-464, 1958.
20. CALIFORNIA DEPARTMENT OF PUBLIC HEALTH, *Alcoholism and California: Follow-up Studies of Treated Alcoholics; Description of Studies* (Publication No. 5; Berkeley, California, 1961).
21. GIBBINS and ARMSTRONG, *op. cit.*
22. S. B. GUZE, V. B. TUASON, M. A. STEWART, and B. PICKEN, "The Drinking History: A Comparison of Reports by Subjects and Their Relatives," *Quarterly Journal of Studies on Alcohol*, 24:249-260, 1963.
23. W. R. LIPSCOMB, "Evaluation in Alcoholism Study," in *Selected Papers Delivered at the Eighth Annual Meeting of the North American Association of Alcoholism Programs*, Berkeley, California, 1957.
24. CALIFORNIA DEPARTMENT OF PUBLIC HEALTH, *op. cit.*
25. GERARD, SAENGER, and WILE, *op. cit.*
26. Five of the 55 patients were not rated owing to insufficient information.
27. ROSSI, STACH, and BRADLEY, *op. cit.*

28. LIPSCOMB, *op. cit.*
29. S. C. FRANCO, *A Company Program for Problem Drinking* (New York: Consolidated Edison Company of New York, 1962; mimeographed); PFEFFER, FELDMAN, FEIBEL, FRANK, COHEN, BERGER, and FLEETWOOD, *op. cit.*
30. PFEFFER, FELDMAN, FEIBEL, FRANK, COHEN, BERGER, and FLEETWOOD, *op. cit.*
31. MINDLIN, *op. cit.*
32. E. P. WALCOTT and R. STRAUS, "Use of a Hospital Facility in Conjunction with Outpatient Clinics in the Treatment of Alcoholics," *Quarterly Journal of Studies on Alcohol*, 13:60-77, 1952.
33. TERHUNE, *op. cit.*
34. PFEFFER and BERGER, *op. cit.*
35. ROSSI, STACH, and BRADLEY, *op. cit.*
36. GIBBINS and ARMSTRONG, *op. cit.*
37. ENDS and PAGE, "Study of Three Types of Group Psychotherapy . . ."; "Group Psychotherapy . . ."; L. H. GLIEDMAN, "Concurrent and Combined Group Treatment of Chronic Alcoholics and Their Wives," *International Journal of Group Psychotherapy*, 7:414-424, 1957; L. H. GLIEDMAN, D. ROSENTHAL, J. D. FRANK, and H. T. NASH, "Group Therapy of Alcoholics with Concurrent Group Meetings of Their Wives," *Quarterly Journal of Studies on Alcohol*, 17:655-670, 1956.
38. WALCOTT and STRAUS, *op. cit.*
39. ENDS and PAGE, "Study of Three Types of Group Psychotherapy . . ."; "Group Psychotherapy . . ."; R. A. MAIER and V. FOX, "Forced Therapy of Probated Alcoholics," *Medical Times*, 86:1051-1054, 1958.
40. D. L. GERARD and G. SAENGER, "Interval Between Intake and Follow-up as a Factor in the Evaluation of Patients with a Drinking Problem," *Quarterly Journal of Studies on Alcohol*, 20:620-630, 1959; D. L. DAVIES, M. SHEPHERD, and E. MYERS, "The Two-Years' Prognosis of 50 Alcohol Addicts after Treatment in Hospital," *Quarterly Journal of Studies on Alcohol*, 17:485-502, 1956; GIBBINS and ARMSTRONG, *op. cit.*

41. Rossi, Stach, and Bradley, op. cit.
42. J. J. Rossi and N. J. Bradley, "Dynamic Hospital Treatment of Alcoholism," *Quarterly Journal of Studies on Alcohol, 21*: 432-466, 1960.
43. Franco, op. cit.
44. W. E. Wilby and R. W. Jones, "Assessing Patient Response Following Treatment," *Quarterly Journal of Studies on Alcohol, 23*:325, 1962.
45. V. Fox and A. Smith, "Evaluation of a Chemopsychotherapeutic Program for the Rehabilitation of Alcoholics: Observations over a Two-Year Period," *Quarterly Journal of Studies on Alcohol, 20*:767-780, 1959.
46. W. W. Wattenberg and J. B. Moir, "Factors Linked to Success in Counseling Homeless Alcoholics," *Quarterly Journal of Studies on Alcohol, 15*:587-594, 1954.
47. For example, Pfeffer and Berger, op. cit.
48. For example, Wallerstein, *Hospital Treatment of Alcoholism.*
49. Ends and Page, "Study of Three Types of Group Psychotherapy . . ."; "Group Psychotherapy . . ."; Wallerstein, "Comparative Study of Treatment Methods . . ."; *Hospital Treatment of Alcoholism.*
50. For example, R. P. Knight, "The Dynamics and Treatment of Chronic Alcohol Addiction," *Bulletin of the Menninger Clinic, 1*:233-250, 1937; "The Psychodynamics of Chronic Alcoholism," *Journal of Nervous and Mental Disease, 86*:538-548, 1937.
51. E. Herzog, *Some Guide Lines for Evaluative Research: Assessing Social Change in Individuals* (Washington, D.C.: Department of Health, Education, and Welfare, Social Security Administration, Children's Bureau, 1959); E. E. Levitt, *Clinical Research Design and Analysis in the Behavioral Sciences* (Springfield, Illinois: Charles C Thomas, 1961); F. J. McGuigan, *Experimental Psychology: A Methodological Approach* (Englewood Cliffs, New Jersey: Prentice-Hall, 1960); F. N. Kerlinger, *Foundations of Behavioral Research* (New York: Holt, Rinehart and Winston, 1964); E. A. Suchman, *Evaluative Research, Principles and Practices in Public Service and*

Social Action Programs (New York: Russell Sage Foundation, 1967).
52. P. FELLIN, "The Standardized Interview in Social Work Research," *Social Casework*, 44:81-85, 1963.
53. J. G. HILL, "Cost Analysis in Social Work Service," in N. A. POLANSKY (ed.), *Social Work Research* (Chicago: University of Chicago Press, 1960), pp. 223-247.

PART TWO: NEW DIRECTIONS IN RESEARCH AND CLINICAL ACTION

Chapter 6
Broadening the Clinical Base: Around-the-Clock Psychiatric Services

The study of alcohol problems can open new vistas and needs. The history of alcoholism treatment, in most instances, has been to apply, perfunctorily, to the alcoholic methods that work for other conditions. The implication is that, if an approach works in one difficult area, it might work with alcoholics.

Two events reverse this process: The Alcoholics Anonymous approach and the creation of innovative approaches, such as the Acute Psychiatric Services at the Massachusetts General Hospital. Alcoholics Anonymous, originating in part from the Washingtonian Movement of the nineteenth century, was created by alcoholics for the neglected alcoholic population of this country, and it has become a major model for helping the sufferers of other ills of man. The Acute Psychiatric Service has a similar history. When application of various techniques of reaching and motivating alcoholics proved fruitful, pertinent questions arose. Are these procedures applicable to the alcoholic alone? Will they work for the total psychiatric population that comes to an emergency setting of a general hospital? The need for special techniques to get and keep the alcoholic in treatment stems from nothing innate in the alcoholically ill. The specialness results from society's prevailing view of alcoholic people and the self-perception of the alcoholic person.

Behavioral disorders in which demonstrable lesions and etiologies are nonexistent, and in which the afflicted person seems to play a part in contributing to his disorder, are viewed with a moralistic and punitive attitude by society. This has two results: On the one hand, when the individual comes to a health facility, caregivers meet the person with a less compassionate and understanding attitude than is supplied to people who are "sick"; on the other hand, the person coming for help with an alcoholic problem perceives himself as second-class and delinquent, and usually anticipates and receives the responses he expects. In other words, the alcoholic person is generally viewed by society as bad and causing his sorry state, and the patient feels the same way about himself. Common experience shows that when the alcoholic person is treated with the respect afforded other patient populations, then he must test out the reality of this response by inviting negative responses; this he does almost in disbelief that anyone could view him as just a person with an affliction. For these reasons, the initial encounter is the crucial determinant of a successful therapeutic alliance.

But, there are other persons who are emotionally and behaviorally ill and who seem not to receive any of the benefits available from psychosocial treatment techniques. These are persons of lower- and lower-middle-class status, who expect tangible provisions from caretakers, who possess limited ability to negotiate the labyrinths of systems of health services, and who have negligible means of communicating with middle-class therapists. These are persons who are all too frequently labeled unmotivated, unreachable, and untreatable.

The importance of an acute psychiatric service in a general hospital is emphasized when we recognize that many patients come with complaints of a physical nature, which mask their psychosocial discomfort. We were not just fulfilling an unmet need, but creating an open door for early identification of problems and the diminishing of chronicity.

The acute psychiatric service, modeled upon our approach to the seemingly unreachable alcoholic, aims to satisfy people's needs to understand themselves and to motivate them to treatment. Patients are persons, and not categories. Helping a patient care for a treasured pet or notifying an interested acquaintance before admission to a hospital can work wonders that no medicine can provide. If nothing more, when we respond to people asking for help by individualizing our approach, we acknowledge that the person is just that, an individual. This attitude is respectful and therapeutic.

There is little question in our minds, as we review the creation of the acute psychiatric service, that this major thrust in the delivery of psychiatric services to a largely neglected patient population emanated from our interests in the problem of alcoholism. And small wonder. There is nothing innate in alcoholic people that should preclude their responding to humane, understanding attempts to help, just as there is nothing innate in lower-middle- and lower-class people that should preclude their desire to achieve surcease from discomfort.

· · ·

6.A. The Effect of a Psychiatric Emergency Service on Motivation for Psychiatric Treatment

Emergency service activities of the Massachusetts General Hospital reflect the same trend for increased services reported elsewhere. Coleman and Errera examined the issue and its relation to psychiatric problems, and concluded that emergency facilities are rapidly becoming the "poor man's doctor," but that psychiatric referrals in an emergency-room setting result in few patients accepting referral to a psychiatric facility, these patients being "present-oriented," rather than "future-oriented."[1] The purpose of this paper is to describe the effect of an emergency psychiatric service on patients' motivation for further treatment in general.

The Acute Psychiatric Service of the Massachusetts General Hospital was established in the light of two factors. First, it is generally recognized that emergency services of general hospitals are increasingly utilized by the community as a substitute for the fast-disappearing general practitioner. This means that emergency services of urban hospitals no longer engage primarily in life-death emergencies but rather assume the role formerly fulfilled by the family doctor. Hence, instead of an emergency service being faced by urgent, life-threatening situations, there has been a marked change—an increase in the proportion of persons seeking treatment for chronic illnesses and for psychosocial problems. There has therefore been a concurrent change from traditional patterns of care involving rapid diagnosis, treatment, and turnover of patients, carrying a sense of urgency, to intervention of a type that includes appreciation of an intensive evaluation of the patient as a whole—medically, psychiatrically, and socially—and treatment planning involving not only the patient himself but family members and extrahospital community resources as well.

Second, the research by our group (see Chapter 2) on methods of motivating alcoholics seen in an emergency service to continued

Section 6.A. written by Morris E. Chafetz.
Notes to Chapter 6 will be found on page 250.

treatment relationships suggested the possibility that such an approach might be applied to a general psychiatric population of lower- and lower-middle-class origins, members of which are often considered "unreachable," "untreatable," "poor therapeutic risks," and so on. The earlier study with alcoholics revealed that the general pattern of patient contact in the emergency service—rapid dispositions and quick turnover—whereby lengthy waits, minimal contact of the physician with accompanying relatives, incomplete history-taking, omission or comprehensive treatment planning, and lack of direct contact with agencies were the all too common rule, resulted in a virtual lack of follow-through and treatment recommendations. When the problems noted above were corrected for the alcoholic population in the emergency service, a strikingly high response to treatment recommendations was observed. Thus an assumption on which the study group operated—that the initial contact a person in crisis has with caretakers is of critical importance in enhancing or inhibiting motivation for treatment—was confirmed.

The guiding philosophy, therefore, of the Acute Psychiatric Service was as follows: (1) Contemporary modalities of psychological treatment for outpatients, suitable for middle- and upper-middle-class patients, may be inappropriate and nonapplicable to lower- and lower-middle-class patients. (2) Previous experience indicates that active reaching out, meeting the expressed needs of patients and engaging other family members in the evaluation and treatment process, reducing reality frustrations, and the caretaker's following through the treatment recommendations can be highly effective in motivating for treatment the lower- and lower-middle-class psychiatric patient who is now becoming typical in an emergency service.

Looking at the extent of change involved in such an emergency psychiatric service may provide perspective to the striking changes occurring in patient attendance. In 1952, 300 psychiatric patients were seen in the emergency service of the Massachusetts General Hospital; in the first year of operation of the Acute Psychiatric Service 3,450 individuals were seen for more than 5,000 visits. Table 15 (Appendix A) illustrates the number of patients, the number of contacts and by whom seen for the first quarter of 1964 (running at an expected rate of 5,000 patients for 7,000 visits, or a 46 percent increase in one year). Table 16 (Appendix A) shows the distribution of type of presenting problem broken down into three broad categories—psychiatric, alcoholic, or medical—and the sex distribution. Table 17 (Appendix A) presents the age by sex distribution of patients. This table reveals that 50 percent of the patient population falls within the age group of 10 to 39 years, emphasizing the potential for early case finding in an emergency psychiatric service. Table 18 (Appendix A) shows the distribution of type of problem by sex distribution and reveals that (contrary to anticipation) alcoholics do *not* make up the greater percentage of patients utilizing the emergency facilities of a psychiatric department. Table 19 (Appendix A) presents extrahospital and intrahospital sources of referral. Extrahospital sources of referral make up 40.4 percent of the referrals to the Acute Psychiatric Service, whereas intrahospital referrals account of 59.6 percent of the patients. Table 20 (Appendix A) presents disposition by type of problem and shows an almost equal distribution between intrahospital and extrahospital dispositions. Table 21 (Appendix A) presents the distribution of intrahospital and extrahospital dispositions respectively by type of problem. These figures demonstrate the wide range of problems, age, sources of referral, and dispositions met in the Acute Psychiatric Service.

The operation and activities of the Acute Psychiatric Service consist of the following: (1) intensive team evaluation of the patient and his primary social system; (2) comprehensive treatment planning that involves the patient and his family with intrahospital as well as community resources; (3) careful utilization of initial contact with patients and family members in order to enhance motivation for continuing care; (4) continuity, cooperation, coordination, and consultation with a variety of community agencies in treatment planning and implementation; (5) an inservice training program for psychiatric residents, psychiatric social work students, and psychology trainees, and a complementary program of training for community agents, lay and professional; and (6) evaluation.

Since the present paper is concerned with the effectiveness of motivation for treatment, only those activities pertaining to this subject will be discussed. The findings of our studies reported in Chapter 2 are relevant in this regard. If alcoholism is largely symptomatic of a psychological disturbance there should be some generality of these findings for psychiatric disorders in general. The findings imply that, like alcoholics, the nonalcoholic patients in the Acute Psychiatric Service can be significantly motivated to follow through treatment recommendations when the initial crisis contact is handled by techniques designed to enhance motivation.

These techniques may vary from case to case and are often spontaneous, but the underlying tone is always the same, that is, interest in the person and respect for his integrity and dignity as an individual. Specific techniques include gratification, within reality limits, of needs expressed by the patient—for example, the patient who is in need of a place to sleep or needs dentures and the like—which needs must be met before he will contemplate therapeutic procedures (this we term constructive utilization of dependency needs); offering a continuous relationship; and recognition and acceptance of feelings, whether directly or indirectly expressed. Another guiding principle, derived from Lindemann's theory of crisis, is that motivation for treatment is greatest at points of psychosocial crisis. Commonly, persons in crisis focus only upon the acute manifestation of a chronic problem, but the assumption that the person is not only asking for help with the immediate crisis but with the underlying problem as well has been a central part of the theory of treatment. Minimal motivation may be enhanced simply by recognizing this with the patient. A third factor in the initial contact that can serve to reduce motivation inhibitions is to keep reality frustrations to a minimum; for example, avoidance of lengthy waits, fragmented contacts with a number of personnel, impersonality, and other behaviors that may be interpreted by the patient as hostile or rejecting.

Those who accompany the patient, often marital partners or relatives, are especially important in the effect they may have in enhancing motivation. Since patients do not live in a vacuum, optimal evaluation and treatment must be developed within the setting of the individual, the family, and the community. When involving key relatives in evaluation and treatment planning, one enlists their aid in enhancing the patient's motivation. Interpretation of aims, giving reassurance, and discussing secondary problems that may arise for relatives because of the treatment plan proposed, are essential to reduce gross or subtle pressure that relatives can exert to influence the patient's decision to accept or refuse treatment. In this way, the family, not the individual alone, becomes the focus of treatment.

A major problem in motivating persons in stress relates to interagency referral procedures and practices. Many interagency referrals are ill-considered and poorly carried out. By ill-considered I mean that one agency refers a patient or family to another agency without clear-cut knowledge of the administrative policies or clinical services of the receiving agency. By poorly carried out, I mean lack of or minimal communications between the two agencies and lack of or minimal preparation of the patient for what he may expect at the receiving agency. What frequently results is interagency or interprofessional tension and conflict, and, as Stanton and Schwartz have shown for the mental hospital, it is the patient who suffers most from this kind of conflict.[2] Often the patient is "dumped" from one agency to another, where a patient can finally start treatment after months or years have elapsed, or never.

Working out interagency referral procedures and practices is difficult but rewarding, in that a tremendous and disorganized consumption of community resources, while patients are receiving little or no help, is avoided. Referral procedures and practices have been worked out in the following ways: First, direct knowledge of the administrative policies and clinical organization of the particular agency is developed. Practical knowledge of each agency's potential permits more effective tailoring of the resources available to the patient's needs and minimizes waste of community resources. Second, working out referrals leads to reaching some understanding and agreement between key personnel in both agencies as to what constitutes a "good" referral, and a mutually agreed-upon set of referral procedures. Third, one should be in a position to offer something to the receiving agency, for example, a reciprocal referral system or informal training or consultation where needed. A simple appeal for effective patient care, although helpful, is usually insufficient. Fourth, the whole process must be a continuing one in which constant reevaluation is necessary to reinforce mutually acceptable referral patterns. Follow-through of referrals is another excellent method of good interagency relations and additionally serves as feedback to the effectiveness of one's own treatment planning.

In discussing effective interagency community referrals, we are obviously referring to lower- or lower-middle-class populations. Middle- and upper-class social positions usually provide sufficient supporting resources so that mobilization of community resources is negligible or readily available. Hence the observation has often been made that many patients in outpatient settings discontinue psychotherapy early, and the dropout rate has been related to low social class position (*see* Chapter 3, Section C). The interpretation of findings regarding dropouts has resulted in two contrasting views. One calls for more careful screening to eliminate "poor therapeutic risks," while the second argues that insight-based forms of psychotherapy may not be best for all psychiatric outpatients and recommends a systematic and continuous search for other kinds of therapy that show evidence of applicability to those patients who now do not enter or who discontinue therapy. The writer believes that the latter approach is the more enlightened one, since the evidence heavily suggests that large numbers of people in psychosocial stress either have not found help forthcoming or have been unable to accept the kinds of treatment offered. Also, as a consequence of the earlier studies of alcoholics, the writer feels that persons of low social class fail to receive treatment because of communication difficulties between such patients and middle-class therapists' value system. Lower-class individuals are generally action-oriented, which runs counter to the thinking-verbal orientation usually found among middle-class therapists. The Alcohol Clinic studies, primarily with lower-social-class persons, indicate that initial action in the form of gratifying the concrete needs expressed by the patient can be highly effective in establishing a therapeutic alliance. Further, emphasis is laid on the need for bold, brave, and barrier-breaking therapeutic approaches to help these individuals in what for many is a resocialization form of therapy. Although it is not within the purview of this paper to examine therapeutic techniques, but merely effectiveness of motivation for therapy, the writer cannot ignore the crying need for new therapeutic approaches to a large segment of the population. And one wonders if many of the reported failures of psychiatric treatment for large populations result from the inability of these patients to be treated or the result of limited therapeutic approaches not applicable to much of the population of psychiatric and social casualties.

In summary, data have been presented that show that emergency services have an increasingly important role in serving the psychiatric needs of communities. Further, the writer has intended to show that by an approach that utilizes a careful initial evaluation of the patient, his family, and his society, coupled with mobilization of intrahospital and extrahospital resources, a greater number of patients can be effectively motivated into a treatment setting. The frequent dropouts from therapy and the number of patients unable to accept treatment recommendations, as the result of rigid therapeutic models, have been discussed.

6.B. Treatment of Psychosocial Crises in the Emergency Service of a General Hospital

With some exceptions, the predominant influences inherited by this generation of American psychiatry are those flowing from the schools of psychoanalytic thought—those based on physiological-biochemical approaches, and more recently those developing from the emphasis on environmental determinants of emotional illness. In this section we describe the establishment of a psychiatric unit in a general hospital emergency service based on the flexible and coordinated uses of these varying conceptual frameworks.

Metropolitan general hospitals throughout the country have been challenged in recent years by ever-increasing demands on the services

---

Section 6.B. written, in collaboration, by Fred H. Frankel, Morris E. Chafetz, and Howard T. Blane.

Notes to Chapter 6 will be found on page 250.

of their emergency facilities, and a considerable proportion of these patients are recognized as having needs of a predominantly psychosocial nature. Traditionally, these usually very challenging problems are handled by residents in training who frequently have neither adequate supervision nor the clinical experience to provide the necessary patient care.

In order to improve the psychiatric attention in the emergency service of the Massachusetts General Hospital, where approximately 60,000 to 65,000 patient visits have been recorded annually in recent years, and where 10 percent to 12 percent of this number are conservatively considered to have predominantly psychosocial problems, the program outlined in the previous Section was put into effect in 1962. As indicated earlier, the program is based on research demonstrating the value of crisis intervention in motivating alcoholics in the emergency service to follow through on treatment in the outpatient alcohol clinic.

Among other things, our clinical approach emphasized the concept of crisis intervention, which provided the framework for the multidisciplinary, flexible, and versatile structure necessary to meet the practical needs of an emergency service while simultaneously supplying the academically cautious with a meaningful rationale.[3]

The word "crisis" implies a challenge to the personality, family, or community created by an altered set of circumstances for which adaptive resources are not readily available. It has long been recognized that mastery of a crisis can result in an enrichment of the personality, which then acquires resources to deal with similar events in the future. Failure to meet the challenge results not infrequently in a maladaptive response, which, too, is likely to be applied to similar challenges in the future—there burdening the personality with a handicap.

Intervention in crisis aims at assisting the individual toward meeting his crisis successfully, and at times entails little more than guidance, advice, or education. When analyzed more adequately, intervention implies an evaluation of the resources within the individual, an evaluation of the resources among those who surround him in the family and the community, and an assessment of his past personal history. This takes into account how he has handled previous crises in his life, his educational, vocational, marital, and social achievements, his preferences and values, and what he expects from professional help. He is then invited, with those around him and involved with him, to examine the strengths that are available to him, and to participate whenever possible in planning the steps immediately necessary for the successful resolution of the crisis.

Two corollaries of crisis intervention have influenced clinical practice in the Acute Psychiatric Service (APS). One assumes that when a patient seeks help for a crisis it is a propitious time to interest him in seeking help for his underlying problems. The other is that the strengthening of the patient's motivation to enter therapy and maintain the relationships is as much the responsibility of the caretaker and the agency as it is the responsibility of the patient. This contrasts quite forcibly with the prevailing attitudes regarding psychotherapy in which the responsibility for motivation lies largely with the patient.

Several psychiatric residents in the first and third years of training respectively are present around the clock to meet the requirements of the service, which is housed in offices not far from the emergency service. The patients come from a large number of sources, and no referral, whatever the source, is refused an evaluation. Many people seek assistance without being sent by others, and either present physical symptoms to the chief medical officer in the emergency service who may then refer them to the APS, or they request help for the psychosocial problems in direct terms and are sent to the APS. Many are sent or brought by relatives, friends, ministers, local doctors, social agency workers, police, and others, and some are referred by residents in the emergency service attached to other services.

Social workers are on duty from 9 A.M. to 9 P.M., with weekend coverage, and whenever possible they interview all patients first, and relatives or friends who accompany them. Supervision by senior personnel is available throughout the day, and by telephone consultation evenings and weekends. Evaluations of the problems are discussed with patients and their relatives, and plans formulated. Return visits, when indicated, are suggested and scheduled. The plans made attempt to meet the individual needs of the patients and include referrals to hospital units such as the psychiatry clinic or the alcohol clinic, and to community agencies. Other hospitals and institutions form essential parts of many dispositional plans, as does medication, advice, and counseling, or reassurance and the recommendation to return home and come in again only if necessary. Teaching conferences take place daily and are run by the senior staff.

A review of all records is undertaken by the coordinator each morning and the previous day's dispositions are reviewed. When indicated, further social service contact with patients or agencies is recommended and executed, and weekly review conferences are held to consider the outcome of these follow-through procedures. Consultation with community agencies prior to referring patients to them is considered mandatory.

Coordination of such a service, dealing as it does with about 600 visits a month (including repeat visits and scheduled appointments), entails the organization, supervision, and direction of personnel from several disciplines, the establishment of office routines, the maintenance of lines of communication among frequently changing staff members, and supervision of data collection for research purposes. Administrative, consultative, teaching, and research activities become inextricably bound up with the role of the coordinator, and the goals of the service have to be kept constantly in mind by him.

To provide adequate help for as many types of psychosocial problems as possible, evaluation must be thorough, the therapeutic orientation flexible and multidisciplinary, and the range of treatment modes wide. It is a happy situation that encourages mobility from one conceptual framework to another when one is more applicable than the other to the circumstances of the problem. Recommendations for hospitalization and electroshock therapy, medication, supportive case work, referral to family agencies, or advice on the problems of adolescence to parents in a struggle with a teen-age child, have to be made with as much care and confidence as that applied to recommendations for intensive psychotherapy. Not infrequently more than one treatment model is used in one case, thus drawing on the concepts from diverse theories.

The dividing lines between good practical psychiatry, mental health, and preventive psychiatry are faint, and in addition to a therapeutic orientation and the preventive aspect of crisis intervention, other opportunities arise for the prevention of maladaptation and maladjustment in patients and their relatives. For example, characterologically disturbed parents of young children at times present themselves on impulse in crisis and thereafter fail to show up for return appointments. Considerable effort has to be expended in trying to motivate them to embark on a suitable program with a community agency, or to return to the service if a further crisis arises. Where little alteration in the attitudes and behavior of such patients is likely to occur, attempts have to be made to modify or support environmental features in order to alleviate stress and minimize the deleterious effects on the children.[4]

In effect, any personal, family, or environmental feature that can be used as a means to alleviate crisis, set in motion the restoration of equilibrium, or contribute to mental health has to be taken advantage of. This applies largely to the unsophisticated public in lower socioeconomic groups, but not solely, as not infrequently members of more privileged socioeconomic groups are prevented by background and personality factors from using intensive psychotherapy, and require equally direct assistance leading to immediate goals.

Within the service itself mutual interdisciplinary regard and respect is of paramount importance. Pathways of communication have to be kept open, and discussion of opinions encouraged. Individual differences of approach among the residents are to be expected and accepted, and they are encouraged by example rather than edict to become aware of the indispensable and complementary nature of social service endeavors.

Successful articulation with other services is essential. Medical and surgical residents, often with little interest or experience in psychiatry, come to appreciate the value of the services of patient care, and their own anxieties are met by reasonable effort, assistance, and, when necessary, education in psychiatric principles. A psychiatric resident who handles a crisis at 2 A.M. instead of evading the clinical responsibility because the patient is either unsuitable for psychotherapy or is not committable performs an indispensable service. Good working relationships are essential when clinical responsibility has to be shared in problems such as attempted suicide or delirium tremens.

In addition, the maintenance of good relationships with community agencies is essential and frequently delicately balanced. Knowing an agency's facilities and scope of activities prevents inappropriate referrals. Little is calculated to disturb interagency relationships as thoroughly as ill-chosen referrals that illuminate the receiving agency's weaknesses instead of its strengths. Keeping the lines of communication open, and constant reevaluation of case dispositions in the light of subsequent events, helps to improve the knowledge of community facilities.

As with any organization involving numerous people who are all committed to a major goal, but whose individual work and accomplishments entail minor goals of secondary importance, the theoretical framework, direction, and coordination of an APS has to be well prepared and effective. For such a service to be competent it must comprise and comfortably absorb several different disciplines and, because it articulates with the public and other branches of medicine, it can offer ideal opportunities to demonstrate the participation of psychiatry in maintaining high levels of community health. In view of our experience, what may we recommend to other hospitals and agencies that plan to establish such services? Attainment of the goals of an emergency psychiatric service will depend largely on the influence exerted by supervisory personnel. This is all the more so when the nature of the setting requires the frequent rotation of most other professional personnel.

There can be little doubt that the competence of senior personnel depends largely on the extent and breadth of their clinical experience. Although advanced formal training in community psychiatry, mental health, and preventive principles are of considerable importance as preparation for such a role, the value of experience in general psychiatry cannot be overestimated. In order to meet the numerous obligations to his patients, colleagues who consult him, and the community agencies asking for guidance, the assiduous practicing general psychiatrist has had to borrow heavily from all psychiatric schools.

If he has ignored either the physiological-biochemical orientation, or the wealth of understanding derived from a grasp of psychoanalytic and dynamic principles, he will not readily qualify for the tasks involved. In an APS he will be called upon to advise on the administration of the most appropriate drugs and the dosage required, in addition to having to supervise and counsel personnel confronted by the challenge of manipulative patients or patients whose life-pattern is governed by the need to be the underdog and fail. If he has an acquaintance with the principles of mental health work, social psychiatry, and preventive psychiatry, his ability will be that much enhanced. Though concepts in some of these areas are new and in the process of development, and though his grasp will have been one largely of width rather than of depth, much of the teaching of the diverse schools distilled by a wide clinical experience will provide him with an uncommon perspective, exceptionally useful in the overall and direct control of the wide range of problems to be encountered in a service aimed at dealing with psychosocial crises. Hospitals and agencies planning to establish such services may profitably look to the range of the flexible and assiduous practicing general psychiatrists for part-time if not full-time assistance.

6.C. Modalities of Intervention in a Psychiatric Emergency Service

The "third revolution" in psychiatry, as it relates to an around-the-clock outpatient psychiatric service, implies a flexible approach to the disturbed individual in his social matrix, a short-term effort at matching his needs with available resources. It also shifts the emphasis from physician-oriented service to an emphasis on "reaching out" to motivate the patient, tailoring service to manifest needs, realignment of interpersonal forces to promote better coping, careful coordination with existing community resources, and constant improvisation.

Section 6.C. written by Alfred J. R. Koumans.
Notes to Chapter 6 will be found on page 250.

It is the intent of this paper to describe four modalities of intervention and their variants that have grown out of the clinical operations of one psychiatric emergency service, that is, the Acute Psychiatric Service of the Massachusetts General Hospital. These modalities are (1) crisis intervention, (2) coordination, (3) liaison, and (4) aftercare. Each modality, with its variants, will be described and illustrated by case material.

Crisis Intervention

Crisis intervention, described by Klein and Lindemann, among others, is particularly well suited to an emergency service.[5] Its aims, through realignment of a patient's inner and outer resources during a period of crisis, are to restore equilibrium and to prevent an acute breakdown from a rigidifying into a permanent one. The instance of Mrs. A., whose alarming situation ameliorated rapidly, illustrates the use of crisis intervention.

> Mrs. A. entered the Acute Psychiatric Service with suicidal wishes, a plan to shoot her husband who had left her, and inability to work and to handle her legal and financial affairs. Until recently, Mrs. A., whose social skills and work history were excellent, felt her marriage to be exemplary. Then she suffered several blows that turned her world upside down: her husband, who had agreed to care for her sick dog while she was at work, had shot the dog; she underwent a hysterectomy; and her husband deserted her. The last straws came when her son was drafted, and she received no presents for Christmas. In the course of three visits to the Acute Psychiatric Service, Mrs. A.'s dependency shifted from her rejecting husband to sustaining friends, her son, and agencies. Her hostility, which alarmed her, was brought into perspective and labeled as "protective" of her family; her obvious assets were used to help her overcome her lowered self-esteem; with legal aid she initiated separation proceedings; help with budgeting was provided; she began to work again. Follow-up three months later confirmed the impression of an adaptive resolution of the crisis.

A modification of classic crisis intervention may be called non-interpretive intervention. In this technique, the goal is resolution of an interpersonal crisis through active intervention by the psychiatrist, without clarification and interpretation to the patient. The approach may be fruitfully used with relatively unsophisticated patients, in which case it is often necessary to give advice or take action based on knowledge of the dynamics involved, without attempting to give the patient insight.

> Mrs. B., a 25-year-old compulsive housewife, came in complaining of inability to handle all that was involved in taking care of a new and larger house. She felt, as she said, that "the roof is cracking"; her marriage, already strained, also showed signs of cracking. She and her husband were seen together in the Acute Psychiatric Service, the precarious relationship was gently probed, and the couple referred for marital counseling in the psychiatric clinic. The couple never contacted the clinic, but Mrs. B. made several contacts with the Acute Psychiatric Service during the following months, and reported increasing stress. Mr. B. was invited to come in again for reevaluation of the situation. At this time, Mrs. B's burdens became more obvious; in addition to running the new house, she was caring for her invalid parents and a dependent sister, and Mrs. B. felt she had no choice in these matters. Her compulsive defenses were not up to coping with the added hostility. She was advised to sell the house, this being considered a way of giving her permission to relinquish the burdens of the house and the care of her parents. With this advice, her underlying hostility came on so strongly that brief hospitalization was necessary. Here integration took place on a more adaptive level and, upon discharge, she was able to reassume her responsibilities, make peace with her husband, and defer selling the house.

A further modification of crisis intervention may be termed concrete intervention, and consists of action in terms that are easily understood by the patient. Such action may include thorough evaluation, immediate relief, imposing controls, the expression of interest through letters and telephone calls, attention to basic needs, and continuity of care. This approach is aimed at providing motivation for behavior change, and an action-oriented, immediate kind of help. Impulsive patients sometimes respond more readily to this approach than to more indirect kinds of help; we have found the technique particularly useful in working with alcoholic patients. The case of Mr. C. illustrates the approach.

> Mr. C., a 50-year-old alcoholic without shelter, job, money, or family, came to the Acute Psychiatric Service asking for help. Since he had no immediate medical problem he was interviewed, given an effective tranquilizer, and sent to the "state farm" to dry out. During the 14 days he stayed there, we telephoned him and asked him to return to the Acute Psychiatric Service. He did so, jittery and without plans. He was given medication and introduced to the nurse of the alcohol clinic, who suggested an employment opportunity, which he took. For several months he maintained his contact with the nurse.

Coordination

A psychiatric emergency service attracts many patients whose problems are not acute; a common problem is the alienated or drifting patient who is involved with other agencies but not "getting anywhere," and who comes to us seeking a temporary and incidental helping agent; often a vain succession of contacts has served only to confuse or block more consistent treatment efforts. When this kind of vagrant helpseeker comes to a psychiatric emergency service, then it can function to sort out the untherapeutic imbroglio, attempt a confrontation, and by consistent effort and policy, allow for the concentration of hitherto random efforts. Often the only intervention needed is some kind of sorting out of contacts; after an assessment of an impasse, agencies may be added or eliminated.

The case of Mr. D. illustrates what we term coordination by concentration.

> Mr. D., the 26-year-old father of five, whose history included addiction, sexual deviation, arrests, and suicide attempts, came into the Acute Psychiatric Service saying

that he wanted to "change." His wife, whom he described as being depressed, had been going out with strangers; the children were neglected and unmanageable. Agencies already involved were two state hospitals, the Department of Public Welfare, a local psychiatric clinic, and a social service agency. None of them was aware of the involvement of the others. The Acute Psychiatric Service staff and a social worker in one of the involved agencies worked out a plan to be administered by the worker. Some of the agency contacts were retained, several were eliminated. Follow-up six months later showed a viable and productive arrangement.

In some cases the help of more than one agency is needed, but their contributions to the care of the individual are effective only if they time and coordinate their efforts. This is called coordination by cooperation, and is illustrated by the case of Mr. E., for whom we planned and coordinated a program involving the Visiting Nurses Association, a state hospital, a clinic, a rehabilitation service, and a training school.

Mr. E., a 47-year-old father, came in at the insistence of a public health nurse who had been caring for his wife. The nurse had noticed that he had a drinking problem, and felt that his wife and daughter seemed to encourage the drinking. After visiting the Acute Psychiatric Service, Mr. E. made an unsuccessful attempt to give up drinking on his own; he was finally admitted to the addiction center of a state hospital. After his discharge, we instituted and supervised a plan of care that included casework and vocational rehabilitation. Since he was afraid to go out when he was not drinking, a counselor made home visits, which focused on the earlier loss of a favorite daughter and permitted a belated grief reaction. After a year of combined casework and counseling, Mr. E. was sober and employed.

Liaison

A somewhat different type of problem frequently seen in an around-the-clock service is that in which the patient is involved with only one other agency, but in which the relationship, for whatever reason, needs outside help. In these cases, we may find ourselves in the position of mediator. For example, the difficulties in treatment of character disorders are notorious, and include the problems of tenuous contact, the need to test, and the multiplicity of people who can become involved. An on-call service is well suited to supplement the treatment relationship with an additional form of personal contact that is not too intense yet always available and that offers continuity even though many different people are involved. An example is the case of Miss F.

> Miss F., who had a long history of desertions by and between her parents and who had on occasion been hospitalized because of suicidal impulses, was in a continuing treatment relation with a social worker in our psychiatric clinic. Miss F. often made visits to the Acute Psychiatric Service, usually prompted by real or imagined separations from her therapist. These contacts provided an opportunity to ventilate the fears and furies that she feared might upset her worker, and served to reinforce and support a beneficial relation to her caseworker.

A somewhat different situation arises when a contact between patient and caretaker has not yet jelled into a therapeutic alliance; liaison work consists of fostering the relationship. In these cases, or in those involving patients who find it hard to obtain help on short notice, an emergency service may become a temporary repository, a bridge, or motivating agency toward ultimately appropriate care. Here, liaison work consists of holding maneuvers, as in the case of Mrs. G.

> Mrs. G. was referred to the Acute Psychiatric Service from a private clinic, where she was awaiting treatment of her depression. Being placed on the waiting list had disappointed her and she was upset. In the Acute Psychiatric Service she was given medication, the policies of overburdened clinics were explained to her, and her fears that she might receive electroshock treatments were allayed. She was given the option of returning to us if she needed to do so.

In the preceding cases, patient-caretaker relationships needed support. In other cases, the relationship is not viable, and a change may be needed. Our service, since it is not a continuous participant, is in an advantageous position for assessing and providing suitable alternatives. An example is seen in the case of Mrs. H.

> Mrs. H., a 22-year-old phobic woman, had been seen for short-term therapy in the psychiatric clinic. A year after termination, she came in to the Acute Psychiatric Service with her original complaints, complicated by intense anger at her husband. She was referred to the clinic again, but became delusional, and had to be admitted to the hospital. After discharge, she was referred for private psychotherapy, which meant that she would have to get a job. Within a week she had made suicidal gestures, became delusional, and began making frantic calls to us. It was obvious that her ego strengths had been overestimated; she was given phenothiazines and a social worker began to see her immediately on a supportive basis. Improvement was rapid, and medication was tapered off as she settled into treatment.

Aftercare

Partly as a consequence of recognition of the discontinuity between life in an institution and life in the community for patients who are discharged from a mental hospital and partly because of a current emphasis on early discharge, plans for aftercare become particularly important when patients seen in an around-the-clock service are institutionalized. Aftercare may be either short- or long-term, as illustrated by the cases of Mr. I. and Mr. J.

> Mr. I. is a 58-year-old deaf widower who was hospitalized because of recurrent suicidal tendencies. He was resentful of personnel in Acute Psychiatric Service, whom he blamed for hospitalizing him, but on the day of his discharge he walked 30 miles from the hospital to the Acute Psychiatric Service to see his doctor, ostensibly to tell him off. This was a turning point for him, because his hostile dependent character allowed him few relationships. The

"guilt" of the Acute Psychiatric Service was gradually expiated as a social worker helped with his financial problems and living arrangements, provided an improved hearing aid, and gave him a donated television set.

Here, a patient's character trait was used to help engage him in an aftercare project. He allowed the social worker to "make up for the injustice of committing him," and received assistance toward a more rewarding life.

One result of current hospital discharge policies is that an increasing number of actively psychotic patients are found in the community. Often one trusted individual serves as their link with reality, and the loss of this person or other disturbing events may precipitate a crisis for the patient. Prompt intervention may prevent rapid rehospitalization, as in the case of Mr. J.

> Mr. J., a chronic schizophrenic, came to the Acute Psychiatric Service and was sent to a mental hospital for custodial care. After his discharge, he found a local physician willing to "treat" him for the "horrible growth of hair" around his orifices. When the doctor moved to another town, Mr. J. again became caught up in psychotic ruminations. He returned to the Acute Psychiatric Service, where it was decided to give him a trial period of ambulatory aftercare, rather than returning him to the hospital; he was put on phenothiazines and urged to return the next day. For several months he had regular, but increasingly spaced, visits with the same doctor in the Acute Psychiatric Service; his need for medication decreased, his concerns shifted to social areas, and he attempted a few odd jobs. He continues on this basis at the present writing.

Both short-term and long-term aftercare require a certain amount of flexibility and inventiveness on the part of an emergency service, but results are often worth the effort required.

Clinical practice has been guided by the thinking of Lindemann and other formulators of community mental health philosophy. As the only available resource of its kind in the community, the Acute Psychiatric Service serves as a testing ground where concept and practice complement each other, and new ideas and practices are developed. Although the original name of the unit has been preserved, the services provided have expanded far beyond its original functions, and truly acute problems constitute a relatively small percentage of its caseload. We have rejected the concept of an emergency psychiatric service as a facility that merely provides rapid evaluation, referral, and drugs, in favor of an approach designed to meet the needs of the community. Thus the crisis approach has been adapted and supplemented by other treatment modalities in order to deal with patients whose problems are neither acute nor mainly personal.

In some cases, this modified approach causes discomfort in an academic center, where residents may hesitate to "adulterate" newly learned attitudes of nondirective probing into more action-oriented stances. Meeting the patient or his family half way by "reaching out" in terms of phone calls, letters, or home visits to remind a patient of his need for help may also require some reorientation.

When a psychiatric emergency service is interested in implementing care, it will soon find itself faced with the chronic patient, including those whose "crises" are manifestations of protracted maladaptive struggles. These patients come to an emergency service for any of a number of reasons. Often they have "missed the therapeutic boat" for other than purely personal reasons Some have attempted contact and been referred elsewhere; some have lost their way in an administrative maze, or have been trailed fruitlessly from one agency to another because of failures in communication; others have been turned away because few clinics cater to long-term cases, and few agencies accept psychotics. Others have "profited" from the abundance of independently operating agencies in urban centers and, gypsy-like, have skimmed these resources without settling. In some cases, if the "crisis" is not viewed as the patient's own concern, a few interventions requiring a minimum amount of time and effort may yield a modicum of effect. In others, only a carefully integrated and time-concert of assistance can provide the services needed, and no single agency, however resourceful and flexible, is sufficient. In either case, an emergency service is well equipped to provide the intervention or the integration of services.

The modality of coordination grew out of the trial-and-error management of these cases; we refused to discharge the responsibility until a referral had taken, or until all efforts had failed. Coordination requires the constant availability of the Acute Psychiatric Service, an active policy of following through on referrals, open communications with other facilities and with members of the patient's social network, a flexible administration, and a working knowledge of the aims and limits of community agencies. We have been able, for example, to replace untherapeutic contacts with more helpful ones, to arrange complex networks of ancillary facilities, and to provide consultation and moral support to other agencies.

Closely related, yet distinguishable from coordination, is liaison work. This term is used to describe our activities in instances in which ongoing relationship between patient and helper suffers from a disruption requiring remedial action. For example, often treatment (at least in the view of the patient) does not allow for certain types of behavior; then the APS may minister to temper tantrums, depressions, or anxieties. Sometimes a caretaker is not available, as happens frequently during summer vacations; perhaps a referral does not "take," and the other agency does not follow through. In these and similar situations, the availability and relatively impersonal nature of the APS (where patients do not always return to the same doctor) makes it particularly suitable for liaison work. We may, for example, support faltering casework contacts, hold patients on a "p.r.n." basis until the therapist returns, or pick up the pieces of broken appointments or other distress indicating a therapeutic mesalliance.

The maintenance of the psychotic person in his community, or his speedy return after brief hospitalization, are explicit objectives of the community mental health approach in psychiatry. This goal necessitates the development of aftercare services, and modalities of intervention tailored to suit this demand. We have met this challenge with the modalities of maintenance (with progress as a bonus), and aftercare proper, with the focus on reestablishing a disrupted social network. Both seem to flourish on the groundwork of an emergency service that provides the combination of rapid assessment, continuity of psychiatric and social service care, and a program adapted to the patient. Thus an around-the-clock outpatient psychiatric service constantly seeks to modify traditional techniques of care and to develop new modes of aiding people who come to the hospital in distress. These are some of the ways whereby the medical profession can provide equally good care to all members of society.

6.D. Current Status of Emergency Psychiatric Services in General Hospitals

In an earlier paper elucidating factors contributing to recent rises in the use of general hospital emergency services, we concluded that ". . . sweeping changes in the distribution of private health services . . . are aggravating long-standing difficulties of lower classes in negotiating private medical treatment and [are] forcing an across-the-board increase in the use of emergency facilities for health problems of all types and degrees."[6]

We further suggested that the sheer increase in numbers combined with a heightened sensitivity on the part of physicians to emotional features in illness has resulted in marked demands for more psychiatric service—even though there appears to have been no rise over the years in the proportion of patients presenting with primary or secondary psychological problems. Psychiatrists, for their part, seem ill-prepared to deal effectively with the unreflective lower-class patient who is the typical consumer of services in emergency settings.

In this section, using the literature as a guide, we will survey the facilities available to care for persons who come to general hospital emergency services with psychosocial problems. We will devote special attention to innovative arrangements that are realistically articulated with the requirements of the kinds of patients usually seen in general hospital emergency settings.

Before we can examine structures and procedures currently available to persons seeking immediate psychiatric care, it will be neces-

Section 6.D. written, in collaboration, by Howard T. Blane, James J. Muller, and Morris E. Chafetz.
Notes to Chapter 6 will be found on page 250.

sary to differentiate among the institutional medical settings in which these persons are commonly seen. These settings may be grouped into three broad (and to some degree overlapping) categories: (1) general hospitals with psychiatry departments, which are usually located in urban areas and are teaching hospitals with residency training programs in psychiatry; (2) general hospitals without psychiatry departments, which may be located in urban, suburban, or rural areas and are not ordinarily teaching hospitals; they may or may not have a psychiatrist on their staffs; and (3) psychiatric facilities per se comprising mental hospitals, both public and private, outpatient clinics, and mental health organizations that are unattached to medical centers. Characteristics of patients who apply for immediate care, as well as features of services offered, are undoubtedly related to type of setting, although any person who is a danger to himself or others will receive at least immediate disposition independent of whether he goes to a psychiatric facility or either type of general hospital.

Systematic, comprehensive information about the nature of services offered in each of the three types of settings is for the most part not available, although there are a handful of reports describing recent attempts to reorganize or institute 24-hour psychiatric services along unique lines in psychiatric and teaching general hospital facilities. The paucity of comprehensive information is especially surprising when one considers that federal regulations governing the construction of community mental health centers—which in most instances will be part of either a general hospital or a psychiatric facility—state 24-hour emergency care to be one of the mental health services required in order to qualify for federal construction and staffing funds. We have summarized the available information below, categorizing it according to type of setting.

General Hospitals with Psychiatric Departments

Until recently, teaching general hospitals have followed the time-honored, traditional practice of handling acute psychiatric problems in the hospital's emergency service by having a psychiatric resident on a stand-by basis. Under this system, the resident is usually called in for only the most gross and obvious cases such as blatant psychotic reactions, which in most instances require mental hospital commitment. Residents, apparently taking a cue from their mentors, see this duty as an onerous and unrewarding task that takes them away from other, more interesting responsibilities or, in the case of night duty, from home.[7]

Indeed, two recent books on general hospital psychiatry, one looking to its "frontiers," contain only passing references to work with psychiatric patients who come to emergency facilities.[8]

BRONX MUNICIPAL HOSPITAL

However, there have been several reports, emanating primarily from a few urban medical centers, of attempts to provide comprehensive and immediate psychiatric services, either through the general emergency service of the hospital or through its psychiatric outpatient clinic, or through a combination of both. It appears that the program instituted in 1956 at the Bronx Municipal Hospital of the Albert Einstein Medical Center was the first of these.[9]

This service is divided into two units, one in the hospital's "emergency room," the other an "emergency clinic" within the hospital's mental hygiene clinic.[10] In the emergency room patients are seen by first- and second-year psychiatric residents at the request of the admitting physicians (medical or surgical residents) assigned to the emergency room. That this is a very active around-the-clock service is indicated by the fact that nearly 9,000 psychiatric emergencies are evaluated annually.[11] Although it is unclear from the published reports, this unit apparently serves primarily as a means of screening patients and routing them to appropriate hospital facilities. It is not evident that routine supervision by staff psychiatrists is part of the unit.

The emergency clinic or psychiatric walk-in clinic is organized along traditional psychiatric clinic lines, with the major exception of providing on-the-spot evaluation and in selected instances short-term intervention—that is, no more than five sessions. Although it is implied in one report that the walk-in clinic is a 24-hour service,[12] Coleman and Rosenbaum state: "For patients who come at night, the Emergency Room of the hospital has a psychiatrist on duty around the clock who will work in conjunction with the Walk-In Clinic, which is open until 5 P.M. each day."[13]

Thus, many of the clinic's referrals come from the emergency room psychiatric facility. The walk-in clinic serves many patients, although in this regard there is some discrepancy between publications describing the service: according to a 1958 report, 3,600 patients were seen annually,[14] whereas a 1963 paper states: "We have been seeing 2,000 to 2,200 new patients yearly for the past several years."[15] Clinical activities in the walk-in clinic take place under staff supervision.

Although it is stated that "a social worker is on call at all times," it is not evident whether this applies to the emergency room unit as well as to the walk-in clinic.[16] It might be added that the relationship between the daytime walk-in clinic and the 24-hour emergency room psychiatric unit at Bronx Municipal Hospital is structurally the same as that between the adult psychiatric clinic and the acute psychiatric service at Massachusetts General Hospital.

ELMHURST

Another early program for psychiatric emergency care is that developed by Bellak at City Hospital, Elmhurst, Queens, New York, which began in 1958.[17] This is a difficult service to summarize because of its rather constant development over a period of years; the most recent description is by Bellak in 1964. The City Hospital program has many similarities to that of the Bronx Municipal Hospital, although until 1962 more emphasis was placed on the Trouble Shooting Clinic (a walk-in clinic) than on emergencies coming to the medical-surgical clinic (the general medical emergency service).

Since 1962 a staff member (it is not clear whether this person is a resident or a staff psychiatrist) has been assigned to all-night duty in the medical-surgical clinic and screens *all* patients admitted to it; in addition, social workers are on duty two nights during the week. This is the only medical-emergency setting other than that of the Massachusetts General Hospital that makes use of social work services in this way. There is presumably daytime psychiatric coverage as well, although it is not clear whether there is daytime social service coverage.

During the evenings, an average of 35 patients per night are screened, one-fourth to two-thirds of whom are "primarily in need of psychiatric care."[18] This means that an annual caseload of more than 12,000 patients with psychiatric problems are referred to appropriate treatment resources, either in the hospital or community; treatment does not appear to be offered in the medical-surgical clinic itself.

The Trouble Shooting Clinic, which is a walk-in facility, is organized similarly to the emergency clinic at the Bronx Municipal Hospital. It is a 24-hour service staffed by psychiatric residents, with experienced psychiatrists, psychologists, and social workers on its staff. Brief treatment—that is, three to five sessions—is available, and other hospital and community resources are used in the event of longer-term problems. As Bellak points out, the "unconventional name was chosen precisely to convey the fact that [the clinic] was designed to offer more than just help in major psychiatric emergencies."

It should be added that Bellak is explicitly aware of the differences between patients who come to the medical-surgical clinic because of a physical problem, "quite unaware of the fact that their problem is psychiatric," and patients who come to the Trouble Shooting Clinic aware that their problem is "emotional," "psychological," or "psychiatric." This distinction, more complex than at first appears, has implications for treatment, data-gathering, and examination of social attitudes.

OTHER EMERGENCY SERVICES

Well-organized emergency psychiatric services along relatively traditional lines were established about 1960 at the San Mateo County General Hospital in the San Francisco area,[19] at St. Vincent's Hospital in New York,[20] and at the Grace–New Haven (Connecticut) Community Hospital.[21]

At San Mateo, "24-hour coverage of the . . . emergency room was started, using residents, and an intake screening device capable of screening patients to the ward, to outpatient service, or back to their own homes."[22] Since its inception, a wide variety of dispositions have been developed, although approximately 60 percent of the annual caseload of 2,500 in 1962–1963 was admitted to the hospital. The aforementioned screening device is not further described, and it is not clear whether staff personnel participate; social work and psychological services do not appear to be available.

The emergency service at St. Vincent's presumably has a very heavy caseload, which is handled by psychiatric residents supported by attending psychiatrists. Unspecified emergency treatment is offered, and when further treatment is indicated, inpatient or outpatient referrals are made.[23] Again, the availability of the skills of mental health personnel other than psychiatrists is not stated.

The program at Grace–New Haven is more completely described than any so far reviewed:

> When a patient comes to the emergency room, he is first evaluated by the medical, surgical, or pediatric admitting house officer, who may, if indicated, request psychiatric consultation. . . . Problem cases are . . . discussed at daily clinic conferences run by staff psychiatrists and attended by psychiatric residents and social workers. Here the resident learns to assess the special requirements in management of the psychiatric emergency room patient.

Second- and third-year residents serve as the consultants in the emergency room. In the year 1960–1961, some 1,555 consultations were requested, accounting for approximately three percent of the total annual emergency room caseload.[24] The daily teaching conferences merit special notice; it is also probable, although not explicitly mentioned, that social work services are available. It is implied, however, that this is an on-call service ("psychiatrists . . . were called to the emergency room"), an implication supported by the fact that the service handles three percent of the total annual emergency room caseload, whereas a similar service at the Massachusetts General Hospital, with on-duty personnel, serves more than ten percent of the annual caseload.

Another emergency psychiatric service, organized along unique lines, is that established at the Massachusetts General Hospital in 1962.[25] This service grew out of the operations and findings of a federally supported demonstration and research grant that sought to provide comprehensive psychological, social, and physical care to alcoholics admitted to the general emergency service (emergency ward) of the hospital.

The unit, which had some 6,200 patient contacts in the year 1964–1965, is staffed by senior psychiatrists, rotating first- and third-year psychiatric residents, psychiatric social workers, a social work assistant, and research and clerical personnel. Each first-year resident is assigned to the unit for a two-month block and is on duty during normal work hours (8:30 to 5, Monday through Friday); his work is supervised by third-year residents who are assigned one day a week to the unit. The third-year residents also see particularly difficult and overflow cases. The first- and third-year resident scheme is also used for night and weekend duty, except that it is completely on a rotating basis. Psychiatric social workers are on duty throughout the day to early evening (up to 9 P.M.), and one is on call weekends. The social work assistant is on daytime duty.

Daily clinical teaching conferences, chaired in rotation by the two senior psychiatrists, the unit director, and two other senior staff psychiatrists, are held to discuss the management of selected patient and family problems. In addition, every morning one of the senior psychiatrists reviews the records of *all* patients seen in the preceding 24 hours; this permits the senior man to evaluate and, if necessary, augment or modify decisions with regard to treatment planning. During the day, a senior psychiatrist is available to discuss clinical problems as they arise; in addition, they supervise the third-year residents' supervision of the first-year men.

When a patient is referred to the unit by the admitting physician of the emergency service (an advanced medical or surgical resident), the patient and anyone who accompanies him is ordinarily first seen by a social worker, who, in addition to gathering information about the patient's problem and social history, makes an assessment of the psychosocial context that mobilized the patient to seek aid at the particular time he did. The resident usually sees the patient after the social worker, or sometimes while the social worker is seeing whoever accompanied the patient. In instances of destructive or grossly disturbed behavior, the resident may see the patient first.

Following contacts with patient and relatives, the psychiatrist and social worker hold an informal conference, calling in supervisory personnel as needed, to work out both an immediate and long-term disposition. Dispositions involve liaison with a wide variety of extrahospital community resources as well as inhospital facilities; usually the social worker handles many of the contingencies involved in out-of-hospital dispositions. The role of the social work assistant, who is a specially trained nonprofessional, is to handle details of such procedures as nursing home placement, telephone calls to various agencies, and to help patients make financial arrangements, all of which frees the trained social worker to use his time in ways (for example, casework) more suited to his skills.

This service aims at preventing crises from progressing into chronic conditions and to centralize care for chronic conditions. The first aim is largely an attempt to reduce the frequency of severe mental health casualties; the second is to lower the incidence of "shopping around," "dumping," and duplications of services that typify the relations of many persons with psychotic, severe characterological, or psychosomatic infirmities to community health services. The tools and tactics used in the attempt to attain these goals are manifold and, in addition to the traditional techniques of mental health workers (individual and group methods of psychological treatment and the chemotherapies), include a variety of innovative procedures.

For example, short-term group work keeps contact with alcoholics referred by the service to a state-supported inpatient facility, the idea being that at discharge these men will not be "dumped" back into the community without resources. A different kind of arrangement has been developed with a state mental hospital in which a social worker works both in the acute psychiatric service and in the mental hospital with patients referred from the service to the hospital, dealing with issues of life after discharge, a process that naturally involves family members.

Another kind of liaison is that with the local Visiting Nurse Association, whereby one of their staff works closely with members of the acute psychiatric service staff to coordinate care of patients in treatment at both places simultaneously. That the goal of centralization is being partially attained is suggested by the fact that during a six-month period, 27 percent of the patients who came to the acute psychiatric service returned for subsequent visits. A further hint of success is seen in the relatively low percentage (16 percent) of patients who were hospitalized for psychiatric reasons upon their first visit to the service.[26] Comparable percentages from Grace–New Haven Hospital (32 percent) and from San Mateo County General Hospital (60 percent) are twice as high and almost four times as high respectively.[27]

One final program that merits mention is the service at University Hospitals in Cleveland, which offers emergency consultation to medical-surgical wards, all outpatient clinics, and to the accident ward of the hospital.[28] This is a well-organized service staffed by resident psychiatrists; it makes use of social workers in initial evaluations. Approximately 50 percent of the on-call consultations involve requests from the accident ward.

In summary, it appears that only a handful of hospitals with psychiatric departments are concerned with innovative, community-oriented programs when it comes to providing care in the emergency service. A majority of hospitals continue to use traditional practices. The programs at Bronx Municipal Hospital, City Hospital at Elmhurst, and Massachusetts General Hospital are the only ones that take advantage of some of the recent advances in social psychiatry; the others represent admirable attempts at careful organization along traditional lines.

GENERAL HOSPITALS WITHOUT PSYCHIATRIC DEPARTMENTS

The attitude of the staffs of most nonteaching hospitals toward emergencies, psychiatric or otherwise, is succinctly summed up by Garetz:

> Although every physician is willing and ready to set aside his own personal needs in order to attend to a true emer-

gency, very few physicians are willing to work at unreasonable times and give up hours with their families, or times from relaxation, to attend to so-called emergencies (pseudo-emergencies) which could easily have waited for more routine management.[29]

This attitude is to some extent understandable when one takes into account small staffs and lack of residents or interns, but arguments based on convenience to professionals and on fine distinctions between "true" and "nontrue" emergencies are misleading and unrealistic. The facts are that even with small staffs, systems of rotation can be worked out that do little violence to convenience and that persons who present themselves are seen whether the emergency is "true" or not.[30] The desire of a majority of hospitals to restrict activities to the care of "true" emergencies, despite the evidence that emergency facilities are widely used for routine medical care,[31] must have its effect on the quality of care patients receive.

When we look specifically at care for psychiatric problems we get no encouragement. First, few hospitals express interest in dealing with psychiatric problems;[32] and second, a survey of more than 5,000 general hospitals revealed that "psychiatric services are most likely to be found in large, short-term voluntary hospitals located in metropolitan areas . . . [and] least likely to be found in small proprietary hospitals located in rural areas."[33] If all psychiatric services are this restricted, provisions for emergency care per se must be almost nonexistent.

We know of only two attempts to provide emergency psychiatric services in nonteaching general hospitals. The first, in Escambia County, Florida, involves a cooperative arrangement among six private psychiatrists and three local general hospitals to provide services for acute psychiatric problems.[34] This arrangement appears to be one means of providing a much-needed service for nonmetropolitan areas. The major defect is that services are not customarily available for persons without the means to pay for them, so that acutely disturbed indigents are more likely to be jailed than hospitalized.[35]

The other, at the Memorial Hospital in North Conway, N. H.,

is a federally supported demonstration project designed to offer comprehensive services to persons with alcohol problems in a rural area.[36] This unit is run by an internist and a social worker with the consultation of a psychiatrist and psychologist; the project is loosely linked for consultative and teaching purposes to members of the psychiatric and social service departments of the Massachusetts General Hospital. Service is provided on a 24-hour emergency basis through the accident ward of the Memorial Hospital. The fact that emergencies are dealt with on an on-call basis is compensated for by the smallness and intimacy of the hospital community. This unit is described in fuller detail in the next Section.

What is most interesting about this project is that after initial growing pains, the community has made increasing demands for similar services to persons with psychosocial problems other than those related to the use of alcohol. The project serves as a model of what can be done in rural settings that lack specialized resources when bridging mechanisms to urban teaching centers are developed.

PSYCHIATRIC FACILITIES

Results of a recent national survey of emergency services in psychiatric facilities[37] show that most hospitals report 24-hour coverage.[38] It is, however, evident that this follows the traditional arrangement of a resident who is called when it is obvious that hospitalization is required or when the patient demands to see him. Only nine percent of the 170 institutions responding (out of 176 contacted) indicated emergency duty as an exclusive assignment in their residency training program, and only seven percent reported the full-time availability of a staff psychiatrist. Nevertheless, these figures are higher than those for general medical settings.

Several walk-in clinic arrangements have been reported; examples are the walk-in clinic at the Massachusetts Mental Health Center in Boston[39] and the "life crisis" clinic at the Rush Center for Problems in Living in Los Angeles.[40] The latter has obvious constraints in that service is limited to state residents over $17\frac{1}{2}$ years of age and to a maximum of six visits per patient; further, the qualification that treatment is begun on the day of application "if possible" suggests that the implication that anyone can get psychiatric attention at any time is misleading.

Another kind of emergency service in a psychiatric facility is represented by the emergency treatment offered to persons applying for admission to Kings County Psychiatric Hospital in New York.[41] Its aim is to reduce the incidence of hospitalization of severely disturbed patients by means of immediately applied outpatient therapeutic measures.

Another program dealing with emergencies that involve severe psychopathology deserves mention, although it does not, strictly speaking, meet the criteria for inclusion in this review. This is an on-call, home-visit team that operates out of the offices of a county health department in a thinly populated area of Maryland; it responds immediately and at any time of day or night to calls for help where behavioral disturbance is reported.[42] Its original aim was to lower the number of disturbed persons who were put in jail until arrangements for mental hospitalization could be made. As it turned out, it became a more general emergency psychiatric service, in all likelihood another manifestation of the phenomenon observed in North Conway, N. H.

Comment

We have seen that psychiatric services in the emergency facilities of general hospitals as well as in those of psychiatric institutions are with few exceptions traditional and conservative. It is perhaps unfortunate that the word "emergency" has been used to denote clinical units in hospitals whose doors are open 24 hours a day—unfortunate because its use so easily leads to the empirical fallacy that if a unit is titled "emergency," then its users should have emergency psychiatric conditions. Translated into policies that govern admission, the "should have" often becomes "have-to-have." The consequence has been a series of sterile arguments and pronouncements aimed at defining the characteristics of the legitimate consumer of emergency services, presumably with an eye toward developing some sort of emergency "means" test to be given to applicants for care at emergency rooms.

Such definitional attempts have run into the further difficulty of reconciling the wish to see only genuine emergencies with the ethical dictum that if a person seeks you out for help he must be seen—an ethic especially difficult to evade in hospitals because of legal ramifications. The entire situation is further complicated by insistence on distinguishing examination and diagnosis from treatment, an arbitrary device perhaps useful for didactic purposes but otherwise a distortion of clinical practice. It is quite possible to conceive that treatment begins when the person decides to see the doctor, and it certainly does begin the moment the patient meets the doctor.

The reality that many fail to recognize is that "true" medical, surgical, or psychiatric emergencies, whether defined by a life-and-death, Dr. Kildare model or by the constraints of Garetz,[43] account for a minor proportion of the business in any metropolitan hospital emergency service—this despite any definitional barriers a hospital attempts to impose. People in distress with headaches, sore throats, chest and stomach pains, in panic, or intoxicated come to emergency rooms because they feel they need attention and need it now, not because they are necessarily in some objective state of emergency. The bulk of patients who come do not want to call beforehand, they do not want to make an appointment, and they wish to come when it is the right time for them—most often between 4 and 8 P.M. These people have always tended to seek medical help this way, and they do so even more now that the neighborhood doctor is no longer available.

Perhaps the wisest course for the medical profession would be to recognize this situation as a permanent part of institutional practice, to stop trying to exclude a patient group that will receive treatment anyway, and to plan rationally for the large numbers of people in distress who use the general hospital emergency room not because they necessarily have medical emergencies but because such usage represents one aspect of the way these people live.

Around-the-clock psychiatric facilities in general hospital emergency services can serve a unique preventive function. If, as we have suggested elsewhere, the act of seeking help is conceptualized as one aspect of a restitutive process, then the way in which we respond to the crisis can detour, impede, or block this process; or our reaction can facilitate, augment, or consolidate it.[44]

Intervention based on recognition of emotional components underlying, complicating, or accompanying physical complaints may be the initial step in preventing the development of a more serious disorder or of a chronic condition. The potential for early casefinding and preventive intervention with persons who tend to think of themselves in physical rather than psychological terms is very high in medical settings, and this preselection makes for a very different kind of patient population from that found in 24-hour settings that are explicitly psychiatric.[45]

Summary

In this paper we have examined 24-hour facilities available in general hospitals to persons in psychosocial distress. Among the urban, teaching hospitals are a few that have instituted innovative around-the-clock services. For the most part, however, urban general hospitals rely on the on-call psychiatric resident who is called in to make a disposition—usually mental hospitalization—only for grossly disturbed patients. In nonteaching hospitals, use of medical facilities on a 24-hour basis tends to be discouraged. Psychiatric facilities appear to be in the forefront as far as innovative arrangements are concerned, but here, too, traditional practices prevail in the vast majority of instances. We suggest that it be recognized that certain large segments of the population will always turn to 24-hour services for care; only this recognition can enable rational planning for service to occur.

6.E. An Alcoholism Treatment Facility in a Rural Area

Providing adequate mental health facilities and services is a vexing problem for the nation as a whole, but doubly so for rural sections. The past quarter-century has witnessed the development of a whole range of new and effective treatment techniques (drug therapies, methods of enhancing motivation, flexible forms of individual and

Section 6.E. written, in collaboration, by Elliot Brown and Charles Taylor.

group therapy, therapeutic communities, crisis intervention, day hospitals, night hospitals, and halfway houses). But major effort is needed if these gains are to be more widely and evenly available. Such implementation requires time, money, community understanding, and support on a broad scale, and more professional mental health staff in all disciplines: psychiatry, public health nursing, psychiatric nursing, clinical psychology, and social work. Recent casefinding studies suggest that a phenomenally large number of people stand in need of some mental hygiene care, but professionally trained staff people who can use the newer treatment techniques seem in perpetually short supply. This is also true for the supply of money to build facilities and finance programs offering newer, more effective, health care patterns.

Trained manpower tends to cluster in a few metropolitan areas. Thus there is a disproportionate geographic dispersion that increases in magnitude as one goes from metropolitan training areas to smaller urban districts, to towns, and to rural areas. Even if there were not this geographic inequity, the size of the mental illness problem requires more personnel than could be adequately trained even if there were more training facilities than there now are. The increasing demand for teachers to train more personnel tends to reduce the already too small ranks of professional practitioners.

In rural areas there are three obstacles to the provision of services so badly needed. These are (1) a tendency to chronic economic distress, (2) low population densities, and (3) remoteness from academic and medical centers. In an experimental effort to provide at least one type of mental health service in a rural area, an alcohol rehabilitation unit has been developed at the Memorial Hospital of North Conway, N. H.

Estimates of the overall rate of alcoholism in New Hampshire have more than doubled in 15 years, from 2,690 per 100,000 in 1944 to 6,030 in 1958. Estimates of the number of alcoholics in New Hampshire have risen from 17,000 in 1953 to 30,000 a few years later. In terms of hospital beds and practicing physicians, New Hampshire is well below the national average. With our undersupply of hospital facilities, we would have trouble planning services even for just acutely ill alcoholics.

Conferences about these problems were held with the Massachusetts General Hospital's Alcohol Clinic and with the personnel of our state program. The present unit was the result of those meetings.

North Conway is a rural village, in Carroll County, the center of the Eastern Slopes Region and a popular ski and summer resort area in northern New Hampshire. The year-round population of the area (including the many small surrounding communities) is about 12,500. The 52-bed hospital provides obstetrical, medical, and surgical care, in addition to the new alcoholism unit. A group of thirteen doctors—general practitioners, surgeons, and pediatricians —from the surrounding area constitute the medical staff. In addition, there is a full complement of nursing, laboratory, x-ray, and other ancillary personnel.

Although the hospital has never refused to admit alcoholics, it has been recognized that physicians in active practice and nurses with many other types of patient to care for lacked the training, interest, and time needed for an effective regimen aimed at rehabilitation of the alcoholic. This realization led to the idea of the Alcohol Rehabilitation Unit, and forms its current rationale. Our experience to date, however, indicates that old ideas about what is wrong with these patients and old habits in defining their needs and caring for them are still prevalent and difficult to modify, and that there are similarities and differences between urban and rural areas in these matters.

In North Conway, few people have really known anything about the nature and usefulness of social casework, psychotherapy, and other rehabilitative measures for alcoholics and their families. In urban centers social workers, psychologists, and psychiatrists are usually part of a hospital staff. Social workers have records, budgets, and accomplishments that are known in the hospital. They have the opportunity for face-to-face contact with members of the medical staff and their mental health colleagues. No such opportunity has existed at North Conway. The director of the welfare department is a trained social worker, but she is virtually office-bound in carrying out her duties and not really visible in her professional role outside the welfare setting.

In the Eastern Slope area and in Carroll County generally, there are no professionally trained mental health personnel. The one hospital with university affiliation is 100 miles away. A state-operated, two-day-a-month clinic for diagnostic evaluation problems in young persons is 70 miles in a different direction. The few psychiatrists in private practice are in Portland (Maine), Lewiston (Maine), Laconia, and Concord, all of which are 60 to 85 miles away. The state hospital is 90 miles away. Not a single inpatient facility for persons with emotional problems exists within the county. Thus, a patient who can use outpatient treatment (with only an occasional brief one- or two-day period in the hospital) cannot be offered this option. He must be maintained completely as an outpatient or enter the State Hospital with its minimum in-hospital period and the major rupture of life at home.

As in urban areas, custodial care for alcoholics (in addition to that provided by general hospitals to patients admitted for delirium tremens, gastritis, and other acute medical manifestations of the illness) has been meted out by nursing homes, jails, houses of correction, and county infirmaries.

Some clergymen in the town, responding to the pressing needs of their parishioners, do an extensive amount of pastoral counseling and when they feel beyond their depth refer patients to the remotely located treatment facilities. These ministers have been articulate in expressing the need in the community for mental health resources. They have formed the community base of support for the alcoholism unit, interpreting the role of the unit to the larger community and encouraging those with the problem to avail themselves of the service.

Beyond a broad educational and community relations effort, consultation with physicians (who may be considering a patient for referral) seems likely to yield the best results. In such encounters the physician has the opportunity to see the social worker's approach to a particular patient's problem, and can be encouraged to deal with his own ambivalence about "whether anything can be done." This same approach is used with relatives or friends of potential patients who come to see what is available and to seek encouragement in their efforts to get help for the alcoholic.

A principal feature of the rural community is its "intimacy." Word of mouth is a major and potent source of information. Informality characterizes the conduct of most businesses nearly as much as it is the main feature of purely social relationships. The staff of the unit has experienced this intimacy as a double-edged sword. The success or failure of the unit in particular instances may become common knowledge, and the potential patient risks exposure and shame in applying for help in the unit. It is yet to be seen whether community interest and concern can be fostered so that seeking help will be not only an acceptable, but also a worthwhile, thing to do.

Emphasis on face-to-face relationships and informality may work some initial hardship on patients seeking help. But it has positive features, too. Because of the informality and dispatch with which most business is conducted, establishing widely effective community relations for the unit has not been difficult. In a brief span of time the unit social worker has developed sound and productive relations with major organizations in the community, with the school system, the service clubs, the clergy, the police, the radio station, and the local offices of state agencies. Even "going through channels" is accomplished quickly, with little red tape. It is a simple matter to get invited to speak to one of the service clubs, to obtain public service time on the radio, or to gain permission to engage in research and teaching in the local high school. All of these have seemed in part related to the need within the community for help with some problems.

The unit's unique therapeutic potential is illustrated by the following case:

> A 50-year-old man had been severely alcoholic for 20 years. His drinking history included the entire range of beverage and nonbeverage alcohol. Recently he had consumed only beer, but his pattern of long binges continued. A preexisting lung condition, long quiescent, was becoming an acute problem again during each binge. Treatment attempts had been made sporadically over the entire span of his manifestly pathologic drinking. These included several admissions to the state hospital, commitment to the

County Farm, a "live-in" occupational arrangement in a neighboring state with attendance at Alcoholics Anonymous seven nights a week, disulfiram therapy as an outpatient without other treatment, and confinement in the local "drunk tank" (frequently at the patient's own request).

At the point of referral to the treatment unit, the patient's situation and health were testimony to the failure of previous treatment attempts. His economic functioning could only be called marginal, although he had an indulgent employer. His wife and one child were living apart from him. The only relief in this bleak picture was that his current employer (while believing that the patient was essentially a "bum") kept him on the payroll despite extensive absenteeism because, when he could work he was an "artist" at the particularly demanding job that he'd learned only after being hired, and the hostile-dependent relationship between the patient and his employer evidently provided some gratification to the latter.

The patient presented himself to the unit as a tremulous, sad-looking bleary-eyed, frightened man who looked much older than 50 years. He related as a child seeking help from an adult. He anticipated a moralistic, punitive response from the caretakers and seemed relieved and surprised when this was not forthcoming. He was despondent about the prospects for therapeutic benefit, since so much effort had been expended on his behalf over a 20-year period.

The treatment program consisted of a meticulous physical examination followed by therapy for his lung condition and for psychomotor seizures. Hospitalization was made immediately available whenever a "slip" occurred. Other measures included psychiatric evaluation; weekly casework treatment for the patient, spouse, and children; occasional "family group interviews"; consultation with the employer; and support of attendance at Alcoholics Anonymous.

In individual casework interviews the patient voiced depressive feelings about his failure to create a wholesome family life. These longings were related to his very deprived childhood in a nearby lumbering community, his father's alcoholism, and his mother's physical and mental deterioration after a massive stroke. His depressive episodes associated with unhealthy drinking behavior would occur following incidents that reactivated his feelings that he had no family life. The goals of treatment were to help him decide what constituted reasonable gratification in his relations with his family and to support his effective functioning as an employee, husband, and father.

In the 16 months since referral many changes have taken place. The wife has been reunited with her husband. A beginning has been made at resolving some of the conflicts in the marriage, some having to do with the husband's drinking and others essentially unrelated to it. The patient's functioning, both as head of the household and as employee, has improved substantially. He is again being consulted about the conduct of family affairs and is actively helping his child (a high school senior) plan the financing of further education. On the job he now feels he really earns his wages, and the hostile-dependent quality of the relationship with his employer has decreased markedly.

While a 20-year, severely pathologic drinking history has not been reversed in 16 months, the patient's drinking is now only one-tenth of what it had been during the past several years. His absenteeism at work has decreased correspondingly. We feel that our success to date in this case (compared with previous attempts) is primarily a function of our direct involvement in the community and our consequent ability to be very active on behalf of the client, to be able to respond immediately and flexibly to any crisis with hospitalization, medication, or a quick home visit, to shore up wavering motivation and hope, and to enlist the aid of many people in the person's life to provide a comprehensive program.

A subject of continuing concern for a treatment unit of this type is the matter of staff recruitment. There exists no real knowledge about the potential of a rural area to recruit from its midst a sufficient number of caretaking and professional personnel to meet its own needs. With regard to recruitment of professional staff, the most promising approach seems to be that of offering a particularly good salary, at or above the level of a metropolitan area, and good fringe benefits (health insurance, travel to professional meetings and so forth) to compensate for the isolation that is the lot of the professional person in a rural facility for the greater part of the time.

A further method for dealing with the issue of professional isolation is an elaboration and extension of the network of relations between rural and urban health centers. For the hospital itself the beginnings already exist; cooperative agreements have been worked out for getting certain kinds of laboratory analyses, consultations on X rays, and special diagnostic evaluation procedures. Similar bridging mechanisms have been incorporated into the organization of the Alcohol Rehabilitation Unit at the Memorial Hospital. We have worked out cooperative arrangements for supervision, consultation, and staff education with the psychiatric and social service staffs at Massachusetts General Hospital in Boston. Thus we can draw on the training and experience of psychiatrists, psychologists, social scientists, and psychiatric social workers there in developing and carrying out the several aspects of our program.

Our psychiatric consultant sees patients directly for evaluation and consults in the treatment and management of all patients. A social casework consultant advises the social work staff on treatment and on the community relations aspects of the program. A research advisor has helped us to develop procedures to evaluate our program and methods of organizing and reporting our findings; he also helped us develop a research inquiry on teen-age drinking attitudes and practices in the local regional high school.

Provision has been made for frequent consultation between the direct service staff, on station, and the consultant and resource staffs in Boston. In addition, emergency telephone consultation is possible, and the facilities at Massachusetts General Hospital are available to unit patients if and when no other resource is nearer.

This model, while basically similar to that used in the provision of medical and surgical care, is apparently unique with respect to the provision of mental health services. We feel that it is a viable model, strikingly more effective than the "traveling clinic" approach. We commend it as a pattern worthy of development for the future.

Notes

1. J. V. COLEMAN and P. ERRERA, "The General Hospital Emergency Room and Its Psychiatric Problems," *American Journal of Public Health*, 53:1294-1301, 1963.
2. A. H. STANTON and M. S. SCHWARTZ, *The Mental Hospital* (New York: Basic Books, 1954).
3. E. LINDEMANN, "The Meaning of Crisis in Individual and Family Living," *Teachers College Record*, 57:310, 1956; D. C. KLEIN and E. LINDEMANN, "Preventive Intervention in Individual and Family Crisis Situations," in G. CAPLAN (ed.), *Prevention of Mental Disorders in Children* (New York: Basic Books, 1961), chap. 13, pp. 283-306.
4. F. H. FRANKEL, "Emotional First Aid," *Archives of Environmental Health*, 2:824-827, 1965.
5. KLEIN and LINDEMANN, *op. cit.*
6. M. E. CHAFETZ, H. T. BLANE, and J. J. MULLER, "Acute Psychiatric Services in the General Hospital. I. Implications for Psychiatry in Emergency Admissions," *American Journal of Psychiatry*, 123:664-670, 1966.
7. COLEMAN and ERRERA, *op. cit.*; M. E. SCHWARTZ and P. ERRERA, "Psychiatric Care in a General Hospital Emergency Room. II. Diagnostic Features," *Archives of General Psychiatry*, 9:113-121, 1963.
8. L. LINN (ed.), *Frontiers in General Hospital Psychiatry* (New York: International Universities Press, 1961), p. 58.
9. N. E. ZINBERG (ed.), *Psychiatry and Medical Practice in a General Hospital* (New York: International Universities Press, 1964).
10. M. D. COLEMAN and M. ROSENBAUM, "The Psychiatric Walk-in Clinic," *Israel Annals of Psychiatry and Related Disciplines*, 1:99-106, 1963; M. D. COLEMAN and D. ZWERLING, "The Psychiatric Emergency Clinic: A Flexible Way of Meeting Community Mental Health Needs," *American Journal of Psychiatry*, 115:980-984, 1959; R. M. GLASSCOTE, D. S. SANDERS, H. M. FORSTENZER, and A. R. FOLEY, *The Community Mental Health Center: An Analysis of Existing Models* (Washington, D.C.: Joint Information Service [APA-NAMH], 1964); M. ROSEN-

BAUM, "Psychiatric Residency in the General Hospital," in L. LINN (ed.), *Frontiers in General Hospital Psychiatry* (New York: International Universities Press, 1961).

11. We have used quotation marks around the names given to these units because of the highly variable use of terms to designate emergency services from one hospital to another. General medical-surgical emergency services are designated by a variety of terms, such as emergency room, emergency ward, emergency clinic, accident ward, and medical-surgical clinic. There is almost as great a variety of terms used to describe emergency services directly linked to psychiatric units within general hospitals (for example, emergency clinic, walk-in clinic, trouble-shooting clinic, acute psychiatric service), although there appears to be a trend toward consensus by naming these "walk-in clinics." It is of interest to note that in later publications the Bronx Municipal Hospital emergency clinic is referred to as the "psychiatric walk-in clinic."

12. GLASSCOTE, SANDERS, FORSTENZER, and FOLEY, *op. cit.*

13. COLEMAN and ZWERLING, *op. cit.*

14. COLEMAN and ROSENBAUM, *op. cit.*

15. COLEMAN and ZWERLING, *op. cit.*

16. COLEMAN and ROSENBAUM, *op. cit.* We are aware from our own experience that such discrepancies can easily occur when reports confuse number of patient visits and number of patients. This is a possible explanation of the discrepancy noted; it is unlikely in these times that the above figures represent a decline in the use of emergency services, although this too is a possible reason for the differences in the two reports.

17. ROSENBAUM, *op. cit.*

18. L. BELLAK, "A General Hospital as a Focus of Community Psychiatry," *Journal of the American Medical Association*, 174: 2214-2217, 1960; "The Comprehensive Community Psychiatry Program at City Hospital," in L. BELLAK (ed.), *Handbook of Community Psychiatry and Community Mental Health* (New York: Grune and Stratton, 1964); M. GOLIN, "This 'Trouble-Shooting Clinic' Strengthening a Community," *Journal of the American Medical Association*, 171:1697, 1959; J. HIRSCH,

"This Trouble-Shooting Clinic Provides First Aid for Emotional Problems," *Modern Hospitals,* 95:102, 104, 1960.
19. BELLAK, "Comprehensive Community Psychiatry Program...."
20. GLASSCOTE, SANDERS, FORSTENZER, and FOLEY, *op. cit.*
21. *Ibid.*
22. COLEMAN and ERRERA, *op. cit.*; P. ERRERA, G. WYSHAK, and H. JARECKI, "Psychiatric Care in a General Hospital Emergency Room," *Archives of General Psychiatry,* 9:105-112, 1963; SCHWARTZ and ERRERA, *op. cit.*
23. GLASSCOTE, SANDERS, FORSTENZER, and FOLEY, *op. cit.,* p. 47.
24. *Ibid.,* p. 176.
25. ERRERA, WYSHAK, and JARECKI, *op. cit.*
26. M. E. CHAFETZ, "Acute Psychiatric Services in the Emergency Ward," *Massachusetts General Hospital News,* 222:1-3, 1963; "The Effect of a Psychiatric Emergency Service on Motivation for Psychiatric Treatment," *Journal of Nervous and Mental Disease,* 140:442-448, 1965; F. H. FRANKEL, M. E. CHAFETZ, and H. T. BLANE, "Treatment of Psychosocial Crises in the Emergency Service of a General Hospital," *Journal of the American Medical Association,* 195:626-628, 1966.
27. This percentage excludes alcoholic patients, since so many of them (45 percent) are sent to a state-supported domicile for alcoholics. To include alcoholics and their hospitalization would inflate the psychiatric hospitalization figure to almost 27 percent; to include alcoholics and not their hospitalization would deflate it to less than 15 percent. It should, however, be noted that slightly more than 9 percent of the alcoholics were hospitalized for psychiatric reasons.
28. ERRERA, WYSHAK, and JARECKI, *op. cit.*; GLASSCOTE, SANDERS, FORSTENZER, and FOLEY, *op. cit.,* p. 59.
29. J. T. UNGELEIDER, "The Psychiatric Emergency: Analysis of Six Months' Experiences of a University Hospital's Consultation Service," *Archives of General Psychiatry,* 3:593-601, 1960.
30. F. K. GARETZ, "The Psychiatric Emergency," *Medical Times,* 88:1066-1070, 1960.
31. J. R. MCCARROLL and P. A. SKUDDER, "Hospital Emergency Departments: Conflicting Concepts of Function Shown in

National Survey," *Hospitals,* 34:35-38, 1960; D. R. MILLER, "The Hospital Emergency Service," *Journal of The Kansas Medical Society,* 63:85-88, 1962.
32. MCCARROLL and SKUDDER, *op. cit.*
33. COLEMAN and ERRERA, *op. cit.*
34. P. H. PERSON, JR., F. L. HURLEY, and R. H. GIESLER, "Psychiatric Patients in General Hospitals," *Hospitals,* 40:64-68, 1966.
35. R. M. GLASSCOTE, E. CUMMING, D. W. HAMMERSLEY, L. D. OZARIN, and L. H. SMITH, *The Psychiatric Emergency: A Study of Patterns of Service* (Washington, D.C.: Joint Information Service [APA-NAMH], 1966); E. S. MYERS, "Comments: Conference on Handling Emergencies," *American Journal of Psychiatry,* 122:224-225, 1965.
36. GLASSCOTE, CUMMING, HAMMERSLEY, OZARIN, and SMITH, *op. cit.*
37. E. BROWN and C. TAYLOR, "An Alcoholism Treatment Facility in a Rural Area," *Mental Hygiene,* 50:194-198, 1966.
38. This section does not pretend to be a comprehensive review of emergency services in psychiatric settings; the interested reader may turn to the recently published survey by GLASSCOTE, CUMMING, HAMMERSLEY, OZARIN, and SMITH, *op. cit.*
39. *Ibid.,* MYERS, *op. cit.*
40. J. R. EWALT, S. ZASLOW, and P. STEVENSON, "How Nonpsychiatric Physicians Can Deal with Psychiatric Emergencies," *Mental Hospitals,* 15:194-196, 1964.
41. M. STRICKLER, E. G. BASSIN, V. MALBIN, and G. F. JACOBSON, "The Community-Based Walk-in Center: A New Resource for Groups Underrepresented in Outpatient Treatment Facilities," *American Journal of Public Health,* 55:377-384, 1965.
42. H. WALTZER, L. D. HANKOFF, D. M. ENGELHARDT, and I. C. KAUFMAN, "Emergency Psychiatric Treatment in a Receiving Hospital," *Mental Hospitals,* 14:595-596, 600, 1963.
43. R. W. CAMERON, "County Psychiatric Emergency Services," *Public Health Reports,* 76:357-359, 1961.
44. GARETZ, *op. cit.*
45. CHAFETZ, BLANE, and MULLER, *op. cit.*
46. BELLAK, "Comprehensive Community Psychiatry Program. . . ."

Chapter 7
Trends
in
Prevention

We have documented, in the preceding papers, the view that alcoholics who receive treatment are likely to be those suffering the most severe ravages of the illness and who are most difficult to treat. Therefore, most of what we know about the genesis and course of alcoholism is based on inquiries with this same group of late-stage alcoholics, and it has never been clear whether the personality, social, and physical factors implicated as causative agents precede the onset of alcoholism, or whether they are caused by it. On the other hand, increasing amounts of information are becoming available about nonpathological drinking patterns and their personality correlates, particularly among high school and college student populations.

Clearly, there is a continuum or gradient between normal drinking and alcoholism yet, with the exception of the McCord's work, neither prealcoholics nor individuals with beginning evidence of alcohol problems have been investigated;[1] obviously, the reason is that such persons do not of themselves come to the attention of investigators. In treatment settings, patients rarely seek evaluation because they are afraid they *might* become labeled as alcoholic, just as patients rarely seek aid for drinking problems that have not as yet interfered with psychological, social, or physical functioning.

If we are to become engaged in prevention, we must change our focus from an exclusive attention to normal drinking and/or full-blown alcoholism, and begin to focus on what we refer to as "alcohol-related problems." In our own work, we use this term to refer to any problem, either medical, social, or psychological, which is accompanied by the use of alcohol, no matter how great or little the amount. We do not assume a causal connection between the alcohol use and the problem, but we use this definition to identify populations of persons in trouble, where alcohol may be implicated. We see such populations as potentially giving rise to a disproportionate number of alcoholics relative to the total population. Naturally, it is only by following samples from such populations over prolonged periods that we will be in a position to justify this assumption.

What are some examples of such alcohol-related problems? College students in academic or administrative difficulty that involves drinking; students who participate in campus affrays after drinking beer;

young people participating, after or during drinking, in public disturbances; persons who don't go to work after a party; persons who commit a crime, or who are involved in automobile or other accidents during or after drinking. These behaviors are not uncommon, and are not necessarily pathological in a psychological sense; it does, however, seem reasonable to expect that the incidence of development of severe alcohol problems will be higher among people with these kinds of alcohol-related behavior than among people who have not exhibited such behavior. It may be that such behaviors are not inevitably transitory or of a single-episode variety, but are prodromal, and signs of an underlying process.

In order to study such populations, we must adopt an active rather than a passive orientation toward casefinding. The papers included in this chapter describe two such efforts on our part, and the rationale for undertaking each study. The first paper includes a description of what we have nicknamed the "court cases" project; this is now nearing completion, but results are not yet available. The second and third papers describe the development and implementation of a program promoting early case-finding and treatment by public health nurses.

7.A. Trends in the Prevention of Alcoholism

The prevention of illness has always been the ultimate goal of the health sciences, and while it has been attained in many physical illnesses this goal has never been reached in mental illness nor in social deviance (unless we consider general paresis and certain toxic psychoses). The social scientist has typically viewed prevention as an elusive will-o'-the-wisp, and infrequently concerns himself with it. In the case of alcoholism, this reluctance on the part of scientists has exerted no restraining influence on temperance workers, legislators, and others who have proposed or instituted preventive programs that reflect little consideration for established fact or appreciation for

Section 7.A. written by Howard T. Blane.
Notes to Chapter 7 will be found on page 291.

social realities. Historically, the effect of such programs on the incidence and prevalence of alcoholism has been imperceptible.

Recently, however, it appears that the scientist is becoming less of a reluctant dragon and more of a cautious optimist in regard to the possibilities of preventing, or at least substantially reducing the incidence and prevalence of alcoholism. The implications of current research and thinking for primary and secondary prevention are beginning to shape up into something of a groundswell. Before looking at some of these trends, it is perhaps helpful to make a distinction between primary and secondary prevention in alcoholism. Primary prevention is the application of procedure(s) to prevent the occurrence of problems associated with the use of alcohol among individuals in a drinking society. Secondary prevention is the application of procedures to stop, or reverse, processes that if continued would, on actuarial evidence, lead to alcoholism. I will not concern myself with tertiary prevention, which is usually thought of as treatment of the full-blown illness, since theoretically it does nothing to reduce incidence and in fact, with respect to alcoholism, does little to reduce prevalence.

What are the signs that point to the possibility of primary prevention, of preventing pathogenic processes from ever getting started? The classic approach to public health problems is epidemiological, that is, the study of the spatial and temporal distribution of an illness in a population. The descriptive epidemiology of drinking practices in the United States, particularly among teen-agers, is virtually complete, and as George Maddox has recently pointed out, longitudinal studies are already under way that will tell us a great deal about the relation between teen-age drinking practices and the development of alcoholism in adulthood.[2] In the meantime, these studies give us promising leads as to the identification of high risk or susceptible groups. This is a point to which I will return. Other studies are under way that examine the association between youthful drinking practices and other personality and social factors. As these interconnections are spelled out it is not at all impossible that critical associations will be found that are amenable to planned change.

Another area that is receiving more attention than before is the study of social perceptions of alcohol, of its use and of its effects, and the relation of these perceptions to behavior. This is an area that has received little systematic attention, although Robert Lindner as early as 1945 coined the phrase, "the romance of alcohol" to denote a set of beliefs, values, and attitudes about alcohol that he presumed to be prevalent in American culture and related to drinking and crime:

> ... Much of overindulgence is engaged upon with the full expectation—and hence the preparation or "set"—for particular effects: and these effects then come about independently of the exertions of the beverage. ... Embodied in this romance are some of the following canards: drinking makes for courage ... enhances sexual attractiveness and prowess ... increases skilfulness ... and makes one happy.[3]

More recently, Kenneth Polk has related alcohol use among teenagers to the value system of the adolescent subculture.[4]

The presence and identification of social perceptions of alcohol raise two questions highly relevant to prevention. First, are such perceptions related to the pathological use of alcohol? It seems plausible that they should be, but the presumed relationship has no sound empirical basis. Second, how are these perceptions transmitted? It seems a likely possibility that negative perceptions of alcohol (for example, "alcohol is bad"; "it will damage your health") are transmitted from generation to generation through parental channels and socializing agents, such as the church and school; but that positive or hedonistic myths (compare Lindner's "romance of alcohol") are transmitted within peer groups and by advertising media. The identification of the content of cultural myths and their chains of transmission opens the way for shortcircuiting those paths that give access to the continuity of irrational, ambivalent conceptions of alcohol that are in all likelihood closely linked with alcohol pathology.[5]

Along somewhat different lines is Chafetz' analysis of drinking behaviors and situations that distinguish national groups that have high rates of alcohol consumption, but markedly different rates of alcoholism.[6] The drinking behaviors he lists include speed of drinking, presence or absence of intoxication, and degree of tenseness or relaxation while drinking. Situational factors include presence or absence of food, presence or absence of another person(s), drinking standing or sitting, and tenseness or relaxation of social atmosphere. Based on his analysis, Chafetz has made concrete proposals that young people be given didactic course materials that focus on experiences with alcohol where the effects of these factors in their various combinations can be seen. He has further suggested that actual drinking experience be undertaken within a neutral education setting; both of these approaches, Chafetz feels, will make for a "practiced drinker" with nonconflicted and guilt-free attitudes toward alcohol. He predicts that such drinkers "will have lower incidence of undesirable effects from alcohol than the unpracticed drinker with guilt and conflict about drinking."

Also in the educational area is the work of Allen Williams and his associates, who have graciously given me permission to report some of their findings prior to their publication elsewhere. Junior high school students took part in small group discussions; some of the groups discussed drinking for one week, while the others discussed current affairs. Measures given beforehand and repeated several times after the groups were dissolved show an initial positive change in attitudes toward drinking; these positive attitudes decay over time. Factual knowledge about alcohol use is increased after group discussion and continues over time. The most important finding, however, has to do with self-reported drinking behavior. Williams' results a year later show that children in the control group who drink have a significantly higher incidence of repeated episodes of intoxication than subjects who underwent the learning experience. These findings tend to complement the position adopted by Chafetz that knowledge about drinking reduces "undesirable" alcohol effects.

The resurgence of interest in primary prevention of alcohol problems is not restricted to social or psychological factors. Lester concludes his recent and duly critical review of research on biological factors in alcoholism with the statement that "the probability has increased appreciably that some of the biological factors involved in an understanding of the genesis of alcoholism may be revealed in the not-too-distant future."[7] Such revelations would naturally carry with them the possibility of application for preventive purposes.

The fermentation of ideas relevant to primary prevention finds its counterpart with respect to secondary prevention. It will be recalled that the goal of secondary prevention is to subvert or reverse processes that if continued would lead to alcoholism. One of the critical problems in secondary preventive work is the identification of individuals in whom traditional clinical manifestations of alcoholism are not yet present and, indeed, may not become present for 15 to 20 years. Much recent work bears directly on the identification of youths who have a high relative probability of becoming alcoholic as adults; these may be thought of as high risks or as susceptibles. Sometimes, they are referred to as pre- or early alcoholics. If we can identify high-risk individuals, then the way is open for early treatment or for intervention.

I have already alluded to the fact that investigations of high school and collegiate drinking practices give us promising information about identifying high risk individuals. Maddox, for example, serendipitously found an association between drinking and accidental injury among college students.[8] Further examination of this finding showed collegians injured while drinking are heavy drinkers who are preoccupied with alcohol and who drink for effect; further they score higher on Park's index of problem drinking than a control group. Maddox suggests that accidental injury while drinking may be an "alerting sign" to problem drinking among young people. Allen Williams administered Park's problem drinking scale to a group of college students and found that problem drinking is associated with self-rated anxiety and depression.[9] When his subjects participated in cocktail parties, Williams found that small amounts of alcohol reduced, but that larger amounts of alcohol increased, anxiety and depression. Studies such as this one and those of Maddox enable us to know more precisely the kinds of characteristics that distinguish self-identified youthful problem drinkers from nonproblem drinkers. From a preventive point of view, such studies suffer in that we cannot measure two factors. First, we do not know how accurately these assessments of problem drinking predict alcoholism. This defect is common to all research dealing with early identification and as Maddox has clearly stated, points up the need for longitudinal studies. The second factor is inherent in any method that relies on the individual to identify himself as a problem drinker; namely, we do not know and probably cannot know the validity of self-identification methods without independent criteria.

Other approaches that do not suffer from this methodological defect may have to make other sacrifices to scientific accuracy. One such approach assumes that alcoholism-prone individuals can be identified on the basis of criteria that are easily observable and relatively public and have been demonstrated on clinical or other empirical grounds to occur with some regularity in the histories of alcoholics.

A prime example of such susceptible individuals are the children of alcoholics. Although the empirical evidence is definitely not clear-cut, there is general agreement that alcoholism may be transmitted, presumably by learning, from one generation to the next. Less frequently stated, but more obvious, is the idea that the child of an alcoholic grows up in an environment that is pathogenic in the broader sense; that is, the chances for the development of some emotional or social deviance are far greater than for a child whose parents are not alcoholic. In a nonsystematic way, this kind of thinking is reflected in practice by development of self-help, Alateen groups, composed of adolescent children of alcoholics. Professional workers have, with few exceptions, shown little interest in studying or in working clinically with children of alcoholics, although there are recent signs that concern is quickening. In a study at our hospital, for example, we found that a disproportionate number of children coming to our child guidance clinic had an alcoholic parent, thus offering support to the idea that psychopathology among children with alcoholic parents occurs more frequently than in the general population. Another of our findings shows that these children tend to have impulse or behavior disorder, as opposed to psychosomatic or learning problems, a result one would expect on the basis of identification. In another survey, we found that 12 percent of a sample of mothers of primary school children reported an alcohol problem in the father. William McCourt, at the level of social action, has proposed that teen-age children of alcoholics might be recruited during summer vacations for a combination work and treatment program.[10] To increase their understanding of alcoholics, they would work as ward aides in an inpatient alcoholism facility, and would meet regularly in small quasi-therapeutic groups to aid them to come to terms with their feelings about their alcoholic parent. McCourt predicts that such experiences would reduce conflict about alcohol use and result in a lower incidence of subsequent alcoholism among these teenagers. More recently, Pauline Cohen and a group of colleagues have begun an evaluative treatment study of adolescent children of alcoholic clients in a family service setting.[11] Other groups of high-risk individuals include the Monday morning absentee, the drunken driver, and the drinking delinquent. With regard to drinking and driving, Waller and Turkel suggest that first-offense drunken drivers should be evaluated and, if necessary, treated rather than punished. They predict that such an approach will reduce the incidence of automobile accidents where alcohol is implicated.[12]

At the Massachusetts General Hospital, we are studying adolescent delinquents whose misbehavior occurs when they are drinking. The project has three major aims: first, to determine if misbehavior while drinking among youngsters is related to the later development of alcoholism; second, to determine whether intervention at an early age will prevent the onset of alcoholism; and third, to examine a theory of prealcoholic personality structure by comparing drinking delinquents and nondelinquents, using later development of alcoholic pathology as the criterion variable.

Our delinquency-while-drinking group is composed of 14- through 16-year-old boys whose current offense involves drinking, or who have been in other trouble while drinking. The association between alcohol use and delinquency is determined either as a matter of court testimony or by a brief interview with the boy. A total of 150 boys who meet the criterion of trouble while drinking have been selected. The first 100 were interviewed and tested, and their parents seen for a social history. Following this each case was presented at an intake conference run along usual child guidance clinic lines, with the following exceptions. After the clinical material was presented and before any discussion of the case took place, each participant in the conference independently predicted whether the boy would, if untreated, become alcoholic, and whether he would become a criminal. Participants were asked to give reasons for their predictions. The case was then opened for discussion and an ideal treatment plan formulated by the conference leader. At this point, the boy was assigned by chance to a treatment or to a nontreatment group. If to the former, treatment was started, following the ideal treatment plan as closely as was practical. If assigned to the no-treatment group, nothing further was done until follow-up one year later.

After selecting the first 100 subjects, we identified but did not evaluate another 50 boys who met the same selection criteria. This gives the following design: (1) 50 boys evaluated and treated; (2) 50 boys evaluated but not treated; and (3) 50 boys neither evaluated nor treated. The third or co-control group acted as a control for the evaluation procedure, which in itself was a fairly intensive process that might carry with it therapeutic effects. Since some of our outcome measures are matters of public record that do not require personal encounters with the subject, we will be able to assess the co-control group.

The project design permits both cross-sectional and repeated longitudinal comparisons to be undertaken. Our measures are derived from several sources and include such unobtrusive measures as state probation records that list appearances for criminal proceedings before any court in the state, attendance at any of the state-supported alcohol clinics, and institutionalization in any state mental hospital. In addition we will survey selected hospitals in the area in which the subjects reside. These measures will provide data on later development of alcoholism, criminality, and health problems associated with alcohol intake.

Measuring instruments involving personal contact with the boy and his family included (1) a psychiatric interview with the subject; (2) a social history of the boy and his family; and (3) psychological test measures. After each initial interview the psychiatrist filled out a rating scale on the interview. Reliability of the items of this scale was determined by having two observers independently rate the interviews. In addition to the usual demographic indices, social history data include an assessment of the extent to which the boy's parents have been able to fulfill their function as role models for their children. The psychological test battery was extensive, and aimed at assessment of the vicissitudes of dependent and counter-dependent needs and behavior at various levels of psychological functioning. In brief, the theoretical underpinning of the tests states that prealcoholics have high need strength with regard to dependence but that the need is blocked from behavioral expression. We predict that our delinquent subjects will show low dependent behavior and high dependent needs relative to a matched nondelinquent comparison group. Tests range from near-behavioral measures of dependency, as in the Dependency Situation Test, specially devised for this project, to measures of dependency as a state-of-mind variable on a TAT-like instrument and the Rorschach. Also included was a measure of field-dependence, the rod-and-frame test as used by Witkin and his associates. I might note here that our orientation has been developed in large part from the work of Edith Lisansky and the McCords on prealcoholic personality structure.[13]

While it is too soon to report results of this project, there are some random but interesting findings. Drinking among these delinquents is a social event, whether it is prepathological or not. Further, solitary drinking is virtually absent. A striking feature in the families of our subjects, as assessed by social history data on the first 30 boys, is that over 60 percent of the fathers either suffered from severe mental or physical illness, including alcoholism, or were absent from the home permanently or for prolonged periods. We have interpreted this to mean that the father has not been available or able to serve as a masculine role model for his children. Finally, with regard to treatment, two things have been noted qualitatively; we will have to wait for more data to make a quantitative statement about them. First, the boys tended to remain in treatment only as long as they were on probation; after they left treatment, despite every effort to divorce ourselves from the police courts and punishment in the boys' minds. Second, boys who enter and remain in treatment even for their probationary period seem to grow; that is, they show less conflicted relations with their parents; they show more adequate school or job performance; and they show less passivity with their peers. At the present time, we are nearing completion of the posttreatment evaluation of our subjects.

In closing, I would like to suggest that recent clinical research activity with implications for primary and secondary prevention of alcohol problems may mean a redistribution of efforts away from a near-exclusive concern with treatment of late stages of alcoholic illness, and a greater emphasis on early interventive approaches with high risk groups and on educational approaches that involve the general population. Such a change in strategy is critical if we are to make perceptible inroads on the incidence and prevalence of alcoholism.

7.B. Public Health Nurses Speak up About Alcoholism

Whether alcoholism is regarded as a specific disorder or as the symptom of a number of underlying emotional problems, it is distinguished from many other psychiatric conditions by its widespread impact on the family and community, as well as on the individual. Traditionally, however, the problem has been treated as though it were a problem of the patient alone. The doctor in a private office and the staffs of clinics and hospital psychiatric wards see the alcoholic patient apart from the environmental conditions that contribute to, and are in part caused by, his problem drinking. Of all the caretaking professions, public health nursing provides perhaps the greatest opportunity to observe the patient in his natural setting at home and with his family.

The public health nurse's professional orientation is toward preventive medicine, and the "public health approach" involves the principles of primary, secondary, and tertiary prevention. The application of these concepts to alcoholism has been described as follows:

Section 7.B. written, in collaboration, by Howard T. Blane and Marjorie J. Hill.

. . . Primary prevention is the use of social, chemical, or biological procedures to prevent the onset of alcoholism. Secondary prevention consists of early intervention in excessive, pathological drinking by medical and/or social means to prevent the major consequences of alcoholism. Tertiary prevention involves rehabilitative efforts for the chronic alcoholic in order to avoid further complications of his illness and prevent the spread of its influence to other members of the alcoholic's environment.

In any of these phases of treatment, it would seem, the public health nurse is in a unique position to identify the problems involved, provide information and assistance to the patient and his family, and thus to serve as a valuable adjunct to treatment resources.

As a part of the research program of the alcohol clinic of the Massachusetts General Hospital, we undertook to interview a number of public health nurses in the Boston area in an attempt to determine the extent of their awareness of alcohol-related problems in the community, their attitudes toward the patient and toward treatment, and their role in identifying and referring alcoholics.

The city of Boston has features that make it especially interesting for the study of alcohol-related problems. It has a large Irish-American population, traditionally a group that contributes heavily to problem drinking, as well as concentrated Italian and Jewish populations, also known to have culturally influenced drinking patterns. The problems of Boston's extensive Skid Row area are currently being complicated by a large-scale urban renewal program.

The Nursing Sample

The nurses in our sample were drawn from the Visiting Nurse Association of Boston, which has a central office, eight district offices, and a professional staff of 75. It "provides nursing care and physical therapy to acutely and chronically ill patients in their homes; instruction in maternal and infant care; family guidance in child development, nutrition, prevention of illness, and advancement of mental and physical health." Although nursing care is provided under doctors' orders, the nurses of the VNA, through their program of health guidance, serve as teachers in physical and mental health, and in this way reach members of the family other than the immediate patient.

One nurse described this program as "a public health nurse's way of adding patients to her caseload. It's a nurse's way of teaching the community without having doctor's orders . . . it can be in any field." Another said, "We can sit down and tell them what conditions need medical attention and where to get help." As the nurses describe the program, it involves instruction in nutrition, in maternal and child care, and in care of the sick at home.

Our study sample included the supervisors of the eight district offices and either one or two staff nurses (depending on the size of the office) who were randomly selected within each district. A total of 20 nurses were interviewed during a period of one month in the summer of 1962, and interviews were tape recorded except in cases of mechanical difficulties or refusal, when shorthand notes were taken.

The nurses ranged in age from 24 through 67, and in length of service with the agency from 6 months to 34 years. Median age of the supervisors was 46, and of the staff nurses, 31. One of the problems of an urban agency of this type is that of rapid turnover of the staff, which means that many nurses do not have the opportunity to acquaint themselves thoroughly with problem areas and the available resources, thus increasing the responsibility of the supervisors. In our sample, we found that, while median length of service of the supervisors was 14 years, 67 percent of the staff nurses had been with the agency for 3 years or less, with a median length of service of 2 years.

Eighteen of the 20 nurses indicated that they drink socially, most very rarely; 6 reported that their families had been strongly against liquor during their childhood. Only 3 nurses indicated that they had never known a problem drinker or an alcoholic personally, and 6 reported problem drinking among their relatives.

Awareness of Problem Drinking

It is interesting to note that in a city that ranks fourth in the nation in rate of alcoholism, most of the staff nurses reported that they rarely encounter cases of alcoholism. The supervisors, however, who direct from four to nine nurses and the areas they cover, generally saw alcohol addiction as a serious problem. The interview material points to several possible reasons for this discrepancy. One of these was the limited nature of our sample, and specific features of the areas covered by the nurses we interviewed. One nurse, for example, reported that 99 percent of her patients are Jewish and drink very little; another, who worked in a district consisting almost entirely of Italian families, told us that she sees much drinking, but no alcoholism. The two nurses who work in Boston's Skid Row area said that they see very little drinking in the homes they visit, although they realize that it is a serious problem in that neighborhood.

A more cogent explanation is that the supervisors, most of whom have been with the agency much longer than the staff nurses, are better able to recognize the problem. As one of them put it, "It takes a while to sort out the problem areas, and by the time they [the staff nurses] know what the problems are, they are likely to leave the agency. So they don't have time to learn to be attuned to alcoholism in the home; being attuned is something one learns. The nurses who stay develop a sensitivity."

The nurses' comments suggest that a lack of sensitivity may result from their tendency to regard drinking behavior as a problem only when it has become extreme. Several reported that their only contact with alcoholics occurred while they were working in hospitals, and this may have led them to identify an alcoholic as one who "can't function," blinding them to symptoms of potential drinking problems. Most of the nurses distinguished between heavy drinkers and alcoholics; for example, "a heavy drinker would drink quite a bit, get drunk, but still be able to hold onto a job and carry out the basic responsibilities of his family life . . . whereas the alcoholic would cease functioning, just drink." Another felt that heavy drinkers become alcoholic "when they lose their responsibility toward their family or their breadwinning . . . or can't control themselves in the community . . . when the community begins speaking of them as always drunk."

When asked for their definitions, some of the nurses again tended to be extreme. "Somebody who doesn't eat, and drinks . . . who disregards nutrition altogether, and will spend his last penny for a bottle of alcohol rather than have something to eat." "Somebody who needs alcohol in order to survive . . . or to carry out, or cope with, day-to-day existence." "They can't stop drinking. They drink from morning till night. They will use up all their financial resources to buy liquor."

The use of extreme definitions is in part a reflection of the first concern of the nurses—to care for the physically ill member of the family who has been referred to them by the doctor. When drinking complicates the medical problem, for example in diabetes, they are quick to recognize it. A supervisor said, "In defense of the nurse, there are so many other things! She's often meeting the needs of the moment, rather than getting involved in a long-term process." The patient, then, tends to be the nurse's first concern, even though she may recognize that other family members have problems that should receive attention. Partly because of the extent of her caseload, she often focuses only on alcoholism in its advanced stages, missing opportunities for preventive teaching and early casefinding.

Alcohol-Related Problems

When we speak of early casefinding, or primary and secondary prevention, we are concerned with what may be called "alcohol-related problems," rather than with extreme alcoholism. These problems are frequently encountered and described by the nurses who find that, once a good relationship has been established with one member of a family, this person often regards the nurse as a confidante who will listen sympathetically to family problems, give advice, and whose professional status makes her a safe person in whom to confide. Many of these problems concern drinking by other family members.

The types of alcohol-related problems that the nurses encounter may be divided into several broad categories. First is the type of patient whose medical condition, for which he is being treated, is either caused or complicated by excessive consumption of alcohol, as, for example, the patient suffering from malnutrition, or one with both arthritis and psoriasis.

In a second type of situation, the patient, usually the housewife, complains to the nurse about the drinking problem of another family member, usually her husband. Although the nurse may never meet the problem drinker, she often gives advice regarding treatment. One supervisor reported, "This woman, who is so sick with cancer, asked the nurse what could be done about her husband. The nurse took the case on for health guidance, for help with alcoholism. We found out that he was a veteran, that he was known to the Veterans clinic, and that they were willing to help."

Least frequently reported by the nurses are patients who themselves ask for help specifically for their drinking problems. In describing such an incident, a nurse related: "Yesterday I had a telephone call from one of our former patients who is in a nursing home, very happy, and doing very well. She wanted to thank the nurse who worked with her and encouraged her to go to a home where she wouldn't have access to the quantities of wine she'd been drinking. The nurse had been seeing her for bouts of diarrhea, nausea, and vomiting."

There is also the case of a drinking problem so severe that it prevents the nurse from seeing the patient at all. Often he is so neglectful of the condition, for which visiting nurse service has been requested, that he fails to cooperate by staying home for the nurse's visits. Among such patients reported by the nurses was a man with an ulcer on his leg that required regular treatment, and a tuberculosis patient much in need of supervision.

In a fifth type of situation, the one which arises most frequently, the nurse is aware of a drinking problem, but is not asked for advice. Sometimes she feels free to initiate a discussion of the subject; in other cases she does not. One of our participants told the following story:

> I visited a young girl who has been drinking since she was an early teen-ager. She said she only went on weekend binges, but she stayed indoors with all the shades drawn, never went out. She was living with a man who was not the father of her baby; the pregnancy was the result of a weekend binge which she was later unable to remember. She didn't say she needed help, but I kept asking her. I brought it up in connection with her being unable to keep

her baby; one of the neighbors had reported her, and she was threatened with the loss of her child. We referred her to a family service, but they wouldn't take her on. And so we decided to resume our visits, but were never able to get into the house again.

Attitudes Toward the Alcoholic

On the whole, the nurses expressed accepting attitudes toward alcoholics "when they are sober," describing them as people who are generally charming, polite, and likable; ". . . these people I've met who drink too much, I find them friendly people, good-hearted." Some nurses saw them as weak people, "little lost sheep," with a loss of self-control, which one nurse described as "character degeneration"; others saw them as sick people in need of medical help, "the same way we would treat any other disease."

The drinking alcoholic, however, elicits a great deal of ambivalence, and some of the nurses were aware of this. One said, "It's easy to sit here and talk about alcoholics whom you see for an hour at a time, but that's entirely different from having to live with them; that would be terrible." A supervisor added, "Suppose that a nurse had, for example, an alcoholic uncle who had caused a great deal of strain, stress, and embarrassment to the family, and she went to take care of other alcoholics. I think it's a rare nurse who would deal with this objectively."

Some nurses recognized, and were frank in expressing, their own negative attitudes: "The alcoholic person . . . becomes rather disgusting in a lot of ways." "I think it's very depressing, working with an alcoholic." Most, however, were more likely to ascribe unfavorable attitudes to other people, and to other nurses. If we assume that it is easier to express one's own feelings when generalizing about the attitudes of others, the ambivalence becomes clear. For example, throughout the interviews there was an undercurrent of fear of violence. Only one nurse expressed this directly, as part of her own experience. Several, however, ascribed fear to other nurses: "I think new nurses are sometimes afraid of them." "They're unpredictable in what they might do, so that we have to be cautious in dealing with them." None of the nurses had heard of an actual case of violence involving a nurse.

Three of the nurses indicated that their own attitudes have changed within recent years, largely as a result of reading and public education programs. One said, "I've changed my feelings about it as I've grown older, and since I've had more experience. I used to think . . . that people could help themselves. When I was younger I never considered it a disease, I just thought of it as an easy way out of things for some people."

Some of the nurses are aware that their attitudes toward the alcoholic may determine their effectiveness in helping him. "I have real feelings about alcoholics," said one. Another admitted: "I just could never, never work with them. I know it, and this may be a failing, but I would never have the patience to. It would not be fair to the patients to force myself to work with them." A third nurse: "In my opinion, it would take a certain kind of person to work with alcoholics, because you're going to have a large number of failures."

Attitudes Toward Treatment

It is not surprising that the public health nurse, like most people in the medical professions, likes to see improvement in her patients, and to bring about observable changes. As a result, she may find no personal satisfaction in work with alcoholics. One of the nurses said: "I think a lot of us tend to feel that it's somewhat unrewarding. Most nurses like to see something that really changes, or that works fast . . . but with alcoholics you don't get this."

Almost half of the nurses interviewed regard treatment of alcohol problems as discouraging and hopeless: "What can you do with people who don't want advice, or who won't help themselves?" One nurse asked another for advice, and was told, "We don't take care of a person like that, because you'd just get them all fixed up and think that you might be getting somewhere, and they'd go out and have another spree, and you have to start all over again." Again, "We have worked awfully hard with some families, and it just sort of went down the drain."

Other nurses find work with alcohol problems to be challenging, and the results of their efforts rewarding. Nine of those we interviewed expressed this viewpoint, saying, for example, "I find it a challenge to work with them, to try to discover what bothers them, and then see if something can be done." Nurses are aware of the impact that alcohol-related problems may have on the family, and the family is usually their first concern. One said: "Maybe the reason that I want to help is that I see what it's doing to the family, not just the patient. . . . I'm not always sure we're thinking that the patient wouldn't have to suffer, but rather that the family would be better off if you helped him."

In reading the cases included in the study, we noted that in some, usually when there was a direct request for help, the nurse was able to work well and successfully with the family. In another group of cases, however, the nurse was aware that alcohol-related problems existed, but did not attempt to deal with them. These cases represent an area in which the nurse may be missing a valuable opportunity to practice preventive medicine, by providing help before the problem becomes so acute that the patient is forced to seek out help or has it forced upon him.

About half the nurses said that they had been asked directly for help in dealing with alcohol problems and had made referrals to Alcoholics Anonymous, clinics, and to hospitals. Although more knew about Alcoholics Anonymous than about any other agency, several mentioned the fact that a successful referral depends on the nature of the patient and the situation. Most suggested that medical treatment be included, often as a readily acceptable steppingstone to getting help with emotional problems.

Concerning treatment facilities, again the nurses saw the situation as a discouraging one. "People who want to join AA know they have to give up liquor. There's got to be coverage for those who won't admit that they're alcoholics." "There are some fine alcoholic clinics in the city . . . but something is wrong with the structural base, because I've heard three people say, 'There were so many people in that clinic that I wouldn't stay.'" "I think the general hospitals, the emergency wards, have a lot of things they could offer that they don't."

Although it is true that treatment facilities are inadequate to the needs of the city, some of the discouragement expressed by the nurses seems due to lack of information. For example, one nurse said: "There is not a clinic to which we can refer a patient who wants psychiatric care without paying a fortune." This nurse also believed that a patient who has been in a state institution is not eligible for outpatient care—a belief that is without basis in fact. Several nurses admitted that they had not been able to provide adequate information about local facilities. This is due, in part, to the rapid turnover of staff. As would be expected, the supervisors were better informed than the staff nurses. However, the prevalent lack of information suggests a certain lack of interest in the problem. All district offices are supplied with literature on community resources for treatment, but few nurses indicated that they had used this material; some were not aware that it existed.

What the Nurse Does

Not unexpectedly, the nurses were unsure of what their role in the treatment should be. They felt that their major function is to provide motivation for treatment. One pointed out that ". . . we can't deal with the things covered by social workers, psychologists, and psychotherapists. Sometimes it's very difficult to appeal to a person to help him to seek help. And we're not equipped for this. All we can do is try to find out if he really wants help, and give him a little push." One nurse pictured her role quite clearly: "They have to depend on you and look to you for guidance. For somebody like me, who's untrained, it's a matter of gently pushing them out on their own to seek help, and to help themselves. At first it would be developing their confidence in me, getting them to listen to me, and to depend on me just so far, and then setting limits and trying to push them the other way, to make them see that they have to do something for themselves." A supervisor's comment: "I'm sure the nurses don't really know where to turn, or what is the best suggestion to make. I think, too, that they probably are interested and would like to help. If we're really going to help people, public health nurses need a lot more help in how to approach families."

If we summarize briefly the material from our interviews, we may say that the public health nurse is in a unique position to serve as an early casefinder, but that she often fails to fulfill her potential—sometimes because she does not recognize the problem, sometimes because she does not know how to handle it, and sometimes because she lacks information and interest. The majority of the nurses we interviewed were interested in alcoholism as a major public health problem but often were unsure of their own role in dealing with it.

When she is specifically asked for help, the nurse often acts effectively; when not asked, she is frequently hesitant to initiate a discussion of the problem. The nurse feels that her job is to provide information and motivation, but she herself often lacks one or both. If she is to work comfortably, as well as effectively, she may also need a chance to examine her own feelings and reactions to problem drinking, so that she may better understand and deal with the feelings of others.

Conclusions

Recent years have brought an increasing awareness of the importance of the public health nurse's role in dealing with alcohol-related problems, in the field of public education, in providing help and support for the family of the problem drinker, and in treatment. As a result, there is a growing body of literature to which the nurse may refer, as well as a number of conferences and seminars planned to assist her in increasing the help she is able to provide.

The interviews we have described, however, suggest the potential value of a more direct approach to training in this field, providing the opportunity for the nurse to become acquainted with community treatment resources and their personnel. A referral made without firsthand knowledge of the agency can seldom be a well-thought-out plan of treatment, and may be less than maximum benefit to the patient. Since firsthand knowledge is often impossible, a possible solution to this problem would be the preparation of a carefully annotated list of facilities, prepared by state agencies dealing with alcoholism. This list should include conditions and restrictions on admission, cost to the patient, procedures for referral, facilities and type of treatment offered, and any other information that would help the nurse to make suitable referrals.

While instruction in recognition and treatment of alcoholism and alcohol-related problems should ideally be provided as part of the basic curriculum in nursing, there is an immediate need to help those nurses who have completed their formal education and are practicing in public health. We suggest the potential value of a carefully planned inservice program aimed at helping the nurse to identify alcohol-related problems, to recognize her own feelings, and to make efficient and effective use of community treatment resources. Such a program could provide the first step toward opening up an important resource for early casefinding and prevention of one of the nation's gravest health problems.

7.C. Public Health Nurses and the Care of Alcoholics: A Study of Attitude Change

An investigation of the attitudes of public health nurses toward alcoholics and alcoholism led us to undertake an in-service training program, as a collaborative effort between the Massachusetts General Hospital and the Visiting Nurse Association of Boston. The project was planned with the close cooperation of both agencies, and with assistance from several other community agencies involved with nursing or the treatment of alcoholism. This paper provides a description of the project in terms of the objectives that were presented in the original grant application.

The general goal of the project was described as follows:

> ... to show that a program of in-service training and education in a community public health nursing agency will increase the use of existing community health services for alcoholics, persons with alcohol-related conditions, and members of their families.

Specific objectives, and activities in regard to each, were as follows:

> *Objective 1:* To aid the public health nurse (a) to identify alcohol problems in the patient or other family members; (b) to assess the effects of the alcohol problem on the

Section 7.C. written by Marjorie J. Hill.

physical, psychological, social, and economic well-being of the family or individual family members; (c) to establish realistic and reasonable treatment and preventive goals with alcoholic patients and their families; (d) to undertake ameliorative measures within the home setting when possible; (e) to prepare the patient and relevant family members for referral to specialized community resources; and (f) to learn of the existence and nature of available community resources for alcoholics and members of their families.

This objective deals directly with the content of the training program; large formal meetings, informal groups, and individual discussions provided the major vehicles for attaining these goals. During the initial phases of the program a series of lectures, followed by discussions, were presented to the entire staff of the Visiting Nurse Association. Topics included an overview of the field of alcoholism, physical and medical aspects, psychological and social aspects, and the role of the nurse in treating alcohol problems.

An experienced psychiatric social worker (hereafter referred to as the "project social worker") held smaller, informal meetings with various groups. The initial meetings were held with supervisors of the eight VNA offices, and provided the opportunity for the social worker to discuss goals of the project, and for supervisors to discuss nurses' problems and attitudes concerning alcohol-related problems, and to describe needs that the program might meet. The project social worker also served as discussion leader at a meeting of supervisors and their assistants, at which a case summary, presented by an assistant supervisor, served as the focus of discussion. This meeting served as the model for a series of discussion groups that were held in the various district offices. These meetings were jointly planned by the social worker and the district supervisor; each meeting included a case presentation by a staff nurse, followed by group discussion. Participation was active, with questions and attitudes freely expressed. Although needs and interests varied among the offices, common concerns and areas of agreement were identified, and active involvement of the nurses was apparent.

In a later phase of the program, the major activity centered on meetings between the project social worker and individual supervisors. These meetings included discussion of individual cases, use of community resources, and problems of policy and supervisory practices.

A final series of small group seminars was designed to enhance and deepen understanding of alcohol-related problems, and to deal with practical aspects of intervention and referral. Approximately one-fourth of the nurses volunteered to take part in these discussions; twelve, representing all district offices, were selected for participation. The series was presented separately to two groups of six nurses each.

> *Objective 2:* To collaborate with the administration of the public health nursing organization, in an attempt to arrive at a reasonable policy for the care of alcoholic patients and families identified at the line level.

Throughout the course of the project there was heavy emphasis on cooperation between the VNA administrative staff and the project (MGH) staff. In the initial phases of the project, a number of meetings were held to familiarize MGH personnel with VNA policy, structure and practice, and to implement planning. Close liaison was established and maintained between the Educational Director for the VNA and the project social worker. Each step in planning was preceded by meetings between the two staffs, at which mutual needs and expectations were discussed.

> *Objective 3:* To collaborate with the staffs of existing community health services around problems of referral from a nursing agency in order to clarify the specific nature of services offered by community agencies, how these are rendered, and the policies that govern the offering of services. To determine the most effective ways in which the public health nursing organization may utilize specialized, nonnursing services offered by these community agencies.

One of the activities planned for the project was to provide a Directory of Community Resources for the VNA. Some of the necessary information was available from the Acute Psychiatric Service of the MGH, which had utilized such a directory for several years. However, this material was often out-dated, and did not refer specifically to the needs of the nursing staff. Therefore, the project social worker and a community social worker visited appropriate community agencies to gather information of specific interest to nurses—for example, how to go about making referrals, the kinds of patients served by the agency, hours and fee policies, and other information. The directory included sections on organizations (e.g., A.A.), clinics and hospitals, other major health services, social welfare services, correctional institutions with alcoholism treatment programs, and resources for information, education and consultation. A sample entry is presented in Appendix B.

> *Objective 4*: To measure the effect of the program by careful accounting of the referrals selected agencies receive during the course of the project period, and by studying changes in nurses' attitudes toward alcoholics; to develop other relevant and feasible measures that will serve to assess the effectiveness of the program.

We originally planned to evaluate the program by the use of three measures: number of referrals from the VNA to other agencies, prevalence studies as a measure of case-finding, and a before-after attitude study. The results of these measures will be described separately.

Referrals

A number of meetings were held at which project staff and VNA administrative staff attempted to formulate a system for recording referrals, making use of the referral form already employed by the nurses. It soon became evident that the number of referrals being recorded was not an adequate measure of the efforts made by the nurses, and that the nurses were less interested in making referrals than in what they themselves could do. It was felt that a measure of this type did not accurately reflect the involvement of the nurse in the case of the patient, and the use of this measure was discontinued early in the project.

Prevalence studies

As a measure of rate of casefinding, we conducted prevalence studies at the beginning and end of the project. Each of the surveys covered a two-week period, in which all nurses were asked to complete a brief report on each patient they saw if an alcohol problem was involved, in either the patient or a family member. As an evaluative measure, the surveys proved disappointing; they did, however, provide some interesting information about the alcohol problems encountered in the VNA caseload. Casefinding, as measured by these surveys, did not increase. The total caseload for the Boston VNA is in excess of 5,000 patients, for an average two-week period; the nurses reported encountering alcohol problems in 35, or less than 1 percent, of their patients; a very conservative estimate would be that such problems exist in 10 percent of the population served by the VNA. This would imply that the nurses are unable to identify alcohol problems, were it not for the fact that 12 percent of the nurses report drinking problems in their immediate families, 13 percent identify the problem in their relatives, and 17 percent report having friends with drinking problems. Since each nurse was counted in only one category, these figures show that 43 percent of the nurses have had experience with drinking problems in family and friends. These figures lend support to our hypothesis that there is a tendency for medical personnel to overlook drinking problems when more "acceptable" or "urgent" medical problems exist.[14]

During the course of the project, the nursing supervisors designed a data collection form for their own use. This was similar to the forms designed for the project, except that it was completed by supervisors from records of the caseloads of each office. Although this survey form was planned to permit intensive study of any health problem that the nurses might encounter, its initial use was for recording drinking problems.

Attitude questionnaire

The major instrument used in evaluation of the program consisted of an 89-item questionnaire designed to tap the nurses' attitudes toward alcohol, alcoholism, and alcoholics. Nurses were asked to indicate their response to each item on a six-point, Likert-type scale, ranging from Strongly Agree to Strongly Disagree; all items were scored so that high scores indicated *less favorable* (more authoritarian, custodial, etc.) attitudes than low scores. Approximately one-fourth of the items were reversed to avoid response set. Items were drawn from a number of sources, which are described more fully in Appendix B. Sources were as follows:

Authoritarianism Scale (F-Scale)—items drawn from the scale developed by Adorno, et al.[15] *Custodial Attitudes Scale* (C.A.I.)—revised version used by Mendelson, et al.[16] *Attitudes toward Immoral Behavior Scale*—from Oram.[17] *Social Drinking Scale*—from Addiction Research Foundation Scales concerned with *Prognosis for Recovery; Alcoholism as an Illness; Alcoholism and Character Defect; Emotional Difficulties as cause of Alcoholism; Social Status of the Alcoholic; Harmless Voluntary Indulgence*—from the Alcoholism Questionnaire, Addiction Research Foundation. In addition, a number of items were written for use in this questionnaire.

The questionnaire was administered to the nurses immediately before the project began, and at the end of a year and a half. Nurses who left the VNA during the course of the project were tested before leaving, and new nurses were tested shortly after their arrival. A control group, consisting of nurses in VNA offices in surrounding cities, was tested at the same time intervals. This permitted us to measure individual change on the part of the project nurses, and to compare them with a group not participating in the project.

Administration of the questionnaire and data analysis were complicated by the very high rate of turnover among VNA personnel; less than half the original sample were with the VNA 18 months later. For purposes of statistical analysis, we found it necessary to break the sample down into groups, depending on length of participation in the project: Group I—49 nurses participating in entire project; Group II—21 nurses in the project at least one year, but not for the entire project; Group III—66 nurses who were with the VNA less than one year during the project; Group IV—35 nurses in the control group, who remained with the VNA for the two years of the project. (See Appendix B.)

Since our questionnaire represents a collection of items that had never been presented together before, we carried out a factor analysis to determine which of the items clustered together in terms of the nurses' responses. The factor analysis was carried out on all pretests ($N = 209$; 161 experimental subjects from the Boston VNA and

48 controls). The ratings on all 89 variables were intercorrelated by the Pearson Product Moment Method, and then factor analyzed by the method of principal components. The analysis yielded five factors.[18] Approximate factor scores for each factor were obtained by summing the ratings on those items that loaded most highly on each factor. Items were selected by rank-ordering the factor loadings of each item within a factor, retaining only those with a loading of .39 or greater. Items that loaded on more than one factor were retained only on the factor on which they loaded highest; in each case, this decision was found to place the item in the factor with which it was most psychologically congruent.

THE FACTORS

The factors, with loadings of each item, are presented in Table 22 (Appendix A). Our interpretations are based on an analysis of the content of the items that composed the factors; in labeling them, we sought to interpret the overall meaning of the items. On the item level, the scale was designed so that a low score reflected a favorable, hopeful, nonauthoritarian attitude, or one in which the nurse is not concerned with issues of morality as they affect her work. We described the factors as follows:

Factor I—Authoritarian Caretaker. A subject with a high score on Factor I may be described as authoritarian (young people sometimes get rebellious ideas . . .; it's hard work that makes life worthwhile; people would be better off if they talked less and worked more). As nurses they bring their authoritarianism to their work (. . . nurses have a responsibility to teach correct social attitudes; nurses treat alcoholics, etc., as well as other people; normal people are ruled by reason, but abnormal people by their emotions). They see alcoholics as a group that needs the guidance the nurse can provide (. . . most alcoholics can't tell right from wrong; one of the main causes of alcoholism is lack of moral strength). This factor included three F-Scale items, three Custodial Attitudes items, and three Morality items, from the original subscales.

Factor II—Unsympathetic. The person who scores high on Factor II is characterized by a lack of sympathy for the alcoholic (. . . we can't be expected to be sympathetic; alcoholics have only themselves to blame; because, if the alcoholic himself doesn't care, why should the nurse? Most alcoholics are completely unconcerned . . . and . . . indifferent to the suffering they cause; most have no desire to stop drinking). Alcoholism is seen as a sign of weakness and not as an illness deserving of understanding (the alcoholic drinks mainly because he enjoys drinking; it is not a disease, but a bad habit, and alcoholics are just weak and selfish).

Factor III—Social Drinking. The nurse with a high score on this factor is characterized by acceptance of moderate drinking as a socially useful and relaxing type of behavior (a few drinks with friends is good for relaxing; social drinking is harmless and an aid to mixing socially).

Factor IV—Skid Row Stereotype. The person who has a high score on this factor may be described as holding the common stereotype of the alcoholic as a bum (. . . usually unemployed, with a poorer education than most people, basically spineless, and there's something about them that makes it easy to tell them from normal people). This attitude is accompanied by a feeling of hopelessness for the future of the alcoholic or his family (he is seldom helped by treatment, will probably end up on Skid Row; his family would be better off without him, and his children are likely to become alcoholics too).

Factor V—Moral Relativism. The items on this factor loaded negatively on the factor; therefore, the individual with a high score rejects the statements included in Factor V, saying in effect that other people's morals are no concern of hers. She is tolerant of what might be considered immoral behavior in others, and does not let attitudes toward morality enter into her professional behavior. She feels, further, that alcoholism is not a moral issue.

Pre-Post Change Scores on the Factors

In order to measure amount of change on factor scores, the following procedure was employed: Individual scores for items appearing in each factor were compared on pre- and posttests, for each nurse. Posttest scores were subtracted from pretest scores; thus a positive

(+) change score indicates change in a *favorable* direction; negative (—) change scores indicate that on the posttest, the nurse was less favorable (or more authoritarian, custodial, etc.) in her attitude. The direction was reversed for Factor V, where negative factor loadings were interpreted as favorable; in this case, change in a negative direction is "favorable" change.

Comparisons were made between four groups: I—Project nurses participating in the entire project; II—Project nurses participating at least one year; III—Project nurses participating less than one year; IV—Controls.

For each factor, a one-way analysis of variance was performed to determine whether the four groups of nurses differed in amount of change on factor scores. The analyses are summarized in Table 23 (Appendix A). Mean change scores are summarized in Table 24, where it may be observed that only on Factor III, that concerned with attitudes toward social drinking, did the groups differ significantly in amount of change ($F = 2.91$, $p < .05$). All project nurses became more favorable toward social drinking, while the control group became less favorable.

Although we have no way of knowing why the control group changed in the direction it did, we may speculate that the project nurses were "on guard" at the time of the pretest; during the course of the project, they became aware that project staff were in favor of controlled social drinking, and the posttest may represent a truer picture of the nurses' attitudes.

All groups showed a tendency toward less authoritarianism on the posttest, although the groups did not differ in amount of change ($F = 1.10$, n.s.). Very little change was demonstrated on Factor II, and the groups did not differ in maintaining their unsympathetic attitudes toward alcoholics. On Factor IV, which indicated an attitude of stereotyping the alcoholic as a Skid Row type, all the nurses became more favorable in their attitudes, although there were no differences between the groups ($F = .91$, n.s.). Factor V, it should be recalled, had negative factor loadings; thus change in a negative direction indicates an increase in rejection of items implying that alcoholism is a moral problem, and, therefore, a concern of the nurse.

In all groups there was an increased tendency to reject these items on the posttest, indicating an even less moralistic attitude; the groups did not differ from each other in amount of change ($F = 1.16$, n.s.).

T-tests were employed to test for significance of change for each group on the various factors. It was found that on Factor I (Authoritarian Caretaker), all three of the project groups showed a significant change on prepost scores in the direction of becoming less authoritarian. (Group I—$t = 3.00$, 48 df, $p < .01$; Group II—$t = 2.88$, 20 df, $p < .01$; Group III—$t = 2.77$, 65 df, $p < .05$). There was no change on this factor for the control group ($t = 1.51$, 34 df, n.s.).

On Factor II (Unsympathetic) only Group I showed a significant change ($t = 2.38$, 48 df, $p < .02$), in the direction of becoming more sympathetic; for the other groups, there was no change. (Group II—$t = .94$, 20 df, n.s.; Group III—$t = .09$, 65 df, n.s.; Group IV—$t = 1.08$, 34 df, n.s.).

On Factor III (Social Drinking) Groups I and III both changed in the direction of being more favorable toward social drinking (Group I—$t = 2.10$, 48 df, $p < .05$); Group III—$t = 2.79$, 65 df, $p < .01$), while the other two groups did not change (Group II—$t = 1.58$, 20 df, n.s.; Group IV—$t = .71$, 34 df, n.s.).

On Factor IV (Skid Row Stereotype), all three of the project groups changed significantly in the direction of less unfavorable stereotyping of the alcoholic (Group I—$t = 2.84$, 48 df, $p < .01$; Group II—$t = 3.95$, 20 df, $p < .001$; Group III—$t = 2.77$, 65 df, $p < .01$). The control group did not change on this factor ($t = 1.63$, 34 df, n.s.).

On Factor V (Moral Relativism), Groups I, III, and IV changed significantly in the direction of increasing rejection of items concerning the nurse's role as arbiter of the patient's moral behavior. (Group I—$t = 4.34$, 48 df, $p < .001$; Group III—$t = 2.09$, 65 df, $p < .05$; Group IV—$t = 3.84$, 34 df, $p < .001$). Group II did not change on this factor ($t = 1.52$, 20 df, n.s.)

Mean change scores for pre- and posttests for each group are summarized in Table 23 (Appendix A). It is evident that there was a tendency for factor scores to change in the expected direction, that is, in the direction of becoming more favorable toward alcoholics, less authoritarian, and less moralistic.

Summarizing the statistical analyses, we find that Group I—nurses who participated in the entire program—had favorable change scores on all factors. Group II—nurses with the program at least one year—changed in a favorable direction on two factors, and did not change on the other three. Group III—with the project less than a year—changed in a favorable direction on four factors, and did not change on the fifth. The Control group changed on only one factor. In order to account for the fact that Group III changed more than Group II, we speculate the following sequence of events: Nurses with brief exposure to the training program bring to it a spurt of enthusiasm, dedication, and hope for help with their day-to-day problems. They have little opportunity, however, to "get their hands dirty," and to become discouraged if newly learned techniques fail to accomplish miracles. Nurses who remain with the program go through a period of disillusionment, finding that it provides no magic answers, and no quick and easy solutions to the problems they encounter with their patients. They become unsure as to their own role in working with alcohol problems and may feel that, despite their best efforts, patients are willfully unmotivated to improve. Initial enthusiasm becomes dulled in contact with the difficult realities of dealing with the alcohol problems, and this is reflected in less favorable attitudes. If, however, the nurse stays with the program, she gets a chance to see her work have effect. She has the opportunity to increase both awareness and experience, and becomes more comfortable in her own role with alcohol problems; her attitudes become correspondingly more favorable.

Another possible explanation of our findings lies in the way in which the program was designed, and the order in which various types of content were presented. In the initial phase, a series of lectures was presented to the entire VNA staff. Following the first two lectures, the project social worker led case discussions in each of the district offices. The program then became focused on meetings and consultation with the supervisors, rather than with the nurses themselves. In the final phase of the program, a special intensive seminar series was presented. Thus, nurses who were in the program at different points in time received widely varying types and amount of contact with project staff. It is possible, then, that the type of content to which nurses were exposed might account for differences in attitude change.

Group I, which showed the greatest amount of change, includes most of the supervisors and assistant supervisors, who received more program content than the staff nurses, and who are in the best position to transmit changed attitudes and practices to present and future staff. We felt that the attitude change indicated by their test scores was also evident in the way these nurses approached and dealt with alcohol-related problems in their practice.

Group II, which demonstrated little favorable attitude change, consisted largely of nurses who came to the VNA after the program had started, and thus were not exposed to any initial enthusiasm, or to most of the lectures. Their average length of stay was 15.9 months; this meant that many of them participated in the group discussions, but left at the time the project staff was working directly with supervisors, and before the final seminars were presented. Compared to the other groups, little was done to make Group II feel a sense of active involvement with the program, and this may have been reflected in their failure to change.

Group III can be subdivided into two groups. Group III-A, then, consists of nurses who were with the VNA at the time the program was initiated, and left soon after (mean length of time in the program = 6.7 months). This group was exposed to very little content; half of them heard only two lectures given to the entire VNA staff. The others attended four or five of the lectures, and had the opportunity of participating in the case discussions that were held in each of the district offices, and which were generally favorably evaluated. Group III-B is composed of the nurses who replaced Group III-A when they left the VNA; Group III-B was exposed to a quite different type of participation. Averaging 7.6 months in the program, these nurses came at a time when meetings with the nurses were no longer being held, and the program was concentrated on work with the district supervisors. In the final phase of the program, six nurses in Group III-B participated in the intensive seminars. Despite these differences, Groups III-A and B did not differ in amount of favorable attitude change. In terms of attitude change, then, the transmission of program content through supervisors seems to be equally effective to working directly with staff.

> *Objective 5:* To explore, should the project appear successful, avenues for extension of the program to other relevant community nursing agencies.

At the present time, the project we have reported here has just been completed; we are not yet thinking in terms of future programs. We have, however, learned a great deal that would be of use in planning similar in-service training, in alcoholism, or in other fields. Outstanding, perhaps, is the need for special planning in order to conduct an effective program in a group in which personnel changes rapidly. Although we were not aware of this problem during the planning stages of our program, it is not unique to the group with which we worked. Morison reports a similar rate of turnover for public health nurses in the Dayton, Ohio area.[19] It seems that there are two ways to avoid some of the problems we encountered. First, a program may be focused almost entirely on supervisors, who will transmit new knowledge and practices to staff nurses. An alternative approach would be to plan a program that would run in short cycles, each cycle including lectures, group discussions, consultation with supervisors, and intensive seminars. In such a system, nurses who had participated in earlier phases of the program might take on teaching roles in later phases.

Before attempting another such program, we would also wish to evaluate the long-term effects of the training provided. Morison, who conducted a similar program, found that "while there was an increase in cases identified during the period the nurse-specialist was in the agencies, the number gradually declined when she was no longer available."[20] Morison felt, however, that continuing change was effected through nursing supervisors.

We feel that our findings point to the need to plan programs in such a way that participants have a chance to apply what they learn, and to see the effectiveness of their own efforts.

Although we would make changes in future programs, we feel that our project has been a successful venture in terms of coordination of efforts between two quite different agencies, each engaged in providing health services. There was some initial resistance to the project, and to the expenditure of time and effort on what some nurses saw as a subject of little benefit in their work. As time went on, however, the nurses showed increasing involvement in the program, and evidenced a great deal of interest in their own roles in working with alcohol problems. The attitude changes reflected in our questionnaire seemed to give a true picture of change in the nurses' dealing with alcohol problems in their patients.

This project emphasizes that a crucial variable in early identification of alcohol problems lies in the attitudes of caretakers. Just as a continuous relation and availability to the patient is essential to the successful treatment of alcohol problems, so is a continuing input of enthusiastic teaching, training, and experience paramount to the caregivers. To teach once and then let go is similar to raising a patient's hopes and then crashing them to the ground with neglect. Our patients are people; so are nurses.

Notes

1. W. McCord and J. McCord, *Origins of Alcoholism* (Stanford, California: Stanford University Press, 1960).
2. G. L. Maddox, "Teenagers and Alcohol: Recent Research," *Annals of the New York Academy of Sciences,* 133:856-865, 1966.
3. R. Lindner, "Alcoholism and Crime," 1945.
4. K. Polk, *Drinking and the Adolescent Culture* (Eugene, Oregon: Lane County Youth Project, 1964; mimeographed).
5. H. T. Blane, "Drinking and Crime," *Federal Probation,* June, 1965.
6. M. E. Chafetz, "Alcohol Excess," *Annals of the New York Academy of Sciences,* 133:808-813, 1966.
7. D. Lester, "Self-Selection of Alcohol by Animals, Human Variation, and the Etiology of Alcoholism. A Critical Review," *Quarterly Journal of Studies on Alcohol,* 27:395-438, 1966.
8. Maddox, *op. cit.*

9. A. F. WILLIAMS, "Social Drinking, Anxiety, and Depression," *Journal of Personality and Social Psychiatry,* 3:689-693, 1966.
10. WILLIAM MCCOURT, personal communication, 1966.
11. PAULINE COHEN, personal communication, 1967.
12. J. A. WALLER and H. W. TURKEL, "Alcoholism and Traffic Deaths," *New England Journal of Medicine,* 275:532-536, 1966.
13. H. T. BLANE, *The Personality of the Alcoholic: Guises of Dependency* (New York: Harper and Row, 1968); E. S. LISANSKY, "The Etiology of Alcoholism: The Role of Psychological Predisposition," *Quarterly Journal of Studies on Alcohol,* 21:314-343, 1960; MCCORD and MCCORD, *op. cit.*
14. H. T. BLANE and M. J. HILL, "Public Health Nurses Speak up About Alcoholism," *Nursing Outlook,* 12, 1964; H. T. BLANE, W. F. OVERTON, JR., and M. E. CHAFETZ, "Social Factors in the Diagnosis of Alcoholism. I. Characteristics of the Patient," *Quarterly Journal of Studies on Alcohol,* 24:640-663, 1963; S. WOLF, M. CHAFETZ, H. BLANE, and M. HILL, "Social Factors in the Diagnosis of Alcoholism in Social and Nonsocial Situations. II. Attitudes of Physicians," *Quarterly Journal of Studies on Alcohol,* 26:72-79, 1965.
15. T. W. ADORNO et al., *The Authoritarian Personality* (New York: Harper and Brothers, 1950).
16. J. H. MENDELSON, D. WEXLER, P. E. KUBANSKY, R. HARRISON, G. LIEDERMAN, and P. SOLOMON, "Physicians' Attitudes Toward Alcoholic Patients," *Archives of General Psychiatry,* 11:392-399, 1964.
17. P. G. ORAM, "Induction of Action and Attitude Change: The Function of Role-Self Values and Levels of Endorsement," doctoral dissertation, Boston University, 1966.
18. The factor matrix was rotated to orthogonal simple structure, using a normal varimax method of rotation.
19. L. J. MORISON and J. M. DEFFENBAUGH, *Integrating an Alcoholism Program into Public Health Nursing: A Project Report and Guide* (Ohio Department of Health, 1968).
20. *Ibid.*

Chapter 8
Making Alcohol Use and Problems Respectable

It is a medical truism that almost no condition has ever been eradicated by treating casualties. This does not mean that treatment of the afflicted should be neglected; it merely recognizes that treatment is a holding effort, that cannot in the long run control or minimize the effects of medical or psychosocial problems. Regardless of how effective our therapies become, treatment will never turn back the alcoholic tide. Prevention has been, and will continue to be, the most effective means of minimizing public health problems.

Prevention means different things to different people. Since we view the alcoholic condition as multidetermined, we believe that an attempt to prevent alcoholism by eliminating its cause is fruitless. If an ill of man results from multiple causes, it is not sensible to seek for the single, "magic bullet" approach. On the other hand, if one views the alcoholic condition as arising from multiple causes, then the approach to prevention revolves around delineating these causes and minimizing their destructive effects. One approach is to define responsible social usage of alcohol. With a clear definition of social usage, the individual whose use of alcohol is beyond the defined limits can recognize the signs of his disturbance, or his deviation can be recognized by members of his immediate environment. The section on clinical syndromes illustrates varying ways in which alcohol can be used psychologically and socially. The next section proposes a set of criteria that may be applied as early indicators of alcohol problems. Certainly others may wish to add or subtract from this list, but this paper is an attempt to face up to the fact that alcohologists have spoken about social drinking practices in vague ways, avoiding specific signs and symptoms except in clinical settings.

In the final section the reader can see the broad outlines of a program of education aimed toward the development of responsible drinking attitudes and behavior. Alcohologists have said for years that alcohol education is the best means of prevention, and prohibitionists have desired to teach the "danger of drink." The educational process should not be based on fear and avoidance nor on the dictum that simply supplying information leads to knowledge. It must provide information, reason, and experience. The early introduction of alcohol education, balanced didactically and experientially, is crucial because, like it or not, alcohol attitudes and judgments are formed early. If responsible attitudes are to be imparted, they must start early, before psychological sets are fixed. Many western societies are ambivalent and conflicted about the use of alcohol; therefore, many parents are confused about what experiences to transmit to their children. For these reasons, educational systems are taking on many responsibilities formerly those of parents and family. Alcohol education, experience, and prevention must be faced directly, with bold ideas, if we are to make any headway in lessening the destructiveness of alcohol problems.

8.A. Alcohol Excess

The concern of society with excess is an ancient one. Rules and regulations have been heaped one upon the other in an effort to protect man from himself—from his desires, his impulses, and his excesses.

Prime among the concerns of society is that with alcohol excess. It should be noted at the outset that excess is a relative term both historically and across cultures. In prohibition eras any use of alcohol is an excess; excess in Russia is different from excess in the United States. Recently, the cry in drinking cultures has been for moderation—the avoidance of excess. As I have written elsewhere, moderation is something everyone talks about without really knowing what it is.[1] Even within the United States, excess does not lend itself as easily to measurement as many presuppose. To a teetotaler, for example, one drop of whiskey is an excess; to someone in the field of advertising where alcohol is part and parcel of the business ritual, a single martini is just a tease. A glass of wine may make a fragile, delicate woman dizzy while a glassful of bourbon may merely quench the thirst of a robust lumberjack.

Other examples of the environment in which the alcohol is used—the emotional state, the physical well-being, and a myriad of known

Section 8.A. written by Morris E. Chafetz.
Notes to Chapter 8 will be found on page 319.

and unknown factors that influence our variable responses to alcohol—could be provided to illustrate that alcohol excess, except at the lethal ends of the continuum, cannot be quantified.

Besides the difficulties of quantification, another facet bears keeping in mind: excess of anything may be destructive! To be in favor of motherhood is a safe position; yet an excess of mothering is harmful. Water, the omnipresent liquid of life, can in excess cause physical destruction and death. I do not believe that I need labor the point that in spite of problems of definition, too much of a good thing can be detrimental.

There are, however, certain aspects of alcohol excess that merit our attention. An individual may by an excess of food intake produce an excess of fat, and we respond with amusement or disgust. We may mount campaigns against this behavior as a threat to a person's health, but we do not become vindictive and punitive. The patient with obesity may not be an admired member of the sick population, but he is a treated one. Of course, many of our slogan and safety programs, I believe, are a mass attempt to imply that we have more effective control over the ever-present threat of personal demise than is actually so. Somehow, somewhere, if we are clean and good and healthy, the grim reaper will pass us by and we shall be safe a bit longer. We do not ask whether the fear of death is worth the deprivation in experiencing life that we suffer. But we have agreed that excess of anything can be detrimental.

What about alcohol excess? What is there about it that makes us self-righteous and punitive, moralistic and inhumane? Even today the attitude toward alcoholic persons is different from that toward other ill individuals. Let any one of us leave this room, go outside to come upon an individual unconscious from an excess of alcohol, and the response of us all—medical and nonmedical person alike—will be to make a wide circle around that fallen person and go on our way. We would not so respond if a person were unconscious from an epileptic fit, nor would we so respond to the plight of an accident victim who might be bloody and broken. No, we would be helpful and kind, and either situation is not a pleasant sight to behold.

The difference in response to alcoholically induced unconsciousness is that we are afraid of what the intoxicated, uncontrolled individual represents. So much effort has been expended by family and society to control us against our inner selves that the person with an infirmity that possesses the aspect of loss of control terrifies and threatens us. For too long we burned, imprisoned, or defiled the mentally ill because they lost control, and now that we have greater understanding, we accept them a bit more as respectable members of our population. Why not the person suffering alcohol problems? We have agreed, albeit reluctantly, that the mentally ill are not responsible for their infirmity, have no control over their condition, and suffer from their sickness. But the alcoholic person is viewed differently; he could stop if he really wanted to; he gets pleasure from his illness, and he tries to get away with behavior that we must ourselves avoid least we too lose hold over our flimsy controls. And so we pontificate and pronounce, moralize about misery, and generally behave in most inhumane ways toward persons with alcohol problems. It would appear, therefore, that the prevailing attitude dictates that, underneath, man is pure beast, always one breath away from total destruction. So he must be protected from himself. A bit of pleasure, a moment of temptation, a taste of the forbidden, and the uncontrollable animal desires will burst forth addicting him to the devil.

These very ancient attitudes, no longer expressed as directly as I have done here, are some of the underlying forces that make us treat the alcoholically sick as punitively as we do.

But the truth is that many cannot stop for the asking, do not enjoy their debauches, and receive no meaningful measure of gratification. It is my contention in conceptualizing any state of ill health that illness and discomfort are foreign to the individual. It is my contention that all men wish to be healthy and successful according to their private definitions of those states, and any behavior or activity that results in self-defeat or self-destruction is evidence of infirmity.

Taking up the issue of illness and when it in fact does exist is important in a consideration of alcohol excess. We assume that the determination of illness is simple—it is not. I view alcohol problems as merely one manifestation of what may be a wide variety of problems, and therefore similar to a symptom. In other words, headaches, fevers, and generalized pain are nonspecific indicators of possible states of illness. Conversely, the presence of these and other disturbances may spontaneously disappear, and we may never learn the cause of the discomfort. Then, too, we cannot state how much headache, how much fever, how much pain the person shall have before he must ask for help for his symptoms. This is most often a private or small social group decision.

What I am contending, to follow my thoughts through, is that anyone who uses alcohol to what is for him an excess-causing illness has at that moment an alcohol problem. So, if any of us yesterday became ill as a consequence of an intake of alcohol, something else may have been wrong with us to produce this unhealthy response. Similarly, if we had a headache, fever, or pain, we must conclude that phenomena were present to produce these signs of disturbed health, although with all these symptoms we may never learn the causes. My proposition, therefore, is that any recognizable discomfort, disequilibrium, or disfunction with alcohol is a symptom of a disturbed state. This contention has nothing to do with amount of excess—it even includes nonconsumption. In my conceptualization, if the mere thought of drinking alcohol produces discomfort or disequilibrium, then an alcohol problem exists.

We must also keep in mind that the determination of an unhealthy state is socially determined, and that this will vary from culture to culture and from era to era. For example, in some societies overt displays of emotion are the norm, whereas in others similar behavior is deemed weakness. Homosexuality has been accepted in certain societies and in others labeled as sickness. Cannibalism is food for survival in some spots and food for repugnance in others. Suicide is sickness in the United States, but in prewar Japan it was an honorable alternative to losing face.

We, therefore, must conclude that alcoholic excesses, alcoholic problems, alcoholism, or any other label you care to affix is produced by complex, multidimensional factors, and that, in fact, there is no such thing as an alcoholic. Just as there is no headache-ic, no fever-ic, no pain-ic, there is no alcohol-ic. I am strongly proposing that to free ourselves from the bondage of subjective statements and dogmatic pronouncements, we must begin to examine the use and nonuse, the meaning and significance, and the implications of alcohol problems as they relate to the total individual and his society, if we hope to achieve understanding in this important field. For too long we have been impaled upon the stereotype of "the alcoholic," and we have not dared to look below the surface.

The reasons for this are important for our consideration. In Chapter 4, Sections A and B, we provided evidence that although highly trained intelligent physicians stated that alcohol problems could exist in any sociocultural group, in actual practice they used the model of the derelict alcoholic person and could not recognize available evidence of alcohol problems in individuals who did not fit this narrow model. This suggests that large numbers of patients go unrecognized and miss early treatment because of the reflection of society's values as manifested through attitudes of physicians.

I believe another factor enters into the need to retain the derelict model. The upper classes who in all societies set the standards and ego ideals have, in my experience, major and extensive alcohol problems. It is class protection and mass denial for them to maintain the derelict image. This class protection is aided and abetted by the caretaking professions, and it is against my colleagues that the major indictment lies. The need to retain the derelict model is enhanced by the demand for total and permanent abstinence as the only meaningful measure of therapeutic success. They furthermore talk mysteriously about "true alcoholics." Perhaps I can illustrate this dilemma by a clinical example.

When caretakers explore the pretherapeutic level of functioning of patients with alcohol problems and find that the individual had social and occupational positions of standing, a family structure that appeared on the surface to be integrated, resources identified by middle- and upper-class values as desirable, and when treatment outcome data by multiple criteria is favorable, the attitude is one that implies that a "truly alcoholic" population was not involved. In other words, if implicitly or explicitly the patient does not fit the stereotype of "the alcoholic," that is, the derelict, one is not treating alcoholism. If a relapse occurs, common to all chronic conditions in medicine, this is taken as evidence that treatment has been wasted.

I should like to state here that when we use the clinical criteria of medicine in evaluating the treatment of alcoholism, we are as successful as the physicians who treat most other chronic conditions in medicine. By those criteria we mean an alteration for the better of the drinking behavior (relief of the symptom), a feeling of well-being and self-respect by the patient, and evidence of social function along the acceptable lines of his subculture and his realistic expectations.

But the issue here is not successful treatment, but rather the parochial attitude of the community that has relegated the patient with alcohol problems to being diagnosed and receiving help only when he has essentially first destroyed himself. Putting it another way, the cancer surgeon does not treat "real" cancer unless he deals with metastatic cancer; unless one treats only the derelict alcoholic, one is not treating an alcohol problem.

At the Massachusetts General Hospital we are trying to readjust our sights. We have concluded, as I have already stated, from our studies and those of others that programs tailored to the needs and resources of the individual are effective. But the treatment comes too late when costly devastation and destruction already exist. We have further concluded that most of us have become mired in the morass of late-stage alcoholism, and that the time is at hand for the investigation of possible early alcohol problems and a systematic study of the natural history of alcohol-related conditions. We further believe that to focus on excess is to wait for the obvious and avoid the subtle. Too much of physical disease and psychosocial crisis must go begging for recognition because we caretakers are too blind, too deaf, too busy, too preoccupied and too disinterested to look and listen. Our level of reliable knowledge in the field of alcoholism is so low (although the dicta and dogmas are plentiful) that even if our efforts provide negative results that have been scientifically achieved, we will add a bit of order to a mountain of chaos.

The intake of alcoholic beverages and episodes of inebriation are common occurrences in the United States. We assume that such intake of alcohol and even periods of inebriation do not for the vast majority of the population result in conditions by which the individual or society "tag" him. By "tagging" I mean admission to an emergency service of a hospital, arrest by a law enforcement agency, loss of occupational or university standing, and so forth, whereby the individual or society expresses concern related to alcohol use.

Since the approach to the study and care of alcohol-related conditions has been so passive, there are many areas of unstudied populations with possible alcohol problems that would lend themselves to active case finding. We have chosen in this study to focus on that population arrested for an alcohol-related offense. By an alcohol-related offense we mean an arrest for intoxication or the commission of antisocial behavior related to alcohol use as designated by a selection system. We hope that by such investigation younger and more socially intact individuals can be studied in earlier stages of alcoholism. We will also be in a position to test out whether or not interventive activity will provide a preventive function. The important point I wish to stress is not the group we study, but rather that we are directing our ideas and operations toward preventive rather than ameliorative significance, and we hope this may be a step in the direction of preventing and reducing the enormous number of casualties due to alcohol-related problems in our society.

Active casefinding requires a frame of reference. We base our approach on alcohol research on the proposition that disease or problems exist when either the individual recognizes within himself, or worries about, malfunctioning and disorder, or when society acts in cognizance of social malfunctioning or disorder in the individual. Some may say that we have no right to intervene until the individual actively seeks specific aid. But if we must wait as we have done until disturbances are so gross and severe as to be obvious to all, as for example metastatic carcinoma or Skid Row alcoholism, then we avoid the larger issue, and we can never reach pragmatic and theoretical understanding of the problem of alcohol-related conditions, much less deal with them effectively.

One of the early interesting findings involves the subject population. In our proposal we assumed that the high-incidence age group would range between the ages of 17–20. However, our surveys revealed that more suitable population for our study falls into the 14–16 age-group level. Furthermore, our preliminary findings confirm that many of society's so-called protective devices of selection—for example, "tagging" fewer boys from the "right" social class—may be doing a disservice. The reason for this disservice is that the studied population does not reveal problems with alcohol use alone, but other evidence of repeated psychosocial disorders. With our penchant for closing our eyes to what we do not care to see, we subject people to the need to send repeated serious signals before we take heed. I should like to emphasize, however, that our study at this time does not indicate that our youth are in danger of massive alcohol problems, nor that the clarion calls of the doom-seekers must be issued against the youth of today. My impression is that the present young generation in the vast majority will continue to be useful human beings to a level at least equivalent to that in the generation that judges them.

Bearing in mind some of the thoughts that I have raised, what measures can we take to reduce the incidence of alcohol-related conditions in our society? Elsewhere I have raised many of these issues, but here I would like to underline them.[2] I am suggesting we learn from other experience and other cultures. We have tried prohibition, and it failed. We have tried campaigns of slogans, and they have failed. We have tried educational programs based on fear of alcohol, and they have failed. Perhaps we ought to face some facts: that the use of alcohol in our society is here to stay; that some cultures use it and have little of the aggravation and much of the benefit; that positive educational experience can be beneficial in reducing but not eliminating problems. I am, therefore, suggesting that we explore methods by which within the home and outside of the home in proper settings, such as school and college, those who are likely to use alcoholic beverages—for example, children of drinking parents—undergo educational and practical experience in the correct as well as the incorrect use of alcohol. As we have reduced the rate of accidents in a high incidence group of traffic-accident-prone individuals by driver-training programs, perhaps we can lower the incidents of unhealthy alcohol use. Let me elaborate. Under ideal circumstances, children should learn healthy attitudes about drink in the familiar surroundings of their homes. But their parents are too confused and too guilty about their own drinking practices to transmit anything beyond their own ambivalence. I believe, therefore, that our educational institutions should provide theoretical information about alcohol and its use. The didactic material should be provided with emphasis on the benefits as well as the deficits of alcohol. They should be taught how different the response will be when a drink is sipped slowly rather than gulped; how different the response will be when drink is consumed with food and while sitting in a relaxed atmosphere, in contrast to drinking without food and standing in tense circumstances; how the use of alcohol provides meaningful experience when partaken with another, while a drink alone is as uncommunicative as talking to oneself; and how intoxication is sickness and not strength.

I would go further. I would serve sherry as well as tea at school functions. Of course, the younger child would be provided a smaller amount of alcohol in a more diluted form. I would provide those students desiring it group experiences in drinking so they might familiarize themselves with their own reactions to alcohol and learn the signals that portend an unhappy drinking experience for themselves or their peers. A practiced drinker with healthy attitudes toward alcohol will have a lower incidence of undesirable effects from alcohol than the unpracticed drinker with guilt and conflict about drinking.

Some will contend that approaches such as I propose will cause a rise in the consumption of alcoholic beverages in this country. I do not believe this to be true. I believe that the evidence from other cultures, whose use of alcohol fits the healthy attitudes I have described, illustrates that healthy use produces less consumption rather than more. I contend that the proper use of alcohol produces less drinking than the improper.

Since we live in a tense, anxious, and frightening period, where new conflicts arise before the old are resolved, alcohol use, if not properly faced, may well lead to problems of increased magnitude. Perhaps, by programs based on understanding rather than fear and guilt, we can lower the possibility of persons using alcohol to solve their life problems.

8.B. Alcoholism
Prevention and Reality

Although drinking problems have troubled mankind over the centuries, only recently have scientific and humane efforts replaced moralism and punishment as measures of dealing with them. But in spite of treatment advances in different places at different times, the pressure of drinking problems continues to grow. One answer for this incongruous situation lies in the nature of alcohol use in society and the ambiguity of definition of problem drinking. As a consequence, it seems that society and its caregivers must wait until late-stage, florid alcoholism exists before diagnosis is made and treatment introduced. Treatment goals are therefore limited and a massive effort must be expended on behalf of the individual and his society because most physical, emotional, and social resources have been dissipated before action is taken. Beyond the individual's sorry state, beyond the caregiver's limited effort, lies the effect upon what I call the "contagion" factor in the production of problem drinking and alcoholism: the spread of irresponsible, unhealthy drinking behavior to the developing and learning young. No effort in social and medical problems can hope to succeed if it is directed solely to treatment of the late stages of a condition. Treatment at best can only slow the flood waters, because the production of people far outruns the production of theaters. Furthermore, as I indicated in the previous section, I believe that if the same criteria are applied to alcoholism as to other chronic conditions dealt with by medicine, the success of treatment is roughly equivalent to that for most other chronic conditions.

For these and other reasons, I believe that the time is at hand for

---

Section 8.B. written by Morris E. Chafetz.

a redirection and reemphasis in the alcoholism field toward the major goal of early diagnosis and prevention. In this communication, I shall briefly explore each of these two avenues of approach to lowering the incidence of problem drinking, basing the conclusions on the following common observations and assumptions:

1. Alcohol as a social instrument is available and used by many large populations, and efforts to remove it have failed.

2. In many cultures that experience minimal alcohol problems, alcohol is used early and often.

3. Studies of drinking cultures without significant alcohol problems, combined with an understanding of the pharmacological action of alcohol, indicate that there are ways of drinking that do not result in alcohol problems.

4. Alcohol need not be used as a means of self-medication in physical, emotional, and social disturbances.

5. The social acceptance of intoxication implicitly or explicitly as a part of drinking behavior usually contributes to a high incidence of alcoholism.

6. Intoxication, its rate of occurrence and temporal sequence, may be arbitrarily used as early evidence of problem drinking.

As noted in assumptions 5 and 6, intoxication can be, when combined with other behavioral and social indices, the end point of the determination of problem drinking. We must remember that all ill states are socioculturally determined and that definitions and delineations, therefore, must be created to aid the individual and his society to know when to ask for help early in a condition and also to provide the impetus for social action. The following limits are proposed for complex, industrialized societies as universals of problem drinking.

1. Anyone who by his own personal definition or by the definition of his immediate society (his family) has been intoxicated four times in a year is a problem drinker.

2. Anyone who goes to work intoxicated is a problem drinker.

3. Anyone who must drink in order to get to and perform his work is a problem drinker.

4. Anyone who is intoxicated and drives a car is a problem drinker.

5. Anyone who sustains bodily injury requiring medical attention as a consequence of an intoxicated state is a problem drinker.

6. Anyone who comes in conflict with the law as a consequence of an intoxicated state is a problem drinker.

7. Anyone who, under the influence of alcohol, does something he contends he would never do without alcohol is a problem drinker.

For too long people have been confused and guilty as to whether their use of alcohol was healthy or unhealthy. It is time that experts in alcohol problems provide realistic guidelines for these determinations. Such guidelines will allow early casefinding and will, at the same time, free the vast majority of problem-free drinkers from doubt and concern about their use of alcohol.

Beyond the issue of early case finding lies the important area of prevention. We have in the past not paid sufficient attention to an obvious fact: Certain cultures use alcoholic beverages and are little troubled by alcohol problems. We know that no society can be free of physical, emotional, and social problems, so we must decide whether or not alcohol problems constitute a sufficiently destructive social force. If, as I believe, alcohol problems are a destructive social force, then we must take social action to prevent or remove the use of alcohol as a means for individuals within a society to express some of their disturbances. What I am suggesting is that the lessening of the use of alcohol in problem-solving, whether the problem be physical, emotional, or social, will not remove the underlying causes but will shift the means of expression and solution, hopefully to a less socially destructive area.

We can do this by changing the attitude toward alcohol and the social significance of drinking in a culture. The feasibility of attitudinal change in a society is not within the scope of this communication, but I believe that it can be done, and perhaps relatively easily in this day of rapid and massive communications.

The change of attitude toward alcohol that in general is preventive concerns on the one hand the development of responsible drinking behavior, based on physiological and societal factors, and on the other hand a negative sanctioning of the intoxicated state. Since I have already dealt in part with this last point, I shall hereinafter only discuss responsible drinking behavior.

The decision to drink is a private, individual decision, but historically most cultures have avoided attempts to deny alcohol to the majority who use it. Cultures that use alcohol with a low incidence of problems drink in a definite pattern: the beverage is sipped slowly, consumed with food, partaken of in the company of others in relaxed, comfortable circumstances; drinking is taken for granted and given no special significance, and no positive sanction is given to prowess in amounts consumed; and intoxication is abhorred. Cultures with a high incidence of alcohol problems drink quickly, often without food, often in solitary and uncomfortable circumstances; drinking tends to have special significance, with guilt conflict and ambivalence prevailing as attitudes; prowess in drinking is supported; intoxication is tolerated.

In times when social units were small and information input limited, social responsibility was centered in the family. Today the dissolution of close, tightly knit social units and the flood of information and stimulation provided by extensive, rapid communication no longer permit the family to provide social responsibility in all areas. For this reason, mass media and educational institutions, for better or for worse, have usurped these responsibilities. In the educational and mass-media worlds lie the potential for creating responsible drinking behavior by those who choose to drink. Furthermore, since attitudes toward alcohol are formed early, educational information and experience should be provided in the hygiene curriculum of schools, and parents should introduce diluted forms of alcohol in small amounts to their children at home, if they, themselves, are drinkers of alcohol.

By providing educational information and experience, along the lines for responsible behavior noted above, with their peers in supervised group settings at school, and by integrating their drinking experience with family use as well, immunization against unhealthy, irresponsible drinking behavior can be provided as a bulwark against alcoholism.

It is time we faced the world as it is and created programs of early identification and prevention based on observable realities. Such an approach would lessen the destructiveness of unhealthy alcohol use.

8.C. Clinical Syndromes of Liquor Drinkers

Alcohol by itself is a simple substance. But when introduced into a human and his environment, it can effect a wide range of variable responses not only between individual and individual, culture and culture, but even within the same person from time to time.

In any examination of the clinical syndromes of liquor drinkers, we must resist the temptation to treat them as those other problems of medicine that more easily lend themselves to categorization; we must take a macroscopic perspective that sees alcohol in relation to society and culture before we can single out for microscopic analysis its action on individuals. Let us begin by looking at the drinking behavior of North Americans.

Many, perhaps a majority of Americans, drink liquor as they live life: rapidly and under tense circumstances. Whether at a cocktail party, a commuter bar, or a private party the general tendency is to achieve rapid, heightened effects from alcoholic beverages. Coupled with this approach to drinking is the desired end point of being "high." Being "high" (or the many other words used to describe this state), as I understand it, is to get to that delicate point of alcohol effect where one is intoxicated but not sick. By intoxicated but not sick, I mean a state where inhibitions are lowered, but where gastric upsets and hangover do not appear. Besides the rapidity of drinking, Americans often drink liquor with little or no food in their stomachs, and in tense, uncomfortable circumstances that often create sufficient anxiety that individuals drink more than intended.

Now the hairline or delicate end point of drink effect I have just described is—especially in the way and where we drink—a tough target to hit. For the variety of influences that can mediate the

Section 8.C. written by Morris E. Chafetz.

imbibing of a definite amount of alcohol are innumerable. The psychological, physical, and social factors that determine our response to a given quantity of alcohol are not consistent from individual to individual, nor within the same person at separate points of time. Since responses to alcohol are unpredictable, you can readily see that drinkers who use alcohol to reach a delicate balance between feeling good and feeling sick often cross the border and suffer the complications.

But you must understand: Our culture does not disdain intoxication. As a matter of fact in our culture to get high or intoxicated (without the unpleasant side effects noted above), is condoned if not acceptable behavior. We conveniently forget that a state of intoxication, even without the unpleasant symptoms, is a state of illness. By a state of illness I mean the partaking of a substance to that state where cerebral and motor controls are severely impaired. We drink, therefore, in the United States with the goal, for the most part, of making oneself sick. This is so strongly engraved in American drinking behavior that one cannot talk about drinking without many people equating it with being drunk.

Recently in a lecture before the New York Academy of Science, I proposed exploration of a preventive approach to alcoholism based on didactic and experiential information on alcohol use in the schools in order to develop responsible drinking patterns in our culture. No one in response—serious or jocular—could discuss my proposal without intimating the students would be intoxicated. Our stage, our television, our writing, most always portray drinking liquor as meaning being drunk. By such a cultural attitude we give sanction to and continually reinforce the proposal that an intoxicated state is acceptable. Does it not appear that our culture permits, seeks and sanctions a sick state with respect to alcohol? And yet we close our eyes to many parts of the world where alcohol is used and where the kind of drinking behavior or acceptance of intoxication I have described is not sanctioned, but where alcohol problems are minimal; whereas other nations whose drinking behavior and attitudes approach our own suffer many alcohol problems.

The attitude of drinking to an intoxicated state has produced one further complication that results in alcohol problems. To counterbalance the desire for drunkenness, there are powerful forces in favor of abolishing all drinking. In other words, extremes of the continuum exist: It's all right to drink to get drunk; it's destructive to touch any alcohol at all. The latter attitude is as conducive to alcohol problems as the former when both coexist in the same culture. And so, you may see the powerful forces operating to produce alcoholism among liquor drinkers in the United States. I should like, before leaving the macroscopic, to reiterate that the causes of alcohol problems are complex and multifaceted and I have filtered out only those major forces operating in nations that have a high incidence of alcoholism.

Bearing the points I have noted above in mind, let us now look at some of the syndromes that exist among liquor drinkers.

To any student of alcohol problems, a common experience is to find, on examination, that the patient uses liquor as a form of self-medication for depression. The etiology of the depression may be related to external causes and be reactive in nature or have more deep-seated roots and be endogenous. Whatever the cause of the depression, the patient begins to use liquor to dull the inner pain and dispel the ugliness within him. The drinking pattern is irregular with these patients: Anniversaries or episodes associated with a loss may lead to a drinking bout; rejection or humiliation, however slight, may similarly nudge the patient to the bottle.

What is striking in these patients, however, is the response to liquor. On the one hand, some patients who take alcohol to alleviate depression find that alcohol actually deepens depression. They respond to the deepened depression by imbibing more and more of the liquor hoping to achieve the relief they seek. Others find that liquor provides what they seek—relief from depression—and become fearful of giving up the bottle for fear that the pain and ugliness will return. Fortunately for the latter, the physical discomfort and illness an excess of alcohol can provide at times, yields them a measure of self-punishment that in itself can temporarily afford relief from depression.

In this age of psychiatric sophistication to focus on the obvious problem of self-medication by liquor and not notice the subtle but causative force of the depression is unfortunate. Careful evaluation of the patient's psychopathology and resources for recovery can provide relief by psychotherapeutic and/or psychopharmacological methods and the need for unhealthy use of liquor can be avoided.

A second kind of liquor user is the person who employs alcohol to blur his perceptions. Such an individual becomes aware that some socially forbidden impulses are operating within him and he develops uncomfortable sensations. An example of this is that individual who has strong homosexual drives that he represses when he is sober. Under circumstances where he becomes homosexually aroused and becomes anxious because these feelings are so close to the surface, the individual may use alcohol heavily. The alcohol use in this circumstance serves a dual function: The liquor may obliterate the discomforting feelings of homosexual arousal on one level or it may dissolve inhibitions on another to permit the drinker to express his homosexual instincts. If homosexual activity—forbidden during sobriety—but practiced during intoxication—occurs, the individual does not consider himself responsible for his actions. He is aware of what has gone on; his responsibilities and desires are masked to him.

A brief clinical history may illustrate this point. A married patient engaged in frequent and intensive extramarital sexual activity; whenever sexual situations arose that could question his masculinity and potency, he would drink heavily. At such times he could perform with a woman partner only if she would describe her sexual experiences with some other man or he would set up situations where he and some other man would presumably share a woman. Under the influence of alcohol, instead of sharing he would engage in homosexual activities. He would deny to himself when he reflected on these experiences their obvious homosexual connotations but would attribute the events to the liquor he had consumed.

This patient and others with similar configurations use alcohol to alter their perceptions of their inner selves and their outer worlds. Here, too, the removal of alcohol without an attempt to deal with the contributing factors toward heavy liquor use will result in a patient developing severe states of anxiety and the onset of various somatic symptoms. My experience with this group of patients has shown me that when they can begin to recognize and deal in different ways with those impulses they make believe do not exist, their need for liquor is significantly lessened.

Another common type of liquor drinker is the individual who uses alcohol to sustain a psychological system of defenses. With this group the often noted "blackout" phenomenon is usual. In other words their repressed unconscious desires become a reality, but they have no recollection when sober of what has transpired. People with a sober characterological attitude of complete kindness, nonexistent hostility, and abject passivity will with liquor become brutal, hostile, and aggressive. A startled employer may find at a company party an intoxicated employee who insults him freely as he would never dare when sober. The employee will not recall once the effects of the liquor have gone and will be incredulous at descriptions of his behavior while intoxicated.

Similarly, the fastidious, prudish woman can, when intoxicated, become filthy in habit, unclean in dress, and promiscuous in behavior. Many a puritan woman has awakened with a shock from an alcoholic slumber to find a man peacefully sharing her pillow, she not knowing how he got there. The secret, repressed desires under the facade of social attitude, respectability, and behavior are obvious.

Less obvious is that subgroup of individuals who although heavily under the influence of liquor do not seem so to the casual observer. These individuals can carry on highly complicated business and social activities and not seem to be any the worse for their drinking. Only when a fall in the blood alcohol level occurs, do they suddenly return to their original state of awareness. These people, when they regain their nondrinking self, do not have an inkling as to people, places, or events that have transpired sometimes for hours, days, or weeks. Where at one moment in time the person may have been the sworn-friend-for-life of another while intoxicated, the "pop" into a sober state brings a response of unfamiliarity startling to all concerned. Not only is the liquor drinker stunned by sudden situations, but innocent sharers of that "other" personality are now confronted with a new individual in an old body.

Treatment in this total group of liquor drinkers is not a simple task. The intensity of denial, the strength of repression, and the alien aspects of behavior make the therapist's task formidable. The dissociative implications that are to a varying degree present in this syndrome suggest serious psychopathology, only a part of which may be amenable to psychiatric treatment.

Since we have just examined a serious syndrome of liquor drinkers, perhaps we ought now to look at one with less ominous prognosis: those who use liquor to break down psychological barriers. From time to time we are called upon to perform an activity we wish to but cannot. Our conscious desire to perform is overwhelmed and incapacitated by unconscious restrictions. Try as we will, try as we must, we cannot do. Liquor for many of these blocked responses is an easy ally; the hounding inhibitions melt quickly before its chemical presence and one can go on. With such cases the lawyer is asked to argue his case before the tribunal with liquor; the actor may bring himself to the otherwise terrifying center stage; the lecturer speak; the author write; the frigid woman respond, and so forth. For this group to drink is to perform and the horrible anxiety and tension pass from the scene.

This group of liquor drinkers is growing because it seems that the demands of increasingly complex social situations require alcohol to ease the way, and the commuter bars are crowded with men who must fortify themselves before they even face their families. Unfortunately, alcohol's dependence on providing the desired relief is fickle and increased amounts to produce the desired-for effect may lead to states of intoxication and responses not appropriate to the circumstances.

Treatment here may or may not be simple. For some a relationship with a sympathetic, understanding, and supporting human being can supply the source of strength formerly furnished by a bottle. For others delving into the source of the fear and developing new—less destructive—methods of handling the anxiety are desirable. In an increasingly complex society, the danger of alcohol fulfilling a tranquilizing role must be guarded against. On the other hand, it may be preferable to relying on a host of other drugs.

Liquor for a certain segment of the population is not unlike the narcosis achieved by the morphine addict. For these liquor imbibers, one goal is worth drinking for: oblivion. The inhabitants of this unhappy drinking state down their drinks to obtain a state of bliss. To them reality is a terror; a dream state of narcosis the only way to continue. Here we see the patient who ends a drinking bout not because he is ill but because he is unconscious. Here we see the person for whom cirrhosis of the liver, esophageal varices, polyneuropathy, loss of family, loss of jobs, loss of self-respect, and loss of life are no threat, no deterrent from drinking. Death is more desirable than life without liquor. To be a habitue of Skid Row with its external social oblivion and internal emotionless life is the all-consuming desire. Although these people are fortunately only a small segment of the problem liquor drinkers, they form the stereotype for most people when they think of alcoholic persons; they also form a major social problem.

Patients who are so bent on self-destruction did not come to this sorry state solely as a result of alcohol. Careful study of their life histories reveal severe disturbances of their prealcoholic personality. Retrospective evidence exists that a disturbance of interpersonal relations revealed itself early. Family adjustment and school performance operated at the extremes of a continuum: overcontrolled or undercontrolled behavior. Goals were seldom achieved and, if accomplished, with unwarranted difficulty. Instability of occupation was common; marriage rates equivalent to that of a nonalcoholic population but with a significantly higher incidence of marital disintegration. In this group the point at which drinking became uncontrolled is diffuse and indefinite and there is some suggestion that social drinking never really existed. Onsets of drinking bouts are unrelated usually to specific external stresses and continue until sickness and stupor ensue. The entire life history pattern as well as the drinking history reveal strong self-destructive and self-defeating behaviors.

Treatment for this group requires a wide gamut of modalities—not because treatment is futile—but because careful tailoring of the therapy to the patient and his resources are essential. Here, too, treatment goals must be based on realistic expectations and perhaps limited objectives. Too often treatment efforts are self-defeating because unrealistic demands are imposed upon patient and therapists. Before leaving this group I must relate an incident told me by a patient. He had been a liquor drinker who essentially fell into the group I have just described and was in a controlled, sober state when he took his wife to Skid Row. His wife was understandably shocked by the sight of intoxicated, oblivious forms lying in doorways and on the street. Noting her response, her husband said, "What is even more shocking is that I envy them their oblivion."

Another clinical syndrome of liquor drinkers we have observed is that in which an individual is more tolerable to his social unit intoxicated than sober. This syndrome is most clearly seen in configurations whereby nonalcoholic, extremely dominating mates or parents exist. On the one hand, the nonalcoholic mate or parent appears on the surface to suffer greatly as a consequence of the alcoholic state of another. If treatment or extraneous events result in sobriety, however, opposition to this state in the so-called healthy members rises. They become proportionately more disturbed as the alcoholic member becomes less alcoholic. What becomes clear is that the pathological drinking behavior of the alcoholic person, socially unacceptable and readily obvious to society, was a cover-up for disturbances in another. Improvement in one exposes the problems in another and the unhealthy drinking in such cases satisfies, in part, emotional needs of another. Furthermore, we see some mates who cannot tolerate the dependency and demands put upon them when the alcoholic person is sober but can readily provide emotional sustenance instead of rejection when he is drunk.

Treatment of this group when directed toward the alcoholic individual alone is self-defeating. The subtle and covert influences that an intimate emotional and social situation can bring to bear in an antitherapeutic way are endless. Unless the symbiotic relationship is understood, treatment will be unsuccessful. Rehabilitation efforts must be directed either toward social manipulation and separation of the patient from his environment or combined treatment of patient and the significant individuals in his society.

The clinical syndrome of liquor drinkers I shall consider last is the one I feel contributes much to unhealthy alcohol use and may give us some clues to preventive measures: the cocktail party. At least in America, and I suspect that it is spreading to other nations as well, the cocktail party epitomizes the essence of unhealthy drinking practice, unfavorable responses to liquor, and unrelating social behavior.

The cocktail party is supreme in emphasizing man's emotional isolation from man; his isolation from what he does, thinks, and feels. People are brought together—many of them unknown to one another—to drink, to talk, to be gay. The drinking is done while standing, gulped rapidly, and with the barest minimum of food, and heightened responses toward intoxication are frequent. All factors conducive to heavy alcoholic use exist in the cocktail party situation. Drinking under these circumstances provides little of the pleasurable responses of relaxation and socialization alcohol can provide. The talk of the cocktail party emphasizes this. People do not listen; they do not care. All of us are familiar with the habitue of the cocktail party who while pouring liquor into himself, pours into our ear his soul: intimate details of his life he would never utter to a close friend. The reason for this is fairly obvious: we do not matter; we probably do not care. It is simpler to share intimate details on one's life with an individual with whom we are not emotionally involved than with those we wish to continue our involvement. Words spoken at cocktail parties are often spoken to oneself rather than to another because excess drinking creates a pharmacological barrier to emotional and social communication while healthy alcohol use facilitates communication. Drinking that points in the direction of isolation—epitomized by the cocktail party and the commuter bar—produce a liquor syndrome for perpetuating and intensifying alcohol problems.

If one reflects on the syndromes I have described, one can see that alcohol use is but one manifestation of a total group of problems of varying intensity, that is, it is symptomatic behavior. True, the destructive nature of alcohol problems can be such that one will only focus on the alcoholic disturbance and not upon the underlying physical, psychological, and social causes. If we are to attempt to reduce alcohol problems on a wide scale, one approach is to understand the factors involved in alcohol's being chosen as a symptom and then systematically to change those factors.

Centuries of evidence have shown us that some societies drink and yet suffer minimal alcohol problems, while others drink with major alcoholic disturbances as a consequence. Obviously, since all societies and cultures exist with problems, the method of coping with the pains of life has been chosen out of the alcoholic context—presumably in a nonalcoholic manner and thereby presumably by less destructive social mechanisms. My preventive approach aims at removing alcohol as a coping tool of society but does not reach the variable and complex causes of alcohol problems. This proposal is based upon my understanding of physiological and pharmacological principles of alcohol use, a study of drinking behavior in nonalcoholic societies, and an understanding of psychological responses to dysequilibrium.

This preventive approach aims to inculcate societies with responsible drinking behavior and to interlard alcohol use with all ordinary social behavior by teaching young people how to drink with responsibility, without ill effects, and for benefit only. This learning experience for those who will choose to drink and those who will not provides factual information about alcohol use during hygiene instruction at school and college levels. This instruction emphasizes the differing effects between drinking rapidly versus sipping slowly; consuming liquor with food in the stomach versus drinking on an empty stomach; drinking under tense circumstances alone or drinking while relaxed, with people and communicating; how intoxication is sickness and is unhealthy behavior. By providing on a voluntary basis group experiences with alcohol under supervision, young people may familiarize themselves with their own responses to alcohol under variable conditions and learn how to avoid disastrous, unhealthy episodes. Finally, I would make alcohol available to all so that the attraction provided by that which is forbidden will be removed.

The day is at hand when many social and human problems we avoided, we can now hope to make positive inroads into. However, we must guard ourselves against the lingering prejudices of ignorance that continually threaten to defeat our purpose. This is the case with alcohol problems. We have a responsibility to open paths of communication so people and societies will no longer need to suffer as much from alcohol problems.

Notes
1. M. E. CHAFETZ, *Liquor: The Servant of Man* (Boston, Massachusetts: Little, Brown and Co., 1965).
2. Ibid.

Conclusion

As we survey the development and range of ten years' work in alcoholism, we are surprised at its substance and directions. The wisdom of hindsight makes us wish that it were part of some grand design, but reflection suggests it was the needs of people with problems rather than a master plan that guided our endeavors. The inception of our work resulted from a need to isolate people with alcohol problems, in order that they might be treated. Only by segregating them from seemingly more attractive, nonalcoholic patients could they be studied and treated. As our sophistication grew, our interest in these people caused others in our hospital to look with less prejudiced eyes, and attitudes began to change. Soon, what was good enough for people with alcohol problems was good enough for the rest of the psychiatric population, so that our alcoholic population could be assimilated into our psychiatric population. It is our contention that real progress will have been accomplished only when alcohol problems are everywhere treated as humanely as any other condition, and the need for segregated facilities no longer exists either in theory or in practice.

What lies beyond the frontiers? There is the need for innovative teaching programs for professionals, preprofessionals, and nonprofessionals. Such teaching programs require new ideas and challenges, rather than a repetition of the catechisms of alcoholism that have so often marked the educational efforts of the present. We need to test our ideas about alcohol and alcoholism, and to be prepared to jettison them when contrary information is provided. We must move away from models exclusively concerned with treatment and from research which is repetitively descriptive, and move toward the implementation of ideas concerning prevention. We must attract people whose interest in the field comes about not through personal tragedy but rather through stimulated interest. We must look more closely at the other cultures which have used alcohol and suffered little from it. Knowledge about the epidemiology and natural history of alcohol problems must be systematically sought. We must study the early signs of alcohol problems, and whether they develop into full-blown alcoholism, or are redirected and compensated for by forces within the individual and the environment. We must investigate the young of alcoholic parents, and study the influence, or protection, that the alcoholic condition delivers to the impressionable. But of course we must never neglect those who are casualties of alcohol problems. They must be understood and treated, treated by approaches that tailor the treatment to the individual; they must not be treated as members of a herd who constitute a category of disease.

As we review the work we present to the reader, we see that much knowledge, attitude, and interest concerning alcoholic people and problems has changed. It is a more refreshing and respectable field in which to labor than it once was. But lest one feel that what is presented here is the ultimate answer we, the editors, remind the reader that frontiers are merely beginnings, and that much remains to be done.

Appendix A
Tables

Notes to Appendix A

Unless otherwise indicated, the statistic employed to analyze the data summarized in the following tables is the x^2 technique. Probability levels uniformly follow this notational scheme:

a: $p \leq .10$
b: $p \leq .05$
c: $p \leq .01$
d: $p \leq .001$

TABLE 1

VISITS, TREATMENT REIATIONS, AND DEGREE OF
ISOLATION BY GROUPS (PERCENTAGES)

	Group Experimental	Control
A. Visits, Isolated Sample	$n = 100$	$n = 93$
Initial Clinic Visit	65.0	5.4[d]
Five or More Visits	42.0	1.1[d]
B. Treatment Relations, Isolated Sample	$n = 100$	$n = 93$
Established	42.0	1.1
Abortive	23.0	4.3
None	35.0	94.6[d]
C. Visits, Less Isolated Sample	$n = 50$	$n = 50$
Initial Clinic Visit	78.0	6.0
Five or More Visits	56.0	0.0[d]

Appendix A

TABLE 2
NUMBER OF VISITS AND CLINIC CONTACTS BY
EXPERIMENTAL PATIENTS MAKING FIVE OR MORE VISITS

	Number of Visits				Number of Contacts				
	5–9	10–14	15–19	20+	Total	5–9	10–14	15–19	20+	Total
Number of Patients	25	8	3	6	42	21	10	2	9	42
Percentage	59.5	19.0	7.1	14.3	99.9	50.0	23.8	4.8	21.4	100.0

Table 3

PATIENTS' AND RELATIVES' VISITS BY GROUPS (PERCENTAGES)

	Group Experimental	Control
A. Patients' Visits	$n = 21$	$n = 24$
Initial Clinic Visit	61.9	20.8[c]
Five or More Visits	26.8	0.0[1]
B. Relatives' Visits	$n = 21$	$n = 24$
Initial Clinic Visits	38.1	12.5[b]
Five or More Visits	9.5	0.0[2]

[1] Fisher's Exact test, $p = .007$.
[2] Fisher's Exact test, $p = .21$.

Table 4

EFFECTIVENESS OF LETTERS AS MOTIVATION FOR TREATMENT (PERCENTAGES)

	Letters Sent	Letters Not Sent
Return to Hospital	50.0 ($n = 50$)	32.0 ($n = 50$)[b]
Return the Same Day	76.0 ($n = 25$)	12.5 ($n = 16$)[d]
Return Sober	80.0 ($n = 25$)	31.0 ($n = 16$)[d]

Appendix A

TABLE 5
ESTABLISHMENT AND MAINTENANCE OF TREATMENT BY SELECTED VARIABLES (PERCENTAGES)

	Establishing Treatment Relations	Maintaining Treatment Relations
Behavioral Dependency		
Dependent ($n = 59$)	61.0	27.1
Counterdependent ($n = 40$)	15.0[d]	2.5[c]
Mode of Entry		
Police ($n = 58$)	32.8	13.8
Other ($n = 41$)	53.7[b]	22.0
Hospitalization		
Hospitalized ($n = 64$)	48.4	25.0
Not Hospitalized ($n = 36$)	30.6[a]	2.8[c]
Current Social Class		
I–II ($n = 0$)	—	—
III ($n = 3$)	0.0	0.0
IV ($n = 16$)	68.8	12.5
V ($n = 67$)	40.3[b]	19.4
Past Social Class		
I ($n = 0$)	—	—
II–III ($n = 13$)	38.5	7.7
IV ($n = 38$)	63.2	26.3
V ($n = 35$)	28.6[b]	11.4
Major Occupational Level		
2–3 ($n = 11$)	18.2	9.1
4–5 ($n = 36$)	66.7	30.6
6–7 ($n = 47$)	34.0[c]	10.6[b]
Social Isolation		
a. Living with Relatives ($n = 26$)	26.9	7.7
Not Living with Relatives ($n = 72$)	47.2[a]	20.8
b. Employed ($n = 38$)	28.9	7.9
Not Employed ($n = 62$)	50.0[b]	22.6[a]
c. Rent-Own Home-Apartment ($n = 30$)	30.0	10.0
Rent Room, Homeless ($n = 65$)	49.2[a]	21.5

TABLE 5 (cont.)

ESTABLISHMENT AND MAINTENANCE OF TREATMENT
BY SELECTED VARIABLES (PERCENTAGES)

	Establishing Treatment Relations	Maintaining Treatment Relations
d. Single ($n = 29$)	20.7	6.9
Married ($n = 11$)	45.4	18.2
Marriage Terminated ($n = 60$)	51.7[b]	21.7
Social Isolation Index		
∅ ($n = 15$)	26.7	6.7
1 ($n = 12$)	33.3	7.7
2 ($n = 21$)	33.3	15.0
3 ($n = 47$)	55.3	25.5
Social Dependence		
a. Hospital Use 1 Year Pre-Admission ($n = 40$)	52.5	25.0
No Hospital Use 1 Year Pre-Admission ($n = 60$)	35.0[a]	11.7[a]
b. Hospital Use 5 Years Pre-Admission ($n = 58$)	50.0	24.1
No Hospital Use 5 Years Pre-Admission ($n = 42$)	31.0[a]	7.1[b]
c. Pension ($n = 27$)	59.3	29.6
No Pension ($n = 73$)	35.6[b]	12.3[b]
d. Social Agency Use 5 Years Pre-Admission ($n = 21$)	57.1	23.8
No Social Agency Use 5 Years Pre-Admission ($n = 79$)	38.0	15.2
e. Arrests 1 Year Pre-Admission ($n = 38$)	47.4	26.3
No Arrests 1 Year Pre-Admission ($n = 62$)	38.7	11.3[a]
f. Imprisonment 1 Year Pre-Admission ($n = 30$)	53.3	23.3
No Imprisonment 1 Year Pre-Admission ($n = 70$)	37.1	14.3
g. Social Dependence Index		
∅ ($n = 21$)	19.0	0.0
1 ($n = 35$)	40.0	14.3
2 ($n = 32$)	50.0	28.1
3–4 ($n = 11$)	72.7[b]	27.3[b]

TABLE 6

BEHAVIORAL DEPENDENCE AS RELATED TO SOCIAL ISOLATION AND SOCIAL DEPENDENCE (PERCENTAGES)

	Behaviorally Dependent
Social Isolation Index ($n=95$)	
∅ ($n=15$)	60.0
1 ($n=12$)	25.0
2 ($n=21$)	57.1
3 ($n=47$)	72.3[b]
Social Dependence Index ($n=94$)	
∅ ($n=21$)	52.4
1 ($n=35$)	48.6
2 ($n=32$)	71.9
3–4 ($n=11$)	72.8

TABLE 7

IDENTIFYING SOCIAL AND MEDICALLY RELEVANT CHARACTERISTICS OF ALCOHOLICS ASSIGNED AND NONASSIGNED TO ALCOHOLISM PROJECT (PERCENTAGES)

	Assigned	Nonassigned
Marital Status	$n=194$	$n=235$
Single	39.7	35.7
Married	26.3	40.0
Widowed	6.7	8.1
Separated, Divorced	27.3	16.2[c]
Marital Status (excl. Single)	$n=117$	$n=151$
Married	43.6	62.3
Widowed	11.1	12.6
Separated, Divorced	45.3	25.2[c]
Employer Listed	$n=185$	$n=23$
Yes	51.8	51.7
No	48.2	48.3
Employer Listed[1]	$n=153$	$n=163$
Yes	58.8	69.9
No	41.2	30.1[b]
Closest Relative	$n=175$	$n=214$
Parent	18.3	21.5
Wife	34.3	47.2
Child	5.1	7.9
Sibling	35.4	17.8
Other Relative	6.9	5.6[c]
Closest Relative[2]	$n=124$	$n=121$
Parent	25.8	38.0
Wife	8.8	5.8
Child	7.3	14.0
Sibling	48.4	32.2
Other Relative	9.7	9.9[b]
Reside with Closest Relative	$n=162$	$n=206$
Yes	42.6	63.6
No	57.4	36.4[d]

[1] Excluding cases over 65 years of age or receiving public assistance.
[2] Excluding current married parents.

Appendix A

TABLE 7 (cont.)

IDENTIFYING SOCIAL AND MEDICALLY RELEVANT
CHARACTERISTICS OF ALCOHOLICS ASSIGNED AND
NONASSIGNED TO ALCOHOLISM PROJECT
(PERCENTAGES)

	Assigned	Nonassigned
Public Assistance	$n=198$	$n=236$
Yes	13.1	25.0
No	86.9	75.0[c]
Medical Insurance	$n=198$	$n=226$
Yes	17.2	38.9
No	82.8	61.1[d]
Mode of Entry to Emergency Service	$n=198$	$n=231$
Police	55.6	35.1
Other	44.4	64.9[d]
Previous Hospital Admission	$n=163$	$n=227$
Yes	62.6	70.5
No	37.4	29.5
Source of Referral Listed	$n=200$	$n=238$
Yes	3.5	18.9
No	96.5	80.1[d]
Patient's Subjective Complaint	$n=200$	$n=238$
Medical	17.5	57.1
Surgical	6.5	13.0
Alcoholic	27.0	1.3
Psychiatric	1.0	1.7
No Complaint Listed	48.0	26.9[d]
Physician's Diagnostic Impression	$n=200$	$n=238$
Medical	6.5	39.5
Surgical	24.5	27.3
Alcoholic	41.5	13.0
Psychiatric	1.5	0.8
No Diagnosis	26.0	19.3[d]
Hospitalization Subsequent to Present Emergency Admission	$n=99$[1]	$n=237$
Yes	18.2	49.4
No	81.8	50.6[d]

Experimental assigned cases were not included in this analysis.

TABLE 8

PERCENTAGE DISTRIBUTION ON SOCIAL INTEGRATION, MEDICAL, AND SOCIAL-MEDICAL INDICES OF ALCOHOLICS ASSIGNED AND NONASSIGNED TO ALCOHOLISM PROJECT

	Assigned	Nonassigned	Nonassigned within Index Position[1]
Social Integration Index	$n=199$	$n=237$	
∅	6.5	0.8	11.0
1	16.6	8.9	34.9
2	21.6	12.2	36.1
3	23.6	18.1	43.4
4	17.6	22.8	56.4
5	10.6	21.9	67.4
6	3.5	15.2[d]	81.3
Medical Index	$n=99$	$n=237$	
∅	40.4	13.5	25.0
1	41.4	19.4	31.9
2	13.1	27.4	67.7
3	4.0	28.3	87.6
4	1.0	11.4[d]	91.9
Social-Medical Index	$n=199$	$n=237$	
.00– .10	12.1	3.0	19.9
.11– .20	20.6	5.1	19.8
.21– .30	19.6	6.3	24.3
.31– .40	17.6	10.1	36.5
.41– .50	15.1	19.0	55.7
.51– .60	11.1	18.1	62.0
.61– .70	3.0	12.7	80.9
.71– .80	1.0	12.7	92.7
.81– .90	0.0	10.1	100.0
.91–1.00	0.0	3.0[d]	100.0

[1] Percentages corrected for unequal n's.

Appendix A

TABLE 9
INTERCORRELATIONS AMONG POSTDICTIVE VARIABLES

	Anger-Sympathy	Anger-Anxiety	Anger-Matter-of-Factness	Sympathy-Anxiety	Sympathy-Matter-of-Factness	Anxiety-Matter-of-Factness	Sophistication about Alcoholism-Psychological Mindedness
Normal Channel							
Male Judges	−.11	.27	−.54	−.09	−.06	−.56	—
Female Judges	−.49	−.19	−.62[a]	−.52	.27	.04	—
Total	−.46	−.03	−.58[a]	−.40	.24	−.38	—
Tone-Only Channel							
Male Judges	−.75[b]	−.00	.07	−.30	−.38	−.09	—
Female Judges	−.72[b]	.65[a]	−.22	−.66[a]	.24	−.67[b]	—
Total	−.77[b]	.44	−.02	−.58[a]	.05	−.67[b]	—
Content-Only Channel							
Male Judges	−.21	−.06	.00	.38	−.07	−.57	.79[b]
Female Judges	−.48	.05	.04	−.24	.25	−.79[b]	.70[b]
Total	−.46	.01	.03	.04	.27	−.75[b]	.78[b]

TABLE 10

MEDIA INTERCORRELATIONS

	Normal Tone-Only	Normal Content-Only	Tone-Only Content-Only
Male Judge			
Anger	.33	.38	.22
Sympathy	.60[a]	−.45	−.27
Anxiety	.13	.34	.55
Matter-of-factness	.04	.88[c]	.38
Female Judge			
Anger	.45	.52	.53
Sympathy	.49	.68[b]	−.06
Anxiety	.46	.52	.18
Matter-of-factness	−.07	.40	−.11
Total Judge			
Anger	.53	.49	.43
Sympathy	.69[b]	.08	−.29
Anxiety	.33	.48	.36
Matter-of-factness	.27	.72[b]	.19
Median	.39	.49	.21

Appendix A

TABLE 11
KENDALL W RELIABILITIES

	Male Judge	Female Judge	Total Judge
Normal			
Anger	.625[c]	.555[c]	.302[c]
Sympathy	.457[b]	.512[c]	.242[b]
Anxiety	.449[b]	.491[b]	.318[c]
Matter-of-factness	.674[d]	.384	.345[d]
Tone-Only			
Anger	.413[b]	.631[c]	.278[c]
Sympathy	.493[b]	.557[c]	.323[c]
Anxiety	.395[b]	.502[c]	.303[c]
Matter-of-factness	.126	.319	.065
Content-Only			
Anger	.256	.329	.212[b]
Sympathy	.492[b]	.417[b]	.106
Anxiety	.493[b]	.719[d]	.481[d]
Matter-of-factness	.282	.509[c]	.188
Sophistication	.688[d]	.694[d]	.369[d]
Psychological-mindedness	.438[b]	.541[b]	.348[d]

TABLE 12
AGREEMENT BETWEEN MALE AND FEMALE JUDGES

	Normal Channel	Tone-Only Channel	Content-Only Channel
Anger-Irritation	.78[b]	.42	.97[d]
Sympathy-Kindness	.42	.61	.06
Anxiety-Nervousness	.81[c]	.84[c]	.98[d]
Matter-of-factness-Professionalism	.71[b]	−.07	.66
Median	.74[b]	.52	.82[c]

TABLE 13

RELATIONSHIP OF SPEECH RATINGS TO REFERRAL EFFECTIVENESS

	Anger	Sympathy	Anxiety	Matter-of-factness	Sophistication	Psychological-mindedness
Male Judge						
Normal Channel	.00	−.13	.75[b]	−.54	—	—
Tone-Only Channel	−.67[b]	.37	−.25	.13	—	—
Content-Only Channel	−.42	−.49	.05	−.50	−.43	−.52
Female Judge						
Normal Channel	−.37	−.27	.49	−.27	—	—
Tone-Only Channel	−.49	.13	−.26	−.10	—	—
Content-Only Channel	−.36	−.34	.04	−.14	−.40	−.45
Total Judge						
Normal Channel	−.24	−.25	.62[a]	−.45	—	—
Tone-Only Channel	−.65[a]	.27	−.27	.06	—	—
Content-Only Channel	−.38	−.57	.05	−.31	−.48	−.50

Appendix A

TABLE 14

COMPARISON OF DIAGNOSED ALCOHOLICS, UNDIAGNOSED ALCOHOLICS, AND NONALCOHOLICS ON MEASURES OF SOCIAL ISOLATION
(PERCENTAGES)

	Diagnosed Alcoholic (D)	Undiagnosed Alcoholic (U)	Nonalcoholic (C)	χ^2 DvsC	DvsU	UvsC
1. Current Social Contact						
a. Currently Married	26.3 ($n=194$)	40.0 ($n=235$)	58.5 ($n=176$)	38.15[d]	8.33[c]	13.10[d]
b. Living with Closest Relative	44.0 ($n=200$)	61.8 ($n=238$)	75.6 ($n=176$)	37.21[d]	13.09[d]	8.19[c]
c. Employer Listed	51.9 ($n=185$)	51.7 ($n=230$)	67.1 ($n=170$)	7.82[c]	ns	8.81[c]
2. Social Stability						
a. Maintained Marriage	54.7 ($n=117$)	74.8 ($n=151$)	90.7 ($n=129$)	39.06[d]	11.03[d]	10.88[d]
b. Employed Where Possible	58.8 ($n=153$)	69.9 ($n=163$)	84.7 ($n=124$)	20.75[d]	ns	7.67[c]
3. Use of Social Resources						
a. Medical Insurance	20.5 ($n=200$)	39.9 ($n=238$)	45.5 ($n=176$)	25.58[d]	18.24[d]	ns
b. Hospital Entry, Self or Referred	44.4 ($n=198$)	64.9 ($n=231$)	84.5 ($n=174$)	62.11[d]	17.30[d]	18.41[d]

Note: Cases for which data were unobtainable differed significantly for measures of living with closest relative (n's for unknown subjects for D, U, C are 38, 32, and 11, respectively), and medical insurance (n's are 20, 22, and 4, respectively). Unknown subjects for these measures were distributed evenly between Yes and No categories before computing the χ^2.

TABLE 15

NUMBER OF PATIENTS, VISITS, AND BY WHOM SEEN
IN THE ACUTE PSYCHIATRIC SERVICE IN A 3-MONTH PERIOD
(JAN. 1–MAR. 31, 1964)

Number of Patients	1,271
Number of Patient Contacts	1,703
Number of Patients Seen by Psychiatrists	1,193
Number of Patients Seen by Social Workers	490
Average Number of Visits Per Patient	1.34

TABLE 16

DISTRIBUTION BY TYPE OF PROBLEM AND BY SEX
OF ACUTE PSYCHIATRIC SERVICE PATIENTS
(JAN. 1–MAR. 31, 1964)

	f	Percentage
Type of Problem		
Psychiatric	723	56.9
Alcoholic	467	36.7
Medical	58	4.6
Unknown	23	1.8
Total	1,271	100.0
Sex		
Men	631	49.6
Women	640	50.4
Total	1,271	100.0

Appendix A

TABLE 17

AGE BY SEX DISTRIBUTION OF
ACUTE PSYCHIATRIC SERVICE PATIENTS
(JAN. 1–MAR. 31, 1964)

	Males f	Males Percentage	Females f	Females Percentage	Total f	Total Percentage
Age						
10–19	30	4.8	44	6.9	74	5.8
20–29	109	17.3	153	23.9	262	20.6
30–39	148	23.5	169	26.4	317	24.9
40–49	133	21.1	143	22.4	276	21.7
50–59	135	21.4	74	11.6	209	16.4
60–69	39	6.2	21	3.3	60	4.7
70–79	24	3.8	19	3.0	43	3.4
80–89	10	1.6	13	2.0	23	1.8
Unknown	3	0.5	4	0.6	7	0.6
Totals	631	100.2	640	100.1	1,271	99.9
Mean Age		42.41		38.49		40.45
Standard Deviation		15.41		15.26		15.58

TABLE 18

TYPE OF PROBLEM BY SEX DISTRIBUTION OF
ACUTE PSYSHIATRIC SERVICE PATIENTS
(JAN. 1–MAR. 31, 1964)

	Males f	Males Percentage	Females f	Females Percentage	Total f	Total Percentage
Type of Problem						
Psychiatric	210	33.3	513	80.2	723	56.9
Alcoholic	380	60.2	87	13.6	467	36.7
Medical	29	4.6	29	4.5	58	4.6
Unknown	12	1.9	11	1.7	23	1.8
Totals	631	100.0	640	100.0	1,271	100.0

TABLE 19

SOURCE OF REFERRAL OF ACUTE PSYCHIATRIC SERVICE PATIENTS (JAN. 1–MAR. 31, 1964)

	f	Percentage
Source of Referral[1]		
Extrahospital	(510)	(40.4)
Self	284	22.5
Relative	89	7.0
Agency	36	2.9
Local Physician	25	2.0
Police	38	3.0
Other	38	3.0
Intrahospital	(753)	(59.6)
Appointment, Acute Psychiatric Service	151	12.1
Chief Medical Officer	339	26.8
Overnight Ward	118	9.3
Medical Emergency Service Consultation	61	4.8
Psychiatric Clinic	23	1.8
Alcohol Clinic	17	1.3
Other	44	3.5

[1] Source of referral unknown for 8 patients.

TABLE 20

DISPOSITION OF TYPE OF PROBLEMS OF ACUTE PSYCHIATRIC SERVICE PATIENTS (JAN. 1–MAR. 31, 1964)

Type of Problem[1]

	Alcoholic f	Percentage	Psychiatric f	Percentage	Medical f	Percentage	Total f	Percentage
Intrahospital	206	44.2	413	57.3	4	7.3	623	50.2
Extrahospital	260	55.8	308	42.7	51	92.7	619	49.8
Total	466	100.0	721	100.0	55	100.0	1,242	100.0

[1] Twenty-nine patients for whom data were not available are excluded from analysis.

Appendix A

TABLE 21

INTRAHOSPITAL AND EXTRAHOSPITAL DISPOSITION OF PROBLEM FOR ACUTE PSYCHIATRIC SERVICE PATIENTS (JAN. 1–MAR. 31, 1964)

	Alcoholic f	Alcoholic Percentage	Psychiatric f	Psychiatric Percentage	Medical f	Medical Percentage	Total f	Total Percentage
Intrahospital								
Return Appointment	49	23.8	112	27.1	2	50.0	163	26.2
Psychiatric Clinic	9	4.4	207	50.1	—	—	216	34.7
Alcohol Clinic	95	46.1	5	1.2	—	—	100	16.1
Other Clinics	11	5.3	12	2.9	2	50.0	25	4.0
Overnight Ward	42	20.4	47	11.4	—	—	89	14.3
Psychiatric Wards	—	—	30	7.3	—	—	30	4.8
Total	206	100.0	413	100.0	4	100.0	623	100.0
Extrahospital								
Home and Return As Needed	83	31.9	143	46.5	13	25.5	239	38.7
Mental Hospital	31	11.9	92	29.9	1	2.0	124	20.1
Hospital for Alcoholics	93	35.8	1	0.3	—	—	94	15.2
Nursing Home	7	2.7	9	2.9	28	54.9	44	7.1
Private M.D.	3	1.2	25	8.1	—	—	28	4.5
Agency	9	3.5	5	1.6	1	2.0	15	2.4
Other	15	5.8	24	7.8	8	15.7	47	7.6
Eloped	19	7.3	9	2.9	—	—	28	4.5
Total	260	100.1	308	100.0	51	100.1	619	100.1

Table 22

FACTORS OBTAINED FROM PRETESTS
(n = 209: PROJECT AND CONTROL NURSES)

Factor I— Authoritarian Caretaker	Factor Loadings	Factor II— Unsympathetic	Factor Loadings
Young people sometimes get rebellious ideas, but as they grow up the ought to get over them and settle down.	.588	The alcoholic drinks excessively mainly because he enjoys drinking.	.651
I feel that nurses have a good deal of responsibility to teach correct social attitudes to patients who are immoral.	.577	Alcoholism is best described as a habit, rather than an illness.	.603
With a few exceptions, most alcoholics don't have the ability to tell right from wrong.	.558	Most alcoholics have no desire to stop drinking.	.561
High incidence of illegitimacy is probably related to high rates of alcoholism.	.527	It's the alcoholic's family, not the alcoholic himself, who suffer because of his drinking.	.539
If people would talk less and work more, everybody would be better off.	.525	We should take proper care of alcoholics, but we should not be expected to be sympathetic with them.	.538
More than anything else, it is good hard work that makes life worthwhile.	.522	Most alcoholics are completely unconcerned about their problems.	.530
I can't help but worry about the morality of some alcoholic and drug addict patients.	.510	The alcoholic has only himself to blame for his problems.	.526
Abnormal people are ruled by their emotions, normal people are ruled by their reason.	.474	I think most alcoholics are indifferent to the suffering they cause.	.494
One of the main causes of alcoholism is lack of moral strength.	.411	Alcoholism is not a disease.	.473
Nurses treat drug addicts, alcoholics, and patients with VD as well as they treat other patients.	.404	Alcoholics have only themselves to blame for their drinking; in most cases they just haven't tried hard enough to stop.	.466
I would expect to find more veneral disease among alcoholics than among nonalcoholics.	.398	Alcoholics are just weak, selfish people, and it is foolish to say that they are sick.	.431

Factor III— Social Drinking	Factor Loadings
The moderate use of alcohol adds to a person's enjoyment	

Appendix A

Table 22

FACTORS OBTAINED FROM PRETESTS
(n = 209: PROJECT AND CONTROL NURSES)

without doing any harm.	.728
A few drinks with friends is good for relaxing.	.715
Alcoholic beverages are an aid to mixing socially.	.706
Drinking can be a respectable habit.	.610
It would be foolish to stop all drinking because a few people abuse the use of alcohol.	.521
It is harmless to take a social drink at a party.	.420

Factor IV—Skid Row Stereotypes	Factor Loadings
You can't really trust an alcoholic.	.501
Alcoholics, on the average, have a poorer education than other people.	.501
The average alcoholic is usually unemployed.	.500
The alcoholic is seldom helped by any sort of medical or psychological treatment.	.431
The alcoholic is basically a spineless person who has found an easy way out of his problem.	.427
In most cases, families of alcoholics would be better off if the alcoholic were removed, either by divorce or being sent to jail.	.427
Because of the progressive nature of alcoholism, most alcoholics end up on Skid Row.	.420
The children of alcoholics are likely to become alcoholics when they grow up.	.412

There is something about alcoholics that makes it easy to tell them from normal people, even when they are sober.	.400

Factor V—Moral Relativism	Factor Loadings
I find it very hard to tolerate the immoral attitudes of some of the patients I work with.	−.660
Sometimes it is hard for me to be tolerant if my friends do things that I consider immoral.	−.657
I sometimes feel uncomfortable around patients whose attitudes I think immoral.	−.640
As a nurse, I would like to correct some of the immoral attitudes I encounter in my work.	−.523
Venereal disease and drug addiction are both the result of immoral behavior.	−.508
Alcoholism and drug addiction are both results of immoral behavior.	−.484
The alcoholic is a morally weak person.	−.464
People who tolerate immoral behavior in others are contributing to the harm that such behavior does to society.	−.453
I can't help but worry about the morality of some alcoholic and drug addict patients.	−.434
Although alcoholics may be sick people, some firm punishment might help them to grow.	−.396

TABLE 23

SUMMARY OF ANALYSES OF VARIANCE OF AMOUNT OF
PRE-POST TEST CHANGE SCORES ON FIVE FACTORS

	Sum of Squares	df	Mean Squares	F
Factor I				
Groups	258.05	3	86.02	1.10
Error	13,012.59	167	77.92	
Total	13,270.64	170		
Factor II				
Groups	111.13	3	37.04	.959
Error	6,451.19	167	38.63	
Total	6,562.32	170		
Factor III				
Groups	304.70	3	101.57	2.91[b]
Error	5,828.25	167	34.90	
Total	6,132.95	170		
Factor IV				
Groups	112.71	3	37.57	.905
Error	6,931.27	167	41.50	
Total	7,043.98	170		
Factor V				
Groups	399.38	3	133.13	1.16
Error	19,232.67	167	115.17	
Total	19,632.05	170		

Appendix A

TABLE 24

MEAN PRE-POST CHANGE ON FACTOR SCORES FOR FOUR GROUPS OF NURSES

	Group I Entire Project ($n = 49$)	Group II At Least One Year ($n = 21$)	Group III Less Than One Year ($n = 66$)	Group IV Controls ($n = 35$)
Factor I: Authoritarian Caretaker	3.27[b]	6.52[c]	2.51[b]	2.74
Factor II: Unsympathetic	1.55[b]	1.76	−.05	1.60
Factor III: Social Drinking	1.75[b]	1.76	1.33[c]	−1.60
Factor IV: Skid Row Stereotype	2.67[c]	4.62[d]	2.03[c]	2.20
Factor V: Moral Relativism	−5.86[d]	−3.84	−3.05[b]	−6.57[d]

Appendix B
Auxiliary Materials for Public Health Nurse Study

SAMPLE ENTRY FROM DIRECTORY OF RESOURCES PREPARED FOR VNA NURSES

Name of Facility: Boston Industrial Home (Pine St.)
Address: 8 Pine St., Boston, Mass.
Telephone No: 426-8483

Description. Large brick building in a neighborhood littered with bottles and refuse. Interior spotlessly clean. Consists of two large dormitories with a total capacity of 195. A portion of one dormitory is reserved for the City of Boston for a small group of men whom the directors are trying to rehabilitate through work. These men have separate, permanent rooms, and help to maintain the building. The Boston DPW provides free lodging here for a number of men nightly. Forty percent of the clientele is permanent; average attendance is 140 per night.

Location. Via MBTA, get off at Boylston, Essex, or Washington Sts., and ask directions; Pine Street is difficult to find.

Services. Clean dorms, bed linens, johnnies for sleeping; decontamination of clothing (via heat treatment); breakfast of hot soup, coffee, pastry; shaving facilities between 9 and 11 A.M.; counsel by clergy of 3 faiths; chapel services; free chest X rays every Monday night.

Eligibility. Men who are sober or nearly sober, and are self-sufficient (there are many stairs to climb). Epileptics who are under medication are acceptable. Men who are in need of medical care or are in very poor shape (e.g., with impending DT's) should not be referred, since the facility is not equipped to meet their needs.

Noneligibility. Men with previous record of undesirable behavior, as, for example, incorrigibly belligerent men, overt homosexuals who try to seduce others, shirkers who constantly ask for free lodging and meal tickets, but refuse to work when asked; agitators; men who arrive after 10:15 P.M.

Procedure. For patients. Boston residents can receive chits from the Department of Public Welfare at 2 Berkeley St. (Station 4), after 5:30 and before 9:00 P.M. (It is advisable to get there as soon after 5:30 as possible, since this office gives out 75 tickets per night, and then closes.) Boston residents are eligible for 6 free nights per

Notes to Appendix B will be found on page 356.

month; nonresidents, for 6 free per year. Patients who do not go through Public Welfare must present I.D. at the desk. Cost is $1.00 per night.

For VNA. If a man has used up his allowable number of nights, and if a nurse has a special plan for a patient that she feels would be enhanced by his being able to stay at Pine St., she may call the managers, and discuss the situation with them.

Sources of Items Used in Attitude Questionnaire

1. *F-Scale.* Six items from the F-Scale were used as a measure of authoritarianism; for example, "People can be divided into two classes, the weak and the strong." These are the items used by Mendelson *et al.* in their study.[1]

2. *C.A.I. Scale.* Fourteen items, adapted by Mendelson *et al.* from the Custodial Attitudes toward Mental Illness Scale of Gilbert and Levinson. Mendelson *et al.* describe them as follows: "The CMI Scale from which the CAI items were adapted was designed to measure the degree to which an individual takes a traditional custodial or "caretaking" attitude toward mental illness as opposed to a humanistic or more actively therapeutic approach. According to Gilbert and Levinson, people who maintain a custodial attitude seek the detention and safekeeping of mentally ill people. They regard the mentally ill patient, in this study, the alcoholic patient, as irrational, dangerous, and incurable. . . ." Sample items are: "One of the main causes of alcoholism is lack of moral strength"; "alcoholics have only themselves to blame for their drinking; in most cases they just haven't tried hard enough to stop."[2]

3. *M-Scale.* Ten items regarding the nurse's perception of her role and attitudes as regards the moral behavior of her patients; for example, "I feel that nurses have a good deal of responsibility to teach correct social attitudes to patients who are immoral."[3]

4. Six scales (21 items) from the Alcoholism Questionnaire, Addiction Research Foundation, Toronto, 1963. *Scale I:* Prognosis for recovery; high scores indicate a belief that most alcoholics do not recover, and cannot be helped to recover from alcoholism. *Scale II:* Alcoholism as an illness; a high score indicates the belief that alco-

Appendix B

holism is not an illness. *Scale III:* Social status of the alcoholic; high scores indicate belief that alcoholics come from the lower socio-economic strata of society. *Scale IV:* Alcoholism and character defect; high scores indicate belief that the alcoholic is a weak-willed person. *Scale V:* Emotional difficulties as cause; high scores indicate belief that emotional difficulties or psychological problems are an important contributing factor in the development of alcoholism. *Scale VI:* Harmless voluntary indulgence; high scores indicate the belief that the alcoholic is a harmless heavy drinker, whose drinking is motivated only by his fondness for alcohol.

5. *S-Scale.* Six items as a measure of attitudes toward social drinking; for example, "A few drinks with friends is good for relaxing."[4]

6. Twenty-six items drawn from the Attitudes toward Disabled Persons Scale.[5] These items were not used in the final data analysis.

7. Nine items drawn from various scales published by the Addiction Research Foundation, and available from the Research Reference Files, # 315.

8. Seventeen items were written for this study, and deal with the family of the alcoholic.

Sample Size and Turnover of VNA Staff

Our method of dealing with the problem of high staff turnover was as follows: When nurses left the VNA, the project staff was notified by the VNA Central Office prior to termination; the questionnaire was individually readministered to each nurse before she left. A similar procedure was followed for new nurses, each of whom was tested during the first two weeks of her employment with the VNA. With the number of district offices involved, and with the need for the VNA Central Office to notify us of personnel changes before they took place, it was inevitable that we would lose some subjects. In 25 cases, we were not notified of a nurse's departure and were unable to administer posttests. For the control group we made no attempt to administer posttests to nurses leaving the VNA during the course of the project; at the end of the two-year period, we retested those control group nurses still with the VNA.

Actual numbers of nurses tested were as follows:

Project Nurses

Pretests
- At beginning of project   105
- Joined VNA during project   56
- Total number of pretests   161

Posttests
- Left VNA, not posttested   25
- Total number of posttests   136

Control Group Nurses

- Pretested   48
- Left during project, not retested   13
- Posttested   35

Notes

1. MENDELSON, J. H., et. al., "Physicians' Attitudes Toward Alcoholic Patients," *Archives of General Psychiatry,* 11:392-399, 1964.
2. *Ibid.*
3. ORAM, P. G., "Induction of Action and Attitude Change: The Function of Role-Self Values and Levels of Endorsement," doctoral dissertation, Boston University, 1966.
4. Alcoholism Research Foundation, Toronto.
5. YUKES, H. E., J. R. BLOCK, and W. J. CAMPBELL, "A Scale to Measure Attitudes Toward Disabled Persons," Human Resources Foundation, 1960.

Appendix C
An Annotated Bibliography of Investigations Evaluating the Effectiveness of Psychotherapeutic Techniques with Alcoholics, 1952–1963

Explanatory Notes

This bibliography systematically summarizes the raw material upon which we based the observations and conclusions set forth in the article entitled, "Evaluation of Psychotherapy with Alcoholics: A Critical Review," which appeared in the *Quarterly Journal of Studies on Alcohol,* Vol. 28, March 1967. As we indicated in that paper, we made every effort to ensure that the bibliography is comprehensive for the decade in question. In the very possible event that it is not, we ask those of you who are aware of other publications describing evaluations of psychotherapy with alcoholics to send the reference to Dr. Blane at the Preventive Intervention Study, Massachusetts General Hospital, Boston, Massachusetts. Each article is annotated under the following headings:

Setting. The place(s) where the evaluation was undertaken; if not otherwise indicated, the setting is inpatient.

Purpose. Since not all reports had evaluation as a primary goal, we have indicated major and minor purposes of each paper.

Cases. Number, sex, and other characteristics of the total, original sample are listed.

Subject selection. The manner in which cases were selected is described.

Controls. Type of control group or measure is described. Although pre-post comparisons are implicit in all studies, "patient as own control" indicates that special attention was given to before-after ratings.

Treatment. Type of treatment is listed.

Length of treatment. Where possible, mean and range of length of treatment are given.

Period from treatment to follow-up. Where possible, length of period, variations in its length, and concurrency with treatment are indicated.

Method of evaluation. Type of measures used are described.

Major criteria. Criteria for assessing change are listed.

Appendix C prepared, in collaboration, by Marjorie J. Hill and Howard T. Blane.

Results. In order to give as much uniformity as possible to the reporting of results, we have in many instances recalculated the findings as reported using the conventions spelled out below. Such recalculations are indicated by an asterisk (*). The first convention we have adopted is the use of a two-point system for reporting outcome: improved *versus* unimproved. The improved category includes such terms as "cured," "recovered," "abstinent," "drank small amounts or intermittently with good adjustment," and so on; the unimproved category includes such terms as "frequently intoxicated," "worse," "drank variable amounts or intermittently with poor adjustment," " little or no progress," and so on. The second convention reflects an arbitrary decision, mitigated by the hope that it permits order in place of chaos. Patients lost to follow-up are placed in the unimproved category; the frequency of patients not followed is given in parentheses. Thus, if 50 patients are listed as unimproved, and this 50 includes 25 unfollowed patients, it will appear as 50(25) in the tabular presentation of results. Third, if the number of patients deceased at time of follow-up is reported these are excluded from our recalculations, unless in the opinion of the author(s) deaths were attributable to alcoholism. We have arbitrarily considered death by suicide to be a treatment failure and have assigned suicides to the unimproved category. Fourth, persons hospitalized at time of follow-up are assigned to the unimproved category, unless the author(s) specifically indicate(s) that hospitalization is unrelated to alcoholism. Contingencies not covered by the above rules have been handled on an individual basis and are indicated by footnotes. Since it would be an injustice to use the above format to summarize the results of certain of the studies, we have in certain instances abstracted the authors' findings in addition to or instead of presenting them graphically.

1. ARMSTRONG, J. D., and R. J. GIBBINS. "A Psychotherapeutic Technique with Large Groups in the Treatment of Alcoholics: A Preliminary Report," *Quarterly Journal of Studies on Alcohol,* 17:461-478, 1956.

Setting. Brookside Clinic, Toronto, Canada.
Purpose. Description of a method of treatment, and evaluation of results.
Cases. 64, presumably all male.
Subject selection. Members of a group in existence (in some form) for more than 2 years at time of study.
Controls. 32 "core group" members (average 15 meetings) compared with 32 patients who attended 3 or 4 times only.
Treatment. Group therapy; 7 of "core group" received long-term individual psychotherapy and 9 "gained help" from Antabuse.
Length of treatment. Study covers 44 weekly sessions over a 12-month period, beginning in third year of group's existence.
Period from treatment to follow-up. Concurrent.
Method of evaluation. Judgment of therapist.
Major criteria. Drinking, psychological attitudes, social adjustment (not further described).
Results:

	Core Group		*Comparison Group*	
	f	%	f	%
improved	23	72	15	47
unimproved	9(7)	28(22)	17(7)	53(22)

2. CELLAR, F. A., and A. H. GRANT. "The Treatment of Alcoholism in an Out-Patient Clinic," *Journal of the Michigan State Medical Society,* 51:722-723, 729, 1952.
Setting. Outpatient clinic of Detroit Committee on Alcoholism.
Purpose. Description and evaluation of program.
Cases. 444, sex not reported.
Subject selection. Total population from April 1950 to June 1951.
Controls. None.
Type of treatment. Individual psychotherapy, not further described.
Length of treatment. Not described.
Period from treatment to follow-up. Not listed systematically, varies from patient to patient.

Method of evaluation. Not described.
Major criteria. Interpersonal relationships, work, drinking.
Results:

	f	%
improved	252	57
unimproved	192 (180)	43 (40)

3. CHAFETZ, M. E. "Practical and Theoretical Considerations in the Psychotherapy of Alcoholism," *Quarterly Journal of Studies on Alcohol,* 20:281-291, 1959.
Setting. Massachusetts General Hospital Alcohol Clinic.
Purpose. Clinical paper; evaluation of results incidental.
Cases. 125 patients, sex not specified.
Subject selection. Of 600 patients referred to the clinic in a five-year period, the 125 in this study were those who "developed and maintained a continuous therapeutic relationship."
Controls. None.
Treatment. Individual psychotherapy.
Period from treatment to follow-up. Not described.
Method of evaluation. Not described; evidently judgment of therapist.
Major criteria. Drinking, "behavior patterns in day-to-day living," and "response to anxiety."
Results:

	f	%
improved	78	62
unimproved	47	38

4. CLANCY, J. "Out-Patient Treatment of the Alcoholic," *Journal of the Iowa State Medical Society,* 51:221-226, 1961.
Setting. Alcoholic Clinic, State Psychopathic Hospital.
Purpose. Description and evaluation of program.
Cases. First 25 patients treated: sex unspecified, probably male.
Subject selection. First 25 patients.
Controls. None.
Treatment. Combination of medical, psychiatric, social service approach with group therapy.
Length of treatment. Not clear.

Appendix C

Period from treatment to follow-up. Six months after initial attendance.
Method of evaluation. Not described.
Major criteria. Attendance, drinking (and others).
Results: Of 11 patients attending at least once every three months:

	f	%
	10	90
	1	9

of 14 patients attending once:

	f	%
improved	7	50
unimproved	7	50

5. DANIELS, R. S. "A Brief Psychotherapeutic Technic for the Treatment of Severe Alcoholism by the Family Physician," *New York State Journal of Medicine,* 58:397-401, 1958.
Setting. Cincinnati General Hospital and a community alcoholism clinic.
Purpose. Description of method, presentation of cases. Evaluation incidental.
Cases. 10 males.
Subject selection. 5 patients "assigned by chance" from inpatient service, 5 "selected" from outpatient clinic.
Controls. None.
Treatment. Individual psychotherapy (for outpatients, 15–20-minute sessions once a week; for inpatients, "seen daily by doctor").
Length of treatment. Presented individually in case histories.
Period from treatment to follow-up. Varies.
Method of evaluation. Not described.
Major criteria. Drinking.
Results:

	f	%
improved	6	60
unimproved	4	40

6. ENDS, E. J., and C. W. PAGE. "Group Psychotherapy and Concomitant Psychological Change," *Psychological Monographs,* 73 (480), 1959.
Setting. Willmar State Hospital, Minnesota.
Purpose. To assess the usefulness of group psychotherapy with alcoholics and to determine the most efficient type and intensity of application.
Cases. At least 134 males to begin with; final groups consisted of 99 subjects, 43 in two experimental groups (28 and 15 each), 56 in two control groups (28 each); attrition due to discharge reported for one E and one C group but not for other two groups.
Subject selection. From those meeting a number of criteria (which are described), random assignment to groups.
Controls. Group receiving same treatment program with exception of therapy.
Treatment. Rogerian group therapy for experimental groups (15-session and 30-session groups).
Length of treatment. 15 sessions and 30 sessions, in period of six weeks.
Period from treatment to follow-up. Follow-up at termination of 15 and 30 sessions of group therapy.
Method of evaluation. Comparison of pre- and posttreatment Q-sorts and MMPIs; also compared for 15 versus 30 sessions.
Major criteria. Shifts in self-concept as measured by self and ideal self Q-sorts; shifts in MMPI scores.
Results: Addition of Rogerian therapy results in significant therapeutic change as indicated by increased self-acceptance; reduced suspiciousness, oversensitivity, and feelings of persecution; and a general pattern of psychological growth. More frequent group sessions result in greater positive change.

7. ENDS, E. J., and C. W. PAGE. "A Study of Three Types of Group Psychotherapy with Hospitalized Male Inebriates," *Quarterly Journal of Studies on Alcohol,* 18:263-277, 1957.
Setting. Willmar State Hospital, Minnesota.

Purpose. To determine which of 3 different methods of group therapy is most economical in improving social functioning in male alcoholics.

Cases. 63 males.

Subject selection. Male admissions, age 25–45, AGCT scores above 40th percentile; 96 patients selected on the basis of a sociometric test. Of these, 63 completed the program.

Controls. The "social discussion" group served as control group.

Treatment. Compares four methods of group therapy: learning theory, psychoanalytic, client-centered, and social discussion controls.

Length of treatment. 15 group sessions.

Period from treatment to follow-up. Q-sort at end of 15th session (five weeks). Follow-up data obtained at 6 months, 1 year, 1½ years after discharge.

Method of evaluation. Q-sort self-ratings by patients. Data from records and county welfare offices.

Major criteria. Drinking pattern, self and ideal self Q-sorts.

Results:[1]

	Learning		Client-centered		Analytic		Control	
	f	%	f	%	f	%	f	%
improved	2	13	8	53	6	40	4	24
unimproved	14(2)	87(13)	7(3)	47(20)	9	60	13	76

8. Fox, V., and M. A. Smith. "Evaluation of a Chemopsychotherapeutic Program for the Rehabilitation of Alcoholics: Observations over a Two-Year Period," *Quarterly Journal of Studies on Alcohol,* 20:767-780, 1959.

Setting. Georgian Clinic, Atlanta, Georgia (in- and outpatient).

Purpose. Description and evaluation of program.

Cases. 214 male, 37 female.

Selection of subjects. 251 admissions seen during an 8-month period.

Controls. None.

---

[1] These refer to drinking pattern; Q-sort changes are also described.

Treatment. Psychotherapy (mostly group), medication, and religious therapy.
Length of treatment. Inpatient—one week to three months; outpatient—varies. The program is planned for six weeks minimum inpatient, followed by outpatient.
Period from treatment to follow-up. Varies. Not specified for first follow-up; second follow-up carried out one year after first.
Method of evaluation. Not described.
Major criteria. Drinking, employment, continued contact with clinic.
Results: First follow-up:

	f	%
improved	97	41
unimproved	139(52)[1]	59(22)

Second follow-up:

	%[2]
improved	54
unimproved	44

9. GERARD, D. L., G. SAENGER, and R. WILE. "The Abstinent Alcoholic," *Archives of General Psychiatry,* 6:83-95, 1962.
Setting. Clinics of the Connecticut Commission on Alcoholism.
Purpose. To investigate factors associated with abstinence through intensive follow-up of 50 abstinent patients. Also describes other groups at follow-up.
Cases. 299, sex not specified.
Subject selection procedure. A random sample of 400 drawn from total of 1,149 cases who first came to clinic in 1950, 1953, and 1956. Sample drawn to give proportional representation to 5 clinics. The 400 cases were arranged chronologically for each clinic and lettered consecutively, A B C D; 4 equivalent samples of 100 cases each obtained.

[1] Four (2%) patients who were deceased and 11 patients (4%) who were considered beyond the scope of the clinic and presumably treated elsewhere are excluded from the analyses.
[2] These are the percentages directly reported by the authors. Due to ambiguities in reporting it is impossible to determine the N involved.

Appendix C 367

Controls. None, but samples selected by random procedure.
Treatment. Social case work and "psychiatry," not further described.
Length of treatment. Not specified.
Period from treatment to follow-up. 2, 5, and 8 years after initial intake.
Method of evaluation. Interviews by social workers, with corroborative data from AA, spouses, relatives, employers.
Major criteria: Drinking.
Results:

	f	%
improved	96	38
unimproved	154[1]	62

10. GIBBINS, R. J., and J. D. ARMSTRONG. "Effects of Clinical Treatment on Behavior of Alcoholic Patients: An Exploratory Methodological Investigation," *Quarterly Journal of Studies on Alcohol,* 18:429-450, 1957.
    Setting. Brookside Hospital, Toronto, Canada, and outpatient clinic.
    Purpose. To improve on usual methods of evaluating treatment and to evaluate treatment program.
    Cases. 96 males, 6 females.
    Subject selection. 102 patients selected (in the same proportions for each of 4 years as occurred in the population) from 235 patients who had been inpatients at least 6 days and attended clinic 3 or more times.
    Controls. Patient as own control; comparison of length of periods of abstinence, pre- and posttreatment.
    Treatment. Group therapy.
    Length of treatment. Minimum of 6 days in hospital, 3 or more clinic visits.
    Period from treatment to follow-up. Varies (see *Results*).
    Method of evaluation. Intensive interviews of patients, relatives, and associates; information from institutions.

[1] 49 patients (17%) were deceased at time of follow-up and have been dropped from this analysis.

Major criteria. Gain in months of abstinence.

Results. Percentage gain or loss is presented for each patient individually.[1] Mean gain for 69 Ss on whom data is complete is 9.8 months.

Months from 1st Admission to follow-up	N	Mean Gain in Months
43-55 ($X = 45.0$)	14	17.9
25-37 ($X = 30.8$)	22	9.0
9-24 ($X = 16.7$)	33	6.9

11. GLIEDMAN, L. H. "Concurrent and Combined Group Treatment of Chronic Alcoholics and Their Wives," *International Journal of Group Psychotherapy,* 7:414-424, 1957.

Setting. Outpatient clinic, Johns Hopkins Hospital.

Purpose. To investigate the role of the marriage, or the family, in the group treatment of chronic alcoholism.

Cases. 9 couples (alcoholic males).

Subject selection. 9 couples who volunteered for treatment, out of 45 contacted.

Controls. None.

Method of treatment. Group psychotherapy.

Length of treatment. Patients—5 months, 2 meetings per week; wives—5 months, 1 meeting per week. Then, four couples participate in three-month series of combined weekly meetings.

Period from treatment to follow-up. At termination of treatment, with follow-up evaluation interviews arranged "whenever this was possible."

Major criteria. Approximate monthly expenditures for alcohol, difference between pre- and posttreatment ratings on adjectives employed by both marital partners when patient was sober and intoxicated.

Results. In 4 out of 5 responding, decreased monthly expenditure for alcohol. In each phase of treatment, increase in number of "good" adjectives used by both partners to describe each

---

[1] Findings would gain in meaning if an angular transformation of the percentages were undertaken.

Appendix C

other during patient's period of sobriety. Authors present a number of findings from checklist.

12. GLIEDMAN, L. H., D. ROSENTHAL, J. D. FRANK and HELEN T. NASH. "Group Therapy of Alcoholics with Concurrent Group Meetings of Their Wives," *Quarterly Journal of Studies on Alcohol,* 17:655-670, 1956.
    Setting. Outpatient psychiatric clinic, Johns Hopkins Hospital.
    Purpose. Clinical study of effect of group therapy on alcoholics and their wives.
    Cases. 7 couples (alcoholic males).
    Subject selection. Of 45 couples contacted, 9 accepted treatment. 2 couples didn't complete treatment.
    Controls. None.
    Treatment. Group psychotherapy.
    Length of treatment. 32 sessions (patients); range, 4-26 sessions; 16 sessions (wives).
    Period from treatment to follow-up. 32 group therapy sessions.
    Method. Before-after ratings by patients and wives on 3 checklists, by therapist on social ineffectiveness scale.
    Major criteria. Checklists completed by both husbands and wives:
    1. Drinking checklist (29 items, 4 ratings for severity)
    2. Symptom checklist (33 psychological items, 4 ratings)
    3. Adjective checklist (5%, commonly applied to alcoholics)
    4. Social ineffectiveness scale (15 items, 5 point scale)
    Results:[1]

	f	%
improved	5	71
unimproved	2	29

13. JENSEN, S. "A Treatment Program for Alcoholics in a Mental Hospital," *Quarterly Journal of Studies on Alcohol,* 23:315-320, 1962.
    Setting. Saskatchewan Hospital, Weyburn, Canada.

[1] These refer to drinking; changes on checklists are also described.

Purpose. Description and preliminary evaluation of program; comparison of patients receiving and not receiving LSD.
Cases. 138 males.
Subject selection procedure. Not described.
Controls. Compares two experimental groups with a "control" group "consisting of patients admitted to the hospital during the same period who received individual treatment by other psychiatrists."
Type of treatment. Milieu, group, and a "minimum of individual" therapy; 58 patients receive LSD, 35 receive therapy without LSD.
Length of treatment. Average of two months.
Period from treatment to follow-up. Varies, covering a 6- to 18-month period.
Method of evaluation. Not described.
Major criteria. Drinking.
Results:

	Full program		*No LSD*		*Controls*	
	f	%	f	%	f	%
improved	41	71	8	23	10	22
unimproved	17(4)	29(7)	27(18)	77(51)	35(23)	78(51)

14. JOHNSTON, M. "Adult Guidance Center, San Francisco," *Public Health Reports,* 68:590-594, 1953.
Setting. Adult Guidance Center, San Francisco.
Purpose. Description and evaluation of program.
Cases. 1,573, ¾ male, ¼ female.
Subject selection. Total clinic population.
Controls. None.
Treatment. Individual and/or group therapy; 78.9 percent—medication only; 21.1 percent—at least one hour individual therapy; 8.9 percent—group therapy; 0.1 percent—concurrent individual and group therapy.
Length of treatment. Average given for each group: A—11½ hours; B—6 hours; C—6¾ hours; D—6 hours.
Period from treatment to follow-up. Varies.

Appendix C

Method of evaluation. Not described.
Major criteria. Drinking, maintaining contact.
Results:

	f	%
improved	456	29
unimproved	1,117 (928)	71 (59)

15. KHOURY, J. and A. W. PEARSON. "Alcoholism: Medical Team Approach to Treatment," *California Medicine,* 95:284-287, 1961.
Setting. Alcoholic rehabilitation clinics, Los Angeles City Health Department.
Purpose. Description and evaluation of program.
Cases. 552, male and female; number of each not specified.
Subject selection. "Selected" from total population of 552 seen from February to June 1959.
Controls. None.
Treatment. Individual and group therapy by psychiatrist, "social supportive" therapy by social workers, "modified medical group therapy," medication.
Length of treatment. Not described.
Period from treatment to follow-up. Evaluation at admission, and approximately one year later.
Method of evaluation. Interviews with "a selected group."
Major criteria. Improvement in economic status, interpersonal relationships, physical and emotional status, drinking pattern.
Results: For a "selected group," number not specified:

	%
improved	76
unimproved	24

16. LEE, K. F. "Alcohol Studies and Rehabilitation in Virginia," *Public Health Reports,* 67:474-478, 1952.
Setting. Virginia State Department of Health Clinic.
Purpose. Description and evaluation of program.
Cases. 816, sex not specified.

Subject selection. Evidently total population in 3-year period.
Controls. None.
Treatment. Not clear. Plan is developed for each patient individually, psychotherapy is available. Evidently both individual and group therapy.
Length of treatment. Not described.
Period from treatment to follow-up. Varies.
Method of evaluation. Not described.
Major criteria. Drinking, family relationships, employment.
*Results.**

	f	%
improved	651	80
unimproved	165	20

17. MAIER, R. A. and VERNELLE FOX. "Forced Therapy of Probated Alcoholics," *Medical Times,* 86:1051-1054, 1958.
    Setting. Georgian Clinic, Atlanta, Georgia.
    Purpose. Description and evaluation of program.
    Cases. 27 male, 2 female, involuntary patients, court referrals on probation.
    Subject selection. Not described, other than that they were between 25 and 60 years of age.
    Controls. None.
    Treatment. Medical, group, and individual therapy by psychologist.
    Length of therapy. 39 meetings during 3-month period.
    Period from treatment to follow-up. Three months after final clinic contact.
    Method of evaluation. Reports from probation office, friends and relatives, other patients, therapist.
    Major criteria. Continued contact, drinking, arrests.
    Results:

	f	%
improved	11	38
unimproved	18	62

Appendix C

18. MILLER, M. M. "Treatment of Chronic Alcoholism by Hypnotic Aversion," *Journal of the American Medical Association,* 171:1492-1495, 1959.
    Setting. Howard University Psychiatric Clinic, private office.
    Purpose. Description and evaluation of method.
    Cases. 19 male, 5 female.
    Subject selection. Not described.
    Controls. None.
    Method of treatment. Hypnotically induced reflex aversion.
    Length of treatment. Average number of treatments = 2.
    Period from treatment to follow-up. Varies; average 9 months.
    Method of evaluation. Not described. Therapist evaluation, patient report.
    Major criterion. Abstinence.
    Results. 3 patients have had relapses, presumably 20 are abstinent.

19. MINDLIN, DOROTHEE F. "Evaluation of Therapy for Alcoholics in a Workhouse Setting," *Quarterly Journal of Studies on Alcohol,* 21:90-112, 1960.
    Setting. Workhouse, Alcoholic Rehabilitation Division of District of Columbia Department of Public Health.
    Purpose. Program evaluation.
    Cases. 100 male workhouse inmates.
    Subject selection procedure. Entire population treated during period of study. (Selection takes place before patient accepted for treatment.)
    Controls. Compared with two other groups on background variables only. Subject as own control, compared with functioning prior to treatment.
    Treatment. Individual and group therapy.
    Length of treatment. 90 days.
    Period from treatment to follow-up. Varies from 3 months to 3 years.
    Method of evaluation. Pooled judgments of five staff members.
    Major criteria. Drinking, work, arrests, attitudes toward therapy.
    Results.

	f	%
improved	32	32
unimproved	68(23)	68(23)

20. MOORE, R. A. and F. RAMSEUR. "Effects of Psychotherapy in an Open-Ward Hospital on Patients with Alcoholism," *Quarterly Journal of Studies on Alcohol*, 21:233-252, 1960.
Setting. Veterans' Readjustment Center, Ann Arbor, Michigan.
Purpose. Program evaluation.
Cases. 100 male veterans.
Subject selection. Entire patient population, 1945–1956.
Controls. None.
Treatment. Psychoanalytic psychotherapy, presumably individual.
Length of treatment. Mean = 162 days; range—2 to 569 days.
Period from treatment to follow-up. Varies; average = 42.2 months.
Method of evaluation. Letters to patients, staff interviews, information from LMD's and referring agencies.
Major criteria. Drinking, insight, control of behavior, marital adjustment, reduction of other symptoms, motivation for improvement.
Results:

Drinking	At Discharge	At Termination of Follow-up	
	f = %	f	%
improved	26	38	41
unimproved	74	55(9)[1]	59(10)
Adjustment			
improved	46	35	38
unimproved	54	58(9)[1]	62(10)

21. MYERSON, D. J., J. MACKAY, A. WALLENS, and N. NEIBERG. "A Report of a Rehabilitation Program for Alcoholic Women

---

[1] Seven patients (7%) were deceased at time of follow-up and are not included in these analyses.

Prisoners," *Quarterly Journal of Studies on Alcohol,* Suppl. 1, 151–157, 1961.
Setting. Out Patient Clinic, Peter Bent Brigham Hospital.
Purpose. Description and evaluation of program.
Cases. 49 alcoholic women prisoners.
Subject selection. "Haphazard"; patients were voluntary, under 45, lived near Boston.
Controls. None.
Treatment. Individual relationship therapy while in prison, followed by supportive therapy at hospital following discharge.
Length of treatment. Not described.
Period from treatment to follow-up. Varies.
Method of evaluation. Judgment of therapist.
Major criteria. Use of clinic, maintaining contact, arrests.
Results:

	f	%
improved	22	45
unimproved	27[1]	55

22. PFEFFER, A. Z. and S. BERGER. "A Follow-up Study of Treated Alcoholics," *Quarterly Journal of Studies on Alcohol,* 18:624-648, 1957.
Setting. Consolidated Edison Consultation Clinic.
Purpose. Evaluation of program.
Cases. 160 patients. Results for 60 patients, 57 male, 3 female.
Subject selection. All patients referred to clinic from February 1952 to December 31, 1954.
Controls. Patient's drinking behavior for one year prior to treatment.
Method of treatment. Individual psychotherapy, directive-supportive and analytic.
Length of treatment. Average duration of clinic contact: abstinent—27 months; changed pattern—23 months; drinking—22 months.
Period from treatment to follow-up. Varies.
Method of evaluation. Phone and letter contact nets 60 patients

[1] Twenty patients failed to contact the clinic after release from prison.

who come in for clinical interview. Also supervisor ratings for 51 Con. Ed. employees.

Major criteria. On basis of drinking, patients divided into three groups; each group rated on 46 factors.

Results:[1]

	f	%
improved	55	92
unimproved	5	8

[1] These are for drinking only. Follow-up information is presented for 46 items. For 51 patients, clinic and supervisor's ratings are compared.

23. PFEFFER, A. Z., D. J. FELDMAN, C. FEIBEL, J. A. FRANK, M. COHEN, S. BERGER, and M. F. FLEETWOOD. "A Treatment Program for the Alcoholic in Industry," *Journal of the American Medical Association,* 161:827-836, 1956.

Setting. Consolidated Edison Consultation Clinic.
Purpose. Description and evaluation of program.
Cases. 180 industrial employees; sex not specified.
Subject selection. Referral through industrial medical departments.
Controls. None.
Treatment. Individual directive supportive, individual analytic, group directive supportive, group analytic psychotherapy. (Table shows percentage receiving each.) All therapy by psychiatrists.
Length of treatment. Range: 1–43 months.
Period from treatment to follow-up. Varies. Includes both those in active treatment and those on follow-up.
Method of evaluation. Medical records, interviews with patients at 6-month check-ups.
Major criteria. Employment, absenteeism, continuing treatment.
Results:

	f	%
improved[1]	135	79
unimproved	36[2]	21

[1] Results are given in terms of those patients who continued, discontinued, and refused treatment, and who retained or lost their jobs. All patients who continued in treatment maintained employment and are regarded as "improved."

[2] Seven patients (4%) were deceased, and 2 (1%) had been hospitalized or referred elsewhere at time of follow-up and are not included in this analysis.

24. PINARDI, N. J. "Helping Alcoholic Criminals: A Pilot Study," *Crime and Delinquency,* 9:71-76, 1963.
   Setting. Four clinics and inpatient facility of the Florida Alcoholic Rehabilitation Program.
   Purpose. To compare characteristics of two groups of patients.
   Cases. 22 probationers and parolees receiving voluntary treatment, and 21 cases referred by usual sources (M.D., AA, family, etc.).
   Subject selection procedures. Not described. The 22 parole and probation cases were "selected" from a total N of 30, treated between 1958 and 1961.
   Controls. 21 cases referred from usual sources.
   Treatment. Individual and group psychotherapy.
   Length of treatment. Not described.
   Length of time from treatment to follow-up. Status at discharge.
   Method of evaluation. Not described; evidently judgment of therapists.
   Major criteria. Not described.
   Results. "Members of both groups had the same prognosis and the same status at discharge. (Half of each group were judged 'improved'.)"

25. PROTHRO, W. B. "Alcoholics Can Be Rehabilitated," *American Journal of Public Health,* 51:450-461, 1961.
   Setting. Grand Rapids, Michigan, Rehabilitation Program (hospital ward plus clinic).
   Purpose. Description and evaluation of program.
   Cases. 614, sex not specified, probably male.
   Subject selection. Total clinic population in 3-year period.
   Controls. None (those receiving treatment once compared to those receiving it more than once).
   Treatment. Individual "medical and social counseling," group therapy.
   Length of treatment. Given only for first hospitalization: median —13 days.
   Period from treatment to follow-up. Varies; covers 2-year period.
   Method of evaluation. Follow-up by public health nurse, social

workers, or correspondence with a "sponsor" to whom patient referred on discharge.

Major criteria. Drinking, socioeconomic status, church and AA attendance, employment.

Results:

Drinking

	f	%
improved	258	44
unimproved	332(129)[1]	56(22)

Socioeconomic status	f	%
improved	154	26
unimproved	436(129)[1]	74(22)

26. Rossi, J. J. and N. J. Bradley. "Dynamic Hospital Treatment of Alcoholism," *Quarterly Journal of Studies on Alcohol,* 21:432-446, 1960.

Setting. Willmar State Hospital and Clinic.

Purpose. Program evaluation.

Cases. Male and Female, number of each not specified for first two follow-ups. Third follow-up—302 males. Number of cases varies for follow-ups (see *Results*).

Subject selection. Entire rural-origin population of hospital over a 5-year period.

Controls. None.

Treatment. Group and individual therapy; psychodrama.

Length of treatment. Program is for 60 days. No indication of how many S spend more or less time.

Period from treatment to follow-up. Varies. After initial follow-up, two more at one-year intervals.

Method of evaluation. Counselor traveled throughout state obtaining information from the patients, judges, sheriffs, county attorneys, police, welfare agencies, AA.

Major criteria. Drinking.

Results:

---

[1] Twenty-four patients (4%) were deceased at time of follow-up and are not included in the above analyses.

Appendix C

	1955[1]		1956[2]		1957[3]	
	f	%	*f*	%	*f*	%
improved:[4]	879	52.6	833	47.8	127	44.7
unimproved:	793	47.4	909	52.2	157	55.3

27. Rossi, J. J., A. Stach, and N. J. Bradley. "Effects of treatment of Male Alcoholics in a Mental Hospital," *Quarterly Journal of Studies on Alcohol*, 24:91-108, 1963.
Setting. Willmar State Hospital, Minnesota.
Purpose. Program evaluation.
Cases. Group I, 208 males; Group II, 45 males.
Subject selection. Over a 20-month period, every seventh admission selected, yielding 243 patients. Selection of the 208 followed is not described.
Controls. Patient as own control; before-after ratings on all criteria.
Treatment. Lecture program, individual and group therapy.
Length of treatment. 60 days.
Period from treatment to follow-up. Ranges from 6 to 36 months, mean 21 months.
Method of evaluation. Patients contacted by research team, social workers, specially trained field workers, cooperating agencies. Measure of reliability obtained by having 95 cases evaluated by two different interviewers, using 5-step rating scale. For absolute agreement, $r = .61$, $p < .001$; 1-step difference, $r = .78$, $p < .001$.
Major criteria. Criteria are complex, including 21 areas of be-

[1] $N = 1724$, all admissions from 77 rural counties, 3/1/50–3/31/55. Fifty-two patients (3%) were deceased at time of follow-up and are not included in this analysis.

[2] $N = 1894$. All admissions from 77 rural counties, 6/1/50–12/31/55. One hundred fifty-two patients (8%) were deceased at time of follow-up and are not included in this analysis.

[3] $N = 302$. Every fifth male admission during the period 6/1/50–12/31/56, from 47 counties. Eighteen patients (6%) were deceased at time of follow-up and are not included in this analysis.

[4] A group categorized as "motivated," and not further described, is included in this group. N. B. Since only rounded percentages and no raw frequencies were reported, the frequencies in the above table have a margin of error as high as plus or minus 9.

havior and a comparison of periods of abstinence pre- and post-treatment. Patients located in first follow-up are divided into "abstinent," "drinking with mild effects," and "drinking with serious effects" groups, and these groups are compared on all criteria. "Mild effects" group reevaluated one year later.
Results:

First follow-up:

	f	%
improved	59	30
unimproved[1]	136(35)[1]	70(18)

Second follow-up:
(of 45 "mild effects" drinkers)

	f	%
improved (or unchanged)	4	9
unimproved (worse)	41	91

28. SAENGER, G. and D. GERARD. "A Follow-up Study of Patients Seen in Out-Patient Clinics Associated with the North American Association of Alcoholism Programs," paper delivered at the 14th annual meeting of the North American Association of Alcoholism Programs, Miami Beach, 1963.
Setting. Pilot study clinics of the North American Association of Alcoholism Programs (9 clinics).
Purpose. To report evaluation research project carried out by NAAAP facilities of nine state-supported alcoholism programs.
Cases. 798, male and female, number of each not specified.
Subject selection. Evidently total population of nine of the "larger and better established" clinics.
Controls. Patient as own control: comparison with preintake status.
Treatment. Group and individual psychotherapy.
Length of treatment. About 51 percent came four times or less; 20 percent attended at least ten times in the year between intake and follow-up.

[1] Thirteen patients (6%) were deceased at time of follow-up and are not included in this analysis.

Appendix C

Period from treatment to follow-up. One year from intake.
Method of evaluation. Clinic records.
Major criteria. Drinking, social adjustment, work, and health.
Results:

Drinking	*f*	*%*
improved	239	31
unimproved	540(173)[1]	69(22)

Interpersonal Relations[2] *f*		*%*
improved	183	35
unimproved	337	65

[1] Nineteen patients (2%) were deceased at time of follow-up and are not included in the above analysis.
[2] Data available for 520 patients.

29. SCHMIDT, E. C. "Alcohol Dependency—Disease or Dilemma," *Wisconsin Medical Journal,* 57:457-464, 1958.
   Setting. Private psychiatric hospital, Wisconsin (inpatient).
   Purpose. Theoretical paper; evaluation incidental.
   Cases. 12 male, 8 female (12 responded to questionnaire and are included in evaluation, sex unspecified).
   Subject selection. Evidently total alcoholic population admitted to one service during two years.
   Controls. None.
   Treatment. "Psychotherapy" not further described; evidently individual.
   Length of treatment. Range—5 to 120 days.
   Period from treatment to follow-up. "A minimum of three months after discharge."
   Method of evaluation. Patients' reports on mail questionnaire.
   Major criteria. Self-reports of drinking, work, and general well-being.
   *Results.**

	f	*%*
improved	11	55
unimproved	9(8)[1]	45(40)

[1] One patient (a suicide) was deceased at time of follow-up and has been included in the "unimproved" category.

30. SCHMIDT, K. T. "A New Testament Service for Alcoholics," *Journal of the Kentucky State Medical Association,* 57:302-304, 1959.
Setting. Alcoholic treatment and rehabilitation unit at Western State Hospital, Kentucky.
Purpose. Description and evaluation of program.
Cases. First 75 patients treated in unit (male).
Subject selection. First 75 patients discharged from alcoholic treatment unit.
Controls. None.
Treatment. Group psychotherapy, pastoral counseling, social casework, AA.
Length of treatment. Approximately one month.
Period from treatment to follow-up. Three months after discharge.
Method of evaluation. Questionnaire.
Major criteria. Drinking.
Results. "Approximately 1/3 remained sober, 1/3 continued to drink, but less excessively, and 1/3 relapsed into heavy drinking."

31. SCHNITZER, K. "The Treatment of Alcoholism in General Practice," *Bulletin of the Orange County Medical Association,* 21:22-23, 1952.
Setting. Outpatient (not specified whether in a clinic or private office).
Purpose. Description of method; evaluation incidental.
Cases. Not described.
Subject selection. Not described.
Controls. None.
Treatment. Psychotherapy "where indicated," medication, AA.
Length of treatment. Not described.
Period from treatment to follow-up. Not described.
Method of evaluation. Not described.
Major criteria. Drinking.
Results. ". . . at least 50% put on this program remained sober up to now [one and a half years] and are enjoying a sense of well-being most of the time."

Appendix C

32. SELZER, M. L., and W. H. HOLLOWAY. "A Follow-up of Alcoholics Committed to a State Hospital," *Quarterly Journal of Studies on Alcohol*, 18:98-120, 1957.
    Setting. Ypsilanti State Hospital, Michigan (inpatient).
    Purpose. Description of patients, identification of prognostic variables, and evaluation of program.
    Cases. 73 male, 25 female (committed).
    Subject selection. Of 131 alcoholic patients admitted from 1/1/48 to 6/30/49, 98 patients without chronic brain syndrome or functional psychosis.
    Controls. None.
    Treatment. "Milieu" therapy with psychiatric interviews, duration and character of which depend on the physician.
    Lenth of treatment. Average duration of hospitalization—4 to 7 months; range—a few days to 28 months.
    Period from treatment to follow-up. Six years following discharge.
    Method of evaluation. Phone or direct contact with patient or surviving relative by social worker.
    Major criteria. Readmission and other hospitalizations, income, residential stability and relations, marital status, acceptance, AA contacts, TB, deaths, abstinence.
    Results.[1]

	f	%
improved	34	35
unimproved	64(15)[2]	65(15)

33. STRAYER, R. "Social Integration of Alcoholics Through Prolonged Group Therapy," *Quarterly Journal of Studies on Alcohol*, 22:471-480, 1961.
    Setting. Bridgeport Clinic, Connecticut Department of Mental Health.

---

[1] These results are for posthospital adjustment (which includes drinking); results on other criteria are also provided.

[2] This analysis includes 18 patients (18%) who were deceased at time of follow-up. Authors do not indicate which category these patients fell in.

Purpose. Descriptive paper; evaluation incidental.
Cases. 19 males (over 11 years, size of group varies from 4 to 7).
Subject selection. Evaluation for suitability for group.
Controls. None.
Treatment. Group therapy, some receive individual therapy.
Length of treatment. Varies.
Period from treatment to follow-up. Evaluation concurrent with treatment.
Method of evaluation. Judgment of therapist.
Major criteria. Behavior in group, total functioning, psychological tests (Wechsler-Bellevue, Rorschach, Sentence Completion, TAT, Figure Drawing).
Results. In terms of group functioning. "Psychological re-testing revealed favorable changes in all the members"; "the members were able to remain abstinent for substantial periods of time."

34. TERHUNE, W. B. "A Method of Treatment of Alcoholism and the Results," *Journal of the Kentucky State Medical Association,* 54:255-260, 1956.
    Setting. Silver Hill Foundation for the Treatment of Psychoneuroses, New Canaan, Connecticut.
    Purpose. Description and evaluation of program.
    Cases. 122 male, 63 female.
    Subject selection. Patients seen in a 14-year period. (Evidently not the total alcoholic population; selection not clear.)
    Controls. None.
    Treatment. Medical and psychiatric reeducation program, "intensive objective psychological reeducation."
    Length of treatment. Basic program covers 10 weeks, followed by three years of outpatient treatment. Whether or not the sample described adhered to this program is not specified.
    Period from treatment to follow-up. Five years and after termination of treatment.
    Method of evaluation. Interviews and correspondence with patients, families, doctors, review of records by "members of our group and a research worker."

Appendix C

Major criteria. Not described; abstinence evidently a key factor.
Results:

	f	%
improved	113	61
unimproved	72	39

35. THOMAS, R. E., L. H. GLIEDMAN, JULIA FREUND, S. D. IMBER, and A. R. STONE. "Favorable Response in the Clinical Treatment of Chronic Alcoholism," *Journal of the American Medical Association,* 169:1994-1997, 1959.
Setting. Six Maryland Alcoholic Rehabilitation Clinics.
Purpose. Description and evaluation of program.
Cases. 57 male, 20 female.
Subject selection. All patients seen during 3-month assessment period.
Controls. Patient as own control; comparison with initial status.
Treatment. Individual and group therapy. Sixty percent get individual therapy; number getting group therapy not specified.
Length of treatment. Average, 19 weeks; range, 2–37 weeks. Average number of treatment sessions, 10.3. Group therapy patients, average 16.7 sessions. Individual therapy patients, average 6.4 sessions.
Period from treatment to follow-up. Varies.
Method of evaluation. Retrospective ratings by therapists, mostly concurrent with treatment.
Major criteria. Drinking, family and social adjustment, work, physical status.
Results:[1]

	Drinking		Family & Social		Occupational		Physical Status	
	f	%	f	%	f	%	f	%
improved	53	69	39	51	32	42	30	39
unimproved	24	32	38	49	45	58	47	62

[1] Results also given separately for 13 patients whose spouses were concurrently receiving treatment.

36. THOMAS, R. E., L. H. GLIEDMAN, S. D. IMBER, A. R. STONE, and J. FREUND. "Evaluation of the Maryland Alcoholic Rehabilitation Clinics," Quarterly Journal of Studies on Alcohol, 20:65-76, 1959.
Setting. Six Maryland Alcoholic Rehabilitation Clinics.
Purpose. Program evaluation as a guide for further program development.
Cases. 57 male, 20 female.
Subject selection. All patients treated in six clinics during a 3-month period.
Controls. Comparison with initial status; patient as own control.
Treatment. Individual therapy (60%), group therapy, also medical care, casework.
Length of treatment. Average 19 weeks. Range—2 to 37 weeks. Mean number of visits—10.3.
Period from treatment to follow-up. Varies (58 percent still in treatment at time of follow-up).
Method of evaluation. Retrospective ratings by therapists.
Major criteria. Drinking, family and social adjustment, work, physical status.
Results:[1]

	f	%
Improved on one or more criteria	53	69
No improvement	24	32

37. THORPE, J. J., and J. T. PERRET. "Problem Drinking: A Follow-up Study," Archives of Industrial Health, 19:24-32, 1959.
Setting. Industrial Clinic.
Purpose. Description and evaluation of program.
Cases. 274 male, 4 female problem drinkers known to Medical Department of Esso Standard Oil Company during period 1948–1956.
Subject selection. Total population of clinic, 1948 through 1956.
Controls. None.
Treatment. Varies; no description of therapy, other than "psychiatric" treatment.

[1] See Thomas et al., above, for analyses of each criterion.

Length of treatment. Not described.
Period from treatment to follow-up. Varies.
Method of evaluation. Review of medical records, information from staff and visiting nurses. "Information on the present status of terminated employees was available in only a few instances."
Major criteria. Drinking, absenteeism, termination.
Results:

Drinking	f	%
improved	130	51
unimproved	125[1]	49

38. VIRGINIA STATE DEPARTMENT OF HEALTH. "Alcohol Rehabilitation," entire issue of *Virginia Health Bulletin*, 7, Series 2, No. 6, 1954.
Setting. Hospital ward and clinics of Virginia Division of Alcohol Studies and Rehabilitation.
Purpose. To publicize and describe program.
Cases. 1,687 patients accepted from 10/48 to 10/53. Sex not specified.
Subject selection. Total population, 10/48 to 10/53.
Controls. None.
Treatment. Psychotherapy, not clearly described. Group, evidently some individual.
Length of treatment. Not described.
Period from treatment to follow-up. Varies.
Method of evaluation. Not described.
Major criteria. Drinking, overall adjustment.
Results:

	f	%
improved	1158	69
unimproved	529	31

39. WALCOTT, ESTHER P., and R. STRAUS. "Use of a Hospital Facility in Conjunction with Outpatient Clinics in the Treatment of

[1] Twelve patients (4%) had retired for reasons not related to alcoholism, and 11 (4%) were deceased at time of follow-up. These 23 patients are not included in this analysis.

Alcoholics," *Quarterly Journal of Studies on Alcohol,* 13:60-77, 1952.
Setting. Blue Hills Hospital and Clinic, Hartford, Connecticut.
Purpose. To examine patient and treatment characteristics related to sustained contact with clinic.
Cases. 402 male, 72 female.
Subject selection. Entire patient population receiving inpatient care during first 12 months of operation (April 1950 through April 1951).
Controls. None.
Treatment. "Psychiatric treatment," not further described.
Length of treatment. Length of hospitalization not specified. Number of clinic visits varies from "no return to clinics" to those still in treatment.
Period from treatment to follow-up. Varies.
Method of evaluation. Ratings based on conferences between staff members of each clinic and one of the authors.
Major criteria. Changes in drinking, social adjustment, attitudes toward problem.
Results:

	f	%
improved	156	34
unimproved	304(190)[1]	66(41)

40. WALLACE, J. A. "A Comparison of Disulfiram Therapy and Routine Therapy in Alcoholism," *Quarterly Journal of Studies on Alcohol,* 13:397-400, 1952.
Setting. Private sanitarium—inpatient and outpatient. (Wallace Sanitarium, Memphis, Tennessee.)
Purpose. Comparative evaluation of 2 programs.
Cases. 49 males, 3 females.
Subject selection. 26 consecutive admissions who request disulfiram compared with 26 consecutive patients not requesting it.

---

[1] Fourteen patients (3%) were deceased or institutionalized for reasons not related to alcoholism at time of follow-up and are not included in this analysis.

Controls. 26 patients receiving disulfiram compared with 26 patients not receiving it.
Treatment. Psychotherapy (not described), medication, plus disulfiram for experimental group.
Length of treatment. Not described.
Major criteria. Drinking.
Results. Given in terms of months of abstinence for each group. Disulfiram group: 12 abstinent at time of report (6–18 months). Of those who relapsed, several had fairly prolonged periods of abstinence. Control group: 17 of 26 patients relapsed within 2 months, all relapsed within 6 months.

41. WALLERSTEIN, R. S. "Comparative Study of Treatment Methods for Chronic Alcoholism: The Alcoholism Research Project at Winter VA Hospital," *American Journal of Psychiatry,* 113:228-233, 1956.
    Setting. Winter VA Hospital, Topeka, Kansas.
    Purpose. To determine relative effectiveness of treatment programs.
    Cases. 178 males.
    Subject selection. Random assignment to groups.
    Controls. A control group is included in the design; its limitations are discussed.
    Treatment. All patients receive individual and group psychotherapy. Also divided into four groups, one control, one getting Antabuse, one conditioned-reflex treatment, one group hypnotherapy (see Paley, *Bulletin of the Menninger Clinic,* 16:1, 1952, 14–19, and Wallerstein, R. S., *Hospital Treatment of Alcoholism* [New York: Basic Books, 1957]).
    Length of treatment. Approximately three months.
    Period from treatment to follow-up. Varies, covers period of two years.
    Method of evaluation. Not described.
    Major criteria. Drinking, social adjustment, subjective feelings of difference (self-assessment), psychiatric changes, continuing treatment.

Results:

	Antabuse $N=47$		C-R $N=50$	
	f	%	f	%
improved	25	53	12	24
unimproved	22(7)	47(15)	38(21)	76(42)

	Hypnotherapy $N=39$		Milieu $N=42$	
	f	%	f	%
improved	14	36	11	26
unimproved	25(11)	64(28)	31(16)	74(38)

42. WALLERSTEIN, R. S. *Hospital Treatment of Alcoholism: A Comparative Experimental Study*, Menninger Clinic Monograph, No. 11 (New York: Basic Books, 1957).
Setting. Winter VA Hospital.
Purpose. To compare effectiveness of different types of therapy.
Cases: 178 males, in four groups.
Subject selection. Patients assigned in order of admission to one of the four groups.
Controls. Control group receiving "milieu therapy" only.
Treatment. Comparison of Antabuse, conditioned-reflex, and group hypnotherapy treatments, and milieu therapy (control group).
Length of treatment. 60 to 90 days.
Period from treatment to follow-up. Regularly scheduled return visits for two years.
Method of evaluation. Interviews with patients.
Major criteria. Drinking, social adjustment, subjective feelings of difference, structural changes in personality configuration.
Results:[1] Appendices give results for each patient. Individual chapters provide detailed results for each type of therapy.

43. WATTERNBERG, W. W., and J. B. MOIR. "Factors Linked to Success in Counselling Homeless Alcoholics," *Quarterly Journal of Studies on Alcohol*, 15:587-594, 1954.

[1] For percentage improved, see Wallerstein (1956) above.

Setting. Out-patient Counseling Center, Detroit, Michigan.
Purpose. Determination of factors prognostic of success in treatment.
Cases. 1,361 homeless males (minus 330 cases discarded because of incomplete recording).
Subject selection. All cases on file, no longer on active status.
Controls. None.
Treatment. Counseling.
Length of treatment. Not described, other than that all had returned for more than one interview.
Period from treatment to follow-up. Six months.
Method of evaluation. Self-report, agency records, contact with employer, landlord, or family member.
Major criteria. To qualify as a success, patient (1) must be locatable in Detroit; (2) by own statement, sober at least six months; (3) with supporting evidence of this from landlord or family member; (4) report from employer of steady job for six months after counseling; (5) police record check shows no arrests for drunkenness or allied charges for past six months.
Results:

	f	%
improved	70	7
unimproved	932(232)[1]	93(23)

44. WEST, L. J. and W. H. SWEGAN. "An Approach to Alcoholism in the Military Service," *American Journal of Psychiatry*, 112:1004-1009, 1956.
Setting. U.S. Air Force.
Purpose. Description and evaluation of program.
Cases. 50 males.
Subject selection. First 50 consecutive cases contacted for experimental program.
Controls. None.
Treatment. Individual psychotherapy, hypnotherapy "in a few cases," AA, medication (gives percentage receiving each.)

[1] Twenty-nine patients (3%) were excluded from the analysis because data was dubious—i.e., reports from various sources differed.

Length of treatment. Not described.
Period from treatment to follow-up. Ranges from 5 to 29 months.
Method of evaluation. Not described, but evidently included questionnaires.
Major criteria. Successful return to duty, drinking.
Results:

	f	%
improved	27	68
unimproved	13[1]	32

[1] Five cases (19%) were transferred overseas prior to follow-up and are not included in the above analysis.

45. WEXBERG, L. E. "The Outpatient Treatment of Alcoholism in the District of Columbia," *Quarterly Journal of Studies on Alcohol,* 14:514-524, 1953.
Setting. D. C. Health Department Alcoholic Clinic.
Purpose. Program evaluation.
Cases. 1455; 1075 voluntary, 380 court referred. Sex not specified.
Subject selection. All registered patients.
Controls. None. Study compared voluntary with court-referred cases.
Treatment. Individual and group psychotherapy (also medical, occupational, and recreational therapy).
Length of treatment. Average number of treatment sessions—18.5 voluntary and 11.7 court-referred.
Period from treatment to follow-up. Concurrent with treatment.
Method of evaluation. Not described.
Major criteria. Drinking, social and psychiatric improvement.
Results:[1]

[1] Results are given for "treated" patients, and includes those who returned for treatment at least 3 times. Those returning only once or twice are considered "registered."

Appendix C

	Voluntary[2]		Court[3]		Total	
Drinking	f	%	f	%	f	%
improved	335	65	133	68	468	65
unimproved	184	35	63	32	247	35
Social						
improved	200	39	65	33	265	37
unimproved	319	61	131	67	450	63
Psychiatric						
improved	99	19	23	12	122	17
unimproved	420	81	173	88	593	83

46. WILBY, W. E. and R. W. JONES. "Assessing Patient Response Following Treatment," *Quarterly Journal of Studies on Alcohol*, 23:325, 1962.
Setting. Clinic of the Alcoholism Foundation of Alberta.
Purpose. To determine relative effectiveness of different periods of time for follow-up.
Cases. 706 patients, sex not specified.
Subject selection. Patients who have had at least 4 clinic visits and were not in treatment at time of evaluation.
Controls. None.
Treatment. Combined medical treatment and psychotherapeutically oriented casework.
Length of treatment. Not described.
Period from treatment to follow-up. 18 months, 24–84 months.
Method of evaluation. Not described.
Major criteria. Drinking, social adjustment.
Results:

	18 months		24–84 months		
improved	482	68	453	64	f %
unimproved	224	32	253	36	

[2] Results for 519 cases "treated" out of 1,075 "registered."
[3] Results for 196 cases "treated" out of 380 "registered."

Bibliography

ABRAM, H. S. and W. F. MCCOURT. "Interaction of Physicians with Emergency Ward Alcoholic Patients," *Quarterly Journal of Studies on Alcohol,* 25:679-688, 1964.

ADORNO, T. W. et al. *The Authoritarian Personality.* New York: Harper and Brothers, 1950.

AMERICAN MEDICAL ASSOCIATION. "Hospitalization of Patients with Alcoholism" (Reports of Officers), *Journal of the American Medical Association,* 162:750, 1956.

Anon. Guide Issue, Part II, *Hospitals,* 32:413, August, 1958.

AULD, F., and J. K. MEYERS. "Contributions to a Theory for Selecting Psychotherapy Patients," *Journal of Clinical Psychology,* 10:56-60, 1954.

BACON, S. D. "Inebriety, Social Integration and Marriage," *Quarterly Journal of Studies on Alcohol,* 5:303-339, 1944.

BAILEY, M. A., L. WARSHAW, and R. M. EICHLER. "A Study of Factors Related to Length of Stay in Psychotherapy," *Journal of Clinical Psychology,* 15:442-444, 1959.

BALES, R. F. "Cultural Differences in Rates of Alcoholism," *Quarterly Journal of Studies on Alcohol,* 6:480-499, 1946.

BELLAK, L. "A General Hospital as a Focus of Community Psychiatry," *Journal of the American Medical Association,* 174:2214-2217, 1960.

———. "The Comprehensive Community Psychiatry Program at City Hospital," in L. BELLAK (ed)., *Handbook of Community Psychiatry and Community Mental Health.* New York: Grune and Stratton, 1964.

BLANE, H. T. *The Role of the Nurse in the Care of the Alcoholic Patient in the General Hospital.* Boston: Division of Alcoholism, Massachusetts Department of Public Health, 1960.

———. "Effectiveness of a Method for Establishing Treatment Relations with Alcoholics" (abstract), *American Psychologist,* 16:366, 1961.

———. "Third-Party Selection of Subjects and Biased Samples," *Psychological Reports,* 13:133-134, 1963.

———. "Drinking and Crime," *Federal Probation,* 29:25-29.

———. *The Personality of the Alcoholic: Guises of Dependency.* New York: Harper and Row, 1968.

———. "Trends in the Prevention of Alcoholism," *Psychiatric Research Report,* 24:1-9. Washington, D.C.: American Psychiatric Association, 1968.

———, and M. J. HILL. "Public Health Nurses Speak up About Alcoholism," *Nursing Outlook,* 12:34-37, 1964.

BLANE, H. T., and W. R. MYERS. "Behavioral Dependence and Length of Stay in Psychotherapy Among Alcoholics," *Quarterly Journal of Studies on Alcohol,* 24:503-510, 1963.

———. "Social Class and Establishment of Treatment Relations by Alcoholics," *Journal of Clinical Psychology,* 20:287-290, 1964.

BLANE, H. T., J. J. MULLER, and M. E. CHAFETZ. "Acute Psychiatric Services in the General Hospital: II. Current Status of Emergency Psychiatric Services," *American Journal of Psychiatry,* 124:37-45, October supplement, 1967.

BLANE, H. T., W. F. OVERTON, JR., and M. E. CHAFETZ, "Social Factors in the Diagnosis of Alcoholism. I. Characteristics of the Patient," *Quarterly Journal of Studies on Alcohol,* 24:640-663, 1963.

BOSTON PLANNING BOARD. *Report on the Income and Cost of Six Districts in the City of Boston.* Boston: Boston Planning Board, 1934.

BRILL, A. A. "Alcohol and the Individual," *New York Medical Journal,* 109:928-950, 1919.

BRILL, N. Q., and H. A. STORROW. "Social Class and Psychiatric Treatment," *AMA Archives of General Psychiatry,* 3:340-344, 1960.

BROWN, E., and C. TAYLOR, "An Alcoholism Treatment Facility in a Rural Area," *Mental Hygiene,* 50:194-198, 1966.

BRUNNER-ORNE, M. "The Role of a General Hospital in the Treatment and Rehabilitation of Alcoholics," *Quarterly Journal of Studies on Alcohol,* 19:108-117, 1958.

BURGESS, E. W. "The Growth of the City," in R. E. PARK, E. W. BURGESS, and R. D. MCKENZIE (eds.), *The City.* Chicago: University of Chicago Press, 1925. Pp. 47-62.

CALIFORNIA DEPARTMENT OF PUBLIC HEALTH. *Alcoholism and California: Follow-up Studies of Treated Alcoholics; Description of Studies.* Berkeley: California Department of Public Health, Publication No. 5, 1961.

CAMERON, R. W. "County Psychiatric Emergency Services," *Public Health Reports,* 76:357-359, 1961.

CARLSON, E. R., and R. CARLSON. "Male and Female Subjects in Personality Research," *Journal of Abnormal and Social Psychology,* 61:482-483, 1960.

CAUDILL, W., and B. H. ROBERTS. "Pitfalls in the Organization of Interdisciplinary Research," *Human Organization,* 10:12-15, 1951.

CHAFETZ, M. E. "Practical and Theoretical Considerations in the Psychotherapy of Alcoholism," *Quarterly Journal of Studies on Alcohol,* 20:281-291, 1959.

———. "A Procedure for Establishing Therapeutic Contact with the Alcoholic," *Quarterly Journal of Studies on Alcohol,* 22:325-328, 1961.

———. "Alcoholism Problems and Programs in Czechoslovakia, Poland and the Soviet Union," *New England Journal of Medicine,* 265:68-74, 1961.

———. "Acute Psychiatric Services in the Emergency Ward," *Massachusetts General Hospital News,* 222:1-3, 1963.

———. *Liquor: The Servant of Man.* Boston: Little, Brown and Co., 1965.

———. "The Effect of a Psychiatric Emergency Service on Motivation for Psychiatric Treatment," *Journal of Nervous and Mental Disease,* 140:442-448, 1965.

———."Alcohol Excess," *Annals of the New York Academy of Sciences,* 133:808-813, 1966.

———. "Clinical Syndromes of Liquor Drinkers," paper presented at the International Symposium on Alcohol and Alcoholism, Santiago, Chile, 1966.

———. "Alcoholism Prevention and Reality," *Quarterly Journal of Studies on Alcohol,* 28:345-348, 1967.

———, and H. T. BLANE. "Alcoholic-Crisis Treatment Approach

and Establishment of Treatment Relations with Alcoholics," *Psychological Reports,* 12:862, 1963.

CHAFETZ, M. E., H. T. BLANE, H. S. ABRAM, J. GOLNER, E. LACY, W. F. MCCOURT, E. CLARK, and W. MEYERS. "Establishing Treatment Relations with Alcoholics," *Journal of Nervous and Mental Disease,* 134:395-409, 1962.

CHAFETZ, M. E., H. T. BLANE, H. S. ABRAM, E. CLARK, J. GOLNER, E. L. HASTIE, and W. F. MCCOURT. "Establishing Treatment Relations with Alcoholics: A Supplementary Report," *Journal of Nervous and Mental Disease,* 138:390-393, 1964.

CHAFETZ, M. E., H. T. BLANE, and J. J. MULLER. "Acute Psychiatric Services in the General Hospital. I. Implications for Psychiatry in Emergency Admissions," *American Journal of Psychiatry,* 123:664-670, 1966.

CHAFETZ, M. E., and H. W. DEMONE, JR. *Alcoholism and Society.* New York: Oxford University Press, 1962.

COLEMAN, J. V. and P. ERRERA. "Acute Psychiatric Problems and General Hospitals: Report of a Preliminary Survey," *Connecticut Medicine,* 25:620-622, 1961.

———. "The General Hospital Emergency Room and Its Psychiatric Problems," *American Journal of Public Health,* 53:1294-1301, 1963.

COLEMAN, M. D., and M. ROSENBAUM. "The Psychiatric Walk-in Clinic," *Israel Annals of Psychiatry and Related Disciplines,* 1:99-106, 1963.

COLEMAN, M. D., and I. ZWERLING. "The Psychiatric Emergency Clinic: A Flexible Way of Meeting Community Mental Health Needs," *American Journal of Psychiatry,* 115:980-984, 1959.

COMMITTEE ON PUBLIC HEALTH RELATIONS, NEW YORK ACADEMY OF MEDICINE. "A Survey of Facilities for the Care and Treatment of Alcoholism in New York City," *Quarterly Journal of Studies on Alcohol,* 7:405-438, 1946.

DAVIES, D. L., M. SHEPHERD, and E. MYERS. "The Two-Years' Prognosis of 50 Alcohol Addicts After Treatment in Hospital," *Quarterly Journal of Studies on Alcohol,* 17:485-502, 1956.

DAVITZ, J. (ed.). *The Communication of Emotional Meaning.* New York: McGraw-Hill Book Co., 1964.

——, and L. Davitz. "Correlates of Accuracy in the Communication of Feelings," *Journal of Communication,* 9:110-117, 1959.
——. "The Communication of Feelings by Content-Free Speech," *Journal of Communication,* 9:6-13, 1959.
Dean, S. I. "Treatment of the Reluctant Client," *American Psychologist,* 13:627-630, 1958.
Dibner, A. S. "Cue Counting: A Measure of Anxiety in Interviews," *Journal of Consulting Psychology,* 20:475-478, 1956.
Durkheim, E. *Suicide.* Glencoe, Illinois: The Free Press, 1962.
Eldred, S. H., and D. B. Price. "A Linguistic Evaluation of Feeling States in Psychotherapy," *Psychiatry,* 21:115-121, 1958.
Ends, E. J., and C. W. Page. "A Study of Three Types of Group Psychotherapy with Hospitalized Male Inebriates," *Quarterly Journal of Studies on Alcohol,* 18:263-277, 1957.
——. "Group Psychotherapy and Concomitant Psychological Change," *Psychological Monographs,* 73, No. 480, 1959.
Errera, P., G. Wyshak, and H. Jarecki. "Psychiatric Care in a General Hospital Emergency Room," *Archives of General Psychiatry,* 9:105-112, 1963.
Ewalt, J. R., S. Zaslow, and P. Stevenson. "How Nonpsychiatric Physicians Can Deal with Psychiatric Emergencies," *Mental Hospitals,* 15:194-196, 1964.
Falkey, D. B., and S. Schneyer. "Characteristics of Male Alcoholics Admitted to the Medical Ward of a General Hospital," *Quarterly Journal of Studies on Alcohol,* 18:67-97, 1957.
Faris, R. E. L., and H. W. Dunham. *Mental Disorders in Urban Areas.* New York: Hofner, 1939.
Feldstein, S., M. S. Brenner, and J. Jaffe. "The Effect of Subject, Sex, Verbal Interaction, and Topical Focus on Speech Disruption," *Language and Speech,* 6:229-239, 1963.
Fellin, P. "The Standardized Interview in Social Work Research," *Social Casework,* 44:81-85, 1963.
Fenichel, O. *The Psychoanalytic Theory of Neurosis.* New York: W. W. Norton and Co., 1945.
Fowler, R. D., Sr. *Studies in Alcoholism.* Montgomery, Alabama: Alabama Commission on Alcoholism, 1960.
Fox, V., and M. A. Smith. "Evaluation of a Chemopsychothera-

peutic Program for the Rehabilitation of Alcoholics: Observations over a Two-Year Period," *Quarterly Journal of Studies on Alcohol,* 20:767-780, 1959.

FRANCO, S. C. *A Company Program for Problem Drinking.* New York: Consolidated Edison Company of New York, 1962 (mimeographed).

FRANK, J. D., L. H. GLIEDMAN, S. D. IMBER, E. H. NASH, and A. R. STONE, "Why Patients Leave Psychotherapy," *AMA Archives of Neurology and Psychiatry,* 77:283-299, 1957.

FRANKEL, F. H. "Emotional First Aid," *Archives of Emotional Health,* 2:824-827, 1965.

———, M. E. CHAFETZ, and H. T. BLANE. "Treatment of Psychosocial Crises in the Emergency Service of a General Hospital," *Journal of the American Medical Association,* 195:626-628, 1966.

FREUD, S. "Contributions to the Psychology of Love. The Most Prevalent Form of Degradation in Erotic Life" [1912], in *Collected Papers.* London: Hogarth, 1925. Vol. IV, pp. 203-216.

———. "Mourning and Melancholia" [1917], in *Collected Papers.* London: Hogarth, 1925. Vol. IV, pp. 152-170.

———. *Three Contributions to the Theory of Sex.* Washington, D.C. Nervous and Mental Disease Publishing House, 4th Ed., 1930.

GARETZ, F. K. "The Psychiatric Emergency," *Medical Times,* 88:1066-1070, 1960.

GARFIELD, S. L., and D. C. AFFLECK. "An Appraisal of Duration of Stay in Outpatient Psychotherapy," *Journal of Nervous and Mental Disease,* 129:492-498, 1959.

GERARD, D. L., and G. SAENGER. "Interval Between Intake and Follow-up as a Factor in the Evaluation of Patients with a Drinking Problem," *Quarterly Journal of Studies on Alcohol,* 20:620-630, 1959.

———, and R. WILE. "The Abstinent Alcoholic," *Archives of General Psychiatry,* 6:83-95, 1962.

GIBBINS, R. J., and J. D. ARMSTRONG. "Effects of Clinical Treatment on Behavior of Alcoholic Patients: An Exploratory Methodological Investigation," *Quarterly Journal of Studies on Alcohol,* 18:429-450, 1957.

GIBBY, R. E., B. A. STOTSKY, E. W. HILER, and D. R. MILLER. "Validation of Rorschach Criteria for Predicting Duration of Therapy," *Journal of Consulting Psychology,* 18:185-191, 1954.

GLAD, D. D. "Attitudes and Experiences of American-Jewish and American-Irish Male Youth as Related to Differences in Adult Rates of Inebriety," *Quarterly Journal of Studies on Alcohol,* 8:406-474, 1947.

GLASSCOTE, R. M., E. CUMMING, D. W. HAMMERSLEY, L. D. OZARIN, and L. H. SMITH. *The Psychiatric Emergency: A Study of Patterns of Service.* Washington, D.C.: Joint Information Service (APA-NAMH), 1966.

GLASSCOTE, R. M., D. S. SANDERS, H. M. FORSTENZER, and A. R. FOLEY. *The Community Mental Health Center: An Analysis of Existing Models.* Washington, D.C.: Joint Information Service (APA-NAMH), 1964.

GLIEDMAN, L. H. "Concurrent and Combined Group Treatment of Chronic Alcoholics and Their Wives," *International Journal of Group Psychotherapy,* 7:414-424, 1957.

———, D. ROSENTHAL, J. D. FRANK, and H. T. NASH. "Group Therapy of Alcoholics with Concurrent Group Meetings of Their Wives," *Quarterly Journal of Studies on Alcohol,* 17:655-670, 1956.

GLOVER, E. "The Etiology of Drug Addiction," *International Journal of Psycho-Analysis,* 13:298-328, 1932.

GOLIN, M. "This 'Trouble-Shooting Clinic' Strengthening a Community," *Journal of the American Medical Association,* 171:1697, 1959.

GOTTSCHALK, L. (ed.). *Comparative Psycholinguistic Analysis of Two Psychotherapy Interviews.* New York: International Universities Press, 1961.

GROUT, J. L., and L. A. HOLUB. "Twenty Years' Experience in Emergency Room Management," *Bulletin of the American College of Surgeons,* 40:210-212, 1955.

GUZE, S. B., V. B. TUASON, M. A. STEWART, and B. PICKEN. "The Drinking History: A Comparison of Reports by Subjects and Their Relatives," *Quarterly Journal of Studies on Alcohol,* 24:249-260, 1963.

HEINBERG, P. "Factors Related to an Individual's Ability to Perceive Implications of Dialogues," *Speech Monographs,* 28:274-283, 1961.

HERZOG, E. *Some Guide Lines for Evaluative Research: Assessing Social Change in Individuals.* Washington, D.C.: U.S. Department of Health, Education, and Welfare, Social Security Administration, Children's Bureau, 1959.

HILL, J. G. "Cost Analysis of Social Work Service," in N. A. POLANSKY (ed.), *Social Work Research.* Chicago: University of Chicago Press, 1960. Pp. 223-247.

HILL, M. J., and H. T. BLANE. "Evaluation of Psychotherapy with Alcoholics: A Critical Review," *Quarterly Journal of Studies on Alcohol,* 28:76-204, 1967.

HIRSCH, J. "This Trouble-Shooting Clinic Provides First Aid for Emotional Problems," *Modern Hospitals,* 95:102, 104, 1960.

HOLLINGSHEAD, A. B. *Two-Factor Index of Social Position.* Mimeographed, no date.

HOLLINGSHEAD, A. B., and REDLICH, F. C. *Social Class and Mental Illness.* New York: John Wiley, 1958.

IMBER, S. D., E. H. NASH, and A. R. STONE. "Social Class and Duration of Psychotherapy," *Journal of Clinical Psychology,* 11:281-284, 1955.

JACKSON, J. K., and R. CONNOR. "The Skid Row Alcoholic," *Quarterly Journal of Studies on Alcohol,* 14:468-486, 1953.

JELLINEK, E. M. *The Disease Concept of Alcoholism.* New Haven, Connecticut: Hillhouse Press, 1960.

JENSEN, S. "A Treatment Program for Alcoholics in a Mental Hospital," *Quarterly Journal of Studies on Alcohol,* 23:315-320, 1962.

JONES, E. *Papers on Psychoneurosis.* Baltimore, Maryland: Ward and Co., 1938.

KAGAN, J., and H. Moss. *Birth to Maturity.* New York: Wiley and Sons, 1962.

KASL, S., and G. MAHL. "Experimentally Induced Anxiety and Speech Disturbances" (abstract), *American Psychologist,* 13:349, 1958.

KAUFFMAN, P. *An Investigation of Some Psychological Stimulus*

Properties of Speech Behavior. Unpublished doctoral dissertation, University of Chicago, 1954.

KELLER, M. "Alcoholism: Nature and Extent of the Problem," *Annals of the American Academy of Political and Social Sciences,* 315: 1-11, 1958.

KERLINGER, F. N. *Foundations of Behavioral Research.* New York: Holt, Rinehart and Winston, 1964.

KLEBANOFF, S. G. "Personality Factors in Symptomatic Chronic Alcoholism as Indicated by the Thematic Apperception Test," *Journal of Consulting Psychology,* 11:111-119, 1947.

KLEIN, D. C., and E. LINDEMANN. "Preventive Intervention in Individual and Family Crisis Situations," in G. CAPLAN (ed.). *Prevention of Mental Disorders in Children.* New York: Basic Books, 1961. Chap. 13, pp. 283-306.

KNIGHT, R. P. "The Dynamics and Treatment of Chronic Alcohol Addiction," *Bulletin of the Menninger Clinic,* 1:233-250, 1937.

———. "The Psychodynamics of Chronic Alcoholism," *Journal of Nervous and Mental Disease,* 86:538-548, 1937.

KOUMANS, A. J. R. and J. J. MULLER. "Use of Letters to Increase Motivation for Treatment in Alcoholics," *Psychological Reports,* 16:1152, 1965.

———, and C. F. MILLER. "Use of Telephone Calls to Increase Motivation for Treatment in Alcoholics," *Psychological Reports,* 21:327-328, 1967.

KRAMER, E. "Judgment of Personal Characteristics and Emotions from Noverbal Properties of Speech," *Psychological Bulletin,* 60:408-420, 1963.

———. "Elimination of Verbal Cues in Judgments of Emotion from Voice," *Journal of Abnormal and Social Psychology,* 68:390-396, 1964.

KURLAND, S. "Length of Treatment in a Mental Hygiene Clinic," *Psychiatric Quarterly* (suppl.), 30:83-90, 1956.

LESTER, D. "Self-Selection of Alcohol by Animals, Human Variation, and the Etiology of Alcoholism: A Critical Review," *Quarterly Journal of Studies on Alcohol,* 27:395-438, 1966.

LEVITT, E. E. *Clinical Research Design and Analysis in the Behav-*

ioral Sciences. Springfield, Illinois: Charles C. Thomas, 1961.

LIEBERMAN, L., H. UNTERBERGER, and D. TUCKERMAN (eds.). *Classified and Alphabetical Directory of Agencies Serving Alcoholics and Their Relatives in Massachusetts.* Boston: Commonwealth of Massachusetts, Division of Alcoholism, 1960.

LIEF, H. S., V. F. LIEF, C. D. WARREN, and R. G. HEATH. "Low Dropout Rate in a Psychiatric Clinic," *AMA Archives of General Psychiatry,* 5:200-211, 1961.

LINDEMANN, E. "The Meaning of Crisis in Individual and Family Living," *Teachers College Record,* 57:310, 1956.

———. "The Psychosocial Position on Etiology," in H. D. Kruse (ed.), *Integrating the Approaches to Mental Disease.* New York: Harper and Brothers, 1957.

LINDNER, R. "Alcoholism and Crime," *Alcohol Hygiene* 1:6, 1945.

LINN, L. (ed.). *Frontiers in General Hospital Psychiatry.* New York: International Universities Press, 1961.

LIPSCOMB, W. R. "Evaluation in Alcoholism Study," in *Selected Papers Delivered at the Eighth Annual Meeting of the North American Association of Alcoholism Programs.* Berkeley, California, 1957.

LISANSKY, E. S. "The Etiology of Alcoholism: The Role of Psychological Predisposition," *Quarterly Journal of Studies on Alcohol,* 21:314-343, 1960.

LORAND, S. "A Survey of Psychoanalytical Literature on Problems of Alcohol: Bibliography," *Yearbook of Psychoanalysis,* 1:359-370, 1945.

LORR, M., M. M. KATZ, and E. A. RUBINSTEIN. "The Prediction of Length of Stay in Psychotherapy," *Journal of Consulting Psychology,* 22:321-327, 1958.

LUDWIG, A. O. "Some Factors in the Genesis of Chronic Alcoholism and Their Bearing on Treatment," in *Papers Presented at the Physicians Institute on Alcoholism of the National State Conference on Alcoholism,* Boston, Massachusetts, March 9-10, 1956.

MCCARROLL, J. R., and P. A. SKUDDER. "Hospital Emergency Departments: Conflicting Concepts of Function Shown in National Survey," *Hospitals,* 34:35-38, 1960.

McCord, W., and J. McCord. *Origins of Alcoholism.* Stanford, California: Stanford University Press, 1960.

McGuigan, F. J. *Experimental Psychology: A Methodological Approach.* Englewood Cliffs, New Jersey: Prentice-Hall, 1960.

Maddox, G. L. "Teenagers and Alcohol: Recent Research," *Annals of the New York Academy of Sciences,* 133:856-865, 1966.

Mahl, G. "Disturbances and Silences in the Patient's Speech in Psychotherapy," *Journal of Abnormal and Social Psychology,* 53:1-15, 1956.

———, and G. Schulze. "Psychological Research in the Extralinguistic Area," in T. A. Sebeok, A. S. Hayes, and M. C. Bateson (eds.), *Approaches to Semiotics.* London: Mouton, 1964. Pp. 51-124.

Maier, R. A. and V. Fox. "Forced Therapy of Probated Alcoholics," *Medical Times,* 86:1051-1054, 1958.

Marcus, A. M. *The Alcoholism Questionnaire: Administration, Scoring, and Interpretation. Studies in Alcohol Education.* Toronto, Canada: Addiction Research Foundation, 1963 (mimeographed).

Massachusetts Department of Public Health. *Classified Directory of Agencies Serving Alcoholics and Their Relatives in Massachusetts.* Boston: Massachusetts Department of Public Health, Division of Alcoholism, 1960.

Mendelson, J. H., and M. E. Chafetz. "Alcoholism as an Emergency Ward Problem," *Quarterly Journal of Studies on Alcohol,* 20:270-275, 1959.

Mendelson, J. H., D. Wexler, P. E. Kubzansky, R. Harrison, G. Leiderman, and P. Solomon. "Physicians' Attitudes Toward Alcoholic Patients," *Archives of General Psychiatry,* 11:392-399, 1964.

Menninger, K. A. *Man Against Himself.* New York: Harcourt, Brace and Co., 1938.

Miller, D. R. "The Hospital Emergency Service," *Journal of the Kansas Medical Society,* 63:85-88, 1962.

Milmoe, S., R. Rosenthal, H. T. Blane, M. E. Chafetz, and I. Wolf. "The Doctor's Voice: Postdictor of Successful Referral of Alcoholic Patients," *Journal of Abnormal Psychology,* 72:78-84, 1967.

MINDLIN, D. F. "Evaluation of Therapy for Alcoholics in a Workhouse Setting," *Quarterly Journal of Studies on Alcohol,* 21:233-252, 1960.

MORISON, L. J., and J. M. DEFFENBAUGH. *Integrating an Alcoholism Program into Public Health Nursing: A Project Report and Guide.* Columbus: Ohio Department of Health, 1968.

MYERS, E. S. "Comments: Conference on Handling Emergencies," *American Journal of Psychiatry,* 122:224-225, 1965.

MYERSON, D. J., J. MACKAY, A. WALLENS, and N. NEIBERG. "A Report of a Rehabilitation Program for Alcoholic Women Prisoners," *Quarterly Journal of Studies on Alcohol,* Suppl. No. 1:151-157, 1961.

NAVIN, R. B. *Analysis of a Slum Area.* Washington, D.C.: Catholic University Press, 1934.

ORAM, P. G. "Induction of Action and Attitude Change: The Function of Role-Self Values and Levels of Endorsement," doctoral dissertation, Boston University, 1966.

PARK, R. E. "The City: Suggestions for the Investigation of Human Behavior in the Urban Environment," in R. E. PARK, E. W. BURGESS, and R. D. MCKENZIE (eds.), *The City.* Chicago: University of Chicago Press, 1925. Pp. 40-46.

PERSON, P. H., JR., F. L. HURLEY, and R. H. GIESLER. "Psychiatric Patients in General Hospitals," *Hospitals,* 40:64-68, 1966.

PFEFFER, A. Z., and S. BERGER. "A Follow-up Study of Treated Alcoholics," *Quarterly Journal of Studies on Alcohol,* 18:624-648, 1957.

PFEFFER, A. Z., D. J. FELDMAN, C. FEIBEL, J. A. FRANK, M. COHEN, S. BERGER, and M. F. FLEETWOOD. "A Treatment Program for the Alcoholic in Industry," *Journal of the American Medical Association,* 161:827-836, 1956.

PITTENGER, R., C. HOCKETT, and H. DANEHEY. *The First Five Minutes.* Ithaca, New York: Paul Martineau, 1960.

PITTMAN, D. J., and C. W. GORDON. *Revolving Door: A Study of the Chronic Police Case Inebriate.* Glencoe, Illinois: The Free Press, 1958.

POLK, K. *Drinking and the Adolescent Culture.* Eugene, Oregon: Lane County Youth Project, 1964 (mimeographed).

POST, J. "Current Research on Problems of Alcoholism. III. Report of the Section on Internal Medical Research," *Quarterly Journal of Studies on Alcohol,* 16:544-546, 1955.

QUEEN, S. A. "The Ecological Study of Mental Disorders," *American Sociological Review,* 5:201-209, 1940.

———, and D. B. CARPENTER. *The American City.* New York: McGraw-Hill Book Co., 1953.

RADO, S. "The Psychoanalysis of Pharmacothymia," *Psychoanalytic Quarterly,* 2:1-23, 1933.

RAINES, G. N., and J. H. ROHMER. "The Operational Matrix of Psychiatric Practices. I. Consistency and Variability in Interview Impressions of Different Psychiatrists," *American Journal of Psychiatry,* 111:721-723, 1955.

REDLICH, F. C., and E. B. BRODY. "Emotional Problems of Interdisciplinary Research in Psychiatry," *Psychiatry,* 18:233-239, 1955.

RIEMER, S. *The Modern City.* New York: Prentice-Hall, 1952.

RILEY, J. W., and C. F. MARDEN. "The Medical Professions and the Problem of Alcoholism," *Quarterly Journal of Studies on Alcohol,* 7:240-270, 1946.

ROBINSON, H. A., F. C. REDLICH, and J. K. MEYERS. "Social Structure and Psychiatric Treatment," *American Journal of Orthopsychiatry,* 24:307, 316, 1954.

ROSENBAUM, M. "Psychiatric Residency in the General Hospital," in L. LINN (ed.), *Frontiers in General Hospital Psychiatry.* New York: International Universities Press, 1961.

ROSENTHAL, D., and J. D. FRANK. "The Fate of Psychiatric Clinic Out-Patients Assigned to Psychotherapy," *Journal of Mental Disease,* 127:330-343, 1958.

ROSENTHAL, R., and K. L. FODE. "Psychology of the Scientists: V. Three Experiments in Experimenter Bias," *Psychological Reports,* 12:491-511, 1963.

ROSSI, J. J., and N. J. BRADLEY. "Dynamic Hospital Treatment of Alcoholism," *Quarterly Journal of Studies on Alcohol,* 21:432-446, 1960.

Rossi, J. J., A. Stach, and N. J. Bradley. "Effects of Treatment of Male Alcoholics in a Mental Hospital: A Follow-up Study," *Quarterly Journal of Studies on Alcohol*, 24:91-108, 1963.

Rubinstein, E. A., and M. A. Lorr. "A Comparison of Terminators and Remainers in Outpatient Psychotherapy," *Journal of Clinical Psychology*, 12:345-349, 1956.

Sachs, H. "The Genesis of Perversions" (abstract), *Psychoanalytic Review*, 16:74, 1929.

St. Louis Planning Commission. *A Year of City Planning*. St. Louis, Missouri: St. Louis Planning Commission, 1937.

———. *Urban Land Policy*. St. Louis, Missouri: St. Louis Planning Commission, 1936.

Sapir, J. V. "Relationship Factors in the Treatment of the Alcoholic," *Social Casework*, 34:297-303, 1953.

Schaffer, L., and J. K. Meyers. "Psychotherapy and Social Stratification," *Psychiatry*, 17:83-93, 1954.

Schilder, P. "Psychogenesis of Alcoholism," *Quarterly Journal of Studies on Alcohol*, 2:277-292, 1941.

Schmidt, E. C. "Alcoholic Dependency—Disease or Dilemma," *Wisconsin Medical Journal*, 57:457-464, 1958.

Schneyer, S. "The Marital Status of Alcoholics. A Note on an Analysis of the Marital Status of 2,008 Patients of Nine Clinics," *Quarterly Journal of Studies on Alcohol*, 15:325-329, 1954.

Schwartz, M. E., and P. Errera. "Psychiatric Care in a General Hospital Emergency Room. II. Diagnostic Features," *Archives of General Psychiatry*, 9:113-121, 1963.

Sherfey, M. J. "Psychotherapy and Character Structure in Chronic Alcoholism," in O. Diethelm (ed.), *Etiology of Chronic Alcoholism*. Springfield, Illinois: Charles C. Thomas, 1955. Pp. 16-42.

Shortliffe, E. G., T. S. Hamilton, and E. H. Norocan. "The Emergency Room and the Changing Pattern of Medical Care," *New England Journal of Medicine*, 258:2-25, 1958.

Singer, E., H. T. Blane, and R. Kasschau. "Alcoholism and Social Isolation," *Journal of Abnormal and Social Psychology*, 69:681-685, 1964.

Slack, C. W. "Experimenter-Subject Psychotherapy: A New

Method of Introducing Intensive Office Treatment for Unreachable Cases," *Mental Hygiene,* 44:238-256, 1960.
SNYDER, C. R. *Alcohol and the Jews.* Glencoe, Illinois: The Free Press, 1958; New Brunswick, New Jersey: Rutgers Center of Alcoholic Studies, 1958.
SOSKIN, W. F., and P. E. KAUFFMAN. "Judgment of Emotion in Word-Free Voice Samples," *Journal of Communication,* 11:73-80, 1961.
STANTON, A. H., and M. S. SCHWARTZ. *The Mental Hospital.* New York: Basic Books, 1954.
STARKWEATHER, J. "Content-Free Speech as a Source of Information About the Speaker," *Journal of Abnormal and Social Psychology,* 52:394-402, 1956.
———. "Vocal Communication of Personality and Human Feelings," *Journal of Communication,* 11:63-72, 1961.
STRAUS, R. "Alcohol and the Homeless Man," *Quarterly Journal of Studies on Alcohol,* 7:360-404, 1946.
———. "Community Surveys: Their Aims and Techniques; with Special Reference to Problems of Alcoholism," *Quarterly Journal of Studies on Alcohol,* 13:254-270, 1952.
———. "Medical Practice and the Alcoholic," in E. G. Jaco (ed.), *Patients, Physicians and Illness.* Glencoe, Illinois: The Free Press, 1958. Pp. 439-446.
———, and S. D. BACON. "Alcoholism and Social Stability: A Study of Occupational Integration in 2,023 Male Clinic Patients," *Quarterly Journal of Studies on Alcohol,* 12:231-260, 1951.
STRAUS, R., and R. G. MCCARTHY. "Non-Addictive Pathological Drinking Patterns in Homeless Men," *Quarterly Journal of Studies on Alcohol,* 12:601-611, 1951.
STRICKLER, M., E. G. BASSIN, V. MALBIN, and G. F. JACOBSON. "The Community-Based Walk-in Center: A New Resource for Groups Underrepresented in Out-Patient Treatment Facilities," *American Journal of Public Health,* 55:377-384, 1965.
SUCHMAN, E. A. *Evaluative Research, Principles and Practices in Public Service and Social Action Programs.* New York: Russell Sage Foundation, 1967.

SULLIVAN, P. L., C. MILLER, and W. SMELSER. "Factors in Length of Stay and Progress in Psychotherapy," *Journal of Consulting Psychology,* 22:1-9, 1958.

SUTHERLAND, E. H., H. G. SCHROEDER, and C. L. TORDELLA. "Personality Traits and the Alcoholic: A Critique of Existing Studies," *Quarterly Journal of Studies on Alcohol,* 11:547-561, 1950.

SYME, L. "Personality Characteristics and the Alcoholic: A Critique of Current Studies," *Quarterly Journal of Studies on Alcohol,* 18:288-302, 1957.

TERHUNE, W. B. "A Method of Treatment of Alcoholism and the Results," *Journal of the Kentucky Medical Association,* 54:255-260, 1956.

THOMAS, W. I., and F. ZNANIECKI. *The Polish Peasant in Europe and America.* New York: Alfred A. Knopf, 1918.

TIEBOUT, H. M. "The Role of Psychiatry in the Field of Alcoholism. With Comment on the Concept of Alcoholism as a Symptom and as Disease," *Quarterly Journal of Studies on Alcohol,* 12:52-57, 1951.

UNGERLEIDER, J. T. "The Psychiatric Emergency: Analysis of Six Months' Experience of a University Hospital's Consultation Service," *Archives of General Psychiatry,* 3:593-601, 1960.

VOEGTLIN, W. L., and F. LEMERE. "The Treatment of Alcohol Addiction: A Review of the Literature," *Quarterly Journal of Studies on Alcohol,* 2:717-803, 1942.

WALCOTT, E. P., and R. STRAUS. "Use of a Hospital Facility in Conjunction with Outpatient Clinics in the Treatment of Alcoholics," *Quarterly Journal of Studies on Alcohol,* 13:60-77, 1952.

WALLACE, J. A. "A Comparison of Disulfiram Therapy and Routine Therapy in Alcoholism," *Quarterly Journal of Studies on Alcohol,* 13:397-400, 1952.

WALLER, J. A., and H. W. TURKEL. "Alcoholism and Traffic Deaths," *New England Journal of Medicine,* 275:532-536, 1966.

WALLERSTEIN, R. S. "Comparative Study of Treatment Methods for Chronic Alcoholism: The Alcoholism Research Project at Winter V. A. Hospital," *American Journal of Psychiatry,* 113: 228-233, 1956.

———, and ASSOCIATES. *Hospital Treatment of Alcoholism: A Comparative Experimental Study* (Menninger Clinic Monograph No. 11). New York: Basic Books, 1957.

WALTZER, H., L. D. HANKOFF, D. M. ENGELHARDT, and I. C. KAUFMAN. "Emergency Psychiatric Treatment in a Receiving Hospital," *Mental Hospital,* 14:595-596, 600, 1963.

WATTENBERG, W. W., and J. B. MOIR. "Factors Linked to Success in Counseling Homeless Alcoholics," *Quarterly Journal of Studies on Alcohol,* 15:587-594, 1954.

WELLMAN, M. W., M. A. MAXWELL, and P. O'HOLLAREN. "Private Hospital Alcoholic Patients and the Changing Conception of the 'Typical' Alcoholic," *Quarterly Journal of Studies on Alcohol,* 18:388-404, 1957.

WILBY, W. E., and R. W. JONES. "Assessing Patient Response Following Treatment," *Quarterly Journal of Studies on Alcohol,* 23:325, 1962.

WILLIAMS, A. F. "Social Drinking, Anxiety, and Depression," *Journal of Personality and Social Psychology,* 3:689-693, 1966.

WINDER, A. E., and M. HERSKO. "The Effect of Social Class on the Length and Type of Psychotherapy in a Veterans Administration Mental Hygiene Clinic," *Journal of Clinical Psychology,* 11:77-79, 1955.

WIRTH, L. "Urbanism as a Way of Life," *American Journal of Sociology,* 19:1-12, 1938.

WITKIN, H. A., S. A. KARP, and D. R. GOODENOUGH. "Dependence in Alcoholics," *Quarterly Journal of Studies on Alcohol,* 20:493-504, 1959.

WOLF, I., M. CHAFETZ, H. BLANE, and M. HILL. "Social Factors in the Diagnosis of Alcoholism in Social and Nonsocial Situations: II. Attitudes of Physicians," *Quarterly Journal of Studies on Alcohol,* 26:72-79, 1965.

WORLD HEALTH ORGANIZATION. *World Health Organization Technical Report Series,* No. 48. Geneva, Switzerland: World Health Organization, Expert Committee on Mental Health, Alcoholism Subcommittee, Second Report, 1952.

YUKER, H. E., J. R. BLOCK, and W. J. CAMPBELL. *A Scale to Meas-*

ure Attitudes Toward Disabled Persons. Human Resources Foundation, 1960.

Zax, M. "The Incidence and Fate of the Reopened Case in an Alcoholism Treatment Center," *Quarterly Journal of Studies on Alcohol*, 23:634-639, 1962.

———, M. Massey, and C. F. Biggs. "Demographic Characteristics of Alcoholic Outpatients and the Tendency to Remain in Treatment," *Quarterly Journal of Studies on Alcohol*, 22:98-105, 1961.

Zigler, E., and L. Phillips. "Psychiatric Diagnosis: A Critique," *Journal of Abnormal and Social Psychology*, 63:607-618, 1961.

Zinberg, N. E. (ed.). *Psychiatry and Medical Practice in a General Hospital*. New York: International Universities Press, 1964.

Zorbaugh, H. W. *Gold Coast and Slum*. Chicago: University of Chicago Press, 1929.

Index

Index

Abram, Harry S., 42–64, 106
Abstinence, 300
  as a research variable, 169–170
Action-oriented therapy, 11–13, 77, 91–92. *See also* Crisis intervention
Acute psychiatric services, 205–213
  operation and activities, 209
  See also Emergency psychiatric programs
Addicted alcoholic
  child-like patterns of, 23–25
  children of, 263–264, 266, 303, 304
  contrasted with schizophrenic, 9–10
  depression of, 10, 311–312
  identification of, 46–47, 306–308
  initial contact with, 14–15, 41–42, 64–66, 82–83, 85–88, 206–208
  prealcoholic personality of, 8–11
  punitive treatment of, 296–298
  therapist, role of, 11–14, 59, 77
  as a type, 26, 78
Addiction Research Foundation, 283, 354, 355
Admission data, 38, 161, 170, 178, 182
Adorno, T. W., 283
Affleck, D. C., 51–52, 56
Aftercare, 225–229
Age-by-sex distributions, *tables*, 343
Agency coordination, 222–223
Albert Einstein Medical Center, 231–232
Alcoholic-as-derelict concept, 106–116, 121, 130–132, 135–136, 300–302. *See also* Skid Row stereotype
Alcoholic intake, reasons for, 311–316
Alcoholics
  classification of, 7–11
  identification of, 46–47, 306–308
  physicians' definitions of, 131–133
Alcoholics Anonymous, 15, 205, 247, 275
  treatment evaluation and, 173–174
Alcoholism as a symptom, 299
American Medical Association, 125
Anomic patients, rate of return, 83
Arrest record, related to treatment, 159, 163. *See also* Police intervention
Attitudes of Americans toward alcoholism, 105–106, 310–311
  See also Drinking cultures
Attitudes of Nurses toward alcoholics, 267–276
  authoritarian, 284
  moral relativism, 285
  Skid Row stereotype, 285
  social drinking acceptance, 285
  unsympathetic, 284–285
  tables, 346–349
Attitudes of patient to treatment, 48–49. *See also* Motivation for treatment
Attitudes of physicians toward alcoholics, 105–109, 113–116, 121, 129–136. *See also* Physicians' attitudes
Attitudes toward Disabled Persons Scale, 355
Attitudes toward Immoral Behavior Scale, 283
Authoritarian Scale, 283, 354
Automobile accidents, 264

Bellack, L., 232–233
Biased sampling, 166–169
Biggs, C. F., 89
Blackouts, 313
Blane, Howard T., 16–28, 42–67, 106–149, 160–186, 213–219, 229–242, 258–269
Bradley, N. J., 174–175, 181
Bridgewater State Hospital, 36–37
Bronx Municipal Hospital, 231–232
Brown, Elliot, 242–249

Caretakers
  follow-up interviews with, 193
  role of, 23–28
  See also Physicians; Public Health Nurses; Social workers; Therapists
Chafetz, M. E., 6–15, 37–67, 105–144, 160–186, 207–219, 229–242, 260–261, 296–318
Children of alcoholics, 263–264, 266, 303, 304. See also Teen-age drinking
Chronic alcoholic. See Addicted alcoholic
Clark, Eleanor, 42–64
Classification of patients, 7–11, 26
Clergyman, role of, 245
Clinic contact, 27, 33–34, 54–55, 64–66. See also Emergency services
Cocktail party syndrome, 317
Cohen, Pauline, 264
Community services
  aftercare, 225–229
  agency coordination, 222–223, 227–228
  Directory of Resources, 280–281, 353–354
  follow-up-related use, 190
  liaison work, 223–225, 228
  in the rural community, 246
  treatment-related use, 57–59, 211–212, 218
Conner, R., 122
Content-filtered speech, 136–139
Control conditions for evaluative research
  biased sampling, 166–169
  control group use, 163–165
  motivation variable, 164–165, 167–168
Counterdependency, 80–81
  mode of entry and, 87–88
  social context of, 83–84
  as a stage, 84
  therapy, effects on, 82–85
Crisis intervention, 214–215, 220
  concrete, 221–222
  as initial contact, 35–36, 42, 64–67
  noninterpretive, 221
Cultures, drinking. See Drinking cultures
Custodial Attitudes Scale (C.A.I.), 254, 283

Danehy, H., 137
Defense mechanism, 313
Demone, H. W., 105–106
Denial, 10, 14
Dependency, 21–23, 28
  behavior, defined, 81–82
  fulfillment of, by personnel, 42–44, 59, 210, 212–213
  mode of entry and, 87–88
  motivational, 79–81
  perceptual, defined, 79
  social context of, 83–84
  as a stage, 84
  as treatment motivation, 34–35
Depression, 10, 311–312
Deteriorated geographic areas, 93–94
Diagnosis
  action, 124–125
  appearance, effects on, 109, 130–132
  criteria for, 46–47
  formal, 124–125
  medical characteristics and, table, 335
  social characteristics and, table, 334
  social factors, effects on, 106–128
  social isolation and, 149
  See also Alcoholic-as-derelict; Physicians' attitudes
Director of Resources (community), 280–281, sample entry, 353–354

Index

Discontinuance of therapy, 56–57
Disposition of patients, *tables,* 344, 345
Doctor. *See* Physician
Dress as diagnostic factor, 109, 130–132
Drinking cultures, 306, 308, 309–311, 318
Drinking patterns, 169–176
Drinking prowess, 22, 80, 308
Driving accidents, 264

Education of hospital personnel, 125–126
Education of prealcoholic youth, 304
Elmhurst City Hospital (N.Y.), 232–233
Emergency psychiatric programs, 230–242
  Bronx Municipal Hospital, 231–232
  Elmhurst (N.Y.), 232–233
  Escambia County (Fla.), 238
  Grace-New Haven (Conn.), 233–234, 237
  Kings County Psychiatric, 240
  Massachusetts General Hospital, 235–237
  North Conway (N.H.), 238–239, 242–249
  Rush Center for Problems in Living (Calif.), 239
  St. Vincent's Hospital (N.Y.), 233–234
  San Mateo County, 233–234, 237
  See also Acute psychiatric services
Emergency service personnel, attitudes toward patients, 15, 55
  immediate treatment methods, 64–66, 214–216
  preventive intervention, 241–242
  project coordination and, 44, 216–218

Emergency services and chronic complaints, 207, 240–242. *See also* Initial patient contact
Employment
  as diagnostic factor, 114, 148
  as evaluation variable, 167, 175–176
Ends, E. J., 165, 185
Escambia County (Fla.), psychiatric program, 238–239
Evaluative research
  abstinence as a variable, 169–176
  biased sampling, 166–169
  bibliography of, 359–391
  control conditions for, 162–165
  pretreatment data, 161, 170, 182
  reporting, 183–186
  subject selection, 165
  time intervals affecting, 180–182
Experimental group patients
  median number of visits, 51
  sociocultural characteristics of, 52–53, 61–63
  subject selection, 45–47, 61–62
  therapeutic relation, 49–51
  See also Evaluative research
Expressive cues of physician, 136–144
Extraclassificatory factors and diagnosis, 106–128

Family unity
  as diagnostic factor, 114–115
  teen-age drinking and, 266
  See also Relatives
Fearfulness, 20–21, 27
Female alcoholics, 39, 40, 166
Fenichel, O., 78–79
Fisher's exact test, 66
Follow-up, 178–182
  caretakers and, 193
  interview methods for, 191–194
  locating patients, 186–191
  relatives and, 192–193

Follow-up (cont.)
    treatment teams for, 186–188
    use of community agencies for, 190
Frank, J. D., 51–52, 56–57
Frankel, Fred H., 213–219
Freud, S., 6

Garetz, F. K., 237–238, 241
Garfield, S. L., 51–52, 56
Gerard, D. L., 173–174, 181, 182
Golner, Joseph H., 42–64
Gordon, C. W., 122
Gottschalk, L., 137
Grace-New Haven Hospital (Conn.), 233-234

Hastie, Elizabeth Lacy, 42–64, 186–194
Hawthorne effect, 165
Hill, J. G., 191
Hill, Marjorie J., 128–136, 160–186, 278–291
Hockett, C., 137
Hollingshead, A. B., 89, 107
Home-visit teams, 240
Homosexuality, 6, 312–313
Hospitalization
    as a diagnostic factor, 117, 118
    mode of entry, effects on, 87–88
    table, 344–345
Hospital personnel, education of, 125–126

Identification of alcoholics, 46–47, 306–308
Inferiority feelings, 19–20
Initial patient contact
    counterdependency techniques in, 82–83
    importance of, 14–15, 34–35, 41–42, 64–66, 206–208
    police intervention and, 85–88

See also Diagnosis
Innovative programs, 230–249
In-service training program, 278–291
Insight-based psychotherapy, 59, 91–92
Insurance use, 115
Interdisciplinary coordination, 213–219
Interjudge reliability, 176–177

Jackson, J. K., 122
Junior high school, 261

Kasschau, Richard, 144–149
Kauffman, P., 136, 137
Kings County Psychiatric Hospital (N.Y.), 240
Knight, R. P., 79
Koumans, Alfred J. R., 67–70, 219–229
Kramer, E., 136–137

Letters, as treatment motivation, 67–68, *table,* 330
Liansky, Edith, 266
Liaison work, 223–225
Lindemann, E., 42
Lindner, Robert, 260
Liquor use
    to achieve oblivion, 315–316
    to alter perceptions, 312–313
    to break psychological barriers, 314
    self-medication, 311–312
    to sustain defenses, 313
Lorand, S. A., 79
Lower class. *See* Social class
Low frustration tolerance, 17–18, 24, 27, 28
Ludwig, A. O., 15

McCord, J., 79–81, 84, 257, 266

Index

McCord, W., 79–81, 84, 257, 266
McCourt, William F., 42–64, 106, 264
Mabel, G., 136
Maddox, George, 259, 262
Male alcoholics, 39, 40, 79–81, 166
Marital status, effects of, 95–96, 114
Marsey, M., 89
Masculine self-image, 22, 80, 308
Massachusetts General Hospital, psychiatric services, 235–237
Measuring instruments, 184
Medical characteristics and referral, 112–113, 116–119, table, 335
Medical diagnosis, 108, 116–119, 121–122, 124, 127, 134–136
Medical index, 119–120, 127–128, table, 336
Medical insurance, 115
Mendelson, Jack H., 37–42, 283, 354
Menninger, K. A., 79
Meyers, William, 42–60, 78–84, 88–98
Miller, Carole F., 68–70
Milmoe, Susan, 136–144
Missed appointments, 52
Mode of entry
 diagnosis and, 115–116
 treatment relations and, 85–88
 See also Police intervention
Morison, L. J., 290
Motivation for treatment
 crisis as, 35–36, 42, 64–67
 dependency needs as, 34–35, 79–81
 letters as, 67–68, table, 330
 as research variable, 164–165, 167
 telephone calls as, 68–70
Muller, James J., 67–70, 229–241

Neurotic alcoholics, 7–8, 26
Nondiagnosed alcoholics, 106–128
North Conway Memorial Hospital (N.H.), 238–239, 243–249

Nurses. See Public Health Nurses

Oblivion syndrome, 315–316
Occupation level and treatment establishment, 91
 See also Employment
Oral perversion, 8–11
Oral stage, 6
Oram, P. G., 283
Outpatient psychiatric care, 57, 67–68, 229–242. See also Emergency psychiatric services
Overton, Willis F., Jr., 107–128

Page, C. W., 165, 185
Park's index of problem drinking, 262
Patient contact
 assessment of, 48
 follow-up, 48–49, 178–182, 186–193
 initial, 15, 34–35, 41–42, 55, 64–66, 82–83, 206–208
 missed appointments, 52
Patient disposition, table, 344
Patient distribution by sex and problem, table, 342
Perceptual dependency, 79
Personality type, 78
Physical environment, 93–94
Physicians' attitudes
 alcoholism as a social stigma, 105–109, 113–116, 121–123, 126–127, 132–134
 education for change in, 125–126, 245
 interview data, 129–136
 preference for medical diagnosis, 108, 116–119, 121–122, 124, 127, 134–136
 See also Attitudes; Diagnosis
Physician-patient relationship, voice as referral factor, 136–144, tables, 337–340

Pittenger, R., 137
Pittman, D. J., 122
Police intervention
  diagnosis and, 115–116
  home visits as alternative to, 240
  as initial contact, 85–88
  related to treatment, 159, 163
Polk, Kenneth, 260
Prealcoholic personality, 264–269
Pretreatment data, 38, 161, 170, 178, 182
Prevalence studies, nurse-related, 281–282
Prevention
  educating youth, 304-305
  primary, 259–262
  secondary, 259, 262–268
Primary prevention, 259–262
Primitive disorder, alcoholism as, 9–11
Problem drinking, criteria for, 306–308
Psychiatric services. *See* Emergency psychiatric programs
Public assistance and diagnosis, 115
Public Health Nurse
  alcohol-related problems of, 271–274
  attitudes toward alcoholics, 273–274, *tables,* 346–349
  attitudes toward treatment, 274–276
  in-service training, 278–291
  prevalence studies, 281–282
  re-education of, 278
  referral to clinics, 276
  See also Visiting Nurse Association
Punitive treatment of alcoholics, 296–298

Rado, S., 79
Raines, G. N., 106–107
Reactive alcoholic, 7–8, 26
Redlich, F. C., 107

Referrals
  interagency, 211–212
  nurse-related, 281
  success related to doctor's voice, 136–144, *tables,* 337–340
Referral source, *table,* 344
Relapse, 41
Relatives
  continuance of therapy of, 65–67
  follow-up interview with, 192–193
  patient motivation and, 210–211
  toleration of the alcoholic, 316
  visits, *table,* 330
  See also Family unity
Reliability in evaluative procedures, 176–178
Reporting, 183–186
Research evaluation, 159–194
Rohmer, J. H., 106–107
Rosenthal, D., 51–52, 56–57
Rosenthal, Robert, 136–144
Rossi, J. J., 174–175, 181
Rural health centers, 238–239, 242–249
Rush Center for Problems in Living (Calif.), 239

Saenger, G., 173–174, 181, 182
St. Vincent's Hospital (N.Y.), 233–234
San Mateo County General Hospital, 233–234
Sapir, Jean, 43
Schilder, P., 79
Schizophrenia contrasted with alcoholism, 8–11
Schroeder, H. G., 78
Schulze, G., 136
Secondary prevention, 259, 262
Self-destruction, 25, 79, 315
Self-medication by liquor, 311–312
Sex type and alcoholism, 39, 40, 79–81, 166, *tables,* 343

Index

Sherfey, M. J., 9
Singer, Estelle, 144–149
Skid Row stereotype, 53, 54, 92, 122–123, 285, 315
Slack, C. W., 57, 83
Social characteristics
  diagnostic referral and, 111–116, *table*, 334
Social class
  counterdependency and, 80–81, 83–84
  diagnosis and, 121, 134
  dropout rate and, 56–57
  establishment of treatment and, 88–92
  interagency referrals and, 211–212
  therapy techniques and, 212–213
  treatment motivation and, 206, 207–208
Social dependence
  defined, 92
  measures of, 95–98
  table, 333
Social factors and diagnosis, effects, 106–128
Social integration index, 119, 127, *table*, 336
Social isolation, 106
  diagnosed *vs.* undiagnosed alcoholics, *table*, 341
  defined, 92
  measures of, 94-98
  relation to alcoholism, 144–149
  table, 333
Socially-intact alcoholic
  diagnosis of, 132–133
  referral practices, 123–125
Social-medical index, 120–121, 128, *table*, 336
Social perception of alcohol, 260
Social stigma, 132, 205
  diagnosis and, 107, 108–109, 113–116

Social work assistant, 236
Social worker, 226, 236
  immediate response of, 64–66, 215–216
Soskin, W. F., 37
Stach, A., 174–175, 181
Stages of alcoholism, 84
Starkweather, J., 136, 137
Strauss, R., 107, 122–123, 125
Subjective complaint and diagnosis, 117–119
Suicide, 25
Superiority attitudes, 18–20
Sutherland, E. H., 78
Syme, L., 78

Taylor, Charles, 242–249
Teaching conferences, 235
Teen-age drinking, 257–258, 259
  children of alcoholics, 263–264, 266, 303, 304
  delinquents, 264–268
  pre-alcoholics, 262–268
  prevention techniques, 260–262
Telephone calls as motivation for treatment, 68-70
Therapist, role of, 11–14, 59, 77
Therapeutic relation, defined, 49–51
Therapy
  action-oriented, 11–13, 77, 91–92, 212–213
  insight-based, 59, 91–92
  techniques for low-social-class, 212–213
Time intervals as evaluative measure, 180–182
Tordella, C. L., 78
Treatment
  arrest record and, 159, 163
  evaluative research, 159–186, 359–391
  immediate availability of, 64–66
  model for rural areas, 242–249

Treatment continuance, counter-dependency and, 83
Treatment maintenance, *tables,* 331, 332
Treatment teams, 47–49, 64–66, 186–188, 240
Trouble-Shooting Clinic, 233
True alcoholic, 300–302
Turkel, H. W., 264

Visiting Nurse Association, 237, 278–279, 353–356. *See also* Public Health Nurse

Visits, 52, *tables,* 328, 329, 330
Voice of the physician as referral factor, 136–144, *tables,* 337–340

Waller, J. A., 264
Wallerstein, R. S., 185
Wile, R., 173–174
Williams, Allen, 261, 262
Witkin, H. A., 79
Wolf, Irving, 128–144
World Health Organization, 78

Zax, M., 89